S0-BEH-735

BIBLICAL INTERPRETATION IN EARLY CHRISTIAN GOSPELS, VOLUME 1

Published under

LIBRARY OF NEW TESTAMENT STUDIES
304

formerly the Journal for the Study of the New Testament Supplement Series

Editor
Mark Goodacre

Editorial Board
John M. G. Barclay, Craig Blomberg, Kathleen E. Corley,
R. Alan Culpepper, James D. G. Dunn, Craig A. Evans,
Stephen Fowl, Robert Fowler, Simon J. Gathercole,
John S. Kloppenborg, Michael Labahn,
Robert Wall, Robert L. Webb, Catrin H. Williams

T&T CLARK INTERNATIONAL
A Continuum imprint
LONDON • NEW YORK

BIBLICAL INTERPRETATION IN EARLY CHRISTIAN GOSPELS, VOLUME 1

The Gospel of Mark

Edited by

THOMAS R. HATINA

t&t clark

BS
2387
.B535
2006
v.1

Published by T&T Clark International
A Continuum imprint
The Tower Building, 11 York Road, London SE1 7NX
80 Maiden Lane, Suite 704, New York, NY 10038

www.tandtclark.com

Copyright © Thomas R. Hatina and contributors, 2006

All rights reserved. No part of this publication may be reproduced or transmitted in any form or by any means, electronic or mechanical, including photocopying, recording or any information storage or retrieval system, without permission in writing from the publishers.

British Library Cataloguing-in-Publication Data
A catalogue record for this book is available from the British Library

ISBN 0-567-08067-6 (hardback)

Typeset by ISB Typesetting, Sheffield
Printed on acid-free paper in Great Britain by MPG Books Ltd., Bodmin, Cornwall

CONTENTS

PREFACE

This collection of essays on the interpretation of Scripture in the narrative of Mark's Gospel is the first in a five-volume series, which will include each of the four canonical Gospels and a final volume on the extracanonical Gospels. The objectives of the series are to situate the current state of research and to advance our understanding of the function of embedded Scripture texts and their traditions in the narrative and socio-religious context of early Christian Gospels. Though methodologically broad, the series aims to bridge the concerns of both narrative and historical critics.

The essays in each volume have not been selected nor have they been organized according to specific predetermined categories, but instead are presented as a single undivided collection that promotes methodological integration and overlap.

I wish to express my heartfelt gratitude to the contributors whose creative efforts, generosity, and enthusiasm have made this ambitious project possible. I am also grateful to Mark Goodacre and Craig Evans, who have seen the value of this project, and to the editorial staff at T&T Clark who painstakingly bring such collaborations to completion. Finally, I would like to express my gratitude to Michael Apodaca for indexing.

This series is dedicated to my colleagues in the Religious Studies department at Trinity Western University whose rich scholarship, friendship, and good humour are cherished.

Thomas R. Hatina
July 2005; Vancouver, Canada

ABBREVIATIONS

AB	Anchor Bible
ABD	David Noel Freedman (ed.), *The Anchor Bible Dictionary* (New York: Doubleday, 1992)
ABRL	Anchor Bible Reference Library
AnBib	Analecta Biblica
ANRW	*Aufstieg und Niedergang der römischen Welt*
ArBib	The Aramaic Bible
AsSeign	*Assemblées du Seigneur*
ATANT	Abhandlungen zur Theologie des Alten und Neuen Testaments
BAGD	Walter Bauer, William F. Arndt, F. William Gingrich and Frederick W. Danker, *A Greek-English Lexicon of the New Testament and Other Early Christian Literature* (Chicago: University of Chicago Press, 2nd edn, 1958)
BBR	*Bulletin for Biblical Research*
BEvT	Beiträge zur evangelischen Theologie
Bib	*Biblica*
BibRev	*Bible Review*
BibInt	*Biblical Interpretation*
BJRL	*Bulletin of the John Rylands University Library of Manchester*
BNTC	Black's New Testament Commentary
BR	*Biblical Research*
CBQ	*Catholic Biblical Quarterly*
ConBNT	Coniectanea biblica, New Testament
DSD	*Dead Sea Discoveries*
EKKNT	Evangelisch-katholischer Kommentar zum Neuen Testament
GNS	Good News Studies
HTKNT	Herders theologischer Kommentar zum Neuen Testament
IEJ	*Israel Exploration Journal*
IBS	*Irish Biblical Studies*
JBL	*Journal of Biblical Literature*
JETS	*Journal of the Evangelical Theological Society*
JGRCJ	*Journal of Greco-Roman Christianity and Judaism*
JJS	*Journal of Jewish Studies*
JSNT	*Journal for the Study of the New Testament*
JSNTSup	*Journal for the Study of the New Testament*, Supplement Series
JSOTSup	*Journal for the Study of the Old Testament*, Supplement Series
JSPSup	*Journal for the Study of the Pseudepigrapha*, Supplement Series
JTS	*Journal of Theological Studies*
NIBC	New International Biblical Commentary
NICNT	New International Commentary on the New Testament
NIGTC	New International Greek Testament Commentary

NovT	*Novum Testamentum*
NovTSup	*Novum Testamentum* Supplement Series
NTOA	Novum Testamentum et Orbis Antiquus
OCD	N.G.L. Hammond and H.H. Scullard, *Oxford Classical Dictionaary* (Oxford: Oxford University Press, 2nd edn, 1970)
OTL	Old Testament Library
PEQ	*Palestine Exploration Quarterly*
PG	J. Migne, *Patrologia Graeca*
PNTC	Pillar New Testament Commentary
PRSt	*Perspectives in Religious Studies*
PVTG	Pseudepigrapha Veteris Testamenti graece
RB	*Revue biblique*
RevQ	*Revue de Qumran*
SBLDS	Society of Biblical Literature Dissertation Series
SBLMS	Society of Biblical Literature Monograph Series
SBT	Studies in Biblical Theology
SC	Sources chrétiennes
SJT	*Scottish Journal of Theology*
SNTSMS	Society for New Testament Studies Monograph Series
SSEJC	Studies in Scripture in Early Judaism and Christianity
STDJ	Studies on the Texts of the Desert of Judah
TDNT	G. Kittel and G. Friedrich (eds.), *Theological Dictionary of the New Testament* (ET; 10 vols.; Grand Rapids: Eerdmans, 1964–76)
VT	*Vetus Testamentum*
WBC	Word Biblical Commentary
WUNT	Wissenschaftliche Untersuchungen zum Neuen Testament
ZAW	*Zeitschrift für die alttestamentliche Wissenschaft*
ZTK	*Zeitschrift für Theologie und Kirche*

LIST OF CONTRIBUTORS

Darrell L. Bock,
Research Professor of New Testament Studies,
Dallas Theological Seminary,
Dallas, Texas

Edwin K. Broadhead,
Associate Professor of General Studies,
Berea College,
Berea, Kentucky

S. Anthony Cummins,
Associate Professor of Religious Studies,
Trinity Western University,
Langley, British Columbia

James R. Edwards,
Professor of Biblical Languages and Literature,
Whitworth College,
Spokane, Washington

Craig A. Evans,
Payzant Professor of New Testament,
Acadia Divinity College,
Wolfville, Nova Scotia

Thomas R. Hatina,
Associate Professor of Religious Studies,
Trinity Western University,
Langley, British Columbia

Larry Perkins,
Professor of Biblical Studies,
Northwest Baptist Seminary/Associated Canadian Theological Schools,
Langley, British Columbia

Stanley E. Porter,
Professor of New Testament,
McMaster Divinity College,
Hamilton, Ontario

Mark A. Proctor,
Lecturer in New Testament,
Houston Baptist University,
Houston, Texas

Tom Shepherd,
Professor of Religion,
Union College,
Lincoln, Nebraska

Jesper Svartvik,
Senior Research Fellow,
New Testament Exegesis, Centre for Theology and Religious Studies,
Lund University,
Lund, Sweden

Introduction

EMBEDDED TEXTS AND MARK'S NARRATIVE: ASSUMPTIONS AND ISSUES IN CURRENT RESEARCH

Over the last two decades the growing interest in literary approaches to the Gospels has led to several studies focusing on the function of embedded Scripture texts in the context of Mark's narrative.[1] While we have witnessed a gradual departure from traditional form-critical and redaction-critical approaches, most scholars who admit to incorporating a narrative approach have retained a strong interest in locating the story firmly within its historical context. As a result, we are currently in an era when the narrative critical (i.e. formalist) questions (e.g. plot, characterization, point of view, time) are bumping up against the historical-critical ones. Moreover, the historical-critical questions which have traditionally tended to focus on composition and history-of-religions are not surprisingly giving way to sociological and anthropological inquiry. While most of the contributions in this collection do not specifically deal with the social-scientific questions, they all in their own way attempt to explore biblical interpretation in the Gospel of Mark from a narrative and (socio-)historical perspective.

As stated in the Series Preface, the essays in this volume are not divided into predetermined categories or sections. All the contributors attempt to integrate narrative and historical concerns, even when focusing on a particular section of Mark. My thinking is that such divisions may formulate assumptions that may be counterproductive in promoting methodological integration.

In the opening essay, Darrell Bock attempts to meticulously discern the presence of allusions in the construction of Mark's passion account by pointing to certain 'trigger terms', parallel themes, and parallel story lines. In addition to acknowledging the influence of the righteous sufferer in Psalm 22, as many others do, Bock argues that Mark has also been influenced by the Suffering Servant motif in Second Isaiah and the Day of the Lord motif in Amos. For Mark, the concepts of Scripture richly form an important backdrop and ultimately a

---

1. The most recent larger studies are J. Marcus, *The Way of the Lord: Christological Exegesis of the Old Testament in the Gospel of Mark* (Louisville: Westminster/John Knox Press, 1992); R.E. Watts, *Isaiah's New Exodus and Mark* (WUNT, 2.88; Tübingen: Mohr, 1997); J. Svartvik, *Mark and Mission: Mk 7.1–23 in its Narrative and Historical Contexts* (ConBNT, 32; Stockholm: Almqvist & Wiksell, 2000); T.R. Hatina, *In Search of a Context: The Function of Scripture in Mark's Narrative* (JSNTSup, 232; SSEJC, 8; London: Sheffield Academic Press, 2002). For a survey of methods since S. Schulz, 'Markus und das Alte Testament', *ZTK* 58 (1961), pp. 184–97, see the first chapter of my *In Search of a Context*.

kind of commentary on the events surrounding Jesus' death. These are important cultural scripts that explain what is taking place. In the weaving together of the Righteous Sufferer, the Servant, and the Day of the Lord, Mark not only evokes ideas that point to the arrival of the eschaton and the coming of judgment, but he also highlights the promise of vindication and the provision for salvation from one who was both a Righteous and Vindicated Sufferer.

Edwin Broadhead argues that the various traditions in the trial scene (Mk 14.53–65), some from within the Gospel and others from external texts, have been reshaped to generate a climactic Christological confession of Jesus as the suffering and dying Son of Man. This image is created through a process that transforms the inherited Son of Man sayings tradition into the Markan image. Broadhead attempts to explain the process by giving attention first to the scriptural traditions (Dan. 7.13; Pss. 2 and 110.1) which serve as the basis for the Markan Son of Man. Broadhead then turns his attention to the realignment of materials from within the Gospel of Mark (which he calls 'intratextuality'). This is followed by an engagement with similar texts from outside the narrative (which he calls 'intertextuality') which reveal that in addition to images of the Righteous One, the Suffering Servant, and the rejected prophet, the trial scene is very much influenced by Jewish apocalyptic thought. Finally, Broadhead draws out the sociological implications of a suffering and dying Son of Man for Jesus' followers.

Tony Cummins focuses on the intriguing episode involving King Herod's birthday banquet and the death of John the Baptist in Mk 6.17–29. Although this episode has been explored from a range of interesting angles, Cummins observes that a comprehensive and integrative assessment of its overall nature and function still requires exploration. In addressing this situation Cummins begins by succinctly explicating his overarching working assumption: namely, that the Gospel of Mark tells of the divine identity and eschatological mission of a Messiah Jesus who in unexpected fashion embodies and establishes the kingdom of God. What then follows comprises two extended and interrelated components. First, Cummins offers a detailed reading which delineates the significant role played by this episode within its immediate context (6.1–44) and Mark's narrative overall, largely in terms of a mutually interpretative and ironic correlation concerning King Herod Antipas, John the Baptist and Messiah Jesus. Second, Cummins' patient analysis is then developed further by considering the ways in which this correlation has been significantly shaped by kingship related motifs and themes evident in various aspects of the Elijah narratives (1 Kings 17–19, 21; 2 Kings 1–2) and the Book of Esther. Cummins' approach invites and enables a vibrant ironic comparison between notable Old Testament types and the Gospel figures of Herod and Herodias, John, and Jesus.

Without focusing on any particular passage, James Edwards argues that the character and activities of Jesus are remarkably similar to those of the Servant and Yahweh in Second Isaiah. Given the quantity and breadth of parallels which are often conceptual and thematic (in the form of allusions) rather than explicitly stated in the form of quotations, Edwards views Second Isaiah as a vital influence in the shaping of Jesus' ministry and passion accounts in Mark's narrative. Thus, according to Edwards, Mark presents Jesus as fulfilling not only the role of the Servant, but also the role of God. Edwards, however, is not content simply to leave the parallels on the literary level. He concludes his essay by arguing that Isaiah's Servant of God which is reflected, for example, in the Parable of the Sower, served as a paradigm for the ministry of the historical Jesus.

While acknowledging that allusions are difficult to substantiate, especially when unrelated Scripture texts are quoted in the immediate context, Craig Evans attempts to demonstrate that Zecharian allusions are not only present in Mark's passion narrative, but have served a vital role in its compositional history. To support his position, Evans draws on three overarching observations. First, he points out that allusions to Zechariah in the passion narrative are numerous – as attested to by other scholars – which would suggest that Mark (and/or earlier tradents) was familiar with the biblical book. Since this is the case, possible allusions should be regarded as plausible ones. Second, Evans observes that some of the allusions in Mark are made clearer in the Gospel parallels. And third, while other Scripture texts, such as the Psalms, are quoted explicitly in the passion narrative, Evans' investigation into the Jewish exegetical traditions of these texts reveals that some have definite associations with Zechariah. Though Evans primarily deals with the scriptural building blocks of narrative, he argues that in some cases the Zecharian influence goes back to Jesus.

In my own contribution, I aim to show that if Mark is taken seriously as narrative art, a search for *the* meaning, and hence *the* echo, of an embedded text that is more allusion than quotation, can be reductionistic and self-defeating because it potentially excludes other layers of meaning which would have been open to the earliest audiences (and should remain open to the modern literary critic). I argue that the announcement of the 'voice from heaven' in Mk 1.11 should be treated as a reverberation of several traditions in early Judaism, as long as each can be incorporated into the narrative. It is the narrative itself within its socio-historical context, which should be the primary arbiter for evaluating a textual or oral-traditional influence. And when several Jewish interpretive traditions cohere with the narrative or narrative features (such as plot, themes, point of view, or characterization), as is the case with the voice's announcement in Mk 1.11, the exegete must in the end remain satisfied with a plurality of options. In my approach I try to build the best possible case for each scriptural influence independently by showing how each can fit (and be the 'best' option) within Mark's story and could have been appropriated by early audiences. The process inevitably deconstructs the traditional historical-critical operating principle that only one stream of influence should be assumed.

Dissatisfied with studies that focus only on the function of embedded Scripture texts in their immediate contexts, Larry Perkins seeks to understand why the Markan author used materials from the Exodus narrative in the composition of his entire story. Perkins tackles such questions as: What is the relationship between explicit quotations from Exodus and Exodus motifs? Do they serve complementary functions or different rhetorical and literary purposes? Does the Markan author desire his readers to understand the Exodus references through the grid of

Isaiah 40–55 and its prophecies about a new exodus? By reflecting upon Israel's exodus experience and Isaiah's prophecies of a new exodus in the light of Jesus' words and deeds, Perkins argues that the Markan author helps his audience understand the person and work of Jesus as Son of God, God's eschatological purposes, and the eschatological role of Jesus' disciples. Perkins also gives attention to the evaluation of allusions, especially since many of the connection he draws are not based on explicit quotations. On several occasions Perkins demonstrates how the larger narrative material can be useful in narrowing otherwise ambiguous allusions which are capable of being connected with more than one Scripture text.

Beginning with basic generic distinctions from the ancients, and their suitability for application to the Gospels, Stanley Porter creatively examines the use of quotation in Mark from the standpoint of its similarities to and differences from the use of citation and quotation in other ancient biographies. But Porter moves beyond the standard comparisons by bringing into the discussion a papyrus manuscript that is often overlooked, and rarely examined in terms of its use of quotation, namely P.Oxy. 1176 which contains a life of Euripides by Satyrus, the biographer. Porter argues that although the fragmentary and incomplete nature of the document makes it problematic for comparison with Mark, with its well-established and well-documented textual history, it nevertheless contains a number of features that show surprising overlap between the ways that quotations are used in the two ancient sources.

Mark Proctor concentrates on the function of Hos. 6.2 in Mark's references to Jesus' resurrection. For Proctor, the significance of Hos. 6.2 for early Christian thought lay in its unique combination of resurrection language with a doubly precise third-day temporal marker. Yet when one compares the importance Paul, Luke, John, and others attributed to the third-day resurrection motif with the wording of Mark's three passion predictions, a distinct peculiarity arises. Whereas the prevailing tradition claimed the Lord arose 'on the third day', Mark has Jesus predict on three separate occasions that he would rise μετὰ τρεῖς ἡμέρας (i.e. 'after three days' or 'on the fourth day'). Proctor claims that good reasons exist for suggesting not only Mark's general awareness of Hosea, but also his specific knowledge of LXX Hos. 6.2 and its Christological significance for the wider tradition. But where Mark's Christian contemporaries found in Hosea's text a temporal marker of sufficient accuracy to suit their theological needs, the second evangelist saw something that might draw his readers' attention away from his main literary goal. Mark's desire to downplay the significance of the empty tomb *vis-à-vis* the story of his protagonist's death thus precipitated an important change of wording in one of the gospel tradition's pivotal exegetical elements. Mark, in an effort to focus his community's attention squarely on the cross and the spectacle of Jesus' ironic demise as the Son of God, used the general temporal phrase μετὰ τρεῖς ἡμέρας instead of the specific temporal marker ἐν τῇ ἡμέρᾳ τῇ τρίτῃ in the passion predictions, and in so doing compromised Hos. 6.2's primary Christological appeal.

The aim of Tom Shepherd's essay is to present briefly the findings of a narrative analysis of Mk 1.1–15 in the standard categories of settings, characters, actions and plot, time relationships, and narrator/implied reader, and to suggest several ways this data may assist the scholarly debate over the passage. Shepherd observes that too often narrative studies present interpretation of the narrative data without providing much of the raw analysis data itself that stands behind that interpretation. He suggests that it is preferable to present as much of the raw data as possible (and as is reasonable) so that others can both have the data in hand, and be able to critique the conclusions drawn from the data. In contrast to some contributors, Shepherd more freely allows narrative features to control the function and meaning of embedded Scripture texts. He shows that Mark tempers the sense of Jesus following John via the Scripture quotation in 1.2–3 which intimates that a greater personage follows those who prepare the way before him. Nevertheless, the terminology for a follower is still used. And Jesus' actions convey weakness. Jesus in the end is depicted as both a strong and weak or submissive character. Shepherd observes that characterization-by-showing in the prologue tends to focus on Jesus' weakness while characterization-by-telling tends to focus on his strength.

Setting the stage by explaining how scholarship needs to rethink embedded texts in light of literary questions, Jesper Svartvik concentrates on the narrative and theological dimensions of causality in the Markan plot. He argues that Scripture is embedded in the Markan text to such an extent that it cannot be removed without destroying the story. The role Scripture plays in the Gospel (and New Testament) is certainly neither a matter of antithesis nor of fulfillment, but rather of a shared symbolic universe. More specifically, Svartvik draws attention to a number of interesting observations, which make it difficult to adhere to the mainstream interpretation of the Pentateuchal food laws in Mk 7.1–23. His textual, effectual and contextual investigations arrive at the following results. (1) Textually, although Mark emphasizes causality to a remarkably high degree in his narrative, an abrogation of the Jewish food laws is not at stake in the trial. The setting, characters and plot suggest that the bread cycle in Mark 6–8 provides a narrative parallel to the Pauline mission to the Gentiles. (2), Effectually, the central saying in Mk 7.15 serves as a warning against evil speech. And (3) contextually, when the saying is compared to rabbinic aggadah it is best understood in a relative sense (*not so much...as*) rather than in an absolute sense (*nothing...*). All in all, Svartvik explains how Mk 7.1–23 is not part of the controversy cycles when it is read within its narrative and socio-religious context.

There are several related issues, representative of broader scholarly thinking, which emerge from this collection of essays. The first issue concerns the meaning of embedded texts in the Gospel narratives. In other words, to what degree does a narrative context aid in determining the meaning of allusions? How do narrative features such as plot, characterization and time affect the interpretation of embedded Scripture texts? Do embedded texts shape narrative in the sense that the narrative attains its structure and meaning from biblical stories or episodes, from which the embedded texts are taken; or does narrative shape and give (new) meaning to embedded texts and by implication to the biblical stories and events they echo? While it could be argued that both processes are at work, one is usually presupposed. Underlying theological assumptions about the unity of the two testaments sometimes tips the scale in favour of the former. As a result, the embedded texts serve as extensions of their prior (ancient Israelite or early Jewish) meaning, even though they are found in a Christian context. Social scientific assumptions are certainly at work with regard to the latter, which would allow for embedded texts to take on entirely different meanings within the larger context of myth-making. This approach has no investment in trying to preserve some kind of theological unity between the testament. The two approaches emerge from the well established distinction between theology and religion.

A second issue – which is closely connected to the first – has to do with the embedded texts' loci of meaning. In other words, in which of the many possible contexts do quotations and allusions attain meaning? Is it in external contexts such as the biblical book from which it is taken, the early Jewish interpretive traditions (and even rabbinic traditions), the historical Jesus, and/or early Christian kerygma? If meaning is found external to the narrative, then the reader must assume that embedded texts are charged with prior meanings that influence the narrative. In this case, Mark can be regarded as an importer of meaning. Or are meanings of embedded texts strictly shaped by their new narrative context? If this is the case, then the reader must allow for the possibility of entirely new and even contradictory meanings to emerge, which function in the service of their new literary context. In this case, Mark can be regarded as in exporter of meaning. Again, one can argue for both importation and exportation of meaning, but in practicality, studies of embedded texts in Mark have tended toward one or the other – usually the former partly because New Testament studies, as a more traditional discipline generally speaking, has not sufficiently interacted with postmodern literary theory, especially its conception of intertextuality.[2]

A third issue, which is of particular interest to historical critics, is the connection between the historicity of the Gospel vignettes – as accurate representations of Jesus' deeds and sayings – and the evangelist's adaptation of Scripture texts in the composition of his narrative. Scholars who are predisposed to preserve the line of continuity between Jesus' religious program and that of the Markan evangelist tend toward acknowledging less literary creativity in the use of embedded texts. But if Scripture is acknowledged as playing a vital role in the shaping of the larger Markan narrative (which supposedly preserves its continuity with the Old Testament), does this not imply that the nature of the Gospel narrative is apologetic, aggadic, or some form of myth-making, which at the same time detracts from its historicity? In other words, the more that one appeals to influence (whether the motive is or is not cohesion), the more one needs to wrestle with historicity. Can we have it both ways? Some attempt to do just that by attempting to connect the embedded Scripture with the historical Jesus whenever possible. This maneuver, however, is certainly contentious among both historical Jesus scholars, narrative critics, and mythologists – to name a few. Nevertheless, it is an issue which emerges and requires attention on literary, historical, and socio-religious levels.

---

2.   See T.R. Hatina, 'Intertextuality and Historical Criticism in New Testament Studies: Is There a Relationship?', *BibInt* 7 (1999), pp. 28–43.

A fourth issue concerns the literacy competence of Mark's audience. Even if the audience was familiar with the Scriptures, as I think we should presuppose, should the audience be primarily located in an oral culture or a chirographic/ literate culture? There are two contrary assumptions regarding the reception of Mark operating in this collection of essays. Some contributors assume that Mark was read by individuals much like we would read Mark today. This means that most embedded texts would have been grasped and interpreted because the audience was well versed in the Jewish Scriptures and interpretive traditions. I say that this is an operating assumption because the competence of the audience is often not explicitly mentioned. Instead, the investigation of embedded texts begins either with the assumption that authorial intent can be recovered or with the assumption of an objectively agreed upon text as a self-contained entity. Whereas other contributors assume that Mark was an oral performance heard primarily by an illiterate audience which would have had mixed abilities in identifying allusions. Certainly, they would have been familiar with biblical stories and their traditions. If it is the case that the audience was largely illiterate, many of the so-called allusions and even some of the quotations (i.e. without formulas) may not have been identified by the hearers at all. How one understands the cultural reception of the narrative and its audience has significance for how one reads embedded texts. In this regard, narrative explorations of embedded texts cannot be separated from sociological/ anthropological ones.

A fifth issue also concerns Mark's audience, but from a different angle. There are two contrary assumptions operating among the contributors with respect to the familiarity of Mark's narrative among its audience. Some contributors begin their investigation with the presupposition that the narrative is fresh, perhaps heard/ read for the first time, and thus they place significant emphasis on reactions such as surprise and suspense. Conversely, some contributors approach the narrative as a repeated performance which would have been familiar to an audience group. From this perspective, interpretations of embedded texts are not entirely dependent on narrative chronological sequence, but are much more multidimensional, incorporating features such as mnemonic devices in the story that allow for interplay among episodes.

A sixth issue which emerges has to do with the nature of allusions. Since so many essays in this collection concentrate on allusions rather than explicit quotations, questions concerning the meaning, extent, and validation of literary allusions inevitably arise and force biblical scholars into the realm of literary criticism and theory where much of the work has been and continues to be done. The philosophical implications stemming from this issue are far-reaching in that they intersect with the nature of text, intertext, the locus of meaning, and the vastness of post-structuralism. As mentioned above, future studies into the function of embedded texts will inevitably have to take such concerns into consideration.

There are certainly many more emergent issues which could be discussed, and each reader of these essays may suggest new ones or revise the ones that are offered here. These are nevertheless offered as an entry way into further discussion.

THE FUNCTION OF SCRIPTURE IN MARK 15.1–39

Darrell L. Bock

1. *Introduction*

A narrator of an account has a variety of ways in which the theme can be revealed. An author can tell us directly with narrative summaries, or can allow characters to act and speak in certain ways. An author can also use 'cultural scripts', that is, allusions to manners, customs, or ideas that only need a trigger to be evoked. This final, subtler manner of presentation can accomplish a great deal in a short space, if the clues are properly read. I often tell my classes that the sentence, 'The Cowboys are going up to the frozen tundra to melt the Cheeseheads', makes a great deal of sense to sports fans in the United States but would be an exercise of frustration to someone learning English in the Middle East. That American football is being addressed without using the term 'football' is an example of a cultural script that often appears. As a result, it is sometimes difficult to be sure when a script is being utilized.

For the Gospels and their theological world, one of the key cultural scripts is the Scripture. The easiest way to evoke this authoritative world is simply to cite the text directly. However, often it is the case that texts are alluded to rather than quoted. As a result, there is debate about whether an allusion is actually present. This situation applies to the discussion of Mk 15.1–39. In these verses, only Ps. 22.2 (22.1 English) is cited in Mk 15.34. All other references to the Hebrew Scripture are allusions, and some are debated. Almost everyone recognizes the connections and use of Psalm 22 in the account. More debated are the potential allusions to the Suffering Servant.[1] Our goal is to proceed through this unit one allusion at a time and see what results. In order to examine whether or not a cultural script is present, we will not only look for specific terminology (keeping in mind that we have just suggested that a concept can be evoked without using a specific term), but we will also see whether a cluster of ideas appears to such a measure as to suggest that a specific image is being used.

---

1. For example, contrast Joel Marcus, *The Way of the Lord: Christological Exegesis of the Old Testament in the Gospel of Mark* (Louisville: Westminster/John Knox, 1992), pp. 186–96, who sees a major influence of the Servant songs on these verses to Howard Kee, 'The Function of Scriptural Quotations and Allusions in Mark 11–16', in E. Earle Ellis and E. Güasser (eds), *Jesus und Paulus: Festschrift für Werner Georg Kümmel zum 70. Geburtstag* (Göttingen: Vandenhoeck & Ruprecht, 1975), pp. 165–88. Kee on pp. 182–83 says, 'There are no sure references to Isaiah 53 and none of the distinctive language of the Suffering Servant is evident'.

As previously stated, our examination will proceed one alleged allusion at a time, and then we shall summarize the results.

2. *Allusions and Citation in Mark 15.1–39*

To Give Over in Mark 15.1, 10, 15

The first allusion is actually a chain of references in vv. 1, 10, and 15. The use of παραδίδωμι in these verses raises the question of whether the language of Scripture is being evoked. In v. 1, the Jewish leadership gives Jesus over (παρέδω-καν) to Pilate. In v. 10, the pluperfect for the Jewish leadership giving Jesus over appears (παραδεδώκεισαν), a remark that reviews v. 1 and points to a stylistic feature of Mark in repeating key points. In v. 15, Pilate gives Jesus over (παρέ-δωκεν) to be flogged.

The debate here is whether the expression 'giving over' is a merely judicial term or whether it has theological overtones emerging from Isa. 53.6 and 12. The argument against the allusion is that one common term does not an allusion make; something else with it needs to trigger the idea of an allusion.[2] The relevant verses in the LXX read as follows:

53.6b καὶ κύριος παρέδωκεν αὐτὸν ταῖς ἁμαρτίαις ἡμῶν
53.12a ἀνθ᾽ ὧν παρεδόθη εἰς θάνατον ἡ ψυχὴ αὐτοῦ
53.12b καὶ διὰ τὰς ἁμαρτίας αὐτῶν παρεδόθη

In Isaiah LXX, the Servant is given over for sin and is given over to death. The language in the Greek varies from the Hebrew, where an encounter or a meeting of a certain fate is meant (פָּגַע is the verb in v. 6 and v. 12b). In the Hebrew, the Lord has sin encounter the Servant (v. 6), his soul was poured out to death, and he made intercession or encountered the transgressors (v. 12). The Greek verb of the LXX appears once in the active (v. 6) and twice in the passive (v. 12). Clearly παραδίδωμι is prominent in this passage. The question is whether Mark picks up on this in these verses. It should also be noted that the passage suggests that it is God who gives over the Servant.

The reuse of παραδίδωμι in Mark does appear to be an allusion. The writer seems to use the word as a literary trigger that reminds readers of the Passion predictions in Mk 9.31, 10.33–34, and 14.21, 41. It is especially important that 14.21 states that the delivery of the Son of Man is something that 'is written of him' (γέγραπται περὶ αὐτοῦ). So the handing over is part of the cultural and

---

2. For example, Douglas Moo, *The Old Testament in the Gospel Passion Narratives* (Sheffield: Almond Press, 1983), pp. 92–96 argues against an allusion here in 15.1, 15 (see his note 3) as does H.E. Tödt, *The Son of Man in the Synoptic Tradition* (London: SCM Press, 1965), pp. 156–61. Tödt's standard is that the term needs to be connected to another phrase in Isaiah 53 to count as an allusion. Moo does see such an allusion in the Passion sayings, a key use to which we shall return. For a theological allusion, see Vincent Taylor, *The Gospel According to St. Mark* (London: MacMillan, 2nd edn, 1966), pp. 578, 584; Raymond Brown, *The Death of the Messiah* (New York: Doubleday, 1994), pp. 211–13, 853; and W. Propkes, *Christus Traditus* (ATANT, 49; Zurich: Zwingli, 1949), pp. 152–69, 180–81.

scriptural script that Mark has alerted the reader to several times before he actually tells the story. The reference in 14.21 frames the account at a literary level. This suggests that the term is likely an allusion to the Servant concept. It also suggests that the standard of more than one term has been met, for the 'handing over' is something that has been written about previously.[3] This case also serves as a reminder that in looking at allusions, we must not let our tendency to consider a text or allusion in small pericope, form critical, or tradition historical units keep us from seeing how a text works at a literary level within a Gospel. For in this case, to lose the story line is to lose the likely, cultural script that the evangelist has continually raised and even framed by an earlier reference.

So we would conclude that the telling of Jesus' handing over by both the Jewish officials and by Pilate is underlaid by allusions to the Servant of Isaiah 53. Even though in the original passage God hands the Servant over, in Mark's telling these foretold events portray both the human and divine elements in the event. The cultural script not only suggests that this act was part of a divine plan where God designed the handing over, but also that such suffering was the call of Jesus. In addition, the script supplies the fact that this death was for sin.

The Silence and Amazement in Mark 15.5

Two potential allusions are the topic of discussion in Mk 15.5. These are whether the issue of Jesus' silence alludes to Isa. 53.7 and whether Pilate's amazement recalls Isa. 53.13–15. Both allusions are debated since the connection is more conceptual than terminological.[4]

What complicates this discussion on the allusion to silence is that this theme appears three times in Isa. 53.7; twice it is said the Servant did not open his mouth, and once it is said that he was dumb. The LXX of this verse runs parallel to the MT on this point, and the three points of contact read in this manner: καὶ αὐτὸς διὰ τὸ κεκακῶσθαι οὐκ ἀνοίγει τὸ στόμα ὡς πρόβατον ἐπὶ σφαγὴν ἤχθη καὶ ὡς ἀμνὸς ἐναντίον τοῦ κείροντος αὐτὸν ἄφωνος οὕτως οὐκ ἀνοίγει τὸ στόμα αὐτοῦ. The emphasis on silence as the Servant is led to his suffering is what causes some to read an allusion here. If the idea is evoked, then the issue of

---

3. W. Marxsen, *Mark the Evangelist* (trans. Roy A. Harrisville; New York: Abingdon Press, 1969), p. 39 n. 33, indicates how important this verb is for Mark. He uses it in an absolute sense of Jesus in 3.19; 14.11, 18, 21, 42, and with some qualification in 9.31; 10.33; 14.41; 15.1, 15. The term is almost like a choral refrain in Mark. Jesus is also the 'one given over' in Mk 14.42, 44. This constant usage only enhances the likelihood that the use is intentional.

4. For example, R.H. Gundry, *Mark: A Commentary on his Apology for the Cross* (Grand Rapids: Eerdmans, 1993) p. 993, rejects an allusion to amazement, arguing that the amazement in Isaiah involves the silence of kings, not the Servant, and that the amazement in Isaiah is not related to the silence of the Servant. On the other hand, C.A. Evans, *Mark 8.27–16.20* (WBC, 34b; Nashville: Thomas Nelson, 2001), p. 479 argues that the allusion by itself is 'not impressive', but it becomes possible when combined with other allusions to Isaiah 53 in the chapter. Taylor, *St. Mark*, p. 580, thinks it 'impossible' not to think of Isa. 53.7 when Jesus' silence is discussed, while many others simply do not mention any allusion here indicating they are not convinced. M. Hooker, *The Gospel According to Saint Mark* (BNTC; London: A. & C. Black, 1991), pp. 367–68, discusses the amazement allusion as possible, but makes no mention of Jesus' silence and Isaiah.

the injustice of the process is also present, since the Servant suffers unjustly.[5] Although this allusion is not certain, the fact that Mark frames the Passion in Servant language (see Mk 10.45 and 14.24) makes a connection more likely, rather than less likely.[6]

An allusion to amazement seems harder to establish, although it is still possible. Gundry's objection is that the amazement is not tied to silence in the Servant song, as in Mark 15, but to the marring and suffering. He underscores this point by noting that it is the kings who are silent.[7] This point is technically correct, but it is probably only half right, since it is a beating at the least and a crucifixion at the most that is being contemplated as Pilate interrogates Jesus. This means that the idea of suffering and marring is what is being contemplated in the context[8]. The amazement in Isaiah has to do with the humble state of the Servant, which is also certainly part of what is at play in the scene in Mark. If there is an allusion here, it is a complicated one where the silence of Isa. 53.7 and the amazement of Isa. 52.13–15 have been combined and collapsed together. There is a terminological overlap to a degree as Isa. 52.15a reads, οὕτως θαυμάσονται ἔθνη πολλὰ ἐπ' αὐτῷ. The verb θαυμάζειν appears in Mk 15.5 as well. The verb in the LXX translates the difficult Hebrew term for sprinkle, so the allusion, if it exists, is closer to the LXX.[9] The difficulty here is that Pilate must be seen as a representative of the nations, if the LXX is the point of contact. This is possible, but the allusion in this case requires more inferences, which is why it is less than clear. In my view, the allusion to silence is more likely than one to amazement, even though the latter has a verbal contact. However, it is the point of verbal contact that makes the second allusion possible, if less than likely.

In sum, it is likely that Mk 15.5 alludes to the Servant at one point, namely that of Jesus' silence, and it also suggests that Jesus suffers unjustly. Less clear is whether a second allusion to Isa. 52.15a appears with Pilate's amazement. If it does, then the silence is reinforced, as Mk 15.5 makes that connection explicit. If the first allusion to silence is present, then Jesus' humble and submissively silent response is the point of the allusion.

The Mocking of the Soldiers in Mark 15.19–20

Allusions in the interrogation by Pilate in Mk 15.1–5 are really not so concentrated. Likewise, there is no significant allusive activity in the exchange of Barabbas for Jesus in Mk 15.6–15. However, everything changes as we enter into the movement to crucifixion, beginning with the soldiers' mocking of Jesus in Mk 15.16–20. Now, allusions will come one after another.

---

5. L. Hurtado, *Mark* (NIBC; Peabody, MA: Hendrickson, 1989), pp. 258–59.

6. Marcus, *The Way of the Lord*, p. 187, calls this allusion probable, although he recognizes a potential overlap with the theme of the righteous sufferer from a text like Ps. 38.13–15. What speaks for the allusion is the way in which Isaiah 53 is evoked elsewhere in the passage.

7. Gundry, *Mark*, p. 993.

8. Brown, *The Death of the Messiah*, p. 734.

9. Moo, *The Old Testament in the Gospel Passion Narratives*, p. 148 n. 2.

The pattern starts with the mocking of the soldiers in Mark 15.19–20, καὶ ἔτυπτον αὐτοῦ τὴν κεφαλὴν καλάμῳ καὶ ἐνέπτυον αὐτῷ καὶ τιθέντες τὰ γόνατα προσεκύνουν αὐτῷ. καὶ ὅτε ἐνέπαιξαν αὐτῷ. In this scene, the soldiers mockingly clothe Jesus in royal purple, which ironically points to Jesus' real identity. The key to establishing the allusions comes from the slapping and spitting. Isaiah 50.6 LXX, a part of the third Servant song, reads: τὸν νῶτόν μου δέδωκα εἰς μάστιγας τὰς δὲ σιαγόνας μου εἰς ῥαπίσματα τὸ δὲ πρόσωπόν μου οὐκ ἀπέστρεψα ἀπὸ αἰσχύνης ἐμπτυσμάτων. The last term mentions spitting. Although with different Greek words, slapping is also noted. Important here is that the passion prediction of Mk 10.34 mentions scourging and spitting.[10] This is important because these predictions have an element of divine design to them. The combination of beating and spitting also occurs in Mk 14.65. These three texts (Mk 10.34; 14.65 and 15.19–20) are the only uses of mocking in Mark. The internal framing by the evangelist makes an allusion to Isaiah here likely.[11] Pesch speaks of a martyr-king in Mark 14–15. He is one who '*von Gott auf dem Thron zu seiner Rechten erhöht werden wird* (14,62); *sein Haupt, das jetzt geschlagen wird, ist zum Martyrium gesalbt worden* (14,3–9). *Er hat den Spott und die Mißhandlung von Juden* (14,65) *und Heiden* (15,16–20b) *erdulden müssen – und ist am Kreuz weiterer Verhönung ausgesetzt* (15,29–32)'.[12] This summarizes well the emphases in Mark, as the reference to Jesus as a King appears six times in Mark 15 (vv. 2, 9, 12, 18, 26, 32), often in ironic mocking.

As we come to the crucifixion proper, we see the Scripture emerging in a manner that appeals to the imagery of the Suffering Servant. However, another portrait of Jesus, that of the Righteous Sufferer, will also become increasingly prevalent, and Psalm 22 plays a central role in this portrait. The key uses involve Ps. 22.18 (v. 24), 22.7 (v. 29), 22.1 (v. 34), the likely use of 22.6 (in vv. 30-31), 69.21 (v. 36), and conceptual allusions in the scorn of onlookers to Isa. 53.3–4. These passages will link the images of the Suffering Servant and the Righteous Sufferer.[13]

Offer of the Drink in Mark 15.23
There is discussion whether the offer of a drink to Jesus recalls Prov. 31.6, which reads: 'Give strong drink to the one who is perishing, and wine to those who are distressed'. There is overlap in one term between Mark and the LXX, the use of

10. Marcus, *The Way of the Lord*, pp. 189–90; J. Gnilka, *Das Evangelium nach Markus* (EKKNT, II/2; Köln/Neukirchen–Vluyn: Benziner and Neukirchener Verlag, 1979), p. 308 sees a conceptual allusion with texts like Pss. 119.51; 31.18–19; 70.4 (all MT). Gnilka appears to have a typo here, citing Ps. 109.15, but 119.51 looks more likely to be correct. If the allusion is conceptual, then the Servant and Righteous Sufferer overlap.

11. But for the view that an allusion here is 'remote at best', see Evans, *Mark 8.27–16.20*, p. 488; while Hooker, *Saint Mark*, p. 370, rejects the connection completely.

12. R. Pesch, *Das Markusevangelium, 2. Teil* (HKNT, II/2; Freiburg: Herder, 1984), p. 474. He argues that this portrait is part of a pre-Markan passion tradition.

13. R.T. France, *The Gospel of Mark* (NIGTC; Grand Rapids: Eerdmans, 2002), p. 640. J.H. Reumann, 'Psalm 22 at the Cross: Lament and Thanksgiving for Jesus Christ', *Int* 28 (1974), pp. 40–41 has charts of the use of Psalm 22 in Mark 15 and in the New Testament. He argues its widespread use is evidence that this association does not belong to Mark but part of a Passion tradition Mark has used.

the verb δίδωμι. There is discussion about whether this is an act of mockery or compassion in Mark, as the Matthean parallel corresponds more closely to the text and seems to be an act of mockery (Mt. 27.34). Pesch calls the allusion in Mark possible, while Brown does not see any echo.[14] An allusion to Scripture here is questionable, as there is no development of a theme tied to concepts in Proverbs beyond the possible connection here. A clearer echo of such a theme comes in Mk 15.36.

The Casting of Lots for Clothes in Mark 15.24

One of the clearest allusions in Mark 15 is to the casting of lots for clothes from Ps. 22.17. Just comparing Mark and the LXX makes this clear. The relevant portion of Mark for casting lots reads, διαμερίζονται τὰ ἱμάτια αὐτοῦ, βάλλοντες κλῆρον ἐπ᾽ αὐτά. The LXX of Ps. 21.19 reads, διεμερίσαντο τὰ ἱμάτιά μου ἑαυτοῖς καὶ ἐπὶ τὸν ἱματισμόν μου ἔβαλον κλῆρον. The extensive verbal contact is obvious. In fact, Brown notes five points of contact: divided up, clothes, for, threw, and lots.[15] The custom involved here is that the crucified forfeited his possessions (Tacitus, *Annals* 6.29). The connection is a clear allusion to the Righteous Sufferer. In the framing of Mark, Jesus suffers as a righteous one and in innocence as King of the Jews, Son of Man (Mk 14.61–62), and Son of God (Mk 15.39). Jesus dies powerless in humiliation.[16]

Crucified with the Thieves in Mark 15.27

More debated and less clear is Mark's possible allusion to either Isa. 53.12 or to Ps. 22.16 in his description of Jesus' crucifixion with the thieves. Such an allusion is made explicit in the textually suspect Mk 15.28, which clearly cites Isa. 53.12, but the earliest manuscripts of Mark lack this verse (א, A, B, C, D). The LXX of Isaiah refers to the 'lawless' (ἀνόμοις), while Mark refers to rebels (λῃστάς). This allusion is less than certain for Mark, given the complete lack of verbal contact, although the use of Isaiah 53 in the chapter and the easy conceptual connection make it possible. If present, it adds to the theme of innocence, but its absence does not detract from anything already present in Mark 15.

Wagging of the Heads in Mark 15.29 and Mocking in Mark 15.31

Some who mock Jesus wag their heads at him, a description that is an allusion to Ps. 22.8. What is present here may actually be an appeal to the Old Testament theme of righteous suffering, as Lam. 2.15 also expresses this kind of an idea. The LXX for Ps. 22.8 (21.8 LXX) reads, πάντες οἱ θεωροῦντές με ἐξεμυκτήρισάν με ἐλάλησαν ἐν χείλεσιν ἐκίνησαν κεφαλήν. The relevant part of Lamentations reads, πάντες οἱ παραπορευόμενοι ὁδόν ἐσύρισαν καὶ ἐκίνησαν τὴν κεφαλὴν αὐτῶν ἐπὶ τὴν θυγατέρα Ιερουσαλημ. Mark 15.29 reads, Καὶ οἱ παραπορευόμενοι ἐβλασφήμουν αὐτὸν κινοῦντες τὰς κεφαλὰς αὐτῶν. The

---

14. Pesch, *Das Markusevangelium 2*, p. 478; Brown, *Death of the Messiah*, p. 943.
15. Brown, *Death of the Messiah*, p. 953.
16. W.L. Lane, *The Gospel According to Mark* (NICNT; Grand Rapids: Eerdmans, 1974), p. 566.

LXX reflects the Hebrew at these points. One can see how the Markan wording of the theme is more like Lamentations, although the corporate nature of Lamentations, with its daughters of Jerusalem, is more distant than the individual suffering in Psalm 22. The fact that Psalm 22 so dominates the Markan account makes it likely that it is the point of contact,[17] but the presence of the theme elsewhere in the Hebrew Scripture has influenced the wording. In fact, the theme is common in the Scripture and in Judaism (Pss. 69.20; 109.25; Jer. 18.16; Isa. 37.22; Sir. 13.7).[18]

This subsequent mocking of Jesus fits the suffering righteous one motif. Mark extends this mocking to the activity of the chief priests and scribes in v. 31, which reads, ὁμοίως καὶ οἱ ἀρχιερεῖς ἐμπαίζοντες πρὸς ἀλλήλους μετὰ τῶν γραμματέων ἔλεγον· ἄλλους ἔσωσεν, ἑαυτὸν οὐ δύναται σῶσαι. This also looks back to Psalm 22 in theme, fitting a pattern of mocking noted in Judaism as well (*Ascension and Martrydom of Isaiah* 5.2–3). The mocking cry to save oneself using οὐὰ in Mk 15.29 may also be an allusive element applying to a theme of suffering (Pss. 35.21; 40.15; 70.4). It could easily be mocking the things that Jesus said that he would do during his ministry. Senior, commenting on the use of Psalm 22 at this point says, 'No biblical piece [Ps. 22] so eloquently expresses the lament of the Just One'.[19] The mocking cry that God might rescue him in v. 32 may be a play on the Jewish idea that God will help the righteous (Wis. 2.17–18). All these details extend the imagery of Jesus suffering as a righteous one at the hands of those who do not go God's way.

Darkness of Creation in Mark 15.33
We have seen Mark use the idea of the suffering Servant and the Righteous Sufferer in Mark 15. In Mk 15.33, we get a third key theme: the use of apocalyptic imagery in the description of the darkness coming over the creation in the sixth hour. This evokes a more ominous element in the event. Darkness and death look back to two keys moments in the Scripture, the death of the first-born in Exod. 10.21–22 and, more significantly, the imagery of judgment of the Day of the Lord (Amos 8.9–10; note also Deut. 28.29; Isa. 13.10; Joel 3.14 [4.15 MT]). Amos 8.9 LXX reads, καὶ ἔσται ἐν ἐκείνῃ τῇ ἡμέρᾳ λέγει κύριος ὁ θεός καὶ δύσεται ὁ ἥλιος μεσημβρίας καὶ συσκοτάσει ἐπὶ τῆς γῆς ἐν ἡμέρᾳ τὸ φῶς. The relevant portion of Mark 15.33 reads, σκότος ἐγένετο ἐφ᾽ ὅλην τὴν γῆν. What is expressed in a verb in the LXX is expressed in a noun in Mark. A reference to the earth is also shared between the texts. The spectrum of divine judgment is tied to the event. In one sense, something is amiss in this death, and the pall of this death impacts the creation, casting a shadow over the earth. With the eschatological note pointing to an act of the Day, salvation and judgment draw near.

17. Moo, *Passion Narrative*, p. 258.
18. Gnilka, *Das Evangelium nach Markus, 2*, p. 320.
19. D.P. Senior, *The Passion of Jesus in the Gospel of Mark* (Wilmington, DE: Michael Glazier, 1984), p. 118.

The Cry of Jesus in Mark 15.34

Of all the allusions to Scripture in Mark 15, none is clearer in its point of contact than Jesus' cry from Ps. 22.2. Mark appears to transcribe the Aramaic here. So we have the Greek transcription of an Aramaic cry from a Hebrew Psalm, a fitting combination given the cultures at play in this event. There is much discussion among commentators of what the original event here was. Did Jesus say it or did Mark add it? If Jesus did say it, what language did he use, given that some hear a cry to Elijah when Jesus has cried out to God? Those issues are not our concern, since we are examining the use Mark makes of Scripture. More important for us is how the Righteous Sufferer theme works here. Is this merely a cry of despair or is there more at work, an appeal to the entire Psalm with its ultimate resolution in faith and hope? This point is heavily discussed with positions ranging the spectrum from a cry of only despair to a cry that sees Jesus dying in both pain and hope following the theme of the entire Psalm.[20]

The key to the issue, as Marcus points out, is the linkage in Psalm 22 between the theme of suffering and the kingship of Yahweh, which is what is at stake in the appeal of the Righteous One.[21] Marcus points out how the reading of Psalm 22 in Judaism involved a linkage between suffering and hope (1QH 5.31; 4QPs^f). The use of the Psalm in the New Testament shows the same emphases in Heb. 2.12–13 and 2 Tim. 4.17–18. When one places this background next to the theme of Jesus' kingship in Mark 15 and next to the echoes of Psalm 22 (see vv. 18, 24, 26, 29, 32, 34, 39), then a connection to God's kingdom work is present (see also 15.43). The centurion's confession climactically evokes this hope and suggests that the use of Ps. 22.27, which states that the ends of the earth will turn to the Lord, points to the triumphant theme of the psalm. So those who claim there is no allusion to the triumph of the Psalm are wrong.

What is difficult in assessing this case is whether one should distinguish what Jesus does in uttering the single verse and what Mark does in framing the cry from a single verse. As the apocalyptic darkness comes, Jesus knows he is headed towards death, but he has an expectation of ultimate vindication (as seen in his examination by the Jewish leadership). Is the cry, then, a recognition of suffering

---

20. For example, Gundry, *Mark*, p. 966, and France, *The Gospel of Mark*, pp. 652–53, see the note of despair and suffering as the sole point here. Gundry notes that the evangelists are capable of making themselves clear and that only a note of despair is here. In contrast, Senior, *The Passion of Jesus in the Gospel of Mark*, pp. 122–23, sees an appeal to the tenor of the whole Psalm, as does Gnilka, *Das Evangelium nach Markus 2*, p. 322. Falling in between these two views are Evans, *Mark 8.29–16.20*, p. 507, and Marcus, *The Way of the Lord*, pp. 180–82. They stress the despair but do not doubt an appeal to the whole Psalm. Evans sees an appeal to the Psalm but with the emphasis in this moment on the pain and despair of death as expressed in the being forsaken by God. Marcus argues that the Psalm is so pervasive throughout Mark 15 that it is evoked by the account as a whole as much as by this verse. He makes the point because many claim that nowhere in Mark 15 is the more triumphant part of the Psalm cited.

21. Marcus, *The Way of the Lord*, pp. 18–82, is defending the thesis of H. Gese, 'Psalm 22 und das Neue Testament: Der älteste Bericht vom Tode Jesu und die Entstehung des Herrenmahles', in *Vom Sinai zum Zion: Alttestamentliche Beiträge zur biblischen Theologie* (BEvT, 64; Munich: Kaiser, 1974), pp. 192–96.

before vindication?[22] This combination, though not certain, seems more than likely. Jesus dies in the pain of suffering, but as the Servant and the Righteous One, he knows that pain is not the end of his journey, even though the pain is real and deep and a cause of incredible despair. Regardless of how one judges Jesus' use of the verse, what is more certain is how Mark frames Jesus' single remark. Mark is saying that even though Jesus cries out in despair, the combination of crucifixion details that point to the Servant, the Righteous Sufferer, and the Day mean that vindication and victory do follow.

Offering a Drink to the Victim in Mark 15.36
The suggested allusion here is to Ps. 69.21 (Ps. 68.22 LXX). The LXX reads, καὶ ἔδωκαν εἰς τὸ βρῶμά μου χολὴν καὶ εἰς τὴν δίψαν μου ἐπότισάν με ὄξος. Again the LXX mirrors the MT here. Mark 15.36 reads, δραμὼν δέ τις καὶ γεμίσας σπόγγον ὄξους περιθεὶς καλάμῳ ἐπότιζεν αὐτόν λέγων· ἄφετε ἴδωμεν εἰ ἔρχεται Ἡλίας καθελεῖν αὐτόν. The key overlapping term here is the reference to ὄξος. Although Pesch rejects this allusion, the use of Psalm 22 throughout the section places the balance in favor of it.[23]

Once again the idea is that enemies have mocked the Righteous One during his suffering. Jesus dies facing mocking to the end. The crucifixion scene ends with a centurion's cry that Jesus was the 'Son of God'. This climactic confession echoes questions raised that led Jesus to the cross in Mk 14.61–62 ('Are you the son of the Blessed One?' Jesus said, 'I am. And you will see the Son of Man seated at the right hand of power and coming with the clouds of heaven'). The centurion's confession forms a bracket with that examination scene. Mark is saying that despite the mocking, suffering, and humiliation that Jesus experienced on the cross, Jesus was who he claimed to be. Scripture and creation, two divine witnesses, indicate this was so.

3. *The Three Key Scriptural Themes of Mark 15.1–39*

We have argued that the three key themes in Mk 15.1–39 are appeals to the Suffering Servant, the Righteous Sufferer, and the Day of the Lord. Bearing the

---

22. I have defended the likely authenticity of the thrust of Jesus' response before the Jewish leadership in detail elsewhere, *Blasphemy and Exaltation in Judaism and the Final Examination of Jesus* (WUNT, II/106; Tübingen: Mohr–Siebeck, 1998), pp. 184–233. The common objection that the Ps. 22.2 cry from the cross is not authentic is because of alleged evidence of a seam between Mk 15.34–35. The crowd hears a cry to Elijah, while Jesus speaks of God, showing a 'disconnect' conceptually. The objection is without real force. It is possible that the cry to God could have led listeners to think Jesus was asking God to send Elijah since Elijah was viewed as a protector and an eschatological agent (Sir. 48.10).

23. Pesch, *Das Markusevangelium*, II, p. 496, says the passage does not have enough contact to establish the allusion. Brown, *Death of the Messiah*, p. 1059, argues Mark is 'much less specific' than Mt. 27.47–49 and Jn 19.28–30, but that the 'whole context of 15.36 echoes Scripture passages, including Psalm 22.2'. He also notes how the mockery is also shared between the scenes. Brown has a full, lucid discussion of the cry-Elijah-offer of vinegar sequence on pp. 1058–66.

burden of this scriptural backdrop are passages from Psalm 22, Psalm 69, and Isa. 52.13–53.12. The use of these images has implications for eschatology, christology, soteriology, and discipleship in Mark.

The study by Marcus has made the point that the use of the Righteous Sufferer and the Suffering Servant carried eschatological implications in the intertestamental period and also for Mark.[24] That this connection also exists for the Day of the Lord is obvious. As he notes, the Sufferer goes from a person suffering in spite of righteousness to one who suffers on account of righteousness but with the expectation of ultimate glory (Wis. 2.12–20; 5.1–7; 4 Ezra; *2 Apoc Bar.*; superscriptions on Psalms 'for the end', 4QPs 37 3.10–13; 1QH 8.32; 5.21, 23–24). The Sufferer is ultimately a figure who is vindicated in the end as God exercises his judgment. The Servant also is a triumphant figure, but oscillates between an individual portrait and a collective one, as Wis. 2.12–20 and 5.1–7 show. Qumran does the same (1QS 8.3–7,10 – 'the elect ones of God's favor', to make propitiation for the land, where the elect one looks back to Isa. 42.1, while expiation looks to Isaiah 53; 1QSa 1.1–3). This backdrop suggests that there is an eschatological element of vindication and victory that hovers over the death of Jesus. His death is not the end, but the beginning and pivot in a movement to the end. Here is the eschatological dimension of Mark's use of Scripture.

At a christological level, the innocent Sufferer and Servant leads to the centurion's confession of Jesus as Son of God and counters the mocking taunts that Jesus shows himself to be king of the Jews. That confession forms a bracket with the Jewish examination of Jesus and affirms that Jesus is the Son of God, the Christ, and the Son of Man. His innocent suffering and coming vindication point to this reality for Mark.

In terms of soteriology, if the allusions to Isaiah 53 early in the passage stand, then there are echoes back to Mk 10.45 and 14.22 which point to Jesus' suffering as substitutionary to a degree. Jesus was given over for sins (53.6b, 12b LXX). It may well be that the one scene that is not explicitly allusive to the Old Testament, the exchange for Barabbas, also fits here. Just as Jesus went in his place, he goes in ours, as a ransom for many.

Finally, there is the example of Jesus' suffering. He suffers the indignity of injustice in a way that those who follow him can model. The implicit corporateness of the Righteous Sufferer and Servant may well point in this direction.

In sum, Mark's appeal to the concepts of Scripture richly forms an important backdrop and ultimately a kind of commentary on the events surrounding Jesus' death. These are important cultural scripts that explain what is taking place. In the weaving together of the Righteous Sufferer, the Servant, and the Day of the Lord, Mark not only evokes ideas that point to the arrival of the eschaton and the coming of judgment, but he also highlights the promise of vindication and the provision for salvation from one who was both a Righteous and Vindicated Sufferer, a man who would be and was a divinely sent king.

24. Marcus, *Way of the Lord*, pp. 177–79, 190–93.

Reconfiguring Jesus: The Son of Man in Markan Perspective

Edwin K. Broadhead

1. *Introduction*

The Christology of the Gospel of Mark is created through a series of narrative structures and processes employed in the characterization of Jesus. Among these techniques is the appropriation of previously existing texts[1] in order to create new significance.[2] This engagement may involve materials from different parts of the same narrative (intratextual), materials from other narratives (intertextual), or both. Such literary moves allow the Gospel of Mark to negotiate among a variety of traditions in order to frame its own unique understanding of Jesus. The product of this negotiation may stand in various relationships to the traditions employed, ranging from emphasis to correction to rejection. In their essence, these moves are formal literary strategies which belong to the morphological and syntactical design of the narrative.[3] While literary traditions are involved, a sociological dimension is also at work: literary traditions imply tradents – people who create, preserve, and transmit such traditions. In a similar way the reconfiguration of existing traditions implies a community for whom this new configuration is important.

This generative process is at work in the scene of Jesus' trial in Mk 14.53–65. Here various traditions, some from within the Gospel of Mark and others from external texts, have been reshaped to generate a climactic christological confession. More specifically, the Markan image of Jesus as the Son of Man is created through this process. Attention will be given first to the intertextual basis for the Markan Son of Man, then to the realignment of materials from within the Gospel of Mark (intratextual), then to the engagement of texts from outside the narrative

---

1. Here I am using the term *text* not only in reference to a string of words, but also to a title, a concept, or a cluster of images. I have labeled this process of appropriation as *metamorphosis* – the creation of narrative significance out of existing materials and traditions. The term *metamorphosis* is discussed in Edwin K. Broadhead, *Teaching with Authority: Miracles and Christology in the Gospel of Mark* (JSNTSup, 74; Sheffield: Sheffield Academic Press, 1992), pp. 49–50. The entire book discusses this technical process in relation to miracle stories.

2. *Significance* is here understood as a formal term for the signs created within a narrative. For the distinction between *significance* and *meaning*, see Broadhead, *Teaching with Authority*, pp. 47–49. The formal interaction of semiotic elements (signs) within a text produces *signification* or *significance*. *Meaning* is what the reader negotiates from these text and its signs.

3. Such moves need not be attributed to an apostolic figure nor even to an imagined redactional genius labeled as the evangelist. Narrative critics describe this need to personify literary moves as *the intentional fallacy*.

(intertextual). Finally, the sociological implications of this process will be considered.

2. *The Intertextual Basis for the Son of Man*

The first trial scene in Mk 14.53–65 reaches its high point in the dialogue between the high priest and Jesus. When false witnesses cannot agree, the high priest puts the question directly: 'Are you the Christ, the son of the Blessed One?' (14.61). Jesus replies, 'I am, and you will see the Son of Man seated at the right hand of the Power and coming with the clouds of heaven' (14.62). The description of the Son of Man in Mk 14.62 draws explicitly upon Dan. 7.13 ('the Son of Man coming with the clouds of heaven") and upon Ps. 110.1 (the image of one seated at the right hand of God)[4] In addition to these citations, concepts articulated in Psalm 2 lie in the background of Mk 14.62. Old Testament images of the Righteous One, the Suffering Servant, and the rejected prophet are also evoked by the first trial scene in Mk 14.53–65. Beyond this, a strong tradition of Jewish apocalyptic thought underlies the trial scene. These various texts and traditions provide the intertextual basis from which the Son of Man imagery of Mk 14.62 is negotiated.

3. *Old Testament Citations and Allusions*

The Daniel citation is drawn from an apocalyptic vision. Daniel gains access to the heavenly court, where he sees four beasts (Dan. 7.2–7). The fourth of these beasts sprouts its eleventh horn, which has human eyes, and speaks arrogant words (7.8). Within this context the Ancient of Days is described, then the scene of judgment begins (7.9–10). In the following scene the fourth beast is destroyed and the power of the other beasts is removed (7.11–12). In what is apparently a separate scene, the Ancient One hands over dominion to a figure who comes with the clouds of heaven (7.13–14). This figure is described as 'one like a son of man'. While this phrase has been interpreted in various ways, it seemingly refers to a heavenly figure who, in contrast to the beasts, bears human visage.[5] Significantly, this figure represents the suffering people of God, and they in turn share in his dominion (7.27).[6] The figure who appears before the Ancient One thus seems to be 'the enthroned heavenly patron of the people of God who have suffered at the hands of the kings, who have rebelled against heaven…'.[7] Daniel 7.13 describes

---

4. Norman Perrin, 'Mark 14.62: The End Product of a Christian Pesher Tradition?', in *A Modern Pilgrimage in New Testament Christology* (Philadelphia: Fortress Press, 1974), pp. 10–22 sees Mk 14.62 as an independent Christian pesher tradition built on the two strands of Scripture (Psalm 110 and Daniel 7).

5. Gabriel also has the appearance of a human in Dan. 8.15. Daniel is called 'son of man' by Gabriel in 8.17.

6. Michael seems to play a similar role in Dan. 10.13, 21; 12.1.

7. G. Nickelsburg, 'Son of Man', *ABD* 4, pp. 137–50 (p. 138).

the heavenly figure as one *like* a human, probably in contrast to the beasts. Other apocalyptic texts describe such a figure *as* the Son of Man.

The language from Ps. 110.1 ('seated at the right hand of the Power') reflects kingship imagery and lies in the background of Jewish messianic thought. This psalm has appeared already in Mk 12.36. Teaching in the temple, Jesus poses a riddle based on Ps. 110.1: if David calls the messiah his lord, how then can the messiah be the son of David? While the Gospel of Mark uses this text to fill out its christological portrait, the presumptions underlying this exegesis are important. The first use of the term κύριος is understood to refer to Yahweh, the second to the messiah. The place of the messiah is understood to be at the right hand of Yahweh. The destiny of the messiah is understood to be vindication in the presence of his foes.

A similar set of presumptions is drawn from Psalm 2, which lies behind the baptismal story (Mk 1.9–11). The kings of the earth conspire against the king of Israel, who is God's anointed (Ps. 2.1–3). Yahweh is described as 'he who sits in the heavens' (2.4). Yahweh laughs in derision at the plotting of the kings, speaks in wrath against them, and terrifies them with divine fury (2.4–5). The king of Israel is enthroned in Zion at the decree of Yahweh (2.6). God's anointed, the king, is also God's son: 'You are my son; today I have begotten you' (2.7). He will bring the judgment of Yahweh upon the nations and rulers (2.8–11).

The trial scene in Mk 14.53–65 invokes these images from the psalms. The high priest's question equates the term messiah ('anointed') with the title Son of God, a connection not firmly rooted in the available Jewish literature. Though Son of Man is not a messianic title in pre-Christian Jewish thought, Jesus' affirmation of the Christ title is connected directly to the work of the Son of Man: 'I am, and you will see the Son of Man…' (Mk 14.62). Because the Son of Man will be seated at the right hand of Yahweh, the Son of Man is the Lord, the King, the anointed (messiah), and the Son. He who sits at God's right hand will be vindicated by God in the presence of his enemies (Ps. 110.1).

The trial scene in Mk 14.53–65 also invokes Old Testament images of the Righteous Sufferer.[8] In his hour of need Jesus is abandoned by his followers: 'My friends stand aloof from my plague, and my kinsmen stand afar off' (Ps. 38.11). His condemnation by religious leaders recalls that 'those who seek my life lay their snares, those who seek my hurt speak of ruin, and meditate treachery all the day long' (Ps. 38.12). He is silent before his accuser 'like a speechless man who does not open his mouth' (Ps. 38.13). The abuse of 14.65, set alongside the declaration of innocence in 14.55–56, evokes images of the Righteous Sufferer.

The image of the rejected prophet is also found in this scene. Jesus is condemned because of an alleged prophecy against the temple (14.57–58). His prophecy about the coming Son of Man evokes the guilty verdict as well as the death sentence (14.63–64). In the scene of abuse, Jesus is taunted with the insistence that he prophesy (14.65). This scene echoes, among others, the story of Jeremiah

---

8.   Rudolph Pesch, *Das Markusevangelium* (HTKNT; Freiburg: Herder, 1980), I, pp. 426, 431–32, finds numerous Old Testament images of the Suffering Righteous One at work in the trial scene.

prophesying against the temple (Jer. 26.1–19). A similar verdict is rendered by the priests and prophets against Jeremiah: 'This man deserves the sentence of death because he has prophesied against this city, as you have heard with your own ears' (Jer. 26.11).

Images of the Suffering Servant of Isaiah may also lie behind the first trial scene. Various terms connect Mk 14.65 to Isa. 50.6: ἐμπτύω ('to spit'), πρόσωπον ('face'), ῥάπισμα ('blows'). Beyond these linguistic ties, the image of the Suffering Servant looms over the trial scene. Like the Suffering Servant (Isa. 53.7), Jesus is silent before his accusers (Mk 14.60). Like the Servant (Isa. 53.8), Jesus is taken away by a perversion of justice (Mk 14.55, 59). He is condemned to be 'cut off out of the land of the living' (Isa. 53.8; Mk 14.64).

Thus, the first trial scene in Mk 14.53–65 draws upon various Old Testament texts and traditions to characterize Jesus. In addition to the titles used in the story – Christ, Son of God, Son of Man – the trial scene also invokes images of Jesus as the Righteous Sufferer of Israel's psalms, as the Suffering Servant of Isaiah, and as the rejected prophet of God. Each of these prior texts has been drawn into the climactic focus on the character of Jesus in Mk 14.53–65.

4. *Jewish Apocalyptic Traditions*

Beyond these citations and allusions to scripture, the confession in Mk 14.62 also participates in another stream of tradition – that of Jewish apocalypticism. This tradition first emerges around 165 BCE in the book of Daniel. Further developments may be seen in the *Similitudes of Enoch* (*1 En.* 37–71). Traces of this tradition, though without the Son of Man title, may be found in the Wisdom of Solomon, in *4 Ezra*, and in *2 Baruch*. Among these, only Daniel 7 can be certified as pre-Christian.

In Daniel 7 the heavenly figure who is like a son of man (in contrast to the beasts described there) is the heavenly patron of the suffering people of God. The apocalyptic image of a heavenly Son of Man has been modified in the *Similitudes of Enoch* (*1 En.* 37–71).[9] The Son of Man of the *Similitudes* is a heavenly figure who represents the righteous and chosen ones in their warfare with the kings and the mighty ones. The Enoch description of the Son of Man is drawn from three streams of Old Testament tradition: Daniel 7; Isaiah 11; and Psalm 2 along with Isaiah 42, 49, 52–53. Various images coalesce in this figure: he is the heavenly Son of Man, the Davidic king, the Servant of the Lord. This Son of Man is pre-existent (*1 En.* 48.3) and bears other traits of Wisdom. Through the Spirit, which he bears, he will judge correctly (*1 En.* 49.1–4). His judgment vindicates the persecuted righteous ones, and they will enjoy eternal life in the presence of the Son of Man (*1 En.* 62–63). A surprising revelation seems to occur in chapter 71, which is probably a later addition. Here Enoch ascends to the heavenly realms and comes before the Lord of the Spirits, where he is addressed by an angel as 'Son of Man'.

---

9. While *1 Enoch* was found at Qumran, the *Similitudes* were not. It is thus difficult to label the *Similitudes* as pre-Christian.

If this passage identifies Enoch himself as the Son of Man, then his heavenly status has been preceded by his earthly travail. The earthly identity of the Son of Man remains hidden until this heavenly judgment. Thus, the Daniel 7 images have been developed into a clear apocalyptic vision of the heavenly Son of Man who comes with judgment and vindication, perhaps after a period of earthly trials.

The Wisdom of Solomon, which dates from around the beginning of the common era, takes part in this stream of tradition. Though the Son of Man title is absent, Wisdom of Solomon 1–5 tells of a Righteous One who is persecuted and killed by powerful opponents. Much to the surprise of his opponents, this righteous person is subsequently vindicated in the heavenly realms. In distinction from the Enoch tradition, this righteous figure is human throughout. He typifies the oppressed righteous one, his vindication is a personal reward from God, and he does not initiate the judgment against his oppressors. The Righteous One of the Wisdom of Solomon is less a heavenly judge and more a model of the ultimate vindication of the righteous.

Echoes of the Daniel tradition may also be found in *4 Ezra*, which is dated from the end of the first century CE. The visions found in *4 Ezra* 11–12 and 13 borrow extensively from the vision of Daniel 7. The four beasts reappear, with the fourth being the most powerful and most arrogant (11.36–46). As in Daniel, this beast is burned (12.3). In 12.11 the vision is connected explicitly to Daniel. A deliverer in the form of a lion is roused from the forest, but this character speaks in a human voice in behalf of the Most High (11.37–38). This lion figure is the messiah, the offspring of David whom God has kept for the end of days (12.31–32). He will judge the wicked oppressors and deliver the righteous remnant (12.32–34).

One who has the figure of a man is also prominent in the vision of *4 Ezra* 13. Though frequently called 'a man', he is addressed by the Most High as 'my son' (13.32, 37, 52). Kept by the Most High for many ages, he will deliver the righteous (13.25–26), he will judge and destroy the wicked through the law (13.38), and he will reconstitute the lost tribes of Israel (13.39–50). Through these developments *4 Ezra* extends the concept of Daniel 7 and engages social and political events near the end of the first century CE.

This tradition appears in *2 Baruch*, also dated near the end of the first century CE. The judgment of the figure from Daniel 7 is directed against the fourth beast in *2 Baruch* (36–39). This figure has traits which make him more than human: he has a glorious appearance (29–30); he is the agent of universal judgment (53–74); he appears in the image of lightning (53–74). In *2 Baruch* the Danielic tradition has been developed in two important ways: the figure is frequently described as 'my anointed', and he is more than human. While the messianic title is an expansion of Danielic tradition, the transcendent nature is an expansion of the Jewish idea of kingship.[10]

Taken in combination, these texts seem to indicate the existence near the end of the first century CE of a rather strong Jewish tradition about a heavenly judge

---

10. So Nickelsburg, 'Son of Man', pp. 137–50 (p. 141).

and deliverer. Nickelsburg describes this as 'a common model that was composed of elements from Israelite traditions about the Davidic king, the Deutero-Isaianic servant/chosen one, and the Danielic "son of man"'.[11] This conceptual line is marked by its ability to conflate various Jewish traditions and by its unique address to situations of persecution.

The difficult question is to know how to read Mk 14.62 in relation to this material. While much is shared in common, lines of influence are difficult to demonstrate, since only the Daniel tradition can be demonstrated as pre-Christian. It is clear, however, that these traditions are connected and that intertextuality is at work. It is quite possible that the use of Son of Man to refer to a coming heavenly judge is first found with Jesus and/or with the early Church. This concept would be an expansion of the Daniel tradition, and it might influence the Enoch, Wisdom, and Baruch traditions. Whatever the direction of influence, it is clear that the Son of Man imagery of Mk 14.62 participates in a complex web of intertextuality.

5. Intratextual Negotiations over the Son of Man

Norman Perrin, in one of his groundbreaking investigations of the narrative dimensions of the Gospels, saw Mk 14.62 as central to the narrative strategy of Mark. Perrin argued that Mk 14.61–62 functions both retrospectively and prospectively. Retrospectively, it is the climax of the christological concerns of the evangelist, and it marks the formal disclosure of the Messianic Secret. Prospectively, it prepares the way for the christological climax of the centurion's confession; it interprets the crucifixion/resurrection of Jesus as the enthronement/ascension of Jesus as the Christ and Son of Man; and it anticipates the parousia. These verses take on a new significance as they are examined from the literary-critical standpoint of their function in the Gospel.[12]

The narrative function first described by Perrin is part of an extensive pattern at work in the Gospel of Mark. In its description of Jesus, various types of texts are employed in Mark: citations and allusions to scripture (1.11; 12.36; 13.26; 14.27); a voice from heaven (1.11); calling stories (1.16–20); miracle stories (2.1–12; 4.35–5.1); sayings (2.10); parables (12.1–12); controversy stories (12.13–17, 18–27); a christophany (9.2-8); prophecies (13.26); titles (Son of God, Son of David, Son of Man, Christ, prophet, others); a passion narrative (14.1–16.8); resurrection predictions (14.28; 16.7). These diverse texts produce a portrait of Jesus marked by complexity, contrast, contradiction. The trial scene in Mk 14.53–65 provides a hermeneutical key which gathers together various strands of characterization and creates a new set of priorities.[13] This proves especially true for the enigmatic Son of Man title.

---

11. Nickelsburg, 'Son of Man', pp. 137–50 (p. 141).
12. Norman Perrin, 'The High Priest's Question and Jesus' Answer', in W. Kelber (ed.), *The Passion in Mark: Studies on Mark 14–16* (Philadelphia: Fortress Press, 1976), p. 95.
13. See E.K. Broadhead, *Prophet, Son, Messiah: Narrative Form and Function in Mark 14–16* (JSNTSup, 97; Sheffield: Sheffield Academic Press, 1994), pp. 128–45.

The Son of Man title has a complex linguistic base. Behind the Greek phrase (ὁ υἱὸς τοῦ ἀνθρώπου) stands the Hebrew *ben 'adam* and the Aramaic *bar 'enas*. This Semitic expression employs a noun for humanity in general, but individualizes the noun through its construction: it may thus refer to 'one who belongs to the human classification'.[14] The phrase may also be used indefinitely to speak of 'someone'. Such use is frequent in the Old Testament, particularly within poetic parallelism.[15] Here the phrase appears in the second part of a synonymous parallelism as emphatic repetition of a term designating a human being.[16] The Hebrew form of this concept (but not the Aramaic) may be used as a form of direct address. The Hebrew term (*ben 'adam*) is used over 90 times in Ezekiel, normally by God to address the prophet. Some argue that *bar 'enas* may also be used as a circumlocution for the speaker.[17] Thus, the linguistic evidence points to four distinct uses for the term: (1) as a generic term it would mean 'a human being'; (2) as an indefinite term it would mean 'someone'; (3) as a circumlocution it would mean 'I' with reference to the speaker; (4) as direct address it could point to a human figure or to one who is more than human.

The literary and conceptual background for the Son of Man title has been sought in various places: Canaanite mythology;[18] the Adam speculation found in rabbinical thought, Philo, the *Pseudo-Clementines*;[19] and in Jewish apocalyptic materials such as Daniel, *Enoch*, Wisdom of Solomon, *4 Ezra*, and *2 Baruch*.

In the Gospels the title is found exclusively on the lips of Jesus, and it is rare elsewhere (Acts 7.55; citations of Daniel 7 and Psalm 8). Three types of Son of Man sayings are found in the New Testament: (1) sayings which refer to the Son of Man as an apocalyptic figure who will come in the future, (2) sayings which refer to the present activity of the Son of Man, and (3) sayings which describe the suffering of the Son of Man.

The Son of Man title is the most frequent of the christological images in the Gospel of Mark. The term occurs some 14 times throughout the narrative (2.10, 28; 8.31, 38; 9.9, 12, 31; 10.33, 45; 13.36; 14.21 [twice], 41, 62), but is primarily found in the last half of the Gospel (8–16), with only 2.10, 28 employing the

---

14. On the linguistic aspects of this title and other issues of the current debate, see G. Vermes, *Jesus the Jew: A Historian's Readings of the Gospels* (London: Collins, 1973); *idem*, 'The "Son of Man" Debate', *JSNT* 1 (1978), pp. 19–32; J. Fitzmyer, *A Wandering Aramean: Collected Aramaic Essays* (Missoula, MT: Scholars Press, 1979), pp. 143–60; *idem*, 'Another View of the "Son of Man" Debate', *JSNT* 4 (1999), pp. 58–68; B. Lindars, *Jesus Son of Man: A Fresh Examination of the Son of Man Sayings in the Gospels* (London: SPCK, 1983); W. Walker, 'The Son of Man: Some Recent Developments', *CBQ* 45 (1983), pp. 584–607; John R. Donahue, 'Recent Studies on the Origin of "Son of Man" in the Gospel', *CBQ* 48 (1986), pp. 484–98.

15. See Nickelsburg, 'Son of Man', pp. 137.

16. See Num. 23.29; Isa. 51.12; 56.2; Jer. 49.18, 33; 50.40; 51.43; Pss. 8.4; 80.17; 146.3; Job 16.21; 25.6; 35.8.

17. Vermes supports this position, but Fitzmyer opposes it for the New Testament era.

18. C. Colpe, 'ὁ υἱὸς τοῦ ἀνθρώπου', *TDNT* 8, pp. 415–20.

19. O. Cullmann, *The Christology of the New Testament* (trans. S. Guthrie and C. Hall; London: SCM Press, 1963), pp. 142–52, sees this line as an important background for the New Testament concept.

term in the first half. Thus, the Son of Man title is a frequent image which increases as the story approaches the passion account.

While all three types of Son of Man sayings are found in the Gospel of Mark, the Markan Son of Man sayings may be more accurately categorized along two conflicting thematic lines. One sequence (2.20, 28; 8.38; 9.9; 13.26) associates the Son of Man with power and judgment. The Son of Man will be raised from the dead (8.31; 9.9, 31; 10.33). He will come with the angels in the glory of his Father (8.38).[20] The Son of Man will be seen coming in the clouds with great power and glory, and he will gather the elect from the corners of creation (13.26–27).

In two instances the power of the Son of Man seemingly belongs to the present age. In Mk 2.10 the Son of Man has authority to forgive sins upon the earth, and in 2.28 he is lord over the Sabbath and its demands. While both verses could refer to the future activity of the Son of Man, the present activity of Jesus provides the most likely point of reference. The Gospel of Mark thus creates a clear association between the Son of Man title and images of power and judgment, mostly in the future.

A contrasting association is framed around the Son of Man title in Mk 8.31; 9.12, 31; 10.33, 45; 14.21 [twice], 41. The Son of Man must suffer much and be rejected by religious leaders (8.31). The suffering and abuse of the Son of Man are foretold in the scriptures (9.12). The Son of Man will be handed over to those who will kill him (8.31; 9.31; 10.33–34). In Jerusalem the Son of Man will be betrayed into the hands of religious leaders, who will condemn him to death and hand him over to the gentiles (10.33). The Son of Man has come to serve and to give his life (10.45). In fulfillment of the scriptures, the Son of Man is handed over and goes up to his death (twice in 14.21). At the end of his prayers in Gethsemane the Son of Man is handed over to sinners (14.41).

The Gospel of Mark makes it clear that the Son of Man, both in his power and in his suffering, is Jesus himself. The power of the Son of Man to forgive is demonstrated in the forgiveness Jesus offers to a paralytic (2.5, 10), and his authority over the Sabbath is seen in Jesus' defense of his disciples' actions on the Sabbath (2.28). The references to the resurrection of the Son of Man in the passion predictions (8.31; 9.31; 10.33–34) clearly refer to Jesus' own destiny. Likewise, the suffering of the Son of Man refers to Jesus: it is at the arrest of Jesus that the Son of Man is given into the hands of sinners (14.41).

If Jesus is the Son of Man in the Gospel of Mark, how is the reader to accept the conflicting images of power and suffering? These two streams of characterization have their confluence in the first trial of Jesus (14.53–65). Here the bounds of the messianic secrecy are broken. Mark 14.62 does what the rest of the Gospel of Mark has steadfastly refused to do; it places explicit christological claims on the lips of Jesus.[21] Previously the messianic identity of Jesus has been veiled in

20. Thus, the Markan Son of Man is also the Son of God.

21. Mark 14.62 is probably not a remembered saying of Jesus, but one constructed in the reflection of the followers of Jesus. The trial scene presents no witness who can convey these events to the disciples. Indeed, the disciples have fled and Peter awaits outside in denial.

secrecy. While secrecy is a traditional motif in miracle stories,[22] much of this secrecy is a Markan literary device which explains the failure to recognize Jesus as messiah during his ministry.[23] The secrecy motif is frequent in the Gospel of Mark (1.24–25, 34, 44; 3.11–12; 4.11–12; 7.36; 8.26, 30; 9.9). Though demons and even disciples sometimes articulate christological claims (1.24; 3.11–12; 8.27–28), Jesus distances himself from these efforts to make public his identity. As a part of its literary characterization of Jesus, the Gospel of Mark accepts traditional christological affirmations with great hesitancy.

The confession in Mk 14.62 provides a dramatic reversal of this literary pattern. The messianic secrecy is broken in the presence of religious leaders and other witnesses. The hesitant acceptance of christological imagery is replaced by a declaration on the lips of Jesus which invokes the name of Yahweh – ἐγώ εἰμί – 'I am'. In one brief stroke the trial scene makes explicit the identity of Jesus: he is messiah, Son of God, Son of Man, prophet of God. Thus the ministry of Jesus is connected to his trial: all of the implied christology of the Gospel of Mark is made explicit through the testimony of Jesus before the religious leaders.

Even here the Son of Man title stands out. The high priest asks Jesus about two titles: 'Are you the Christ, the son of the Blessed One?' Following the answer of ἐγώ εἰμί, Jesus extends the question. Not only does the priest stand in the presence of the Christ, the Son of God; he also stands before the Son of Man who will come with power and judgment (14.62). Jesus is the one who, amidst cosmological tremors, will come in the clouds with great power and glory to gather the elect from the corners of earth and heaven (13.24–27). Mark 14.62 thus provides the most triumphal image of Jesus in the Gospel.

The context of this confession provides the decisive hermeneutic for understanding the Markan portrait of Jesus. Precisely at the moment of his arrest and condemnation, on the eve of his execution, the character of Jesus is endowed with the full authority of the Son of Man. Two central images – the Son of Man who suffers and the Son of Man who reigns – have been joined to create a new image: those who wish to know the power and glory of the Son of Man must see him as the crucified one.

Beyond this nuanced intratextual development, the Gospel of Mark links various other images to the Son of Man title. In the first trial (14.53–65), Jesus claims openly and explicitly that he is the Christ and the Son of God. Further, the image of Jesus as the rejected prophet is developed in this scene. His previous predictions of his death (8.31; 9.31; 10:33–34) begin to unfold, and he is abused as a false prophet (14.65). Images of the Servant from Isaiah circulate around this scene. Images of the Righteous One are drawn from the Psalms. Thus, the trial scene draws the Son of Man title into a web of character traits: rejected prophet, suffering Servant, suffering Righteous One, messiah, Son of God. All of these images are brought under the controlling hermeneutic of the death of Jesus.

22. See Ulrich Luz, 'Das Geheimnismotiv und die markinische Christologie', *ZNW* 56 (1965), pp. 361–64.

23. William Wrede, *The Messianic Secret* (trans. J.C.G. Greig; Cambridge: James Clark, 1971 [1901]).

This end result is not a unilinear correction which extinguishes the prior texts and traditions. The engagement of text against text in the Gospel of Mark creates a pattern of reciprocity which realigns all traditions about Jesus.[24] This intra-textual strategy is clearly at work in the Son of Man title.

6. *Intertextual Negotiations over the Son of Man*

The intramural debate within the Gospel of Mark over the Son of Man is, in reality, a staging ground for an intertextual debate with the Sayings Tradition (Q). The Son of Man title is found ten times in the Sayings Tradition (6.22 [Lk. only]; 7.34; 9.58; 11.30; 12.8 [Lk. only]; 12.10; 12.40; 17.24; 17.26; 17.30).[25] These sayings may be divided into two streams: the present work of the Son of Man (6.22; 7.34; 9.58; 11.30; 12.10) and his future work (12.8; 12.40; 17.24; 17.26; 17.30).

The present activity of the Son of Man is associated with rejection. He is considered a glutton and drunkard, a friend of tax collectors and sinners (7.34). He has no place to lay his head (9.58). Like Jonah, his presence is a sign of impending judgment (9.58). A word spoken against the Son of Man may be forgiven (12.10). His followers may suffer insult and persecution (6.22). But no crucifixion, no execution, no death is connected to the Son of Man in the Sayings Tradition.

The future coming of the Son of Man brings final scenes of judgment. He will come, as in the days of Noah, with a sudden and unexpected judgment (12.40; 17.24; 17.26; 17.30). He will vindicate his followers (12.8).

The present and future destiny of the Son of Man cohere in the Sayings Tradition. Jesus has come among the people as a messenger of the final judgment. He has cast his lot with outcasts and wanders as a homeless person, but his presence is decisive. His followers may be likewise rejected in this age, but they will be vindicated in his coming. The earthly presence of the Son of Man is of one piece with his future appearance; he has come to offer a final warning before the coming judgment.

While the Son of Man title is limited to ten sayings, the image of the Son of Man pervades the larger portrait of Jesus in the Sayings Tradition. Here Jesus is the final envoy from God whose message of judgment and salvation is decisive. The coming of God's judgment and sovereignty is imminent. The present age is a moment of crisis in which the final call is issued. Because of this, those who travel from village to village need make no provisions for the future. How one

---

24. For an extended analysis of how the story of Jesus' death stands in a reciprocal interpretive relationship with the story of his life, see Broadhead, *Prophet, Son, Messiah*. For the way in which the larger narrative world defines the role of the titles in the Gospel of Mark, see E.K. Broadhead, *Naming Jesus: Titular Christology in the Gospel of Mark* (JSNTSup, 175; Sheffield: Sheffield Academic Press, 1999).

25. I am using the reconstruction of the Sayings Tradition presented in J. Robinson, P. Hoffman and J. Kloppenborg (eds), *The Critical Edition of Q* (Leuven: Peeters, 2000). In accordance with scholarly practice, versification of the Sayings Tradition is based on the Lukan order and versification.

decides about Jesus, his message, and his messengers in this final time is determinative for the age to come.

The Gospel of Mark cannot ignore or reject the portrait of the Son of Man
sketched out in the Sayings Tradition. The Sayings Tradition accurately echoes
the form of Jesus' teaching (pronouncements) as well as its content (the imminent
crisis of the coming reign of God). This tradition has its home in the earliest circle
of Jesus' followers; it has been preserved, practiced, and transmitted by disciples
who knew Jesus.

What the Gospel of Mark can – and does – do is to incorporate this material
through a pattern of strategic reconfiguration. The essential message of the Sayings Tradition is accepted: Jesus is the Son of Man whose end time appearance
culminates the work of God, and association with him in this age is determinative
for the future age. But the Markan Son of Man is unveiled first and only in the
moment of his trial, in the presence of his opponents, on the eve of his execution.
In the gospel of Mark the central image of the Sayings Tradition has been incorporated, but it now operates under the control of another strategy and another text
– the Son of Man who came to serve and to give his life.

7. *Sociological Implications behind the Markan Son of Man*

Those who create and transmit the Gospel of Mark have before them a wide
range of options about the story of Jesus. Echoes and remnants of these traditions
remain: miracle collections, teaching units, parables and sayings, controversy
stories, Petrine traditions, stories of the Twelve, women's stories, a passion narrative, and resurrection accounts. It is clear that the Gospel of Mark is built
around a framework which narrates the story of Jesus from his baptism to the
empty tomb. This story is told in episodes and employs a variety of forms and
traditions. The genius of the Gospel of Mark is that it represents the first attempt
to draw upon multiple strands of tradition in order to present a coherent narrative
account of Jesus.

While the Gospel of Mark draws upon various traditions, oral and written, it is
important to recognize that texts are held by communities. Thus, the Gospel of
Mark represents not only a negotiation between pieces of literature, but more so
between the communities of faith which sponsor those traditions.

I wish to suggest that the Gospel of Mark is shaped in large measure through
negotiations with tradents of the Sayings Tradition. Seen from the standpoint of
sociology, the Sayings community (or Q community) has a distinct advantage.
The traditions it preserves and transmits go back to the oral teaching of Jesus and
to the memory of those who accompanied him from village to village. At some
point these sayings were translated from Aramaic to Greek. These traditions were
eventually reduced to written form, though they retained the ethos of orality.
Even in their written Greek form, these Sayings were interchangeable, transport-
able, and subject to development. They also engage the hearer in an experience
of immediacy: to be present to the words of Jesus is, in some sense, to experience
the ongoing presence of Jesus as the exalted one.

Werner Kelber has investigated the contrast between orality and writing and its effect on early Christian tradition.[26] For Kelber, the Sayings Tradition operated under a powerful oral hermeneutic. Its two-pronged christology emphasized both the present authority of Jesus as the Son of Man and his future return. The Jesus of the Sayings Tradition is an authoritative prophet, and suffering and death play no role in this christology. This perception guided those who transmitted the Sayings: they were not bound to a historical figure of the past, but were authorized by a Jesus who continues to speak through their words. Kelber insists that 'In the oral, prophetic mode of Q the power of speech united the earthly and the future Son of man into the present efficacious one'.[27]

Kelber believes that the Gospel of Mark intends to counter this orality and its effects by placing the story of Jesus in a fixed, written narrative form which culminates in the passion story. Kelber says that

> Nowhere in early Christianity is it more obvious than in the Gospel of Mark that preservation of oral tradition is not a primary function of writing. The Gospel's reserved attitude toward sayings, its displacement of all oral authorities, its christological framework, its extensive narrative explication of Jesus' death, and the silence it ascribes to the risen Lord are all features that go against the grain of basic oral impulses. Both in form and content the written Gospel constitutes a radical alternative to the oral gospel.[28]

If the Gospel of Mark represents a conscious displacement of the Sayings Tradition, a different strategy is practiced in the Gospel of Matthew and in the Gospel of Luke. They include extensive content from the Sayings Tradition, but make it a part of a written account of Jesus' life and death based on the framework of the Gospel of Mark.

Further evidence that early Christianity sought to domesticate the Sayings Tradition and its community may be found in the *Didache*, a book of Christian instruction from the end of the first century CE. Here instruction is given concerning the presence of 'apostles and prophets' (11.3). True prophets will stay only for a few days and accept only a daily ration of food (11.4–6). Ecstatic prophets are to be judged by their actions (11.7–12). If such prophets wish to settle in the community, they may, and they are to be supported by the community (13.1–7). Gerd Theissen and others see here the remnants of the wandering charismatic prophets of the Sayings Tradition.[29] Their status is still high, for the *Didache* reminds the community that bishops and deacons must be held in respect alongside the prophets and teachers (15.1–2). Thus, the *Didache* seems to know

---

26. Werner Kelber, *The Oral and Written Gospel* (Philadelphia: Fortress Press, 1983). The idea of Mark's Gospel as an alternative to oral, prophetic speech was first developed by M. Eugene Boring in 1977 in 'The Paucity of Sayings in Mark: A Hypothesis', *SBL Seminar Papers* (Missoula, MT: Scholar's Press, 1977), pp. 371–77. His theory is further developed in *Sayings of the Risen Jesus: Christian Prophecy in the Synoptic Tradition* (SNTSMS, 46; Cambridge: Cambridge University Press, 1982), pp. 195–203.

27. Kelber, *The Oral and Written Gospel*, p. 203.

28. Kelber, *The Oral and Written Gospel*, p. 207.

29. Gerd Theissen, *Social Reality and the Early Christians* (Minneapolis: Fortress Press, 1992).

tradents of the Sayings Tradition, and it insists these people are to be treated with both respect and caution.

The Markan negotiation over the Son of Man title fits well into this larger picture, but with significant nuance. I have suggested that Mk 14.62 has been constructed through an intratextual negotiation with other images of the Son of Man. I have further suggested that this intratextual process is the staging ground for an intertextual engagement with the Sayings Tradition and thus with its sponsoring community. What is distinct about this engagement over the Son of Man is that here the Gospel of Mark does not always distance itself from the Sayings Tradition in the manner Kelber describes. Rather than avoiding the portrait of the Son of Man which forms the central christological image of the Sayings Tradition, the Gospel of Mark has appropriated it. The Son of Man who has authority upon the earth and who will come with heavenly authority inhabits the Markan world, but in a radically different form. Following three predictions of his passion (Mk 8.31; 9.31; 10.33–34), the Son of Man is given into the hands of sinners (14.41). He is abandoned, arrested, abused, condemned to death (Mk 14.43–65). The destiny of the Son of Man is tied directly to his mission as the Christ, the Son of God, the Righteous Sufferer, the Suffering Servant, the rejected prophet. In this way, the Son of Man of the Sayings Tradition is transformed into the suffering and dying Son of Man, and the implications for his followers are clear.

8. *Conclusion*

The Gospel of Mark invokes a variety of traditions and texts in its portrayal of Jesus. These previously existing texts have been appropriated under a guiding hermeneutic whose effect is not correction, but reciprocity. This is most evident in the reconfiguration of the Son of Man which is completed in Mk 14.53–65. Accomplished within the story through an intratextual strategy of reciprocity, the reconfiguration of Jesus in the Gospel of Mark belongs ultimately to the intertextual dialogue through which early Christian tradition was shaped, refined, preserved, and transmitted.

INTEGRATED SCRIPTURE, EMBEDDED EMPIRE: THE IRONIC INTERPLAY OF 'KING' HEROD, JOHN AND JESUS IN MARK 6.1–44

S. Anthony Cummins

The intriguing episode involving King Herod's birthday banquet and the death of John the Baptist in Mk 6.17–29 continues to preoccupy and puzzle commentators. It has been explored from a range of interesting angles, but arguably often in ways that have yet to provide a comprehensive and integrative assessment of its overall nature and function. In addressing this situation this article begins by making some brief observations about antecedent evaluations. It then explicates as succinctly as possible an important and overarching working assumption: namely, that the Gospel of Mark tells of the divine identity and eschatological mission of a Messiah Jesus who in unexpected fashion embodies and establishes the kingdom/rule of God. What then follows comprises two extended and interrelated components. First, I offer a detailed reading which delineates the significant role played by this episode within its immediate context (6.1–44) and Mark's narrative overall, largely in terms of a mutually interpretative and ironic correlation concerning King Herod Antipas, John the Baptist and Messiah Jesus.[1] Second, this patient analysis is then developed further by considering the ways in which this correlation has been significantly shaped by kingship related motifs and themes evident in various aspects of the Elijah narratives (1 Kings 17–19, 21; 2 Kings 1–2) and the Book of Esther.

In this way it will be shown that this curious retrospective scenario involving King Herod's myopic mistreatment of Jesus' precursor John, not least as informed by Elijah and Esther, attests to the incapacity of Herod – and, indeed, the Jewish and Roman authorities overall – to recognize and receive Messiah Jesus himself, and thus to envisage and enter into the divine empire emerging in their midst. Here, as throughout the Gospel of Mark, emblematic aspects of the Old Testament have been inextricably integrated into a New Testament document in service of an embedded king and kingdom, all this according to scripture and to the unfolding universal economy of God.

---

1. This is, of course, Herod Antipas, ruler of Galilee and Perea from 4 BCE to 39 CE (cf. Mk 3.6; 8.15; Lk. 3.1; 23.6–12), one of the sons of King Herod the Great of Judea (Mt. 2.1–20; Lk. 1.5).

1. *The Nature and Function of Mark 6.17–29: Antecedent Approaches and Estimations*

Scholars have examined Mk 6.17–29 and its immediate context from a number of critical standpoints.[2] Synoptic studies, usually assuming Markan priority, have compared Mark's lengthy and dramatic description with Matthew's abbreviated and austere report (14.3–12) and Luke's rather perfunctory notice (3.19–20), tackling a range of puzzling issues.[3] Historical critics have delineated and discussed in great detail the differences between the Markan (and Synoptic) versions and the account of Herod's execution of John found in Josephus (*Ant.* 18.116–19), usually concluding that the latter is historically much more reliable.[4] Attempts to account for these differences have given rise to various proposals on the possible source and tradition-history of Mark's material; these have included conjectured (and often conflicting) reconstructions of the circuitous routes by which an originally independent (and perhaps non-Christian) piece could have found its way into Mark's narrative.[5] The structure of the passage as now found in Mark

2.   See especially the comprehensive study by M. Hartmann, *Der Tod Johannes' des Täufers: Eine exegetische und rezeptionsgeschichtliche Studie auf dem Hintergrund narrativer, intertextueller und kulturanthropologischer Zugänge* (Stuttgarter Biblische Beiträge, 45; Stuttgart: Katholisches Bibelwerk, 2001).

3.   These have included the difference in Herod's title ('king' in Mark, 'tetrarch' in Matthew and Luke); questions about the identity of Herodias' unnamed daughter and her precise relationship to Herod; and the varied depiction of the motives, concerns and character qualities of the principal figures. See H. Hoehner, *Herod Antipas* (SNTSMS, 17; Cambridge: Cambridge University Press, 1972), pp. 149–71, whose analysis of such issues has been variously taken up by later commentators.

4.   Hoehner, *Herod Antipas*, pp. 124–49 provides a thorough (and conservative) assessment, tackling significant problems related to chronology; the precise identity of Herodias' former husband (whether Philip or Herod); Herod's motives for arresting John (whether personal or political); and the location of John's imprisonment and execution (whether in Galilee or Machaerus). J.P. Meier, *A Marginal Jew*. II. *Mentor, Message, and Miracles* (ABRL; New York: Doubleday, 1994), pp. 171–76, largely eschews any attempts to reconcile the accounts, much preferring Josephus as a historian. He is followed by most recent commentators on Mark. Hartmann, *Der Tod Johannes' des Täufers*, pp. 254–355, offers an excellent extended analysis of Josephus' depiction of John on its own terms. For other notable historical reconstructions of the death of John the Baptist, drawing on both the Synoptic Gospels and Josephus, see R.L. Webb, *John the Baptizer and Prophet: A Socio-Historical Study* (JSNTSup, 26: Sheffield: JSOT Press, 1991), pp. 366–77, and J.E. Taylor, *The Immerser: John the Baptist within Second Temple Judaism* (Studying the Historical Jesus; Grand Rapids: Eerdmans, 1997), pp. 213–59.

5.   J. Marcus, *Mark 1–8* (AB, 27; New York: Doubleday, 2000), pp. 397–98, is representative of many commentators who think it likely that 6.17–29 existed largely in its present form before being incorporated into Mark. There are a number of elaborate and varied tradition-historical proposals. R. Aus, *Water into Wine and the Beheading of John the Baptist: Early Jewish-Christian Interpretation of Esther 1 in John 2.1–11 and Mark 6.17–29* (Brown Judaic Studies, 150; Atlanta: Scholars Press, 1988), pp. 67–71, posits that an original Aramaic account arrived in a bilingual Jewish Christian setting (such as Syria); it was then translated into Greek by those who recognized its dependency on Judaic haggada on Esther and who incorporated terminology from the LXX version of Esther into their translation; and it finally reached the author of Mark probably in its Greek form. G. Theissen, *The Gospels in Context: Social and Political History in the Synoptic Tradition* (Minneapolis: Fortress

has also been subject to varied assessment.[6] Accompanying all of this have been form critical and genre analyses of this passage which have produced a bewildering range of literary classifications: for example, 'legend' (Bultmann), 'anecdote' (Dibelius), 'novella' (Lohmeyer), 'midrash' or 'etiological haggada' (Aus), 'martyr report' (Gnilka), 'court tale' (Theissen), 'historical parable' (LaVerdiere), and various combinations thereof.[7] Such considerations have led many to conclude that this passage is comprised of a 'historical core' concerning John's execution due to his condemnation of Herod's unlawful marriage to Herodias, which 'has been greatly embellished by folkloristic features and theological tendencies'.[8]

These wide-ranging and varied analyses have issued in an assortment of estimations concerning the episode's role within Mark.[9] It might simply be a curious digression with little or no obvious linkage to its wider context; or perhaps an entertaining interlude while the disciples conduct their mission (cf. 6.13, 30). More substantively it may be a forewarning of the failure and/or cost of that mission; or offer the resolution to the earlier notice of John's arrest (1.14) by providing the reason for and manner of his execution; and thus it might also reinforce John's portrayal as a faithful prophet who upholds the Torah and traditions of Israel. Extending beyond John, it offers a disturbing foreshadowing of Jesus' own arrest, suffering, and martyrdom; or an empathetic portrayal of an outwitted Herod which anticipates and somewhat exonerates Pilate's role in Jesus' death. Perhaps

Press, 1991), pp. 81–97, argues on the basis of a series of purported 'displacements' that this 'popular folk tradition' (p. 85) was significantly shaped by changes occurring between 30–70 CE, before being found by the evangelist in the form of a popular (Palestinian) tradition influenced by ongoing anti-Herodian sentiment. Hartmann, *Der Tod Johannes' des Täufers,* pp. 234–38, suggests that this once independent piece had three stages of development, from an orally transmitted story about John's execution as told by his disciples, to its inclusion in a court scene context which supplied the rationale for his death, to the acquisition of its theological dimension as it was combined with the other material in Mark's final narrative.

6. Hartmann, *Der Tod Johannes' des Täufers*, pp. 119–38, surveys six evaluations. In his own view 6.17–29 is tripartite, comprising exposition, the main body, and a conclusion (in verses 17–20, 21–26, and 27–29 respectively), pp. 116–18.

7. See Hartmann, *Der Tod Johannes' des Täufers,* pp. 221–28, for an overview of the main proposals and representative proponents. To these may be added E. LaVerdiere, *The Beginning of the Gospel: Introducing the Gospel According to Mark.* I. *Mark 1–8.21* (Collegeville, MN: Liturgical Press, 1999), pp. 163–64, who considers the passage 'a historical parable'. The view of J. Gnilka, 'Das Martyrium Johannes des Täufers (Mk 6,17–29)', in P. Hoffmann, N. Brox, and W. Pesch (eds), *Orientierung an Jesus: Zur Theologie der Synoptiker: Festschrift fur J. Schmid* (Freiburg: Herder, 1973), pp. 78–92, that the passage is a 'martyr report' has been influential, but not everyone is persuaded due to the absence of any depiction of exemplary piety and suffering (so, for example, Theissen, *The Gospels in Context*, p. 81, n. 53). The possibility of a complex tradition-history has lead some to conclude that we have a mixed form, perhaps a combination of a 'martyr report' and 'court tale'; so K. Berger, *Formgeschichte des Neuen Testaments* (Heidelberg: Quelle, 1984), p. 334.

8. So Marcus, *Mark 1–8*, p. 400.

9. Cf. the convenient and succinct summary by J.C. Anderson, 'Feminist Criticism: The Dancing Daughter', in J.C. Anderson and S.D. Moore (eds), *Mark and Method: New Approaches in Biblical Studies* (Minneapolis: Fortress Press, 1992), p. 118.

most notably, it could be seen as an episode which assists the reader's understanding that it is Jesus, not Herod who is the rightful king.[10]

Finally, it may be noted that there has been a general recognition amongst commentators that this passage may owe something to Old Testament antecedents, perhaps principally to Esther.[11] However, the often disparate methods employed and varied evaluations reached have obscured the nature of and extent to which this is the case. As will become evident, there is more to be said about the rich contribution of the Old Testament to the resonant role of this passage about King Herod and John the Baptist within Mark's overall narrative concerning Messiah Jesus and the kingdom of God.

2. *Mark's Narrative: Messiah Jesus and the Coming Kingdom of God*

The Gospel of Mark concerns 'the gospel of Jesus Christ, the Son of God' (1.1) who proclaims and establishes the long-awaited eschatological 'kingdom of God' (1.14–15).[12] The remarkable identity and mission of the protagonist, and the enormity of the universal divine dominion which he reveals, only emerges as the narrative unfolds, with each element (including our own passage) playing an integral role. However, the programmatic prologue does offer the discerning reader a privileged perspective from the very outset. This Messiah Jesus – and God's coming kingdom – are according to Scripture (1.2–3); prepared for by the prophet John and his baptism of repentance (1.4–8); empowered by an eternally enthroned God whose sent Spirit is present with his beloved Son (1.9–11); and will assuredly overcome all vain attempts by Satan to substitute a counterfeit empire (1.12–13).

Yet from the ensuing narrative of Jesus' activity in a Galilee governed by Herod Antipas, it is all too evident that the other participants in this unfolding drama – the disciples, the people, and the authorities – struggle to discern and/or actively resist what is taking place before them.[13] Certainly Jesus invites and

---

10. This last proposal is that of L.W. Hurtado, *Mark* (NIBC: Peabody: Hendrickson, 1989), p. 96, and here will receive greater consideration than his succinct commentary allows.

11. Cf., for example, Anderson, 'Dancing Daughter', pp. 127–30; Aus, *Water into Wine*; Hartmann, *Der Tod Johannes' des Täufers*, esp. pp. 201–14; and B.D. Schildgen, 'A Blind Promise: Mark's Retrieval of Esther', *Poetics Today* 15 (1994), pp. 115–31.

12. While it cannot be argued for here, I take 'Christ' (Χριστός) to carry its titular sense of 'Anointed One/Messiah', which in Jewish tradition connotes a pre-eminent human agent of God, a redeemer/royal figure in the tradition of King David, who is to deliver Israel from its ongoing subjugation under foreign rule and inaugurate 'the kingdom of God' – that is, the sovereign eschatological rule of God over all of humanity and creation. This King-Messiah figure was also seen in terms of divine sonship in the Old Testament (cf. 2 Sam. 7.14; Pss. 2.7; 89.27–28), is variously attested as such at Qumran (4QFlor; cf. 1QSa, 4Q369, and perhaps 4Q246); and there are also later Jewish references to a messianic 'son of God' (*1 En.* 105.2; *4 Ezra* 7.28–29; 13.32, 37, 52; 14.9). Amongst the vast literature documenting and discussing such matters, see especially W. Horbury, *Jewish Messianism and the Cult of Christ* (London: SCM Press, 1998); and J.J. Collins, *The Scepter and the Star: The Messiahs of the Dead Sea Scrolls and Other Ancient Literature* (ABRL; New York: Doubleday, 1995). With reference to Jesus and early Christianity, see L.W. Hurtado, *Lord Jesus Christ: Devotion to Jesus in Earliest Christianity* (Grand Rapids: Eerdmans, 2003).

13. While the demons also resist Jesus, due to their supra-human role in relation to Satan they at

initiates his disciples into the mystery of the kingdom;[14] and they clearly constitute the nucleus of an eschatological people of God who are to continue his mission.[15] Yet even as 'insiders'[16] they are ambiguous characters unable to recognize Jesus' identity and role as a Messiah who is also a suffering Son of Man (8.27–33; 9.30–32; 10.32–34). This is apparent in their fear (4.40; 6.50), false expectations (10.35–45), and eventual falling away (14.50).

On a wider scale, the people at large are drawn to and readily welcomed by Jesus as he teaches, heals, and casts out demons (1.39, etc.). The abundance of his provision is dramatically manifest as he hosts and feeds many thousands (6.30–44; 8.1–10) or simply shares a meal with smaller gatherings of tax collectors and other sinners (2.15–17). Indeed, it is particularly in his intense encounters with often marginalized figures that we see an emerging faith indicating their entrance into the Jesus-centered kingdom of God which is unfolding in their midst (e.g. 5.25–34; 9.14–29). Nevertheless, in the end there remain many among the crowds who, stirred up by their counterfeit leaders, call for Jesus' crucifixion (15.6–15).

This brings us to the Jewish and Roman authorities comprised of scribes, Pharisees, Sadducees, chief priests, Herodians, and their overseers in Jerusalem and ultimately Rome.[17] In the face of Jesus' growing fame they are motivated by a complex set of variables ranging from a mistaken sense of their own divine right to rule to self-serving attempts to preserve their hold on power. Early on it is intimated that they are aligned with Satan and a collapsing household/kingdom that is being bound over to one who is more powerful than they are (1.7; 3.22–27; cf. 12.1–12).[18] As such they are collectively incapacitated, proving unable to read Scripture aright or to recognize God's kingdom power at work around them (12.24–27). Characterized as functioning on fear rather than faith, together they question, confront, inform on, entrap, and finally arrest and crucify this so-called 'King of the Jews' (15.9, 26). Yet, paradoxically, it is precisely through his death and resurrection that this suffering Son of Man is vindicated as the Messiah-Son-of-God who participates in the creation-wide lordship of God.[19]

---

least recognize who it is they are up against – 'the Holy One of God' – and that he has come to destroy them and their ruinous attempts to take possession of God's creation (cf. 1.23–25, 34; 5.1–13; 9.14–29).

14. This is soon indicated, for example, by the call narratives (1.16–20; 2.13–17; 3.13–19) and the revealing parable of the Sower (4.1–20, especially 4.10–12).

15. The earliest notable example of this is at 6.6b-13, on which see further below.

16. On their 'insider' status, cf. 4.33–34; 7.17; 9.28; 10.10; 13.3.

17. Cf., for example, 2.6; 3.6; 8.15; 11.27–28; 12.13; 14.1–2.

18. The intense encounter between Jesus and the scribes at 3.20–30, with its charges and counter-charges as to who really is possessed by 'Beelzebul, the ruler of demons', is a sharp-edged reminder that the conflict between Jesus and his adversaries is a function of a cosmic-wide battle between God and Satan.

19. Cf. J. Marcus, 'Mark 14.61: "Are you the Messiah-Son-of-God?"', *NovT* 31 (1988), pp. 125–41. Taking 'Son of the Blessed One' at Mk 14.61 as equivalent to 'Son of God' (cf. Mt. 26.63), and rendering ὁ Χριστὸς ὁ υἱὸς τοῦ εὐλογητοῦ as 'the Messiah-Son-of-God', Marcus argues that in this expression the phrase 'Son of God' is not simply a synonym for 'Messiah' (such that the question concerns only whether Jesus is 'the royal Messiah, the Messiah-Son-of-David', p. 138); rather, as the immediate context indicates, it carries even greater significance as a term which implies 'participation

In sum the Gospel of Mark is all about Jesus' divine identity and eschatological mission, disclosing and declaring that 'it is in Jesus that we are to see God coming as king'.[20] It is with this enormous claim that each one of the participants in Mark's narrative must contend – including, not least, King Herod Antipas.

3. *A Subverted Empire: King Herod, John the Baptist and Messiah Jesus in Mark 6.1–44*

Mark's account of King Herod's banquet and John's execution (6.17–29) and the preceding transitional passage (6.14–16) are strategically intercalated between Jesus' sending and the subsequent return of the disciples on their first mission (6.6b–13; 30–31).[21] Moreover, this section is itself bracketed by illuminating accounts of Jesus' rejection in Nazareth (6.1–6) and the continuance of his ministry amongst the people who are characterized as sheep without a shepherd (6.30–44). As such, the immediate context of this episode invites and entails a close and mutually interpretative correlation involving the respective leadership roles of Jesus, his disciples, Herod and John the Baptist. Of course, Jesus and John have been closely connected from the outset; and in between the Baptist's removal (1.14) and now retrospective return the reader has seen the development of Jesus' Galilean activities and the onset of the kingdom of God.[22] Thus, this wider backdrop must also be kept in view, even as we now engage in a close analysis of this particular section (6.1–44), especially the myopic and ironic role played by King Herod (6.14–29).

The reader privy to the prologue and the ensuing narrative is able to recognize various unfolding associations. For example, consistent with his own family's earlier misreading of his ministry (3.21; cf. 31–35), we observe that the synagogue in Jesus' hometown of Nazareth takes great offence at his wise teachings and 'mighty works', and seeks to put their native son 'in his proper place' rather than believe in his divine powers (6.1–6a).[23] Thus the reader is not surprised when King Herod, whose dysfunctional family is soon to be seen, likewise 'misplaces'

---

in God's cosmic lordship (14.62; cf. Ps. 110.1)' and thus incurs the charge of blasphemy from the high priest, p. 139. It suggests 'an approach to equality with God that infringes the incommensurateness and unity of God' (p. 141).

20. So R.T. France, *Divine Government: God's Kingship in the Gospel of Mark* (London: SPCK, 1990), p. 25.

21. For earlier notable examples of this so-called 'sandwiching' compositional technique, see 3.20–35 and 5.21–43.

22. Following the initial announcement that 'after John was arrested, Jesus came to Galilee' (1.14), the recurring references to Galilee (1.16, 39; 3.7) – and also to Capernaum (1.21; 2.1) and Nazareth (1.24; cf. 6.1) – have shown the reader that Jesus is now in the process of taking over Herod's territory (even as he conspicuously avoids the capital Tiberius), confronting human misrule with the kingdom of God.

23. Jesus' telling rebuke that 'prophets are not without honor, except in their hometown, and among their own kin, and in their own house' (6.4), evokes further associations: for example, with John the Baptist's treatment and Jesus' earlier remarks about 'a house/kingdom divided against itself' (3.24–25), and thus censure Herod's conduct and forecast his fate.

Jesus by mistaking him for John the Baptist raised from the dead (6.16), and so also fails to grasp the magnitude of all that is transpiring.[24]

In the scenario which follows an undeterred Jesus extends his ministry among the villages of Galilee (6.6b), and then also sends forth the twelve disciples to represent and replicate his preaching and wonder-working (6.7–13). Their depiction and call for repentance is reminiscent of John the Baptist (cf. 1.4–6; 6.8–12), and also heralds the divine redemption and rich provision of the eschatological exodus now manifest in the way being taken by Messiah Jesus (cf. 1.1–3).[25] King Herod's ensuing birthday banquet thus pales by comparison, ironically subverted by features such as Herod's own 'sending forth' in the form of an order for the head of John the Baptist (cf. 6.7, 27). However, as attested by the effort expended and resistance encountered by both Jesus and now the disciples (6.8–11), God's kingdom will not come without self-denial and considerable self-sacrifice, nor will it always be welcomed.[26] This too finds ironic juxtaposition in Herod's ostentatious and self-serving birthday celebration, which carries with it his failure to give a further hearing to an ostracized John and which comes at the terrible cost of the prophet's life. This, of course, anticipates the suffering and death of Jesus himself which will undo all such pretentious and passing human misrule and establish the glorious and eternal rule of God.

If alert readers are able to make such associations the same cannot be said for a confused King Herod (6.14–16). He has heard, presumably via official reports and/or hearsay, about the disciples casting out demons and healing the sick (cf. 6.13 and 6.14).[27] Moreover, the narrator makes it clear to the reader that the broadcasting of the disciples' activities is due to the fact that '*Jesus*' name had become known' (6.14; cf. 1.28; 3.7). Herod, however, asserts that the powerful mission of Jesus and his disciples is attributable to the fact that (literally rendered) 'the one I beheaded, John, this man has been raised from the dead' (6.16). Certainly Herod

24. Even the vision of an imprisoned John the Baptist is somewhat impaired, requiring reports from his disciples concerning Jesus' identity and activity (so Mt. 11.1–6; Lk. 7.18–23). Note also Jesus' affirmation of John as 'the Elijah who is to come' (on which see further below) and his reference to the violent men who seek to seize the coming kingdom by force, including a possible allusion to Herod Antipas in his pejorative references to 'a reed shaken in the wind' and 'those who wear soft robes [and who] are in royal palaces' (cf. Mt. 11.7–15; Lk. 7.24–27; and Theissen, *The Gospels in Context*, pp. 26–42, who argues that the reed was an emblem of Herod, appearing on his coinage and earning him the epithet 'wavering reed' or 'shaken reed', a 'title of ridicule and recognition', p. 38).

25. That Jesus instructs the disciples 'to take nothing on their journey except a staff; no bread … but to wear sandals and not to put on two tunics' (6.8–9) evokes various aspects of Israel's Exodus and wilderness wandering (cf., for example, Exod. 12.11; Deut. 8.2–5; 29.5–6). See further, Marcus, *Mark 1–8*, p. 389.

26. The disciples' entrance into houses which may not always welcome their presence (6.11) evokes comparison with Jesus' earlier parable about a divided and unstable house/kingdom occupied by Satan who will be overcome (3.23–27); one anticipates that such will be the fate of Herod's corrupt household/kingdom which is presently under Satan's control. On the disciples' later ongoing costly mission in the face of warring and collapsing kingdoms, cf. 13.3–13.

27. Herod's informants could well have come from among the scribes, Pharisees, chief priests and Herodians noted above. While little is known about the Herodians, it is likely that they were supporters of Herod Antipas and the Herodian dynasty, and thus also allies of Rome (12.13–17).

is not alone in misidentifying Jesus: some of the people likewise think Jesus is John raised,[28] others that he is Elijah, and still others that he is 'a prophet, like one of the prophets of old' (6.14–15).[29] However, in Mark a self-possessed Herod is emphatic ('the one *I* beheaded') that the person he is hearing about is a resurrected John the Baptist.[30] At best this indicates considerable confusion; at worst, it denotes a decided incapacity to recognize the competing powers of a rival King-Messiah Jesus and his increasingly active followers.[31] It is from this standpoint that we are to appreciate the nature and significance of the immediately ensuing flashback to King Herod's banquet and the execution of John (6.17–29). This earlier myopic mistreatment of Jesus' precursor John is indicative of and contributes to Herod's incapacity to recognize and receive Jesus himself, and thus to envisage and enter into the divine empire embedded and emerging from within his own Galilean jurisdiction.[32]

On one level, the entire episode depicted at 6.17–29 manifestly revolves around King Herod. Certainly that seems to be *his* perspective on the matter. At the outset we are told that 'Herod himself' had sent his men to arrest, bind and imprison John (6.17). It was Herod who then 'protected' the righteous and holy prophet from his wife Herodias, and who on occasion liked to listen to what he had to say (6.19–20). It is Herod's birthday banquet which is the setting and focal point of the entire drama. Finally it is Herod who, if rather reluctantly, orders John's execution. Of course, significant 'supporting' roles are played by Herodias and the unnamed daughter. Herodias had been working behind the scenes for some time, nursing a grudge against John's denunciation of her illegal marriage to Herod.[33]

28. This is the case if we follow ἔλεγον ('they [the people] said') rather than ἔλεγεν ('he [Herod] said') at 6.14c; so R.T. France, *The Gospel of Mark: A Commentary on the Greek Text* (NIGTC; Grand Rapids: Eerdmans, 2002), p. 251, who notes that on either reading the flow of the text at 6.14–16 remains rather awkward.

29. These people at least recognize that Jesus' ministry aligns him with the Old Testament prophets and the prophet John (see 8.28 where similar opinions are expressed); but this still falls short of understanding his full significance. Herod's emphatic pronouncement indicates that his shortsightedness is all the more severe.

30. In Luke's account Herod appears to be more perplexed: 'John I beheaded; but who is this about whom I hear such things?' (Lk. 9.9).

31. Inasmuch as Herod's assertion that John had been raised (6.16) is tied directly to the retrospective account of the prophet's execution (6.17–29), it would appear that Herod (and those sharing his position) held a literal view of resurrection, however precisely this would have been conceived. Perhaps he thought in terms of claims made for the Roman emperor as *redivivus*, as in the case of Nero (cf. Tacitus *Histories* 2.8; Dio Chrysostom *Orations* 21.10; *Sib. Or.* 4.119–24). In any event, it is all the more ironic that Herod is unable to identify Jesus rather than John as *the* embodiment of such life-giving divine power.

32. The irony is further accentuated by the use of the divine passive ('he has been raised', 6.16c) whereby from Herod's own mouth is expressed a sentiment which recurs in Acts: '*You* killed him [Jesus] ... but *God* raised him up' (Acts 2.23–24; 3.15, etc.). See also Marcus, *Mark 1–8*, p. 393.

33. Herod's relationship with Herodias, who is his niece and wife of his half brother Philip, is incestuous (cf. Lev. 18.16; 20.21), even if it serves to extend the Herodian family's political influence and control. Rulers typically employed marriage in such a fashion; and it may be that the couple was concerned that John's condemnation could undermine such efforts by arousing popular sentiment against their alliance (cf. Josephus, *Ant.* 18.116–19).

Thus she readily seizes upon the opportunity provided by the banquet to do away with the troubling prophet.[34] Employing her daughter to entice and then exploit her husband's reckless offer of 'half of [his] kingdom' (about which more below), Herodias is finally able to have her way. A 'deeply grieved' Herod can only rue his rash oath and acquiesce to John the Baptist's execution (6.26–27). One wonders whether the reader is to envisage the elite guests looking upon the unfolding drama with a mixture of bemusement (at the household intrigue) and/or consternation (at what it says about the governance of Galilee). Whatever their perspective, it remains one viewed by those 'on the inside' together with Herod's family, in contrast to an imprisoned John the Baptist who is clearly 'on the outside'. However, the reader knows that the reverse is true concerning their respective positions in relation to the kingdom of God (cf. 4.10–12), which is about to make a violent and disturbing entrance into the banquet – and thus into Herod's household/kingdom – in the form of John's severed head.

Notwithstanding Herod's mismanagement of his household/kingdom, it would be wrong to conclude that Herodias was the real power behind the throne, and that poor Herod is positively portrayed as kindly disposed towards John, willfully manipulated by his wife, and thus all but absolved of responsibility in the prophet's death.[35] His depiction is much more complex and sinister than that.[36] That Herod 'feared' John as a righteous and holy man indicates at best a grudging awe and at worst a realization that his own faithless character and conduct paled by comparison. That he 'protected him' carries considerable irony inasmuch as this consisted of the prophet's incarceration and ever-present threat of execution on a ruler's whim.[37] That he 'liked to listen' to John yet was 'greatly perplexed' by what he heard only anticipates his later incapacity to differentiate Jesus from John and to understand their combined message about an emerging kingdom of God which stood over and against his own (again, cf. 4.11–12).

That he then allowed his kingdom to be threatened by his scheming wife and dancing daughter is indicative of his inability even as a merely human ruler. That he was 'deeply grieved/distressed' at the request for John's head owes less to the loss of the prophet and more to being entrapped and embarrassed by his own family before his elite subjects.[38] That he acted on rather than overrode his own reckless and damaging oath indicates that trying to save face was more important than saving the life of John the Baptist. That he silenced his adversary in such a reprehensible and violent fashion, demonstrates that he is typical of those who

34. Cf. εὔκαιρος ('opportunity') at 6.21 and the adverb εὐκαίρως at 14.11 in reference to Judas looking for an 'opportunity' to betray Jesus. An ironic contrast might also be made with Jesus' programmatic exhortation at 1.15: 'the time (ὁ καιρὸς) is fulfilled, and the kingdom of God has come near; repent and believe in the good news (εὐαγγελίῳ)'.

35. So, for example, Marcus, *Mark 1–8*, pp. 399–400; Taylor, *The Immerser*, pp. 245–46.

36. According to Luke, John rebuked the king not just for his illegal marriage but 'because of *all the evil things* that Herod had done' (Lk. 3.19).

37. Matthew suggests that it was only Herod's fear of John's popular support that held him back from putting him to death (Mt. 14.5).

38. There is a further irony here in that Herod's distress stands in stark contrast to Jesus' genuine grief in Gethsemene (cf. περίλυπος at 6.26 and 14.34).

'are supposed to rule' (10.4) but who actually lord it over their subjects. Yet, ironically, in all this he is simply showing himself to be on the losing side in the much wider struggle wherein Satan's vain rule is being undone from within by the coming kingdom of God (again, cf. 3.20–27). This is foreshadowed by the closing reference to John's disciples coming to take his body and lay it in a tomb (6.29), which clearly anticipates the similar action of Jesus' followers after his atoning death (15.46).

At this point the second and shorter section of Mark's stylistic 'sandwich' arrives in the form of Jesus' returning disciples who first report on 'all that they had done and taught' (about the kingdom of God) and then retire with Jesus to rest (6.30–32). Reference to 'a deserted place' evokes both John the Baptist's earlier ministry and also Jesus' initial victory of Satan's wilderness temptation; and it may also signify the need for the disciples to be divinely empowered so as to remain resolved in their own ongoing mission[39] – an undertaking that is so demanding that they have little time for much needed divine sustenance (6.31d; cf. 1.6, 13c), in contrast to Herod's lavish and languid banquet.

That Herod's self-indulgence is symptomatic of his corrupt misrule is then further accentuated as it is bracketed by another telling comparison with Jesus: his exemplary governance and provision in the form of the feeding of five thousand men (cf. 6.1–6 and 6.30–44).[40] In various respects this gathering and meal stands in stark contrast to Herod's birthday banquet.[41] It takes place outside in the open spaces of Galilee rather than within the closed quarters of a palace banquet room. It is attended by a great crowd of people who recognize Jesus rather than an elite few who misidentify him (and will 'recognize' only themselves). The protagonist acts out of compassion as he provides abundantly for both heart and mind (with his teaching) and body (with divinely multiplied food), rather than from selfish motives in a meal which atrophies into a final spare course consisting of a severed head. By his actions Jesus ties this meal to his last (cf. 6.41 and 14.22) and so foreshadows his own self-sacrifice, an act which is ironically anticipated by Herod's self-serving execution of John. Indeed, Jesus' distribution of the loaves, anticipating the Lord's Supper, has its gruesome counterpart in John's head being passed around on a platter (6.28), suggesting this scenario 'is meant to be seen as a kind of demonic eucharist'.[42]

Moreover, the poignant fact that Jesus finds the people as 'sheep without a shepherd' (6.34) evokes notable Old Testament instances of this important motif (derived from ancient Near Eastern royal ideology) in relation to the leadership or lack thereof in Israel. Thus, for example, God instructed Moses to appoint

39. Cf. ἔρημος at 6.31 and 1.3–4, 12–13, 35, 45; also 6.35; 8.34.

40. Matthew reinforces the linkage between Herod's execution of John and the ongoing ministry of Jesus by adding that after John's disciples had buried him they 'went and told Jesus' (14.12b), and that 'when Jesus heard this [report], he withdrew…to a deserted place by himself' (14.13a).

41. Cf. Hartmann, *Der Tod Johannes' des Täufers*, pp. 159–162.

42. So Marcus, *Mark 1–8*, p. 403, who notes that the same verb ἐπέταξεν ('he commanded') is used in reference to the 'false king's' order to execute John (6.27) and the 'true king's' command to the crowds to sit down (6.39).

Joshua as his successor 'so that the congregation of the Lord may not be like sheep without a shepherd' (Num. 27.17).[43] God's prophet Ezekiel issues a scathing indictment against Israel's false kings who have fed themselves rather than the people; ignored and oppressed the sick and injured and lost; and so let the flock become scattered and food for wild animals (Ezek. 34). The prophet admonishes that God himself will rescue his scattered flock, feed them abundantly on the mountains of Israel, and set up over them a new Davidic shepherd (Ezek. 34.23–24).[44] A similar sentiment is expressed in Zechariah's condemnation of false prophets (Zech. 10.1–12). But perhaps the most notorious example is Israel's King Ahab who, together with his counterpart King Jehoshaphat of Judah, learn from the prophet Micaiah that they are to be defeated in battle and 'all Israel scattered…like sheep that have no shepherd' (1 Kgs 22.17). In this dramatic scenario (1 Kgs 22.1–28), Micaiah had been summoned before these two splendidly enrobed and enthroned kings, only to relate his dramatic vision of the heavenly throne room and God's decision to deceive and defeat Ahab by means of a lying spirit in the mouth of his own false prophets. An astounded Ahab orders Micaiah to be put in prison and fed reduced rations (1 Kgs 22.27), and then goes off to an assured defeat and death (1 Kgs 22.29–40).

The various instructive correspondences between such Old Testament antecedents and our narrative comprising Herod's banquet and dealings with an imprisoned John (6.17–29), as bracketed by the ongoing story of his successor Jesus (6.1–6, 30–44), further indicate that it is King Herod's misrule which is center stage and exposed at this point in Mark's drama. Even in John's death and the similar fate that awaits Jesus, Herod's confused and corrupt rule is being subverted and overcome by God's emerging empire. Nonetheless, Herodias does still play an important role in all this.[45] Indeed, as already intimated, together their opposition to the prophet John evokes various associations with the notorious Old Testament example of King Ahab and Queen Jezebel in their dealings with the prophet Elijah. Additionally, the banquet scene also evokes another significant Old Testament precedent provided by the book of Esther and its key characters King Ahasuerus and Queen Esther. A detailed consideration of the ways in which these Old Testament antecedents inform our episode will further enrich our understanding of the embedded nature of the divine empire which confronts and overcomes King Herod's merely human rule.

4. *An Embedded Empire: Elijah and Esther in Mark 6.14–29*

At various key points in Mark's narrative John the Baptist and Elijah have been identified with one another, while also being associated with Jesus. The prologue's depiction of John at the Jordan dressed 'with a leather belt around his

---

43. Cf. John's commissioning of Jesus as his successor, providing Israel with God's true leader.

44. Cf. Jer. 23.5; 30.8–10; 33.17–26; Isa. 9.6–7; Hos. 3.5; Amos 9.11.

45. Their combined kingship aspirations are well attested in Josephus (*Ant.* 18.240–56), with the ill-fated outcome (exile by emperor Gaius Caligula) attributed to divine punishment due to Herodias' jealous motives and Herod's willingness to listen 'to the silly talk of a woman' (*Ant.* 18.255).

waist' is akin to the way in which the prophet Elijah is described to and recognized by an ailing King Ahaziah (2 Kgs 1.8).[46] The one to whom John points may himself evoke associations with Elijah in that Jesus is said to be waited upon by angels during his forty-day wilderness temptation, just as Elijah is attended by angels who provide food and drink during his forty-day flight from Queen Jezebel (1 Kgs 19.1–10); and, as noted, there were those who wondered whether Jesus was Elijah (6.15). However, after Elijah (and Moses) appears with Jesus during his transfiguration (Mk 9.2–8), Jesus indicates to his disciples that it is in fact John the Baptist who is the latter-day Elijah (9.9–13), fulfilling the role of the long awaited eschatological precursor to the Messiah (cf. Mal. 4.5–6).[47]

In view of the foregoing it is likely that evocations of various aspects of the Elijah-related narratives (1 Kings 17–19, 21; 2 Kings 1) in Mark's depiction of Herod's banquet and the death of John should be regarded as illuminating rather than merely arbitrary.[48] Elijah, whose very name ('my God is the Lord') aptly expressed the nature of his divine mission, is sent to bring about faith rather than fear in Israel, and to indicate the abundant provision available to those who truly serve God.[49] It is in this capacity that he also demonstrates himself to be 'the prophet *par excellence* of conflict with oppressive royal power'.[50] It is John the Baptist who stands in his stead in his own encounter with King Herod.[51] Thus, for example, John's initial arrest is precipitated by his strong denunciation of Herod's marriage as illegal (cf. Lev. 18.18; 20.21). In this he cuts a zealous Elijah-like figure (cf. 1 Kgs 19.10, 14), risking his life by confronting the king with the word of the Lord (cf. 1 Kgs 21.17–24; 2 Chron. 21.12–19). Moreover, just as Elijah's zeal precipitates a cunning Jezebel swearing a solemn oath to seek his death (1 Kgs 19.1–2),[52] so John's censure of Herodias' marriage to Herod

---

46. Elijah condemns the king for inquiring after the Philistine god Baalzebub rather than the God of Israel concerning the outcome of his injuries (2 Kgs 1.3, 6, 16). Commentators speculate whether this may provide part of the background to the otherwise obscure reference to 'Beelzebul' in Mk 3.22. If so, given that Herod may be included among those whose household/kingdom will not stand (see above), then he may be associated with disreputable Old Testament rulers such as King Ahaziah, just as John may be aligned with Elijah.

47. See below for more on Mk 9.9–13. A final reference to Elijah occurs in the account of Jesus' death (Mk 15.33–36).

48. Among brief but helpful analyses of Elijah-John connections in this passage, cf. Anderson, 'Dancing Daugher', pp. 129–30; Hartmann, *Der Tod Johannes' des Täufers*, pp. 219–20; and LaVerdiere, *The Beginning of the Gospel*, pp. 160–61.

49. A notable case in point being his provision of food for the widow of Zarephath (1 Kgs 17.8–16; cf. Mk 6.30–44, on which see below); and also his revival of her son (1 Kgs 17.17–24; cf. Jesus' revival of Jairus' 'girl [κοράσιον]', Mk 5.22–24a, 35–43; see below concerning κοράσιον in connection with Herodias' 'girl', Mk 6.22, 28).

50. So J.R. Donahue and D.J. Harrington, *The Gospel of Mark* (Sacra Pagina, 2; Collegeville: Liturgical Press, 2002), p. 196.

51. The prophet confronting a king motif also evokes other Old Testament antecedents such as Nathan's bold engagement of King David (2 Sam. 12.1–2); Jeremiah's exchange with King Zedekiah (Jer. 38.14–28); and the Daniel's appearance at King Belshazzar's feast (Daniel 5). More broadly, see Hartmann, *Der Tod Johannes' des Täufers*, pp. 170–75.

52. This is all too consistent with the fact that she had been 'killing off the prophets of the Lord' (1 Kgs 18.4).

incurs her desire to kill him which finds its fulfillment via Herod's oath (6.19, 23, 26).[53]

Certainly the scheming of both Jezebel and Herodias undermines the rule of their respective husbands.[54] Nonetheless, it is *Ahab* who fails to recognize in Elijah a true prophet of God rather than a 'troubler of Israel' (1 Kgs 18.17),[55] just as *Herod* entertains but cannot understand John, and compounds his incomprehension by confusing John and his successor Messiah Jesus. It is Ahab who sought far and wide to capture an elusive Elijah,[56] requiring 'an oath of [each] kingdom or nation' that the prophet had not been found there (1 Kgs 18.10), just as it is Herod's oath which ensures John's execution, even as the divine mission of both John and Jesus thereby eludes him. Moreover, it is Ahab who Elijah holds responsible and condemns for his abuse of power, and who thereby brings disaster upon his entire household (cf. 1 Kgs 21.17–29; 22.29–40). Likewise we are to see that it is Herod who is ultimately accountable for his decision to execute John the Baptist, an action that is indicative of the disastrous rule of the Herodian dynasty. Of course, in both scenarios the interpersonal antagonism between the prophet and the king and queen are but a function of much more wide-ranging matters: kings who are lead astray into idolatry, aligned with Satan's designs, and who are thus condemned by the Lord of Hosts (1 Kgs 18.15; 19.10, 14) who will ensure the downfall of all evil and the establishment of his eschatological kingdom (cf. Mk 13.24–27).

If Herod has difficulty in recognizing the nature and significance of the Elijah-John identification, an scripturally informed exegesis of this episode is later provided by Jesus himself at Mk 9.9–13. Here, just as John had born witness to Jesus in his life and death under Herod, so Jesus draws upon Elijah in testifying to his disciples about John.[57] While Jesus' transfiguration has just further divinely affirmed his identity as God's beloved Son (9.2–8; cf. 1.9–11), he tells his disciples that he is so precisely as the Son of Man who must suffer and only thence rise from the dead (9.9–10). Confused, they respond with a fumbling question: 'why do the scribes say that Elijah must come first?' (9.11). Jesus replies with an exegetical tour-de-force which reveals John's role in relation to

53. On Jezebel's pronounced hatred of Elijah, see 1 Kgs 16.29–19.3; 21.1–29. While Jezebel fails in her attempts to kill Elijah, she does manage to arrange the murder of the faithful Israelite Naboth so that King Ahab can seize his vineyard (cf. Mk 12.1–12).

54. In the case of the Canaanite Jezebel this is symptomatic of her 'entertaining' other gods, including the hundreds of false prophets of Baal and Asherah 'who [ate] at Jezebel's table' (1 Kgs 18.19); compare Herodias' intervention into Herod's banquet and its disastrous outcome.

55. This is a case unlike Ahab's prime minister Obadiah who rightly recognizes and reveres Elijah (1 Kgs 18.7).

56. Elijah's dramatic appearances and disappearances are due to the Spirit of the Lord at work in him (1 Kgs 18.7–16; 2 Kgs 2.16); cf. the ironic 'appearance' in Herod's banquet (Mk 6.28) of an otherwise elusive John, and an equally absent Jesus and the mysterious kingdom of God which likewise escape Herod's grasp.

57. The following reading of Mk 9.9–13 is indebted to the illuminating analysis of J. Marcus, *The Way of the Lord: Christological Exegesis of the Old Testament in the Gospel of Mark* (Edinburgh: T&T Clark, 1992), pp. 94–110.

Jesus, including the part played by his deadly encounter with Herod. Jesus allows that the scribes correctly interpret the Scriptures (viz. Mal. 4.5) as indicating that Elijah would return before the coming Messiah and 'restore all things'; that is, bring about the healing of a broken humanity (9.12ab). However, asks Jesus, how can this be reconciled with the fact that 'it is written' about the coming Son of Man that he will suffer at the hands of a contemptuous (and thus far from restored) humanity (9.12c)? He immediately resolves the matter by interpreting Elijah's role in relation to its fulfillment by John the Baptist (which anticipates Jesus' fate): 'But I tell you that Elijah has come, and they did to him whatever they pleased, as it was written about him'(9.13).[58] Therefore, John the Baptist suffers at the hands of an unwitting Herod because he is participating in the paradoxical outworking of God's purposes through a crucified King Jesus. Moreover, as the Elijah allusions intimate and the additional associations with Esther (below) will further confirm, all of this is according to Scripture.

Herod's banquet and John's execution also invites quite complex and ironic comparisons with various aspects of the book of Esther, with kingship related motifs again playing a prominent role.[59] The story of Esther tells of an orphaned Jewish girl who, while concealing her origins, replaces a recently deposed Queen Vashti as the wife of the Persian King Ahasuerus; then, aided by her cousin Mordecai, she uses her influence and ingenuity to rescue her fellow diaspora Jews from the genocidal plot of the wicked official Haman. This immensely popular story of divine deliverance is celebrated thereafter in the Festival of Purim.[60] Esther's intricate plot is entirely structured around a series of banquets, with two central scenes involving the three main figures (Esther, Ahasuerus and Haman), and various other banquets/feasts attended by nobility and/or portions of the population at large.[61] As such it provides the most extended and instructive Old Testament precedent to Mark's very distinct depiction of Herod's birthday banquet with its principal characters and elite guests.

Esther is 'a young virgin [κοράσιον]' who joins Ahasuerus' harem and 'pleases' the king such that he makes her his queen. Herodias' dancing daughter

58. No Old Testament text refers to a returning Elijah suffering violence. See Marcus, *The Way of the Lord*, p. 107, who argues that 'as it was written about him' refers to Jesus' own exegesis in which '9.13ab [functions] as the syllogistic conclusion that reconciles the scriptural expectations expressed in 9.11 and in 9.12c'; thus 'written' in the sense that 'it harmonizes the biblical idea of a forerunner with the biblical idea of a suffering Messiah'.

59. For helpful comparative analyses, cf. Anderson, 'Dancing Daughter', pp. 128–29; Hartmann, *Der Tod Johannes' des Täufers*, pp. 201–14; and Schildgen', A Blind Promise'. Aus, *Water into Wine*, p. 40, argues at great length that the 'narrative of the beheading of John is dependent on Hebrew and Aramaic Judaic haggadic traditions on Esther, primarily chapter 1'. While some of the connections are intriguing, not all of his disparate evidence and wide-ranging arguments are equally convincing; nor does his analysis extend to any estimation of the role of 6.17–29 within Mark's narrative overall.

60. Schildgen, 'A Blind Promise', p. 116, rightly observes that 'Esther's recensions, redactions, colophons, and haggadic commentary tradition show that the story was [later] deployed in numerous settings'.

61. On the central scenes, see 5.4–8; 7.1–10 (cf. 3.15). On the more widely attended banquets/feasts, cf. 1.2–4, 5–8, 9; 2.18; 8.17; 9.17–19.

is also described as 'a young girl [κοράσιον]' (6.22, 28),[62] probably indicating that she was of marriageable age, and is likewise said to have 'pleased' Herod and his guests.[63] Esther's position as queen paves the way for the critical scene in which she enters the King's court and prompts Ahasuerus' repeated remarks: 'What is your request? It shall be given you, even to the half of my kingdom' (cf. Est. 5.3, 6; 7.2). Similarly it is the pleasing performance by Herodias' daughter which leads to Herod's reckless offer: 'Whatever you ask me, I will give you, even half of my kingdom' (6.23).[64] It has often been noted that, in spite of Mark's exceptionally concentrated use of 'king' (βασιλεύς) at 6.14, 25, 26, 27, Herod was not actually a 'king', but technically only a tetrarch (so Mt. 14.9 and Lk. 9.7). Additionally, as a mere vassal ruler of Rome, he was in no position to offer any part of his 'kingdom'. However, it is likely that these prominent and otherwise puzzling features are due less to the use of 'popular terminology' or a courtesy extended to Herod, and are more indebted to the book of Esther with its extensive 'king' terminology in reference to Ahasuerus and his empire.[65] If the ambiguity of his title places a deficient Herod in ironic juxtaposition with a benign and at times benevolent (Gentile) King Ahasureus, the contrast is all the more stark in relation to Jesus of Nazareth, the significance of whose own ambiguous titles as 'Messiah' and 'Son of God' are being worked out within Mark's wider narrative.[66]

Of course, whereas King Ahasuerus' offer to Esther is then used to save the lives of her people (Est. 7.3), Herod's offer is quickly seized upon by Herodias and her daughter to achieve a self-serving outcome which is symptomatic of Israel's injurious misrule. The most dramatic and darkest moment in Esther arrives in yet another banquet scene which brings about the downfall and ignominious death of the offensive and wicked Haman who is hanged on the gallows meant for Mordecai (Est. 6.14–7.10). The climactic end to Herod's banquet comes with the gruesome execution of the righteous John the Baptist and the arrival of his head on a platter (Mk 6.27–28).[67] It is possible that at this point

62. While used very frequently in Esther LXX (especially in chapter 2), κοράσιον is found in the New Testament only in reference to Herodias' daughter (Mk 6.22, 28; Mt. 14.11) and the daughter of Jairus (Mk 5.41–42; Mt. 9.24–25).

63. In Esther 'pleasing the king' is a recurring motif, and includes sexual connotations (e.g. Est. 2.4, 9) as elsewhere in the Old Testament (cf. Gen. 19.8; Judg. 14.1–3, 7). This and Herod's male-only birthday banquet make the daughter's dance and the onlookers' pleasure appear more sensual than otherwise (contra Hartmann, *Der Tod Johannes' des Täufers*, pp. 162–68, who finds no evidence of eroticism in the text itself, while allowing that it was later read in such a way; and Donahue and Harrington, *The Gospel of Mark*, pp. 198–99, who appeal to the use of κοράσιον at Mk 5.42 in suggesting that the dance 'could conceivably depict a child's performance').

64. Since the phrase 'half a kingdom' occurs within an offer-request-oath feature common to both Mark and Esther, and this is itself set within a wider range of comparative motifs, it is unlikely that it is merely being used as a proverbial expression for a king's generosity.

65. Contra Hoehner, *Herod Antipas*, p. 150 (who also suggests 'Herod' had become a dynastic title); with, amongst others, LaVerdiere, *The Beginning of the Gospel*, p. 165 (who notes that no Old Testament book uses the title 'king' with greater frequency than Esther).

66. Especially at 8.27–30; 12.35–37; 14.53–56; cf. Marcus, *Mark 1–8*, p. 399.

67. There is biblical precedent for beheading: the future king David slays and decapitates Goliath,

comparison could be made with the later rabbinic *Midr. Esther* 1.19–21 which relates how the head of the former Queen Vashti was brought to King Ahasuerus on a platter.[68] In any event, the demise of the wicked Haman and the righteous John the Baptist are both accomplished by a divine hand discernible only to those faithfully aligned with the rule of God. Throughout the unfolding drama Esther's Jewish identity and divinely directed undertaking is concealed from King Ahasuerus and the Persian empire, and is disclosed only when victory is assured and can be celebrated. Similarly Herodias' scheming is only revealed at the last moment to a beguiled King Herod; in this instance, however, the hollow victory of John's death, foreshadowing that of Jesus, is a function of the mysterious coming of the kingdom of God in the form of Jesus' unfolding Galilean ministry. It is evident, then, that woven into our passage are various interrelated and evocative allusions to Elijah and Esther, who are faithful representatives of God and his people in the face of human misrule, whether foreign or as found within Israel itself. As such these figures function variously in typological and ironic relation to a righteous John the Baptist and a corrupt King Herod and, by extension, in relation to an obedient Messiah Jesus who confronts all corrupt human authorities, whether Jewish or Gentile. However, if Elijah and Esther managed to survive their risky undertakings, John and Jesus experience the full force of human resistance to divine rule. In Jesus' case this becomes all the more apparent as Mark's narrative takes us to Jerusalem.

In his final days in Jerusalem, as his own authority continues to be questioned, Jesus condemns the Jewish authorities for their inability to acknowledge the divine origin and character of John's mission (11.27–33), thus aligning them with Herod's earlier incapacity to understand the Baptist and indeed intimating their complicity in his execution. This thinly-veiled accusation is quickly underscored by the parable of the wicked tenants (12.1–12) with its killing of successive servants (the prophets, latterly John) and the son (Jesus).[69] In the immediately ensuing debate over paying taxes, Jesus adeptly aligns the Pharisees and Herodians with Rome, thereby reinforcing the fact that Herod's earlier actions against John were an attempt to preserve his puppet government, and also symptomatic of widespread opposition amongst the Jewish authorities to the prophet's role within the unfolding purposes of God. All this comes to a head in the various mutually interpretive parallels between the Herod-John episode and Jesus' climactic confrontation with the Jewish and Roman authorities.[70] The leaders are clearly threatened by a dimly perceived divine claimant to their self-serving misrule, and so their ongoing scheming moves inexorably towards its deadly end (cf. 6.19, 26; 3.6 and

---

and then takes his head to Jerusalem (1 Sam. 17.48–54; cf. 2 Sam. 4.7); and, most notably, Judith outdoes Esther in a scene which includes beguiling, a banquet and the beheading of King Nebuchadnezzar's general Holofernes, thereby saving the Jewish people (Jdt. 13.1–10a).

68. See the wide-ranging and variable arguments in Aus, *Water into Wine*, pp. 59–64.

69. Cf. Taylor, *The Immerser*, pp. 255–56, who presses for a reading of the parable that places even greater emphasis on John the Baptist.

70. See especially the detailed comparative analysis in F. Matera, *The Kingship of Jesus: Composition and Theology in Mark 15* (SBLDS, 66; Chico, CA: Scholars Press, 1982), pp. 98–100.

14.1ff.). Those in positions of highest authority (the high priest, Herod, Pilate),[71] who have entertained but also failed to understand the protagonist's identity and mission, order and are thus finally accountable for his execution (cf. 6.26–27; 15.15).[72] The victim is arrested, bound, ignominiously put to death, and buried by followers (cf. 6.17, 27–29; 15.16–47). Thus it is that, paradoxically, John's execution as a persecuted prophet, and Jesus' crucifixion as a Messiah-Son-of-God faithfully fulfills their respective roles in the divine drama which unexpectedly establishes the long awaited eschatological kingdom of God. That this kingdom will overcome and replace all vain residual resistance, including that of King Herod, is affirmed by Jesus' post-resurrection reassurance that he is 'going ahead of [his disciples] to Galilee'(16.7).[73]

6. *Conclusion: Integrated Scripture and an Embedded Empire*

At the outset it was observed that varied approaches to our intriguing yet puzzling passage have led to disparate estimations of its nature and role within Mark's narrative overall. Here, it has been argued that it is first crucial to recognize all that is entailed in the fact that the Gospel of Mark concerns Messiah Jesus and the coming kingdom of God. When viewed within this wider framework, Herod's banquet and execution of John the Baptist, especially as read within its immediate context (6.1–44), can be seen as concerning the ironic correlation between Herod's misrule and the emerging empire being heralded by John and established by Jesus. Moreover, it was also noted that commentators have generally underestimated the important role played by certain notable strands of the Old Testament in all of this. In part this has perhaps been due to a general tendency in Markan (and New Testament) studies to isolate and analyze individual Old Testament citations and allusions in rather atomistic fashion, thus failing to attend adequately to the wider role played by such texts and their Old Testament setting(s) as then integrated into Mark's narrative.[74]

With respect to our particular passage, we have seen that the influence and appropriation of the Old Testament is a much more subtle and broader phenomenon than is often allowed. In the case of the Elijah narratives we are dealing with wide-ranging and variable associations in terms of character portrayal, setting,

---

71. In Lk. 23.6–12 Herod and Pilate, former rivals, are drawn into close alignment as they conspire together in Jesus' trial and in the process become 'friends with each other' (23.12; cf. Acts 4.26–27).

72. Just as it was earlier argued that Herod's portrayal is more complex and sinister than has often been allowed, the same may be said of Pilate's depiction. Notwithstanding his purported protestations, he executes Jesus under a publicly posted charge ('the king of the Jews', 15.26) which ironically indicates both his overriding sense of self-preservation (cf. 8.35) and his complete inability to recognize how his so-called authority is thereby entirely subverted and overcome.

73. The longer ending of Mark depicts Jesus exhorting his disciples towards this end as they together share a meal/banquet (16.14).

74. See T.R. Hatina, *In Search of a Context: The Function of Scripture in Mark's Narrative* (JSNTSup, 232/SSEJC, 8; Sheffield: Sheffield Academic Press, 2002), for an extensive analysis of and an illuminating response to such considerations.

plot development, themes, motifs, and underlying theological concerns. The same is also true for the Esther narrative, even if in this case particular allusions and verbal echoes may emerge more clearly into view.[75] Moreover, while the extent to which here Elijah and there Esther are in play may just be discernable at certain points, any consistent differentiation is decidedly impossible to achieve. The Elijah and Esther (and any other Old Testament) elements are inextricably interwoven into Herod's banquet scene (6.17–29) and its preface (6.14–16). The resulting rich associations are then extended as this central section is itself bracketed first by the sending and return of the disciples (6.6b–13, 30–32) and then by Jesus' prior rejection at Nazareth and the ensuing feeding of the five thousand (6.1–6b, 30–44). As noted, taken together this invites and enables the vibrant ironic comparisons between our notable Old Testament types and the Gospel figures of Herod and Herodias, John and Jesus. Additionally, as Mark's narrative progresses we are provided with Jesus' own scripturally-informed exegesis of the central event in which he remarkably affirms that John's death, foreshadowing his own, is according to Scripture. Taken together, *all* of this contributes to and is confirmed by Mark's overall Old Testament-shaped narrative which is itself a witness to and an instrument of Messiah Jesus' establishment of the kingdom of God.

To press the point further, it might therefore be said that Herod's banquet and John's execution, as set within Mark's narrative, is illustrative of and functions within the wider interplay of the Old Testament and the emerging New Testament, which together operate in service of the unfolding Jesus-focused economy of God. Emblematic aspects of the Old Testament are interactively integrated into a Gospel text in ways that extend the Old Testament – and all that it envisages concerning the Elijah and the King-Messiah who are to come, even as it is embraced by the Gospel and its witness to John the Baptist and Jesus of Nazareth. Finally, inasmuch as this Jesus is the Messiah-Son-of-God – that is, the one who participates in the creation-wide lordship of God – this two-testament Scripture discloses an embedded eschatological empire which has overcome and will finally replace all oppressive human misrule.

75. Cf. Hartmann, *Der Tod Johannes' des Täufer*, pp. 200–21, who observes three different types of 'intertextuality' in 6.14–29: in 6.15 a broad and imprecise use of the Elijah tradition; in 6.18 an unemphasized and unmarked evocation of the Holiness Code (cf. Lev. 18.16; 20.21); and in the Herod-daughter dialogue the recollection of specific vocabulary and motifs evident in Esther.

THE SERVANT OF THE LORD AND THE GOSPEL OF MARK

James R. Edwards

1. *Introduction*

Isaiah's Servant of the Lord provided the early church with an interpretive key for understanding Jesus. Four passages in the book of Acts attest that the first believers declared the significance of Jesus in Servant of the Lord imagery. In a sermon Peter is recorded as saying, 'The God of Abraham, the God of Isaac, and the God of Jacob, the God of our ancestors has glorified his servant Jesus, whom you handed over and rejected in the presence of Pilate...' (Acts 3.13).[1] This reference to Jesus as God's servant is joined by three others in Acts (3.26; 4.27, 30), all four of which are attributed either to Peter or the fledgling church in their first public pronouncements and prayers about Jesus in the temple in Jerusalem. The only other New Testament passage where Jesus is called the Servant (παῖς) of God is in an extended quotation of Isa. 42.1–4 in the Gospel of Matthew. According to Matthew, Jesus' popular appeal, his public healings, and his subsequent warnings not to disclose his identity were a fulfillment of Isaiah's Servant of the Lord, 'Here is my servant, whom I have chosen, my beloved, with whom my soul is well pleased...' (12.18–21).[2]

Oscar Cullmann and others are correct in saying that 'the "Servant of God" is one of the oldest titles used by the first Christians to define their faith in the person and work of Christ'.[3] Nevertheless, although Servant of the Lord imagery was employed early, it was used only sparingly and did not sustain itself in early Christian literature The five texts cited above are the sum total of the title in the New Testament, and in the succeeding century the title appears only another eleven times in three different texts.[4] Moreover, the Apostle Paul does not use the

---

1. Unless otherwise noted, Biblical quotations are from the NRSV.

2. On the function of this quotation in Matthew, see A. Schlatter, *Der Evangelist Matthaeus: Seine Sprache, sein Ziel, seine Selbstaendigkeit* (Stuttgart: Calwer, 1948), pp. 401–402.

3. O. Cullmann, *The Christology of the New Testament* (trans. S. Gutherie and C. Hall; Philadelphia: Westminster Press, 1963), p. 51. Likewise, J. Jeremias, 'παῖς θεοῦ', *TDNT* 5, p. 709: 'the Christological interpretation of the servant of the Lord of Dt. Is. belongs to the most primitive age of the Christian community, and very soon came to be fixed in form'. Again, R. Bultmann, *Theology of the New Testament* (trans. K. Grobel; New York: Scribner's, 1951), p. I.51: '...so it appears to have been early, at any rate, that [Servant of God] was taken into the liturgical vocabulary of the Church'. Finally, Larry Hurtado, *Lord Jesus Christ: Devotion to Jesus in Earliest Christianity* (Grand Rapids: Eerdmans, 2003), p. 193: '...we probably have here an authentic item of the christological vocabulary of early Jewish Christian circles'.

4. Jeremias, 'παῖς θεοῦ', p. 700. The three texts are *Didache*, *1 Clement*, and *The Martyrdom of*

title of Jesus. This is surprising since Isaiah's Servant of God is the only person-ality in the Old Testament who suffers vicariously for others, and the vicarious sacrifice of Christ on the cross is a major Pauline theme. In select Pauline pas-sages (e.g. 1 Cor. 15.3, Phil. 2.7, Rom. 4.25; 5.12ff.) there are allusions to the vicarious suffering of the Servant of God, but not once does Paul directly cite a suffering Servant of the Lord passage with reference to Jesus' atonement. Why was Servant of the Lord used sparingly in Christian vocabulary, and why did it suffer an early demise? And what can we know of its origin? Were Peter and the early Jewish Christians in Jerusalem the originators of the title, or did they inherit the concept (if not the term itself) from Jesus?

Before turning to these questions, let us begin by recalling that the overwhelm-ing consensus among New Testament scholars is to associate Servant of God with the passion of Jesus. This is true of any number of standard treatments of the Servant-title in New Testament Christologies.[5] As a rule, interest in the Servant of God begins and ends with its explanatory significance of the death of Jesus on the cross. There may be passing references in discussions of the title to its signifi-cance for the ministry of Jesus, but they tend to be sporadic and seldom explored. The investigation of the title inevitably makes a long jump over the ministry of Jesus and plants its heels firmly in the passion accounts, or sayings of Jesus related to the passion accounts (e.g. Mk 10.45).[6] 'Unfortunately', notes Larry Hurtado, 'scholarship has been primarily occupied with the question of whether *pais* reflects the "suffering" servant passages/idea in Isaiah, and thus has not adequately considered other matters'.[7]

This observation brings me to the first thesis of this study, and also to its rele-vance for the Gospel of Mark. When we compare the Gospel of Mark with the Servant of God in Isaiah we find a number of instances where the Servant informs the *ministry* of Jesus as well as the passion. A review of Mark shows Servant of God imagery equally evident in the ministry of Jesus, and particularly in the first half of Jesus' ministry in Mk 1.1–8.27. To be sure, this imagery is present pri-marily by way of allusion rather than direct quotation. That is scarcely an argu-ment against its authenticity, however, for the Servant of God imagery relating to Jesus' passion also operates by way of allusion rather than direct quotation.

Polycarp. In all eleven instances the title occurs in the liturgical prayer formula, 'through Jesus Your servant'.

5.   For example, Cullmann, *Christology of the New Testament*, pp. 51–82; G. Bornkamm, *Jesus of Nazareth* (trans. I. and F. McLuskey with J. Robinson; New York: Harper & Row, 1960), pp. 226–27; F. Hahn, *Christologische Hoheitstitel. Ihre Geschichte im frühen Christentum* (Göttingen: Vanden-hoeck & Ruprecht, 1974), pp. 54–66; W. Kaspar, *Jesus the Christ* (trans. V. Green; New York: Paulist Press, 1977) pp. 119–23. Jeremias, 'παῖς θεοῦ', pp. 700–12.

6.   See J. Meier, *A Marginal Jew: Rethinking the Historical Jesus*. II. *Mentor, Message, and Miracles* (New York: Doubleday, 1994), pp. 106–107; or M. Hooker, *The Gospel According to Saint Mark* (BNTC; Peabody: Hendrickson, 1991), pp. 248–49. Cullmann declares that 'the *ebed* con-sciousness came to [Jesus] very probably at the time of his baptism', indeed that it 'has its origin with Jesus himself' (*Christology of the New Testament*, p. 68). Nevertheless, Cullmann does not discuss the relevance of the title for Jesus' ministry.

7.   L. Hurtado, *Lord Jesus Christ*, pp. 190–91.

Isaiah's Servant of God imagery appears to have provided Mark with a template or prototype for the presentation of Jesus as 'the gospel of God' (Mk 1.14), in both his ministry and death.

2. *The Baptism: Jesus as Son of God and Servant of God*

Nearly all New Testament scholars agree that the baptismal accounts in the Synoptic Gospels reflect Servant of God imagery. This is particularly true in the divine declaration, 'You are my Son, the Beloved; in you I am well pleased' (Mk 1.11). The Synoptic baptismal stream consists of several different tributaries, including the inauguration of the Israelite king in Ps. 2.7 (also *T. Jud.* 24.1–3), the messianic priest of *T. Levi* 18.6–8, and also the sonship imagery of Gen. 22.2, 12, 16 and Exod. 4.22–23.[8] But the most important tributary arguably derives from Isaiah, and particularly Isaiah's Servant imagery. The prelude to the divine declaration is the tearing apart of heaven and the descent of God's Spirit on Jesus, both of which have clear precedents in Isaiah. The rending of heaven appears to echo Isa. 64.1 (LXX 63.19), 'O that you would tear open the heavens and come down'. The Hebrew word for 'tear open', קָרַע) is actually translated in the LXX by a milder verb 'to open' (ἀνοίγω), but its true force is captured by Mark's σχίζω, meaning 'to tear' or 'to rend'. Such rending often depicted cataclysmic events in the Old Testament: Moses cleaving the waters of the Red Sea (Exod. 14.21), or the rock in the wilderness (Isa. 48.21); or the Mount of Olives being rent asunder on the day of the Lord (Zech. 14.4). 'To tear open' is equally momentous at the baptism: the heavens are rent asunder so that God's Spirit may descend on Jesus.

The descent of the Spirit also echoes Isaiah. In an early messianic prophecy Isaiah declared that, 'the spirit of the Lord shall rest on [the descendent of Jesse]' (11.2).[9] That prediction takes specific form in Isa. 42.1, where God declares, 'I have put my spirit upon [my servant]'. This is actualized in turn at the baptism where Jesus saw 'the heavens torn apart and the Spirit descending like a dove on him' (Mk 1.10).

The baptism of Jesus is thus framed by three texts from Isaiah, two of which relate to the Servant of God. The climax of the baptism comes in the divine declaration to Jesus, 'You are my Son, the Beloved, with whom I am well pleased' (Mk 1.11). This saying is widely understood by New Testament scholars to combine the divine declaration to the Israelite king as God's son at his enthronement (Ps. 2.7, 'You are my son') and the divine declaration to the Servant of God from Isa. 42.1 ('my chosen, in whom my soul delights'). I do not disagree materially with this consensus, but I should like to argue that another Servant of God text provides a more conspicuous parallel to Mk 1.11. In Isa. 49.3 God says to his servant, 'You are my Servant, Israel, in whom I will be glorified'. The similarity of this verse to the divine voice at the baptism is immediately obvious: 'You are my Son, the

---

8. See J. Edwards, 'The Baptism of Jesus According to the Gospel of Mark', *JETS* 34 (1991), pp. 43–57.

9. For a discussion of the similarities between Isaiah 11 and the Servant of God, see John Walton, 'The Imagery of the Substitute King Ritual in Isaiah's Fourth Servant Song', *JBL* 122 (2003), p. 742.

Beloved, with you I am well pleased' (Mk 1.11). In Greek, the two declarations are remarkably parallel, both structurally and thematically. In both, the commission is contained in the call. Both contain a declaration, followed by a description, followed by an explanatory clause. Apart from three changes (servant/Son; Israel/-Beloved; glorified/well pleased) the wordings of the declarations are virtually identical.

The major difference between Isa. 49.3 and Mk 1.11 is the reference to the Servant as 'Israel', whereas Jesus is called 'my Son'. Already in Israel's history there is an intriguing convergence of 'Israel' and 'Son', however. In Exod. 4.22–23, God sends Moses to announce to Pharaoh, 'Israel is my firstborn son... "Let my son go that he may worship me". But you refused to let him go; now I will kill your firstborn son.' This important text defines the nature of God's relationship with Israel in terms of a father–son relationship. In calling his people into existence, God first defines who they are in relation to him, and then calls them to worship and serve him. Identity precedes function; naming determines commission. This corresponds to the divine proclamation at the baptism. The baptism declares Jesus to be both God's Son and God's Servant, but sonship and servanthood are not parallel. Rather, Jesus' servanthood derives from his divine Sonship. What Jesus does as the Servant of God is meaningful only because of who he is as the Son of God. The baptism signals the confirmation of Jesus' divine Sonship and the commencement of his servanthood. Jesus is the fulfillment of the ideal of Israel, the true Israel, Israel reduced to one. In the Exodus and the baptism, the Father first defines the sonship-relationship with Israel/Jesus, and subsequently commissions Israel/Jesus to worship and serve according to servant categories.[10]

3. *The Mighty One Who Vanquishes the Strong Man*

The Gospel of Mark begins with a carefully crafted Old Testament quotation. The first half of the quotation is a conflation of Exod. 23.20 and Mal. 3.1, introducing a messenger who will prepare the way of God, 'See, I am sending my messenger ahead of you who will prepare your way' (Mk 1.2). The second half of the quotation reproduces nearly exactly the Septuagint version of Isaiah 40.3: 'the voice of one crying in the wilderness: "Prepare the way of the Lord, make his paths straight"' (Mk 1.3).

The quotation is significant, first, because Mark seldom quotes from the Old Testament. This was presumably due to the fact that Old Testament proof texts could not be expected to carry the same weight of persuasion with Gentile audiences that they did with Jewish audiences. In spite of this, Mark begins his Gospel with a complex tapestry of Old Testament texts. This indicates the significance in his mind of the Old Testament story for his Gentile readers, regardless how dubious the choice may have seemed to them. The Gospel of Mark imparts to his Gentile readers that their salvation originates not from their story but from

10. Further on the correlation of Israel and royal messianic connotations, see L. Hurtado, *Lord Jesus Christ*, pp. 191–92.

the redemptive story of Israel. The salvation proclaimed to Gentiles is not inherent in themselves, but is an 'alien righteousness', to quote the Reformers. Gentiles are heirs of salvation that is extended to them from God's saving activity in Israel. Their salvation depends on their being grafted into God's saving root in Israel (Rom. 11.13–24).

The quotation tapestry is doubly significant, however, because it culminates with mention of Isaiah, 'As it is written in the prophet Isaiah (Mk 1.2)'. The passage quoted is the dramatic announcement of Judah's deliverance from a half-century of exile in Babylon. The quotation heralds an eschatological event, nothing less than salvation to captive Judah.[11] The quotation comes from chapter 40, the major juncture in Isaiah's prophecy where God intervenes directly in Judah's historical experience, no longer as judge, but rather as gracious deliverer. To be sure, Isa. 40.3 proclaims the deliverance of Yahweh, but Yahweh's deliverance is repeated in the immediate context of Isaiah's first Servant hymn in 42.16 in essentially the same terms: 'leading the blind', 'laying waste mountains and hills', and 'turning rough places into level ground' (42.16). The deliverance of Yahweh, in other words, is closely associated with the deliverance of the Servant of Yahweh.

A third aspect of Mark's opening quotation is also relevant for the Servant of God. The fortieth chapter of Isaiah, from which Mark quotes the dramatic announcement to 'Prepare the way of the Lord', rehearses God's deliverance of Judah from Babylonian captivity by way of leveled paths and straightened roads in the wilderness. In Isaiah, the references to 'your way' and 'his paths' are naturally references to 'the way of the Lord', namely Yahweh. As employed by Mark, however, the same pronouns refer to *Jesus'* way, as announced by John the Baptist. At the outset of his Gospel, therefore, Mark signals that the way of Yahweh is fulfilled in the way of Jesus, that Yahweh's epochal deliverance of Judah from Babylonian captivity foreshadowed a final deliverance in the gospel of Jesus Christ.

This extraordinary transfer of Yahweh's way to Jesus' way becomes a *leitmotiv* in Mark's presentation of Jesus. In Mk 1.8, John the Baptist announces Jesus as the 'more powerful' one, just as Yahweh is the 'mighty one' who delivers Judah (Isa. 42.13; 49.26; 10.16). The true nature and magnitude of Jesus' might becomes evident in Mk 3.27: 'No one can enter a strong man's house and plunder his property without first tying up the strong man; then indeed the house can be plundered'. This brief but nuclear parable comes as a response of Jesus to the scribes from Jerusalem who accused him of being in league with Beelzebul. The meaning of 'Beelzebul' is not entirely certain, but it appears to refer to Baal's abode, or to Baal as the lord and prince of the abode.[12] The claim that Jesus is in cahoots with Beelzebul, the chief of demons, is self-refuting, says Jesus. *Au contraire*, 'How can Satan cast out Satan?' (Mk 3.23). Jesus is in *conflict* with Satan, as Mk 3.27 graphically illustrates. Jesus is the 'more powerful' one who binds the strong man and plunders his goods.

---

11. See T.R. Hatina, *In Search of a Context: The Function of Scripture in Mark's Narrative* (JSNTSup, 232; SSEJC, 8; London: Sheffield Academic Press, 2002), pp. 182–83.

12. J.R. Edwards, *The Gospel According to Mark* (PNTC; Grand Rapids: Eerdmans, 2002), p. 120.

The image of binding a tyrant and emancipating his captives was not hatched in a vacuum. Snippets of the same image can be found elsewhere in the Hebrew tradition,[13] but none corresponds to Mk 3.27 as closely as does Isa. 49.24–26:

> Can the prey be taken from the mighty,
> or the captives of a tyrant be rescued?
> But thus says the Lord:
> 'Even the captives of the mighty shall be taken,
> and the prey of the tyrant be rescued;
> for I will contend with those who contend with you,
> and I will save your children.
> I will make your oppressors eat their own flesh,
> and they shall be drunk with their own blood as with wine.
> Then all flesh shall know
> that I am the Lord your Savior,
> and your Redeemer, the Mighty One of Jacob.'

The similarity of Isa. 49.24–26 to Mk 3.27 is widely acknowledged. The evil one in Mark is called Beelzebul, Satan, and the Strong One; in Isaiah the evil one is גבור and עריץ ('mighty warrior' and 'tyrant', respectively) and in the LXX γίγας and ἰσχύοντος ('giant' and 'powerful one', respectively). All these terms depict a violent and terrifying adversary, but his power is no match for Yahewh, who identifies himself emphatically as 'I, the Lord your Savior and Redeemer, the Mighty One of Jacob' (Isa. 49.26). Just as the Mighty One of Jacob despoils the evil one, so too Jesus plunders the house of the strong man and liberates his captives. The verbal similarities between the two texts are not exact, but the thematic similarities are so striking that a parallel between these two passages can scarcely be doubted. The organic relationship between the two texts is reinforced by the absence of a comparable picture of a strong man freeing captives of a tyrant anywhere else in the Old Testament.[14]

An invective against idols and idolatry is a running theme in Isaiah 40–55. The invective is directed, in part, at the absurdity of idols: objects made by the hands of fallible humans are deaf, dumb, uncomprehending, and useless (44.9–20). A greater danger of idols, however, is in their power of confusion. They tempt people to pray to gods that cannot save, and they distract people from praying to the God who can. God abhors the compromise that idols pose to his saving character and purpose: 'I am God, and there is no other; I am God, and there is none like me' (45.20–46.13). These dangers are equally present in the confusion of Jesus and Beelzebul in Mk 3.20–30. There is, to be sure, the manifest illogic of the matter: how can Satan and his dynasty prosper if Satan is fighting against himself? But the offence exceeds illogic. To confuse the purposes of the evil one with the Righteous One; to attribute Jesus' miraculous ability to an unclean spirit, and the malice of Satan to Jesus, is blasphemous, an unforgivable offence. The

---

13. 'No one takes plunder away from a strong man" (*Pss. Sol.* 5.3); '…by setting [Sarah, daughter of Raguel] free from the wicked demon Asmodeus' (Tob. 3.17).

14. See M. Hooker, *Jesus and the Servant* (London: SPCK, 1959), p. 272; R.E. Watts, *Isaiah's New Exodus in Mark* (Grand Rapids: Baker Academic, 2000), pp. 148, 284–87.

severity with which Jesus rejects the Beelzebul-connection is reminiscent of Yahweh's acid denunciation of idols in Isaiah.

In discussing Mk 1.2–3 and 3.27 we have seen that the attributes of Yahweh are transferred in a direct and undiminished way to Jesus. That is quite remarkable when one recalls Isaiah's insistence that 'There is no other god besides me, a righteous God and a Savior; there is none besides me' (45.21). To no other figure in Scripture are God's attributes transferred – and transferred so inherently – as they are to Jesus. A particularly revealing example of this transfer is in the ability to forgive sins. In Isa. 43.25 Yahweh reserves the prerogative of the remission of sins to himself: 'I, I am He who blots out your transgressions for my own sake, and I will not remember your sins'. This text emphatically identifies the forgiveness of sins not in extrinsic sacrifices but *in Yahweh's own nature* ('for my own sake').

This unique authority is also evident in Jesus – and only in Jesus. When Jesus declared the sins of a paralytic forgiven, the attending scribes accused him of blasphemy: 'Who can forgive sins but God alone?' (Mk 2.7). The scribes were, of course, entirely correct in their assumption, for in the received tradition God alone could forgive sins. According to Mark, Jesus proceeded to heal the paralytic 'so that you may know that the Son of Man has authority on earth to forgive sins' (Mk 2.10). Like Yahweh, Jesus willed that his hearers recognize his unique authority, and attribute it to no other than himself. Jesus did not pronounce forgiveness in the name of a sacrifice, or even of Yahweh. He pronounced it in his own authority, which was equivalent to the authority of God.

The Mighty One who binds the strong man and ransacks his habitation possesses eschatological messianic authority. Two Jewish texts corroborate this interpretation. In *T. Levi* 18.12 we read, 'And Beliar shall be bound by [the messianic high priest], and he shall grant to his children the authority to trample on wicked spirits'. Likewise, a first-century BCE Qumran text portrays Melchizedek apotheosized to the divine pantheon as a heavenly prince who, like the archangel Michael, 'will carry out the vengeance of God's judgments, [and on that day he will free them from the hand of] Belial and from the hand of all the sp[irits of his lot.]' (11Q13 [Melch] 2.1.13).

Our discussion of Mk 1.2–3 and 3.27 has shown multiple moorings with Isa. 40–55. But are there specific moorings with *the Servant of God*? The Servant, after all, has not been expressly mentioned in the foregoing discussion. In this instance anonymity should not be understood as absence, for a clear line of demarcation cannot be drawn between the work of God and the work of the Servant in Isaiah 40–55. Isaiah's Servant hymns are traditionally identified with four passages,[15] but mention of the Servant of God is not limited to those four.[16] The interplay between God and the Servant permeates large parts of Isaiah 40–55, where the redemptive work of both is expressed in virtually the same imagery. That is certainly true of Isa. 49.24–26, where God's mighty deliverance parallels that of the

---

15. Isa. 42.1–4; 49.1–6; 50.4–11; 52.13–53.12.
16. Isa. 41.8–16; 42.5–9, 19; 48.16.

Servant in 42.6–7, who is 'a light to the nations, to open the eyes that are blind, to bring out the prisoners from the dungeon, from the prison those who sit in darkness'. Again, in Isa. 53.12, the climax of the final Servant hymn, the Servant is described as 'dividing the spoil with the strong'. Finally, in Isa. 42.22, Judah is described as 'a people robbed and plundered, all of them are trapped in holes and hidden in prisons; they have become a prey with no one to rescue, a spoil with no one to say, "Restore!"' No one, that is, except God who, along with his Servant, defeats the powers of darkness and liberates the captives. In all these passages there is reciprocity between God and the Servant. Mark's depiction of Jesus as the promised Mighty One who brings salvation by destroying the works of the devil (1 Jn 3.8) is properly understood against this background.

4. *The Compassionate Provider*

The dominant theme of Second Isaiah is set in chapter 40: ' "Comfort, O comfort my people", says your God. Speak tenderly to Jerusalem (Heb: speak to the heart of Jerusalem) … "In the wilderness prepare the way of the Lord" … He will feed his flock like a shepherd, he will gather the lambs in his arms, and carry them in his bosom, and gently lead the mother sheep' (40.1, 3, 11). God's compassion and shepherding of his troubled people through hostile wastelands echoes like a refrain throughout Isaiah 40–66. 'Comfort' or 'compassion' (נחם in the Piel) occurs a half-dozen times in Second Isaiah.[17] The same is true of the wilderness motif (מדבר). In the wilderness God provides a way for his pilgrim people (40.3; 43.19); the wilderness will be flushed with pools of water (41.18; 43.20), and verdant as Eden (41.19; 51.3).

Compassion for harried crowds is a central theme in the first half of Mark's Gospel as well. And often, as in Second Isaiah, the compassion occurs in deserted places. Mark's opening announcement of the good news of God occurs in the wilderness. John the Baptist appears not in the Holy City but, quoting Isa. 40.3, as 'the voice of one crying out in the wilderness' (Mk 1.3). The theme is repeated in the following two verses: 'John the baptizer appeared in the wilderness, proclaiming a baptism of repentance for the forgiveness of sins. And people from the whole Judean countryside and all the people of Jerusalem were going out to him, and were baptized by him in the river Jordan, confessing their sins' (Mk 1.4–5). God's attributes are again transferred to Jesus, for the compassion demonstrated by Yahweh in Second Isaiah is demonstrated by Jesus in the Gospel of Mark.

In one instance Jesus showed compassion on a man who not only lived in a wasteland, but was a wasteland. A leper approached Jesus, asking to be healed. Jesus' compassionate healing of the pariah brought about an unanticipated role-reversal: the man who had been banished to the wilderness was rehabilitated into society, but Jesus 'could no longer go into a town openly, but stayed out in the country' (Mk 1.40–45). Specifically, in Greek, Jesus had to 'stay outside in deserted places'. In yet another wilderness – a ritual wilderness on the border

---

17. Isa. 40.1; 49.13; 51.3, 19; 52.9; 61.2; 66.13.

between Israel and Phoenicia – Jesus had compassion on a desperate father by healing his epileptic son (Mk 9.14–29).

The theme of compassion for people in distress comes into sharper focus elsewhere in Mark. A salvation-in-the-wilderness text, Isa. 43.19–20, declares, 'The wild animals will honor me, the jackals and the ostriches; for I give water in the wilderness, rivers in the desert'. This text may evoke Mark's temptation narrative where, in addition to the test of Satan, Jesus 'was with the wild beasts; and the angels waited on him' (Mk 1.13). There is no exact parallel to this curious statement in all the Bible. The one reference to 'wild beasts' (θηρία) in the Gospels, however, repeats the same word in Isa. 43.20 (LXX). Whether 'wild beasts' should be understood in an amicable sense in Mark's temptation narrative is disputed,[18] but a not implausible case can be made that it should be.[19] If so, then Mark's temptation narrative could be understood as an eschatological fulfillment of the peaceable kingdom (Isa. 11.6–9), in which all creation, wild animals included, rightfully honor their creator. Once again, the honor due to God would be received by the Son of God, Jesus the Messiah.

A stronger allusion to Yahweh's compassion in Second Isaiah occurs in Mark's two feeding miracles, particularly the Feeding of the Five Thousand. The compassion of God for wilderness wayfarers is again the theme. According to Isa. 49. 9–10, God will call those who are hungry to himself and feed them: 'They shall feed along the ways, on all the bare heights shall be their pasture; they shall not hunger or thirst, neither scorching wind nor sun shall strike them down, for he who has pity on them will lead them, and by springs of water will guide them'. In both the Feeding of the Five Thousand (Mk 6.31–44) and Four Thousand (Mk 8.1–9) Jesus miraculously feeds great numbers of people in 'deserted places' (Upper Galilee in 6.31–32; the Decapolis in 8.1). Like Yahweh's 'feed[ing] his flock like a shepherd' (Isa. 40.11), Jesus 'had compassion on them, because they were like sheep without a shepherd' (Mk 6.34). Again, 'I have compassion for the crowd, because they have been with me now for three days and have nothing to eat. If I send them away hungry to their homes, they will faint on the way –and some of them have come from a great distance' (Mk 8.2–3).

The compassion of Yahweh for errant Israel and the compassion of Jesus for shiftless crowds are atypical of the *hesed*, the covenant faithfulness, enjoined by the Deuteronomic perspective and the Wisdom tradition. According to these two traditions, God's faithfulness with Israel was contingent on Israel's obedience. Job's friends testify to this inexorable logic: if Job is suffering the punishment of God, it must be because he has sinned against God. This same understanding popularly prevailed in Jesus' day: 'We know that God does not listen to sinners, but he does listen to one who worships him and obeys his will' (Jn 9.31).

---

18. Edwards, *The Gospel According to Mark*, pp. 40–42.

19. See R. Bauckham, 'Jesus and the Wild Animals (Mark 1.13): A Christological Image for an Ecological Age', in J. Green and M. Turner (eds), *Jesus of Nazareth: Lord and Christ. Essays on the Historical Jesus and New Testament Christology* (Grand Rapids: Eerdmans/Carlisle: Paternoster, 1994), pp. 3–21; also K. Barth, *CD* 3.1, p. 180.

The compassion of Yahweh in Second Isaiah and the compassion of Jesus in Mark scandalously break the traditional rule, however. In both instances, compassion is shown to those who have forfeited and forsaken it. In Second Isaiah and in Mark, to say that one is a sinner is not to say that one is abandoned by God, but rather that one is the object of God's compassion. The unconditional nature of God's compassion expressed in Second Isaiah is singularly parallel to the compassion of Jesus in Mark.

5. *Revelation through Hiddenness*

In Isaiah, the Servant is sent as 'a light to the nations'. Each time this phrase appears it refers to the Servant of God (Isa. 42.6; 49.6; 51.4). According to Luke, that light was recognized by Simeon the Seer when the baby Jesus was presented in the temple: 'My eyes have seen your salvation... a light for revelation to the Gentiles and for glory to your people Israel' (Lk. 2.30–32). 'The consolation of Israel' (Lk. 2.25) for which Simeon hoped was the consolation promised by God to his people and to the nations[20] in Isaiah (e.g. 46.13; 49.13).

In the Gospel of Mark, 'the light to the nations' is more paradoxical and mysterious than in Luke's infancy narratives. This paradox is reflected in the Servant hymns themselves. The Servant-hymn that bears the strongest resemblance to Mark's presentation of Jesus is Isa. 49.1–7. There the mission of the Servant unfolds contrary to all expectation. The mission begins in 49.1–3 with a description of the Servant's lofty destiny to reveal the glory of God. The audience is not simply Israel, but 'the coastlands' and 'peoples far away', that is, the nations of the world. The Servant is aware of his destiny ('The Lord called me before I was born, while I was in my mother's womb'), and of his unique endowments to fulfill it. His words will be effective ('He made my mouth like a sharp sword') and far reaching ('he made me a polished arrow'). Through the Servant God will be glorified in Israel (49.3).

There is a tormenting discrepancy, however, between the above ideal and the Servant's experience. Though his mouth is like a sharp sword, God has not brandished the sword in victory, but hidden it in the shadow of his hand (49.2). A polished arrow he may be, but rather than being set on the bowstring as the warrior advances in battle or the hunter to the kill, he is hidden away in the quiver. At every turn the Servant's experience belies his destiny. 'I have labored in vain, I have spent my strength for nothing and vanity', he laments (49.4). Nevertheless, the Servant does not falter or fail, but commits his 'cause with the Lord, and my reward with my God' (49.4). The Servant does not rebel against his fate as do Abraham and Moses and Jeremiah and other servants in Israel. Rather, the humiliation of Judah in exile is mysteriously reflected in the humiliation of the Servant. He is submissive to his destiny of suffering, and his submission becomes the vehicle of God's unexpected work through him. The plot seems tragically contrary, like a coach who inexplicably keeps a star player on the bench during a championship game.

---

20. The term τὰ ἔθνη means both 'the nations' and 'the Gentiles'.

God exacerbates this predicament by a final mystifying response. 'It is too light a thing that you should be my servant, to raise up the tribes of Jacob and to restore the survivors of Israel' (49.6). To anyone familiar with the history of Israel, this statement is an oxymoron *par excellence*. The outstanding problem of the Old Testament has been the restoration of Israel. Until now no one has succeeded in healing Israel's chronic disobedience – not David or Elijah or Isaiah or God himself. God now informs the Servant that the unfulfilled objective of salvation history is, in fact, 'too light a thing'. The Hebrew קלל implies that the original plan of saving Israel was a 'trifling matter' that 'pales in comparison' to the new plan of salvation for the nations. Contrary to all logic, the Servant who has failed in the smallest of tasks will be selected for the greatest task, to be 'a light to the nations'. To be sure, the restoration of Israel is still part of God's plan, but it is not the sum of it. God wills that salvation be extended beyond Israel 'to the end of the earth (49.6)'. The one rejected by Israel will, by a divine irony, redeem Israel; the one 'abhorred by the nations' will be worshipped by the kings and princes of the nations (49.7).

Mark's portrait of Jesus' ministry strangely resembles this unique figure in Israel. Jesus attracts large crowds, but he is not understood by them. He wonders among the crowds, but seems to have no lasting fruit among them. Systematic opposition from religious leaders in far away Jerusalem dogs his mission. He crisscrosses the Sea of Galilee and travels extensively, but he goes nowhere. He makes a long circuitous journey into Gentile territory and ends up where he was before. The misunderstandings and impediments of the masses are accentuated in his own disciples, and even his own family, who fail to understand him and who frustrate his ministry. He is dead-tired, but has virtually nothing to show for his labors.

The Parable of the Sower (Mk 4.1–9) is a revealing commentary on the seemingly abortive mission of Jesus. A farmer sows widely and indiscriminately in an open field, as if to symbolize Jesus' ministry. The risks of sowing are not warranted or rewarded, however. Seed is gobbled up by birds; it falls on rocky soil and is scorched by the sun; it is choked by thorns and brambles. Fully three-quarters of the seed is lost, and all hope of a harvest seems dashed. The labor of the farmer seems to symbolize the ministry of Jesus, who, like Isaiah's Servant, also has 'labored in vain...and spent his strength for nothing' (Isa. 49.4).

And yet, the Parable, like the Second Servant hymn, does not end in defeat. A fraction of the seed bears so much fruit that all the wasted seed suddenly becomes irrelevant. It is 'too light a thing' to be considered any more. There is a harvest beyond compare – 'thirty, sixty, and a hundredfold' (Mk 4.9). The ineffectual labors of the Servant were, by the mercy and miracle of God, transformed into a miraculous mission, a light to the nations. The disastrous losses of the farmer – and of the ministry of Jesus – are, by the same divine mercy, transformed into a miraculous bumper crop. One cannot judge the effect of the Servant's ministry or of Jesus' ministry by the present state of affairs. Both have trusted irrevocably in God, and their reward will be great.[21]

21. This interpretation of the Parable of the Sower speaks to the experience of pastors, missionaries,

According to Mark, the Parable of the Sower is not simply one parable among many, but the key to understanding all Jesus' parables. 'Do you not understand this parable?' says Jesus. 'Then how will you understand all the parables?' (Mk 4.13). Parables, moreover, provide windows of understanding of Jesus' ministry and mission. Could the Parable of the Sower be the key to Jesus' ministry precisely because it plumbs the mystery of hiddenness foreshadowed by Isaiah's Servant? The reward will be great because of the power of God, of course, but also because of the hiddenness of the Servant. Not in spite of his hiddenness, but *because* of it. Through smallness, weakness, misunderstanding, and even suffering, the Servant – and Jesus – becomes the inexplicable victory of God.

Significantly, in Isaiah's Servant hymns צדק, which normally means 'just' or 'right', takes on the meaning of 'salvation' (Isa. 41.2, 10; 42.6, 21; 45.8, 13, 19; 51.1, 5). In humiliation, insignificance, and even suffering, the Servant, who acts contrary to all human designs, conforms to a deeper impulse of rightness and justice in the divine economy, and supremely achieves God's saving purposes for Israel and the nations. Through the weak and foolish, God has worked not only his wisdom and power, but his *salvation* for Israel and the nations.

6. *The Servant of God and the Gospel of Mark*

So far in our discussion we have omitted passages in Isaiah 40–55 that relate to the passion of Jesus. We have done this not because we question their relevance, but because a correspondence between the Servant of God and the passion of Jesus is widely acknowledged, even by scholars who minimize its significance.[22] For the sake of completeness, however, we should mention those passages in Second Isaiah that evidently influenced Mark's passion narratives. The reference to the insults, spitting, and physical abuse of the Servant in Isa. 50.6 appears to be echoed in the third passion prediction of Jesus in Mk 10.34, as well as in the description of the abuse of Jesus by the Sanhedrin (Mk 14.65) and by the Roman soldiers (Mk 15.16–20). The silent suffering of the Servant of Isa. 53.7, likewise, seems to have foreshadowed the silent suffering of Jesus before both the Sanhedrin (Mk 14.60–61) and Pilate (Mk 15.4–5). The numbering of the Servant with transgressors (Isa. 53.12) is also suggestive of Jesus' crucifixion between two criminals (Mk 15.27); and the references to the suffering of the Servant for 'the many' (Isa. 53.10–12) are likewise reminiscent of the vicariousness of Jesus suffering in Mk 10.45 and the Last Supper (Mk 14.22–24). Less clear, but not improbable, are also the reference to the 'cup of wrath' in Isa. 51.17, 22, and Jesus' Gethsemane prayer to have the 'cup' removed from him (Mk 14.36). Likewise, the reference to the vanishing of heaven and earth in Isa. 51.6 strikes a

and evangelists as well. God brings for a harvest, despite our personal inadequacies and the inevitable oppositions to ministry

22. Even Morna Hooker (*The Gospel According to Saint Mark*, p. 249), who thinks 'the influence of Isaiah 53 on [Mark 10.45] has…been grossly exaggerated', admits that 'the theology of Isaiah 40–55 as a whole is certainly an important part of its background'.

chord with Mk 13.31, where Jesus says that although earth and heaven will perish, his words will not.

Even without further discussion it is apparent that these passion references, like the references to Jesus' ministry, depend on allusion rather than on direct quotation. This same observation, incidentally, characterizes the New Testament as a whole, where 'astonishingly few' Servant of God passages, to quote Jeremias, are expressly applied to Jesus.[23] This does not imply, however, that the relationship between Servant of God and the Gospel of Mark is thereby less actual. It simply means that the allusions are *sine litteras*, that is, conceptual rather than literal. An allusion need not be less definite than a quotation, however. Indeed, a direct quotation is usually required to evince the existence of a dubious relationship, whereas an allusion suffices to recall an established relationship. The first conclusion of this study, then, is that interpreters will fail to recognize the significance of Isaiah's Servant of God in the Gospel of Mark if they look only to direct quotations. The relationship between Isaiah's Servant and Mark's story of Jesus, as elsewhere in the New Testament, is typically allusional rather than literal.

A second conclusion has been to argue that Isaiah's Servant of God has played an important role in shaping Mark's story of Jesus' *ministry*, just as it has in shaping the passion narratives. There are as many allusions to the Servant of God in the first half of the Gospel with reference to the ministry of Jesus as there are in the passion narratives in the second half of Mark. The presence of these allusions throughout the Gospel of Mark requires an expansion of our understanding of the hermeneutical function of Isaiah's Servant of God: it encompasses Mark's *entire* Gospel. The profile and mission of the Servant, which are unique among Old Testament personalities, were seen by Mark as a unique prefigurement of both the ministry and passion of Jesus, and in roughly equal measure. The enigmatic Servant of God, who in a mysterious way embodies the good news of God's deliverance of Judah from Babylonian captivity, also prefigures the good news of Jesus as the 'light to the nations', from his baptism to his crucifixion.[24]

Third, not all of Mark's allusions to Isaiah 40–55 recall explicit Servant of God imagery. Yahweh's forgiveness of sins and saving mission in the world, for example, are transferred in the Gospel of Mark directly to Jesus. This correspondence surpasses the correspondence between Jesus and the Servant, for it implies that the nature and mission of Yahweh were regarded by Mark as being present and fulfilled in Jesus of Nazareth. Jesus fulfilled not only the role of the Servant of God, but in the above respects also the role of the God who sent him. Jesus did not simply 'proclaim the good news of God' (Mk 1.14); he *was* the good news of God.

Fourth and finally, if the Parable of the Sower reflects the mission and experience of Isaiah's Servant of God, and if, as nearly all scholars agree, parables reflect the mind of Jesus (whether *ipsissima verba* or *vox*), then it seems justified to assume that Jesus found within the profile of Isaiah's Servant a paradigm for

---

23. See the passages noted in Jeremias, 'παῖς θεοῦ', pp. 705–706.

24. In the early church, Servant of God images were likewise employed as examples for Christian virtues: Mk 10.45 for humility and service; Phil. 2.5–11 for unselfishness; 1 Pet. 2.21–25 for willingness to suffer without cause; *1 Clem.* 16.1–17 for humility.

his own ministry. The relationship between Isaiah's Servant and the Gospel of Mark, in other words, appears to derive from Jesus rather than the early church.[25] This conclusion is reinforced by the use of Servant of God in Judaism, and to a certain extent also in the early church. It seems doubtful, as Michael Grant argues, that the early church would have invented the connection between Jesus and the Servant of God, for the idea of a Suffering-Servant-Messiah 'remained so far from the central themes of Jewish doctrine, so contrary both to the prevailing official and popular conceptions, that it would scarcely have established itself in the tradition of the early Christian Church unless it had been too authentic to jettison'.[26] It is important to remember that there is no known pre-Christian Messianic text in Judaism that speaks of a *suffering* Messiah.[27] The popular conception of the Messiah, whether at Qumran or in the *Psalms of Solomon*, depicts a Messiah mighty in word, wise in the Holy Spirit, endowed with miraculous powers, holy and free of sin, and above all, the destroyer of God's enemies and liberator of Jerusalem and the temple from Gentiles. But there is no mention of a *suffering* Messiah; and given the above range of ideas, seemingly no possibility of such.[28] It would be difficult to find an Old Testament text on which Jewish and Christian interpretations historically have differed so dramatically.[29] The concept of a suffering

25. Many scholars recognize that Jesus regarded his impending death (e.g. Mk 10.45) according to Suffering Servant imagery. See the material and reasons gathered in Cullmann, *Christology of the New Testament*, pp. 79–80; and in Jeremias, 'παῖς θεοῦ', pp. 712–17.

26. M. Grant, *Jesus: An Historian's Review of the Gospels* (New York: Scribner's, 1977), pp. 137–38. Grant continues, 'The Church did not like [the concept of the Suffering-Servant-Messiah]; the whole Suffering Servant range of ideas as reformulated in relation to Jesus proved unassimilable, and soon disappeared. Yet it was so manifestly part of the original record, and authentic, that the Gospels could not omit it altogether.'

27. Contra Jeremias, 'παῖς θεοῦ', p. 699. Jeremias rightly notes, 'It is remarkable that in this rich material [the understanding in Israel of the atoning power of the deaths of certain righteous individuals] there is no reference to Is. 53', but wrongly concludes that the silence is due to a preexisting association of the two concepts in the Jewish mind. The reason there is no association of Messiah and the Suffering Servant of Isaiah 53, rather, is because the two concepts were incompatible in the Jewish mind. Martin Hengel's conclusion is certainly correct.'A crucified messiah, son of God or God must have seemed a contradiction in terms to anyone, Jew, Greek, Roman or barbarian, asked to believe such a claim, and it will certainly have been thought offensive and foolish' (*Crucifixion* [trans. J. Bowden; Philadelphia: Fortress Press, 1977], p. 10).

28. The Targum to Isaiah 53 identifies the Servant of God with the Messiah by wholly suppressing the aspect of suffering! The Targum depicts the Servant, as do the *Psalms of Solomon*, as a victorious Messiah who would drive out the Romans and restore the temple. In a different vein, John Walton has noted the motif of a servant who vicariously suffers on behalf of the king in ancient Assyrian contexts ('The Imagery of the Substitute King Ritual', pp. 734–43), but he has not shown how these or other Assyrian ideas might have influenced Judah. Moreover, in Isaiah the Servant suffers on behalf of the people, and not, as in Assyria, on behalf of the king.

29. See Herbert Haag, *Der Gottesknecht bei Deuterojesaja* (EdF, 233; Darmstadt: Wissenschaftliche Buchgesellschaft, 1985). More recently, W. Bellinger, Jr, and W. Farmer (eds), *Jesus and the Suffering Servant: Isaiah 53 and Christian Origins* (Harrisburg: Trinity Press International, 1998). Judaism is generally indifferent to the figure of the Servant of God, as reflected in Abraham Heschel's two-volume study *The Prophets* (New York: Harper & Row, 1962), where discussion of the Suffering Servant of Isaiah receives a scant page of comment.

servant and saviour figure is so unprecedented in Judaism that the early church can scarcely have inherited the concept, either historically or theologically, from Judaism. There is no plausible explanation for its presence in early Christian tradition except to ascribe it to Jesus himself.

The above complex of ideas allows us to postulate why Servant of the Lord, although employed early in the church's proclamation, was used only sparingly and soon dropped out of use altogether. The Servant of God concept clearly guaranteed the experience of humiliation and suffering in both Jesus' ministry and passion, but it failed to encompass the exaltation of Jesus' person, particularly as a result of the resurrection. The title, in other words, was inadequate to incorporate both humiliation and exaltation (e.g. Phil. 2.6–11). Other titles, especially 'Lord', 'Christ', and 'Son of God', were more adequate for the Christological task before the church. In the Gospel of Mark, in particular, 'Son of God' is the load-bearing Christological title, within which Servant of God is subsumed. Appearing in the opening verse (1.1) and final scene at the crucifixion (15.39) of Mark, Son of God is the supreme expression of Mark's portrayal of Jesus as the divine Son of God who lives and dies as the humble Servant of God.[30]

---

30. In the preparation of this study I have profited from the research of and conversation with my teaching assistant Geoffrey Helton.

ZECHARIAH IN THE MARKAN PASSION NARRATIVE

Craig A. Evans

In a previous publication I treated the question of what input, if any, the prophecy of Zechariah may have had in the thinking and activities of Jesus, especially toward the end of his life.[1] The challenge in that study was in determining what points of contact with Zechariah arose from Jesus himself and what may have been the creative contribution of the evangelists. I return to this question in the present essay, this time specifically inquiring into the degree of influence Zechariah may have had on the evangelist Mark.

Before investigating the presence of Zechariah in Mark, a list of the quotations and allusions to Zechariah in the three Synoptic Gospels will be helpful. They have been tabulated in the standard Greek New Testament editions as follows:

UBSGNT:

Zech. 1.1	Mt. 23.35
Zech. 2.6, 10	Mk 13.27
Zech. 2.6	Mt. 24.31
Zech. 8.6 (LXX)	Mk 10.27 = Mt. 19.26
Zech. 9.2–4	Mt. 11.21–22 = Lk. 10.13–14
Zech. 9.9	Mt. 21.5; Jn 12.15
Zech. 9.11	Mk 14.24 = Mt. 26.28 = Lk. 22.20
Zech. 10.2	Mk 6.34 = Mt. 9.36
Zech. 11.12–13	Mt. 27.9–10
Zech. 11.12	Mt. 26.15
Zech. 12.3 (LXX)	Lk. 21.24
Zech. 12.10	Mt. 24.30; Jn 19.37
Zech. 12.14	Mt. 24.30
Zech. 13.4	Mk 1.6
Zech. 13.7	Mk 14.27, 50 = Mt. 26.31, 56; Jn 16.32
Zech. 14.5	Mt. 25.31

NA[27]:

Zech. 1.1	Mt. 23.35 = Lk. 11.51
Zech. 1.5	Jn 8.52
Zech. 2.6	Mk 13.27
Zech. 2.10	Mt. 24.31
Zech. 3.8	Lk. 1.78

---

1. C.A. Evans, 'Jesus and Zechariah's Messianic Hope', in B.D. Chilton and C.A. Evans (eds), *Authenticating the Activities of Jesus* (NTTS, 28/2; Leiden: Brill, 1999), pp. 373–88.

Zech. 6.12	Lk. 1.78
Zech. 7.9	Mt. 23.23
Zech. 8.6 (LXX)	Mk 10.27 = Mt. 19.26
Zech. 8.17	Mt. 5.33; 9.4
Zech. 9.9	Mk 11.2; Mt. 21.5; Jn 12.15
Zech. 9.11	Mk 14.24 = Mt. 26.28 = Lk. 22.20
Zech. 11.12	Mt. 26.15
Zech. 11.13	Mt. 27.9
Zech. 12.3	Lk. 21.24
Zech. 12.10, 12, 14	Mt. 24.30; Lk. 23.27
Zech. 12.10	Jn 19.37
Zech. 13.3	Mk 3.21
Zech. 13.4	Mk 1.6
Zech. 13.7	Mk 14.27 = Mt. 26.31; Jn 16.32
Zech. 14.4	Mk 11.1 = Mt. 21.1; Mk 11.23 = Mt. 21.21
Zech. 14.5	Mt. 25.31
Zech. 14.7	Mk 13.32 = Mt. 24.36
Zech. 14.8	Jn 4.10; 7.38
Zech. 14.21	Mt. 21.12; Jn 2.16

To these one should probably add:

Zech. 14.5	Mk 13.8; Mt. 27.51
Zech. 1.1	Mt. 23.35[2]

As we work our way through the relevant passages in Mark, we can glance at the above tabulation for comparison with Matthew and Luke.

Interest in Zechariah's contribution to the New Testament Gospels has been modest, though a few important studies have been published.[3] Ten Markan passages and clusters will be considered below. The first passage (8.31–9.8) falls outside of the Passion Narrative proper, but scholars agree that this material either contains passion and Easter tradition, or at least elements related to passion tradition.

---

2.   Matthew's 'Zechariah the son of Barachiah' may have in mind the prophet, rather than 'Zechariah the son of Jehoida the priest' (2 Chron. 24.20).

3.   R.M. Grant, 'The Coming of the Kingdom', *JBL* 67 (1948), pp. 297–303; C.A. Evans, '"I Will Go before You into Galilee"', *JTS* 5 (1954), pp. 3–18, esp. pp. 5–8; F.F. Bruce, 'The Book of Zechariah and the Passion Narrative', *BJRL* 43 (1960–61), pp. 336–53; idem, *New Testament Development of Old Testament Themes* (Grand Rapids: Eerdmans, 1969), pp. 100–114; R.T. France, *Jesus and the Old Testament* (London: Tyndale, 1971), pp. 103–10; S. Kim, 'Jesus – the Son of God, the Stone, the Son of Man, and the Servant: The Role of Zechariah in the Self-Identification of Jesus', in G.F. Hawthorne and O. Betz (eds), *Tradition and Interpretation in the New Testament: Essays in Honor of E. Earle Ellis for his 60th Birthday* (Tübingen: Mohr; Grand Rapids: Eerdmans, 1987), pp. 134–48; J. Marcus, *The Way of the Lord: Christological Exegesis of the Old Testament in the Gospel of Mark* (Louisville: Westminster/John Knox Press, 1992), esp. pp. 154–64; B.D. Chilton, *A Feast of Meanings: Eucharistic Theologies from Jesus through Johannine Circles* (NovTSup, 72; Leiden: Brill, 1994), esp. pp. 186–88; idem, *The Temple of Jesus: His Sacrificial Program within a Cultural History of Sacrifice* (University Park: Penn State Press, 1992), esp. pp. 135–36; H.J. de Jonge, 'The Cleansing of the Temple in Mark 11.15 and Zechariah 14.21', in Christopher Tuckett (ed.), *The Book of Zechariah and its Influence: Papers of the Oxford-Leiden Conference* (Aldershot: Ashgate, 2003), pp. 87–100. The studies by Marcus and de Jonge are especially helpful.

1. *The Transfiguration (Mark 8.31–9.8 – Zechariah 3–4)*

Some commentators have suggested that the Transfiguration narrative was originally an Easter appearance, relocated to the pre-Easter life of Jesus, either by the Markan evangelist himself, or by an earlier tradent.[4] It is not necessary in the present study to weigh the evidence for or against this suggestion. The possibility, even probability, that the story of the Transfiguration has been colored by the Easter appearance stories justifies examination of the passage.

Scholarly interest in the Transfiguration story seems to be as great as ever.[5] The Jewish tradition is appreciated, with scholars usually appealing to Moses and Sinai as the principal backdrop. However, in recent studies John Poirier has argued that the visions of Zechariah 3–4, more than the theophanic traditions associated with Sinai, have given shape to the Transfiguration narrative.[6] Poirier's studies are complex and cannot be fully assessed here. Although I remain convinced that the Sinai tradition is the primary point of reference,[7] Poirier's

---

4.   For a few examples, see C.E. Carlston, 'Transfiguration and Resurrection', *JBL* 80 (1961), pp. 233–40; T.J. Weeden, *Mark – Traditions in Conflict* (Philadelphia: Fortress Press, 1971), pp. 118–26; W. Schmithals, 'Der Markusschluß, die Verklärungsgeschichte und die Aussendung der Zwölf', *ZTK* (1972), pp. 379–411, esp. pp. 384–93; M. Coune, 'Radieuse transfiguration. Mt 17,1–9; Mc 9,2–10; Lc 9,28–36', *AsSeign* 15 (1973), pp. 44–84; F.R. McCurley, Jr, '"And after Six Days" (Mark 9.2): A Semitic Literary Device', *JBL* 93 (1974), pp. 67–81; J.M. Robinson, 'Jesus: From Easter to Valentinus (or the Apostles' Creed)', *JBL* 101 (1982), pp. 5–37; F. Watson, 'The Social Function of Mark's Secrecy Theme', *JSNT* 24 (1985), pp. 49–69, here p. 55. The identification of the Transfiguration as an Easter appearance has been vigorously challenged by R.H. Stein, 'Is the Transfiguration (Mark 9.2–8) a Misplaced Resurrection-Account?' *JBL* 95 (1976), pp. 79–96.

5.   For a sample of recent work, see H.W. Basser, 'The Jewish Roots of the Transfiguration', *Bible Review* 14.3 (1998), pp. 30–35; J.P. Heil, *The Transfiguration of Jesus: Narrative Meaning and Function of Mark 9.2–8, Matt 17.1–8 and Luke 9.28–36* (AnBib, 144; Rome: Biblical Institute Press, 2000); S.C. Barton, 'The Transfiguration of Christ According to Mark and Matthew: Christology and Anthropology', in F. Avemarie and H. Lichtenberger (eds), *Auferstehung–Resurrection: The Fourth Durham-Tübingen Research Symposium: Resurrection, Transfiguration and Exaltation in Old Testament, Ancient Judaism and Early Christianity (Tübingen, September, 1999)* (WUNT, 135; Tübingen: Mohr–Siebeck, 2001), pp. 231–46; C.H.T. Fletcher-Louis, 'The Revelation of the Sacral Son of Man: The Genre, History of Religious Context and the Meaning of the Transfiguration', in Avemarie and Lichtenberger (eds), *Auferstehung–Resurrection*, pp. 247–98; P.A. de Souza Nogueira, 'Visionary Elements in the Transfiguration Narrative', in C. Rowland and J. Barton (eds), *Apocalyptic in History and Tradition* (JSPSup, 43; Sheffield: Sheffield Academic Press, 2002), pp. 142–50; P.-Y. Brandt, *L'identité de Jésus et l'identité de son disciple: Le récit de la transfiguration comme clef de lecture de l'Évangele de Marc* (NTOA, 50; Fribourg, Switzerland: Éditions Universitaires; Göttingen: Vandenhoeck & Ruprecht, 2002); C.R. Moss, 'The Transfiguration: An Exercise in Markan Accommodation', *BibInt* 12 (2004), pp. 69–89; J.C. Poirier, 'Jewish and Christian Tradition in the Transfiguration', *RB* 111 (2004), pp. 516–30.

6.   Poirier, 'Jewish and Christian Tradition in the Transfiguration', pp. 516–30; *idem*, 'Two Transfigurations (Mark 8.31–9.8 and Zechariah 3–4)' (unpublished paper, read at the Colloquium Biblicum Lovaniense XLV, 1996).

7.   The parallels are too numerous and too precise to be set aside as general theophanic elements. The principal elements, which have been pointed out by several scholars, include (1) the reference to 'six days' (Mk 9.2; Exod. 24.16), (2) the cloud that covers the mountain (Mk 9.7; Exod. 24.16),

interesting appeal to Zechariah, along with what may be related tradition in Revelation 11 and 2 Peter 1, may help explain the presence of the second heavenly person, namely Elijah.

I review here what I think is Poirier's best evidence for Zechariah's possible contribution to the story of the Transfiguration. This includes the rebuke of Satan, being clothed in rich apparel, the reference to 'those standing here', the messianic significance of the epithet 'Branch', and the figures of Moses and Elijah.

Shortly before this strange event Jesus had rebuked Peter: 'He rebuked [ἐπετίμησεν] Peter, and said, "Get behind me, Satan [σατανᾶ]! For you are not on the side of God, but of men"' (Mk 8.33). Poirier calls attention to Zech. 3.2: 'And the Lord said to Satan [שָׂטָן], "The Lord rebuke [גְּעַר] you, O Satan [שָׂטָן]!"' The vocabulary does constitute a formal parallel, to be sure. But there really is no contextual or exegetical parallel. The context of Zechariah 3 suggests that Satan accuses Joshua the high priest, because his garments are filthy, thus disqualifying him from performing his priestly functions. Satan is rebuked and Joshua is then clothed 'with rich apparel' (Zech. 3.4). The latter detail, according to Poirier, parallels the transformation of Jesus' garments in the Transfiguration: 'his garments became glistening, intensely white, as no fuller on earth could bleach them' (Mk 9.3). But the Markan story gives no hint that Jesus has been accused or that he and/or his appearance is somehow deficient. The contextual parallel at this point seems quite strained.

In Greek Zechariah, the wording of the rebuke is a bit different: 'The Lord said to the devil [τὸν διάβολον], "May the Lord rebuke [ἐπιτιμήσαι] you, O devil [διάβολε]!"' The language of the Greek version parallels closely the tradition quoted in Jude 9, which most scholars believe came from the *Assumption* (or *Testament*) *of Moses*: 'But when the archangel Michael, contending with the devil [τῷ διαβόλῳ], disputed about the body of Moses, he did not presume to pronounce a reviling judgment upon him, but said, "The Lord rebuke [ἐπιτιμήσαι] you"' (Jude 9). The formal parallel here is quite similar to the one just considered. In this case, however, the parallel with the *Assumption of Moses* means that our rebuking of Satan parallel is just as close to Mosaic tradition as it is to Zecharian tradition.

Indeed, the parallel is strengthened in a later patristic tradition: 'When on the mountain Moses died, Michael was sent that he might transport the body. Then while the devil was speaking against the body of Moses, charging (him) with murder, on account of striking Egypt, the angel did not hold the blasphemy against him. "May God rebuke [ἐπιτιμήσαι] you", he said to the devil [τὸν διάβολον]'.[8] What is significant here is that the devil has accused Moses of murder. The role

---

(3) God's voice from the cloud (Mk 9.7; Exod. 24.16), (4) three companions (Mk 9.2; Exod. 24.1, 9), (5) a transformed appearance (Mk 9.3; Exod. 34.30), and (6) the reaction of fear (Mk 9.6; Exod. 34.30).

8. A.-M. Denis, *Fragmenta Pseudepigraphorum quae supersunt graeca* (PVTG, 3; Leiden: Brill, 1970), p. 67. Denis derives the text from J.A. Cramer (ed.), *Catenae graecorum patrum in novum testamentum* (Oxford: E. Typographeo Academico, 1844), p. 163.

of the devil as accuser is closer to Satan's role in Zechariah 3, where he accuses Joshua the high priest.

We have here the possibility of linkage between Zechariah 3 and later Moses tradition, where Satan accuses God's servant (Joshua in Zechariah, Moses in the *Assumption of Moses*) and then is rebuked, either by God or by his angel. What is not clear is that this accusation and rebuke tradition has colored the story of the Transfiguration. Perhaps it has; but if it has, it has done so very indirectly.

It is also difficult to see how clothing Joshua the high priest 'with rich apparel' (Zech. 3.4) truly parallels the transfiguration of Jesus' clothing and appearance. Joshua has not been transfigured. There is nothing supernatural or heavenly about his new clothes. His new 'rich apparel' is of fine quality, but it is earthly. In contrast, Jesus' 'garments became glistening, intensely white, as no fuller on earth could bleach them'. Moreover, Jesus himself is said to be transformed (μετε-μορφώθη), which recalls various apocalyptic traditions, in which we hear of saints with shining faces (cf. 2 Esd. 7.97, 125; *1 En.* 37.7; 51.5; see also Mt. 17.2 and Lk. 9.29, which specifically mention Jesus' face), or saints with shining clothing (cf. Dan. 12.3; Rev. 4.4; 7.9; *1 En.* 62.15). Later interpreters may well have thought of Zechariah 3 in these terms, so the text may be relevant. But it is hard to see how this aspect of the Transfiguration story specifically recalls Zechariah 3.

More promising is Mark's odd-sounding 'some of those standing here [τινες ὧδε τῶν ἑστηκότων]' (9.1), which could be seen as an allusion to God's promise to Joshua the high priest: 'If you will walk in my ways and keep my charge, then you shall rule my house and have charge of my courts, and I will give you the right of access among *those who are standing here* [בֵּין הָעֹמְדִים הָאֵלֶּה / ἐν μέσῳ τῶν ἑστηκότων τούτων]' (Zech. 3.7; emphasis added). Zechariah's 'those who are standing here' are heavenly beings that stand in God's presence.[9] This parallel gains credibility, if Bruce Chilton's interpretation of Mk 9.1 is correct, in which it is argued that 'those standing here', who 'will not taste death', are none other than Moses and Elijah.[10]

Whatever we are to make of that parallel, the diarchic orientation of Zechariah 3–4 is more promising, for in this we may finally have an explanation for the appearance of Elijah, in a setting that is primarily Mosaic. In Zech. 3.8 God assures Joshua the high priest that he will bring his servant 'the Branch'. This diarchy is elaborated in the following chapter, by the metaphor of the two olive trees on the right and the left of the lampstand (Zech. 4.3, 11). The prophet is told that these two trees are the 'sons of oil', 'who stand by the Lord of the whole earth' (Zech. 4.14). The quotation of this material in Revelation is very interesting: 'I will grant my two witnesses power to prophesy... These are the two olive trees and the two lampstands which stand before the Lord of the earth' (Rev. 11.3–4).

---

9. C.L. Meyers and E.M. Meyers, *Haggai, Zechariah 1–8* (AB, 25B; New York: Doubleday, 1987), p. 197: 'the members of the Heavenly Court'.

10. B.D. Chilton, 'The Transfiguration: Dominical Assurance and Apostolic Vision', *NTS* 27 (1981), pp. 114–24. Chilton rightly appeals to biblical and post-biblical traditions that either assert or imply the immortality of Moses and Elijah. Appeal to Zech. 3.7, it seems to me, would strengthen Chilton's argument.

That the two witnesses in Revelation 11 are Moses and Elijah is likely, in view of what is said of them in Rev. 11.6: 'They have power to shut the sky, that no rain may fall during the days of their prophesying, and they have power over the waters to turn them into blood, and to smite the earth with every plague, as often as they desire'. We have here clear allusions to the plagues that preceded the Exodus (cf. Exod. 7.17–21) and the drought during the ministry of Elijah (cf. 1 Kgs 17.1). If the two olive trees are Moses and Elijah, who, according to Zech. 4.14, 'stand by the Lord', then their relevance for the Transfiguration story, where Moses and Elijah come into the presence of Jesus, takes on new possibilities.[11]

The association of Zechariah's lamp and the two prophetic witnesses, who are probably Moses and Elijah, may also explain the reference to the Transfiguration in 2 Peter. After the allusion to the event in 2 Pet. 1.16–18, the author assures his readers: 'And we have the prophetic word made more sure. You will do well to pay attention to this as to a lamp shining in a dark place, until the day dawns and the morning star rises in your hearts' (2 Pet. 2.19). The appearance of 'prophetic' and 'lamp' could be clarified by Zech. 4.2, 11 (cf. *Tg. Zech.* 4.8–9 'a word of prophecy…sent me to prophesy').

In my judgment, the Moses-Sinai tradition remains the principal background, in the light of which the Markan Transfiguration story should be studied. However, the presence of Elijah, with Moses, may well be part of an eschatological dual-witness tradition that grew out of Zechariah 3–4 and that is attested faintly in 2 Peter 1 and explicitly in Revelation 11. Even if I cannot accept all of Poirier's very creative exegesis, I do think he may have shed important light on one of the more difficult aspects of the Transfiguration narrative.

2. *The Triumphal Entry (Mark 11.1–11 – Zechariah 9.9)*

According to Mark, Jesus commands his disciples to enter a village, where they will find a tethered colt (πῶλος), which they are to collect (11.1–3). Having done this, they 'threw their garments on it; and [Jesus] sat upon it' (11.4–7). With fanfare and shouting, the mounted Jesus and his disciples enter the city of Jerusalem. Nowhere does the Markan evangelist quote or paraphrase Zech. 9.9 ('Rejoice greatly, O daughter of Zion! Shout aloud, O daughter of Jerusalem! Lo, your king comes to you; triumphant and victorious is he, humble and riding on an ass, on a colt the foal of an ass'), although the shouting of the crowd in Mk 11. 9–10 clearly alludes to Ps. 118.25–26.

That Zech. 9.9 is in some way behind this event is hardly in doubt. The Matthean and Johannine evangelists recognize the passage and quote it, with formal introduction (Mt. 21.4–5; Jn 12.14–15). Mark's description of the activities of Jesus' disciples – throwing garments on the animal, spreading garments and leafy branches on the road – all have scriptural and historical precedents (e.g. 1 Kgs 1.38–40 [Solomon on David's mule]; 2 Kgs 9.13 [garments laid on steps

---

11. In this connection, see also J.C. Poirier, 'The Endtime Return of Elijah and Moses at Qumran', *DSD* 10 (2003), pp. 221–42.

before Jehu]; 1 Macc. 13.49–51 [palm branches and singing]; 2 Macc. 10.7 [waving palm fronds and singing hymns]). In other words, Mark's narrative is rich with allusions, yet surprisingly, there are only minimal allusions to the primary text most Jewish readers would have readily recognized. Mark's 'colt…on which no one has ever sat' (11.2) probably alludes to the Old Greek's πῶλον νέον ('new colt'). But it may also be implied by the Hebrew's עַיִר בֶּן־אֲתֹנוֹת ('a colt, the foal of an ass'), in that the animal is young and (it would be assumed) untried. In any case, one can hardly argue that the Markan evangelist is dependent on the Greek tradition, since he does not in fact describe the animal on which Jesus sat as a πῶλος νέος. Moreover, it is not made clear in Mark that Jesus was actually mounted on an ass, as it is in Matthew and John, who have quoted the scriptural text, in which words for ass or donkey appear.[12] In short, it is not certain that the evangelist Mark was conscious of the contribution that Zech. 9.9 made, either to Jesus (which I think is the case), or to the tradition that the evangelist inherited.

One cannot be dogmatic in this instance; the Markan evangelist may have been aware of the Zecharian prophecy, but felt no need to cite it formally (which, in any case, the evangelist tended not to do).[13] If the evangelist was aware of Zechariah's prophecy, there is no indication that the entrance narrative was created from it.

3. *The Temple Demonstration (Mark 11.15–18 – Zechariah 14.20–21)*

Jesus' action in the temple precincts has featured prominently in recent scholarly discussion of what prompted the Jewish authorities to arrest Jesus and call for his death. E.P. Sanders placed the story squarely in the spotlight with his novel interpretation, an interpretation that few have followed.[14] Several studies have appeared in the last two decades, as scholars debate the significance of the action. The Markan narrative reads as follows (11.15–18):

> And they came to Jerusalem. And he entered the temple and began to drive out those who sold and those who bought in the temple, and he overturned the tables of the money-changers and the seats of those who sold pigeons; and he would not allow any one to carry anything through the temple. And he taught, and said to them, 'Is it not written,

12. πῶλος means 'colt' and could refer to a horse.

13. This is the principal thesis of A. Suhl, *Die Funktion der alttestamentlichen Zitate und Anspielungen im Markusevangelium* (Gütersloh: Mohn, 1965). In my opinion, Suhl overstates the case. See the concise overview in M.D. Hooker, 'Mark', in D.A. Carson and H.G.M. Williamson (eds), *It is Written: Scripture Citing Scripture. Essays in Honour of Barnabas Lindars* (Cambridge: Cambridge University Press, 1988), pp. 220–30.

14. E.P. Sanders, *Jesus and Judaism* (London: SCM Press; Philadelphia: Fortress Press, 1985). Sanders argues that Jesus did not demonstrate against priestly corruption, but overturned the tables to signify the approaching eschatological change in Israel's administration. Sanders's point about Jesus' eschatological concerns has merit. His assumption that perceptions of corruption played no role is the problem. I have challenged this position by setting forth what I think is substantial evidence that many Jews in the first century, or thereabouts, regarded the Herodian temple establishment as corrupt and, in some cases, as in danger of judgment. See my 'Jesus' Action in the Temple: Cleansing or Portent of Destruction?', *CBQ* 51 (1989), pp. 237–70.

"My house shall be called a house of prayer for all the nations?" But you have made it a
den of robbers'. And the chief priests and the scribes heard it and sought a way to destroy
him; for they feared him, because all the multitude was astonished at his teaching.

The principal problem with Sanders' interpretation is that in failing to see how
Jesus' actions in v. 16 ('he would not allow any one to carry a vessel through the
temple') and utterances in v. 17 ('Is it not written, "My house shall be called a
house of prayer for all the nations?" But you have made it a den of robbers')
make sense in the context of the temple establishment of the early part of the first
century, he dismisses the material as secondary. All that survives is the action of
v. 15 ('he entered the temple and began to drive out those who sold and those
who bought in the temple, and he overturned the tables of the money-changers
and the seats of those who sold pigeons').[15]

One recent and very helpful study comes from Henk Jan de Jonge, who has
reconsidered what connection, if any, the story of the temple action has with
Zech. 14.21.[16] With precision and economy de Jonge traces the interpretation of
the verse, especially with reference to כְּנַעֲנִי/ Χαναναῖος, which in the Hebrew
and Greek probably originally meant 'Canaanite'. It is noted that in biblical
Hebrew כנעני also means 'trader' (as in Isa. 23.8 and Prov. 31.24), which facili-
tated later interpretive developments. Aquila translated the כנעני of Zech. 14.21
with μετάβολος, whose cognate μεταβολή means 'exchange, barter, traffic'
(LSJ). The Targum translates כנעני with עָבֵיד תִּגְרָא ('a worker of trade'). Indeed,
later rabbinic tradition insists that כנעני in Zech. 14.21 did not mean 'Canaanite',
but 'trader' (cf. *b. Pesah.* 50a). From this evidence, de Jonge rightly concludes
that there was an ancient tradition that understood Zech. 14.21 as prophesying that
in the Day of the Lord traders would no longer be present in the temple precincts.[17]
This is the case, not because trade was seen as impure or immoral, but because in
the Day of the Lord the whole city of Jerusalem will be holy, and every pot and
vessel will be pure. Nothing will have to be exchanged; no business activities
will be necessary.[18]

15. Others have taken even more radically skeptical approaches, claiming that the entire narrative
is a Markan creation, as in, for example, D. Seeley, 'Jesus' Temple Act', *CBQ* 55 (1993), pp. 263–83.
With reference to this skepticism, P.M. Casey ('Culture and Historicity: The Cleansing of the Temple',
CBQ 59 [1997], pp. 306–32) wryly comments: 'The unfortunate effect of Seeley's method is that he
regards as unhistorical anything which he does not understand. The trouble with his execution is that
there is too much which he does not understand; consequently, he ends up with too little historical
event' (p. 325).

16. de Jonge, 'The Cleansing of the Temple in Mark 11.15 and Zechariah 14.21', pp. 87–100. De
Jonge is not, of course, the first to appeal to Zech. 14.20–21; many have. In addition to studies listed
in footnote 3 above, see also C. Roth, "The Cleansing of the Temple and Zechariah xiv 21," *NovT* 4
(1960), pp. 172–79. The study by Chilton (*Temple of Jesus*, pp. 135–36) also sheds important light on
the meaning of Zech. 14.20–21 in Jesus' action and is consistent with the position taken here.

17. De Jonge, 'The Cleansing of the Temple', p. 90.

18. If de Jonge's interpretation is correct, then at least one part of Sanders's interpretation may be
correct, after all. Sanders had argued that Jesus' actions implied that the temple's normal trade should
come to an end because of the arrival of the kingdom of God. Ironically, in setting aside Mk 11.16,
which probably reflects an understanding of Zech. 14.21, Sanders has disregarded an important
element that would have modified but also supported his thesis.

Accordingly, the business activities that Jesus encountered when he entered the temple precincts not only denied the presence of the Day of Lord – the arrival of which Jesus had been announcing since the beginning of his public ministry – but high priestly avarice and violence undermined the very divinely appointed task of the temple establishment. By stopping traffic, Jesus both protested the avarice and called for his contemporaries to move toward the prophetic ideal envisioned by Isaiah and Zechariah.

This is my interpretation; not de Jonge's. He concludes that Zech. 14.20–21 inspired the cleansing story in the pre-Markan, but post-Easter tradition. The tradition may be early, he thinks, but it does not reach back to Jesus himself.

I agree with de Jonge that it is pre-Markan. Mark's 'he would not allow any one to carry a vessel [σκεῦος] through the temple' is not likely an allusion to the wording of Zech. 14.21 (which refers to λέβητες, 'cauldrons', and φιάλαι, 'bowls'). But it does realistically describe what one would do, if one wanted to enforce the vision of Zech. 14.21. If the story grew out of scriptural apologetics and imagination in early Christianity, then I should think verbal traces, if not explicit quotation of the text of Zech. 14.20–21, would be in evidence. The later version in the fourth Gospel may offer just such a verbal trace, when the Johannine Jesus says: 'Take these things away; you shall not make my Father's house a house of trade' (Jn 2.16). But this is not what we find in Mark. The influence of Zechariah is pre-Markan, as de Jonge rightly says, but it probably reaches back to Jesus himself, who appealed to it as part of his positive vision for the temple, on the one hand, and as part of his criticism of the temple establishment, on the other. Instead of a 'house of prayer for all the nations', as Isaiah's oracle promised – a holy house in a holy city, where merchants and traders were no longer needed – the temple had become a 'cave of robbers', exploiting the temple trade.[19]

4. *The Mount of Olives (Mark 11.1, 23 – Zechariah 14.4)*

The Markan evangelist contextualizes Jesus' entrance into Jerusalem in a somewhat clumsy fashion: 'And when they drew near to Jerusalem, to Bethphage and Bethany, at the Mount of Olives, he sent two of his disciples' (Mk 11.1). Mention of the Mount of Olives hardly seems necessarily, from a strictly geographical or topographical point of view. Accordingly, some commentators have wondered if

---

19. C.A. Evans, 'Jesus and the "Cave of Robbers": Toward a Jewish Context for the Temple Action', *BBR* 3 (1993), pp. 93–110. Casey's conclusion ('The Cleansing of the Temple', pp. 331–32) is generally supportive of the position that I have taken here. He rightly concludes that Jesus acted in accordance with the oracles of Isaiah and Jeremiah and that Mk 11.16 does fairly reflect Jesus' actions. I doubt that post-Easter reflection on Zech. 14.20–21 would give rise to a fictive story of Jesus demonstrating in the temple. Why would early Christians want to suggest that Jesus advocated the holiness of the temple? Why would early Christians invent a story, which provides grounds for his subsequent arrest and execution? It is more plausible to see the demonstration as authentic and as reflecting Jesus' concern, not the concern of the post-Easter community.

the reference was in fact an allusion to Zech. 14.4: 'On that day his feet shall stand on the Mount of Olives which lies before Jerusalem on the east...'.[20]

The context of Zech. 14.4 does not encourage us to think we have an allusion in Mark 11 to this prophecy; nor do later interpretive traditions.[21] Moreover, the awkward reference to the Mount of Olives may be no more than the evangelist's way of alerting his readers to the place where Jesus will later teach, pray, and be arrested (cf. Mk 13.3; 14.26). (The reference to the Mount of Olives in the eschatological discourse, however, may well be a different matter. This will be considered below.)

After finding the fruitless fig tree withered (Mk 11.12–14, 20–21), Jesus remarks, as part of a teaching on faith: 'Truly, I say to you, whoever says to this mountain, "Be taken up and cast into the sea", and does not doubt in his heart, but believes that what he says will come to pass, it will be done for him' (11.23). Because the saying is independent and may have been placed in its present context by the evangelist, we may rightly wonder if the mountain cast into the sea is an allusion to the Mount of Olives, perhaps again understood in the light of Zech. 14.4, this time quoting the second half of the verse: '...and the Mount of Olives shall be split in two from east to west by a very wide valley; so that one half of the Mount shall withdraw northward, and the other half southward'.

Does Jesus' saying allude to Zechariah? To speak of moving mountains is proverbial,[22] so that is hardly a distinctive feature. What is distinctive in the saying is relating the proverb to *faith*. There is nothing about the saying that makes us think of Zechariah 14, or the Mount of Olives, for that matter. Indeed, the mount just visited, which has occasioned Jesus' anger and which the fruitless fig tree represents, is the temple mount. It is possible that the Markan evangelist, or an earlier tradent who combined the sayings in Mk 11.22–26, saw the proverb as tying Jesus' utterances on faith to his disappointment with the temple establishment. To what degree the Markan evangelist may have edited this material, it seems doubtful he intended his readers to think of the Mount of Olives.

5. *Jesus' Entry into the Temple Precincts (Mark 11–12 – Zechariah 4.14)*

In previous publications I have explored the significance of the diarchic messianism of Haggai and Zechariah, especially as seen in the statement in Zech. 4.14, in which an angel explains the significance of the two olive trees: 'These are the two sons of oil who stand by the Lord of the whole earth'.[23] What I find especially

20. M.D. Hooker, *The Gospel According to Saint Mark* (BNTC; London: A. & C. Black, 1991), p. 258.

21. As has been pointed out by R.H. Gundry, *Mark: A Commentary on his Apology for the Cross* (Grand Rapids: Eerdmans, 1993), p. 633.

22. See *T. Sol.* 23.1, where a demon says to Solomon: 'I am able to move mountains'; *b. Ber.* 64a: 'Rabbah was an "uprooter of mountains"'; *b. Sanh.* 24a: 'you would think he was uprooting mountains and grinding them against each other'; *b. B. Bat.* 3b: 'I will uproot mountains'; and *Lev. Rab.* 8.8 (on Lev. 6.13): '[Samson] took two mountains and knocked them one against another'.

23. The RSV's 'These are the two anointed...' is misleading. Later interpretation will take the

intriguing is the appearance of the distinctive line, 'two sons of oil', in the context of a Qumran commentary on Jacob's testaments for his sons Levi and Judah (cf. 4Q254 frg. 4).[24] The 'two sons of oil' are understood in a messianic sense in some rabbinic midrashim (e.g. *Sifra* §97 [on Lev. 7.35–38]; *'Abot R. Nat.* A 34.4; *Num. Rab.* 14.14 [on Num. 7.84]), but it is the contextualization of the passage in the Qumran pesher that indicates that this unusual epithet was taken in a messianic sense as early as the time of Jesus.[25]

What makes this passage potentially relevant for the study of Jesus and Mark is that the diarchic interpretation of Zech. 4.14 coheres with the Aramaic interpretation of Ps. 118.19–27, parts of which are cited in the entrance narrative (Mk 11.9–10; cf. Ps. 118.26) and at the conclusion of the parable of the Wicked Vineyard Tenants (Mk 12.10–11; cf. Ps. 118.22–23). The Aramaic version transforms this part of the Psalm into the narrative of David – Jesse's son who was initially rejected by the priesthood but later accepted and declared worthy to be 'king and ruler' – portraying a picture of David the king and Samuel the priest serving the Lord faithfully. Here we have a portrait of the kind of diarchic messianism envisioned by Haggai and Zechariah.

The coherence between the Aramaic orientation of Psalm 118 and Jesus' actions and teachings in the temple precincts strongly suggests that this psalm did indeed inform Jesus' self-understanding.[26] Because Jesus' actions in other settings also appear to have been shaped by texts and themes from Zechariah, we must wonder if the messianic interpretation of Zech. 4.14 made a contribution here as well. This must remain no more than speculation, because there is no discernible trace of this distinctive passage anywhere in Mark. All that we can say is that given the several meaningful points of contact between Jesus and Zechariah, perhaps diarchic messianism, to which later interpretation of Zech. 4.14 and Psalm 118 made a contribution, also played a role in Jesus' thinking and activities in Jerusalem, especially in the temple precincts.

---

language in this sense (i.e. two personages anointed for service), but the actual wording, 'two sons of oil', refers to the fruitfulness and productivity of the two personages. Prosperity for Israel will flow from them. It is to that dimension the 'oil' imagery refers.

24. G.J. Brooke, '4Q254 Fragments 1 and 4, and 4Q254a: Some Preliminary Comments', in *Proceedings of the Eleventh World Congress of Jewish Studies* (Jerusalem: World Union of Jewish Studies, 1994), pp. 185–92.

25. C.A. Evans, ' "The Two Sons of Oil": Early Evidence of Messianic Interpretation of Zechariah 4.14 in 4Q254 4 2', in D.W. Parry and E. Ulrich (eds), *The Provo International Conference on the Dead Sea Scrolls: Technological Innovations, New Texts, and Reformulated Issues* (STDJ, 30; Leiden: Brill, 1998), pp. 566–75; *idem*, 'Diarchic Messianism in the Dead Sea Scrolls and the Messianism of Jesus of Nazareth', in L.H. Schiffman, E. Tov, and J.C. VanderKam (eds), *The Dead Sea Scrolls: Fifty Years after their Discovery. Proceedings of the Jerusalem Congress, July 20–25, 1997* (Jerusalem: Israel Exploration Society and the Israel Antiquities Authority, 2000), pp. 558–67.

26. For the details and argument in support of this interpretation, see C.A. Evans, 'The Aramaic Psalter and the New Testament: Praising the Lord in History and Prophecy', in C.A. Evans (ed.), *From Prophecy to Testament: The Function of the Old Testament in the New* (Peabody, MA: Hendrickson, 2004), pp. 44–91, here pp. 81–85.

6. *The Eschatological Discourse (Mark 13.3–4, 8, 14, 27, 32 – Zechariah 14.5; 2.6; 14.6–7)*

Joel Marcus thinks mention of the Mount of Olives in Mk 13.3–4 and 14.26 has something to do with the messianic expectations that came to be associated with Zech. 14.1–5.[27] He may well be correct. The primary passage is Mk 13.2, the setting of the eschatological discourse, of which readers of Mark are reminded when Jesus retires for prayer after the supper. In the discourse of Mark 13 many points of contact with Zechariah suggest themselves. Jesus prophesies the destruction of Jerusalem, which coheres with Zech. 14.2 ('I will gather all the nations against Jerusalem to battle, and the city shall be taken…'). Jesus' discourse implies that a remnant – the elect – will survive the period of tribulation, a point that also coheres with the rest of Zech. 14.2 ('…half of the city shall go into exile, but the rest of the people shall not be cut off from the city'). Jesus also speaks of nations and earthquakes (Mk 13.8), which may allude to Zech. 14.2 ('I will gather all the nations against Jerusalem to battle') and 14.5 ('earthquake'). In Mk 13.14 the warning to flee the coming danger may echo Zech. 14.5 ('you shall flee'; cf. 2.6 'Flee from the land of the north'). In Mk 13.27 the anticipation that the elect will be gathered from the 'four winds, from the ends of the earth to the ends of heaven', may echo Zech. 2.6 ('I have spread you abroad as the four winds of heaven'). And finally, the assertion in Mk 13.32 that 'of that day or that hour no one knows, not even the angels in heaven, nor the Son, but only the Father', may echo Zech. 14.6–7 ('On that day…it is known to the Lord').

The allusions are vague and imprecise, with little actual wording in common. Yet their number and coherence strongly suggest that that these are indeed allusions to Zechariah. What is not clear is that they derive from the evangelist Mark. Some of this material probably derives from Jesus, and some of it probably originated in the post-Easter community.[28] That the evangelist Mark edited the material – especially in view of the impending Jewish war – is probable.

7. *The Blood of the Covenant (Mark 14.24 – Zechariah 9.11)*

In his final meal with his disciples, Jesus says: 'This is my blood of the covenant, which is poured out for many' (Mk 14.24). Commentators have heard in this utterance echoes of several passages. 'Blood of the covenant' recalls Exod. 24.8: 'Behold the blood of the covenant which the Lord has made with you in accordance with all these words'. Some see allusion to Jer. 31.31: 'Behold, the days are coming, says the Lord, when I will make a new covenant with the house of Israel and the house of Judah'. Jeremiah's adjective 'new' probably accounts for the variation in the Pauline and Lukan versions of the words of institution:

---

27. Marcus, *Way of the Lord*, pp. 156.

28. Again, I am in general agreement with Marcus, *Way of the Lord*, p. 163, who states: 'most of these allusions stem from pre-Markan tradition'.

'This cup is the new covenant in my blood' (1 Cor. 11.25); 'This cup, which is poured out for you, is the new covenant in my blood' (Lk. 22.20). Many also hear an echo of Zech. 9.11: 'As for you also, because of the blood of my covenant with you, I will set your captives free from the waterless pit' (RSV). What the RSV translates 'my covenant' is literally 'your covenant' (בְּרִיתֵךְ). Zechariah's text is not garbled, but it is somewhat awkward (which the RSV is trying to rectify). The Greek version reads: 'And you – by the blood of your covenant – have sent forth your prisoners out of the pit that has no water'. The problem in the Hebrew is in the apparent lack of agreement between the first person verb ('I will send', i.e., 'set free') and the second person suffix that qualifies 'blood' (i.e. 'your blood').

The confusion notwithstanding, it is clear that the covenant, to which reference is made, is God's covenant with his people (or, in the context of Zechariah 9, with Jerusalem). Zechariah himself may well have alluded to Exod. 24.8 (as also is probably the case in Jer. 31.31).[29] Likewise, Jesus' 'my blood of the covenant' may allude to Zechariah's 'blood of my/your covenant'.[30]

The final clause, 'which is poured out for many', probably echoes (Hebrew not Greek) Isa. 53.12: 'he poured out his soul to death…he bore the sin of many'. The pouring out of the blood of the Sinai covenant (as in Exod. 29.12: 'and the rest of the blood you shall pour out at the base of the altar') encourages associating the phrase from Isaiah 53 with allusions to the blood-covenant passages already considered.

Jesus' appropriation of these blood-covenant passages is remarkable. There are other texts and traditions, in which the suffering, blood, and death of the righteous redeem or in some way benefit Israel (e.g. 1 Macc. 6.44 [Eleazar 'gave himself to save his people']; 2 Macc. 7.33, 37–38 ['I give up body and life for the laws of our fathers…and through me and my brothers to bring to an end the wrath of the Almighty']; Ps.-Philo, *Bib. Ant.* 18.5 ['on account of his blood I chose them']; *T. Mos.* 9.6–10.1 [Their 'blood will be avenged before the Lord. Then his (God's) kingdom will appear… Then the devil will have an end']). But the appropriation of the blood-covenant language appears to be distinctive. Again, it seems best to regard the saying as pre-Markan and, probably, as reaching back to Jesus himself.

8. *The Kingdom of God (Mark 14.25 – Zechariah 14.9)*

Following the words of institution, Jesus solemnly vows to his disciples: 'Truly, I say to you, I shall not drink again of the fruit of the vine until that day when I drink it new in the kingdom of God' (Mk 14.25). Marinus de Jonge believes that this saying may very well derive from Jesus, though the Markan evangelist has probably edited it (cf. Lk. 22.15–16). De Jonge thinks it probable that the saying

29. D.L. Petersen, *Zechariah 9–14 and Malachi* (OTL; Louisville: Westminster John Knox Press, 1995), p. 60.

30. The appearance of the pronoun 'my' may derive directly from Zechariah; cf. Bruce, 'Book of Zechariah', p. 347; Marcus, *Way of the Lord*, p. 157.

reflects Jesus' restorative expectations.[31] I am inclined to agree.[32] Zechariah's influence may yet be felt again. Not only do Jesus' words in v. 24 allude to this prophetic book, but reference to drinking wine 'in the kingdom of God' may also allude to Zech. 14.9, which looks forward to the day when 'the Lord will become king over all the earth', that is, when the kingdom of God (cf. *Tg. Zech.* 14.9, 'the kingdom of the Lord shall be revealed') will have come in its fullness.[33]

9. *The Striking of the Shepherd (Mark 14.26–31 – Zechariah 13.7)*

Henk de Jonge regards the paraphrase of Zech. 13.7 in Mk 14.27 as probably deriving from post-Easter tradition: 'Jesus said to them, "You will all fall away; for it is written, 'I will strike the shepherd, and the sheep will be scattered'"'.[34] He could be correct. What makes it difficult to determine is that the Markan evangelist gives us little to go on. The evangelist was not in the habit of introducing and quoting scripture, 'as it is written', and so forth. Therefore, we have little, with which to make comparisons.

I am inclined to agree with F.F. Bruce, with whom de Jonge disagrees, although I cannot share the degree of Bruce's conviction, when he says, 'I have no doubt at all that Mark is right in ascribing this interpretation of the prophecy to Jesus'.[35] I have some doubts, but not as many as de Jonge. I think the appeal to Zechariah's stricken shepherd was, again, part of Jesus' effort to find a scriptural explanation for his impending fate. To assert that Jesus did not or would not have pondered the meaning of his death is simply gratuitous. Equally gratuitous and improbable is to assert or assume that had Jesus given his death some thought and spoke about it, his disciples would have remembered nothing.

More positively stated, I think Jesus spoke these words in the press of the moment, because it does not give the impression of a carefully thought-through exegesis. Would early Christians, or the evangelist Mark, appeal to a prophetic text that reads: '"Awake, O sword, against my shepherd, against the man who stands next to me," says the Lord of hosts. "Strike the shepherd, that the sheep may be scattered; I will turn my hand against the little ones"'? Would the early

---

31. M. de Jonge, 'Mark 14.25 among Jesus' Words about the Kingdom of God', in W.L. Petersen *et al.* (eds), *Sayings of Jesus: Canonical and Non-Canonical. Essays in Honour of Tjitze Baarda* (NovTSup, 89; Leiden: Brill, 1997), pp. 123–35.

32. I am puzzled by the strong skepticism expressed in Hooker, *Mark*, p. 342: 'it seems impossible that Jesus himself could have used these words about the wine'. Various festival foods – not least the foods of the Passover meal – all carried symbolic meanings. Why should not Jesus attach symbolic meaning to the wine, as part of his attempt to explain to himself and to his disciples the meaning of his impending suffering and death?

33. See also Marcus, *Way of the Lord*, pp. 156–57. The Aramaic diction, 'kingdom of the Lord/of our God shall be revealed' (cf. *T. Isa.* 40.9; 52.7), is reflected in Jesus' proclamation: 'The kingdom of God is at hand' (Mk 1.15).

34. de Jonge, 'Cleansing of the Temple', p. 89.

35. Bruce, 'Book of Zechariah', p. 343.

community – struggling to mount a scriptural defense of its understanding of Jesus' saving mission – apply a prophetic passage to him, in which the figure is the object of God's wrath? It seems unlikely. Moreover, Jesus faced death by execution, and he probably suspected it would be crucifixion, not death by combat or war (i.e. by the sword). More troubling, the prophetic passage envisions God turning his wrath against his own people; not only against his own shepherd. Would Christians perusing the Scriptures apply such a passage to Jesus?

However, Jesus himself just might see in such a passage a prophetic explanation of what was about to overtake him (and so the imperative of Zech. 13.7 [הַךְ/ πατάξατε[36]] becomes a future in the words of Jesus [πατάξω]). Because of the nation's sin and because of her ruling priests' rejection of Jesus, God's messenger, Israel now faces judgment. Part of that judgment will fall on the aristocratic priestly establishment (Mk 12.10–12; 13.2), to be sure, but part of it will fall on the Lord's shepherd himself.

Admittedly, we cannot rule out the possibility that this interpretation and application of Zech. 13.7 developed in the early community and perhaps even in the Markan evangelist's own creative thinking. But I think that on the whole it is less problematic to see it as an *ad hoc* exegesis of Jesus, rather than as an exegesis that developed more gradually and deliberately in the post-Easter community.

10. *The Resurrection of the Shepherd (Mark 14.28 – Zechariah 14.4 and 13.8–9)*

After his remarkable appeal to the stricken shepherd of Zech. 13.7, Jesus tells his disciples: 'But after I am raised up, I will go before you to Galilee' (Mk 14.28). Marcus sees here an allusion to Zech. 14.4 ('On that day his feet shall stand'), which in Jewish interpretation came to be understood as a prophecy of future resurrection: 'At that time the Lord will take in his hand the great trumpet and will blow ten blasts upon it to revive the dead' (Targum, *apud* Codex Reuchlinianus);[37] and: 'When the dead rise, the Mount of Olives will be cleft, and all Israel's dead will come up out of it' (*Tg. Song* 8.5).[38]

This tradition may well account for the odd Matthean addition to Mark's story of Jesus' death. Mark says only that when Jesus died, 'the curtain of the temple was torn' (Mk 15.38). At the parallel place in Matthew, we find a remarkable addition: 'and the earth shook, and the rocks were split; the tombs also were opened, and many bodies of the saints who had fallen asleep were raised, and coming out of the tombs after his resurrection they went into the holy city and appeared to many' (Mt. 27.51b–53). This odd tradition, which could be an early

36. The Greek reads in the plural: 'Awake, O sword, against my shepherds...strike the shepherds'.

37. As cited in K.J. Cathcart and R.P. Gordon, *The Targum of the Minor Prophets* (ArBib, 14; Wilmington: Glazier, 1989), p. 223 n. 7; cf. Marcus, *Way of the Lord*, p. 155.

38. Also cited by Marcus, *Way of the Lord*, 155.

scribal gloss,[39] is almost certainly inspired by the resurrection interpretation of Zech. 14.4–5.[40]

But the allusion to Zechariah in Jesus' saying is contextual only, not linguistic. Not one word actually alludes to Zech. 14.4. However, if Zechariah was understood to have spoken of the resurrection, then Jesus' direct appeal to Zechariah's stricken shepherd in Mk 14.27, immediately followed by a statement expressing hope for his own resurrection in 14.28, suggests that here again we have an allusion to Zechariah, even without the presence of vocabulary distinctive to Zechariah.

Although it is possible that the saying goes back to Jesus himself, the matter-of-fact tone seems odd. Moreover, the disciples do not react to what would have been a remarkable statement: 'But after I am raised up, I will go before you to Galilee'. Peter's reply, 'Even though they all fall away, I will not' (14.29), is a response to what Jesus said in 14.27b: 'and all the sheep will be scattered'. It is therefore very probable that the presence of 14.28 is due to the evangelist's editorial activity. Nevertheless, the saying itself may in some form have originated in Jesus. I am open to this possibility because the language of this saying does not agree with the formulaic predictions of death and resurrection encountered earlier in the Gospel of Mark. In these predictions, which have been heavily edited and probably expanded from one remembered utterance to three, employ the word ἀναστῆναι ('after three days to arise'; cf. Mk 8.31; 9.31; 10.34). However, in the saying in Mk 14.28 the word is ἐγερθῆναι. In itself this is not conclusive, but I think it does leave open the possibility that the saying may have originated with Jesus, perhaps in a somewhat different context.

Concluding Comments

Analysis of the presence and influence of the book of Zechariah is a complicated and frustrating task. What one encounters time and again is uncertainty if the tradition originated with Jesus, or emerged in the post-Easter community, or was created by the evangelist. In my view, the evidence for the most part suggests that several scriptural matrixes, some of which were drawn from Zechariah, had their origin in Jesus' teaching. These matrixes (especially from Psalms, Isaiah, Daniel, and Zechariah) were edited and expanded by the post-Easter community and then were edited, glossed, and expanded still further by the evangelists (especially so in the case of Matthew).

Because we do not possess Mark's sources, a lack that has always bedeviled exegesis of this Gospel, we cannot easily distinguish the evangelist's *redaction* from his *sources*. But the tendency of editing and expanding is more obvious when one has better controls, as in comparing Matthew to Mark. We have seen how

39. I suspect this insertion is post-Matthean, because of its awkward chronological fit, in that the dead saints are raised at the time of the earthquake (Friday), but cannot exit their tombs until Jesus himself has done so (Sunday). The Matthean evangelist has proven himself to be a far more sophisticated editor of the Markan tradition.

40. Matthew's 'earth shook' alludes to the 'earthquake' in Zech. 14.5.

Matthew expanded the Zecharian tradition of resurrection, alluded to in Jesus' saying in Mk 14.28. Yet another example is seen in how Mark's mention of Judas' agreement with the priests to betray Jesus for money (Mk 14.10–11) becomes in Matthew an elaborate story of Judas receiving 30 pieces of silver (Mt. 26.15), which are later cast into the temple and are used to purchase the potter's field (Mt. 27.3–10), an imaginative expansion assisted in part by Zechariah (cf. 11.12–13).

In the case of Mark, I am left with the impression that the evangelist usually understood the tradition that he inherited, sometimes clarifying and embellishing it, but not indulging in the more imaginative expansions seen in Matthew and John. I think it is fair to describe the Markan evangelist as a conservative tradent, who shaped the materials he inherited into a story he hoped the Christian and non-Christian world would find compelling in the Roman world. The witness of Scripture was important – indeed, he begins his narrative with an appeal to Isa. 40.3, 'as it is written', thus casting the entire story of Jesus, in whom the good news has its beginning, in the context of the witness of Scripture. But the Markan evangelist is no proof-texter or midrashist.

EMBEDDED SCRIPTURE TEXTS AND THE PLURALITY OF MEANING: THE ANNOUNCEMENT OF THE 'VOICE FROM HEAVEN' IN MARK 1.11 AS A CASE STUDY

Thomas R. Hatina

1. *Introduction: The Complexity of Context*

In Mk 1.11, Jesus emerges from the water to a heavenly voice announcing σὺ εἶ ὁ υἱός μου ὁ ἀγαπητός, ἐν σοὶ εὐδόκησα. While there is widespread agreement that the announcement is either an allusion to or a quotation of scripture, there is broad disagreement concerning the specificity of the scripture text. This allusion, as I will call it, serves as an apt example of how historical-criticism has tended to be myopic when confronted with diversity of opinion on the meaning of an embedded scripture text – whether it concerns the search of a specific underlying scripture text as is the case here, or the search for the meaning of an agreed upon embedded text. The myopic principle is the same in that the focus is on the recovery of single text or a single exegetical tradition.

As I have tried to show elsewhere, the embedding of scripture texts within a new narrative complicates the search for a specific interpretive antecedent since the meaning of the embedded text is necessarily determined by its new literary context.[1] The new meanings, however, usually do not deviate too far from contemporary early Jewish interpretations of the given embedded scripture texts. But when several options are possible, methodological considerations become the focal point in the evaluation process. For some, the meaning of an embedded scripture text is determined by reconstructing the evangelist's alleged *Sitz im Leben*. The reconstruction then serves as the context for reading a given quotation or allusion. For others the determining factor is the evangelist's redactional agenda. In other words, if a given quotation or allusion is deemed to be a redactional unit, in contrast to a traditional unit, it is read in light of a theological theme expressed through the redactional activity of the evangelist. Still others attempt to determine the meaning of an embedded scripture text by appealing to its exegetical tradition within early (and Rabbinic) Judaism. If a common tradition is found, it serves as the interpretive key for reading the same scriptural reference in the new context where it is embedded. That is to say, if a given scripture text means such and such consistently in early Jewish writings, it must have the same meaning in its new context. When the interpretive traditions are diverse, and allow for two or

---

1. T.R. Hatina, *In Search of a Context: The Function of Scripture in Mark's Narrative* (JSNTSup, 232; SSEJC, 8; London: Sheffield Academic Press, 2002).

more options, prior assumptions of the evangelist's *Sitz im Leben* or his redactional agenda usually tip the balance. Finally, a few critics focus on the 'original' context of the scriptural quotation or allusion; that is, the literary context of a given biblical book. In this approach, the function of a given text in the original biblical book becomes the interpretive key for understanding the function of the same text embedded in Mark's context. Despite the contextual diversity, the meaning of the text is assumed to remain constant (usually for *a priori* theological reasons). What is common to all of these historical-critical approaches is the insatiable drive to arrive at *the* meaning.

My aim is to show that if Mark is taken seriously as narrative art, a search for *the* meaning, and hence *the* echo, is reductionistic because it potentially excludes the other layers of meaning which would have been open to the earliest audiences (and should remain open to the modern literary critic). I argue that the announcement of the 'voice from heaven' in Mk 1.11 should be treated as a reverberation of several traditions in early Judaism, as long as each can be incorporated into the narrative. It is the narrative itself within its socio-historical context, which should be the primary arbiter for evaluating a textual or oral-traditional influence. And when several Jewish interpretive traditions cohere with the narrative or narrative features (such as plot, themes, point of view, or characterization), as is the case with the voice's announcement in Mk 1.11, the exegete must in the end remain satisfied with a plurality of options. This is not to say that a search for the best option should be discouraged, for history is a series of arguments that requires debate (as opposed to a body of data or a set of facts to be recorded or memorized) and as such it moves its practitioners to formulate the best argument.[2] Historical-critics have tended to be uneasy with the casting of such a large net and prefer to focus their study on the disclosure of *the* or *the primary* influential tradition. Yet many historical-critics would acknowledge the common claim of literary critics that it is next to impossible to ascertain the evangelist's overarching intention in the writing of his story (let alone the intention of a single quotation and even more so an allusion), or whether he assumed more than one intention. Moreover, it is equally difficult to establish the early audiences' reading(s) of these embedded texts, if indeed they were even recognized as such by all hearers.

Jewish audience members who heard and saw the story of Mark performed may well have picked up on several allusions whether they were or were not intended by the evangelist. Retellings of figures and events from the scriptures in early Jewish writings clearly demonstrate that social memory, especially during the Roman occupation, was very active and diverse – and indeed provided the basis for much of early Christian reflection. A reading of a text like the one in Mk 1.11 where a *bath qôl* announces 'you are my beloved son, in you I am well pleased' would have not only triggered one or more biblical accounts, but more importantly it would have triggered some kind of eschatological expectation, as will be shown below.

2.   R.W. Winks and S.P. Mattern-Parkes, *The Ancient Mediterranean World: From the Stone Age to A.D. 600* (Oxford: Oxford University Press, 2004), p. ix.

The search for *the* echo is further complicated when we consider how Mark's story would have been communicated to and comprehended by the earliest audiences. When the final form of Mark's story was first read/performed and heard, a degree of prior aurality and orality would have communicated much of the content of Mark. Hearers would have listened with a *Vorverständnis*, a 'fore-understanding' of the totality of the story. And Mark certainly would not have intended a single hearing. In this sense, the implied hearer becomes the re-hearer who is sensitized to echoes within the story, and especially so if they are similar in diction, discourse and concept.[3] However, if the earliest renditions of Mark's story were performances – whatever the actual interaction between orality and textuality – then retrospective connections must not be equated with rigid dictional parallels as if the story were written for private reading. Oral performances in oral-aural cultures were not fixated on verbatim re-presentations or re-tellings, even if the general story remained the same.[4] Retellings of Mark could have conceivably generated new connections. The achievement of new insights and new associations on the part of audience members who hear, view or even read the same story two or more times is well established. We need not go any further than recalling our own experiences when watching a film for the second time. Simply knowing how a plot unfolds has an impact on the subsequent viewing of a film. How repeated performances engender new interpretations is, of course, much more complex, but for the present purpose it reveals the potential uncertainty of interpreting embedded scripture texts.

2. *The Announcement of the Voice from Heaven and the Uncertainty of Meaning*

The voice in Mk 1.11 and in 9.7 resembles the rabbinic *bath qôl* (lit. 'daughter of a voice') which, according to Joel Marcus, conveys an echo of God in contrast to a direct mediated speech from God or even the Holy Spirit (e.g. *t. Sota* 13.2).[5] That the *bath qôl* is an echo of God is certainly possible, but more often in rabbinic writings and the Targums it is a circumlocution for ministering angels and the Holy Spirit.[6] Such is probably the case here given the subsequent Temptation account in which the Spirit casts Jesus into the wilderness where he is ministered to by the angels.

---

3. On rereading in the Markan community, see F. Kermode, *The Genesis of Secrecy: On the Interpretation of Narrative* (Cambridge, MA: Harvard University Press, 1979), pp. 70, 88–89; E.S. Malbon, 'Echoes and Foreshadowings in Mark 4–8: Reading and Rereading', *JBL* 112 (1993), pp. 211–30.

4. W.J. Ong, *Orality and Literacy: The Technologizing of the Word* (New York: Routledge, 2002), ch. 3.

5. J. Marcus, *Mark 1–8* (AB 27; New York: Doubleday, 2000), pp. 160–61.

6. M. McNamara, *Targum Neofiti 1: Genesis* (The Aramaic Bible 1A; Collegeville: Liturgical Press, 1992), p. 39; *idem, Targum and Testament. Aramaic Paraphrases of the Hebrew Bible: A Light on the New Testament* (Shannon: Irish University Press, 1972), pp. 113–14. See also *2 Bar.* 13.1; *b. San.* 11a, 94a' 104b; *b. 'Erub.* 13b; *b. Ta'an.* 25b; and *b. Mak.* 23b.

The proclamation of Mark's *bath qôl* and its specific scriptural parallel has endured much debate over the years and thereby serves as an ideal case study demonstrating the impasse generated by a hermeneutic oriented toward a single meaning. The most frequently discussed parallels are Ps. 2.7; Isa. 42.1; and Gen. 22.2, each of which conveying a different meaning.[7] The differences are more nuanced when the exegesis of each is traced within the early Jewish and rabbinic contexts. Assuming that these traditions are not conflated, it is difficult to say exactly with which exegetical tradition Mark's audiences would have been familiar. For the purposes of demonstrating a plurality of options as a viable position – and the search for a single echo as reductionistic – I attempt to cast the net widely. Where possible I will try to show that each exegetical tradition, whether known or unknown by the audiences, can be integrated within Mark's narrative. In other words, my aim is not to provide a full exegesis of Mk 1.11, but to legitimize as many exegetical traditions as possible, which could serve as parallels, and thus enhance the interpretative task. All in all, the tactic deconstructs prior attempts to verify a singular textual influence.

The Servant of Deutero-Isaiah

Perhaps the most debated proposal for the primary literary influence behind Mk 1.11 has been Isa. 42.1 which in the LXX reads, Ιακωβ ὁ παῖς μου ἀντιλήμψομαι αὐτοῦ Ισραηλ ὁ ἐκλεκτός μου προσεδέξατο αὐτὸν ἡ ψυχή μου ἔδωκα τὸ πνεῦμά μου ἐπ' αὐτόν κρίσιν τοῖς ἔθνεσιν ἐξοίσει.[8] In the Isaian context, the servant (παῖς) is identified with the messenger (Isa. 41.27; 42.19) of the heavenly court who has reached his decision and pronounced a guilty verdict for the charge of idolatry.[9] The servant's mission is to establish justice and righteousness on the earth (42.1–4) and to be a light to the nations (vv. 5–9, cf. Isa. 49.1–6; 50.3–9; 52.13–53.12). By contrast, his identity does not appear to be as important as his divinely ordained role.[10]

The obvious similarity between Mk 1.9–11 and Isa. 42.1 is the anointing of the Spirit, even though the overall terminology and the recipients are not the same. In Mark it is ὁ υἱός who is anointed; whereas in Isa. 42.1 it is ὁ παῖς. This dissimilarity, however, is not dissuasive. Those who argue for the priority of Isa. 42.1 in Mark's baptism scene usually suggest that παῖς, a translation of עֶבֶד, can mean either 'servant' or 'son' as is the case in Wis. 2.13–18 where both terms are used interchangeably.[11] Since παῖς (2.13) and υἱός (2.18) both appear together against

---

7. Another parallel, which has not received as much attention, is Exod. 4.22–23 where God refers to Israel as his first-born son. See P.G. Bretscher, 'Exodus 4.22–23 and the Voice from Heaven', *JBL* 87 (1968), pp. 309–11. I do not mean to discount the legitimacy of this view. While its inclusion would have added to my overall position, I exclude it simply due to length restrictions.

8. The LXX adds 'Jacob' and 'Israel' to the MT most likely because עֶבֶד was already identified with Jacob and Israel in 41.8–10.

9. J.D.W. Watts, *Isaiah 34–66* (WBC, 25; Waco, TX: Word Books, 1987), p. 119.

10. Taking into account subsequent passages, such as 44.28 and 45.1–4, the author probably has in mind Cyrus as the primary agent of God's justice and salvation.

11. B.M. Metzger and R.E. Murphy (*The New Oxford Annotated Apocrypha: The Apocryphal/*

a background of Deutero-Isaiah's servant typology in Wisdom 2, then it is suggested that the original עבד (in Isa. 42.1) gave way to the use of these two Greek terms.[12] Jeremias has argued that παῖς θεοῦ in LXX Isa. 42.1 underlies the heavenly voice at Jesus' baptism (and at the transfiguration, 9.7) and thus, removes any possibility of a conflated quotation with LXX Ps. 2.7 (which, like Mark, has υἱός μου).[13] Jeremias, taking up the arguments of Bousset and Dalman, gives support to his thesis by pointing to several considerations. First, the purpose of the heavenly voice is to explain the impartation of the Spirit in the previous verse (Mk 1.10). The voice communicates to Jesus that the promised Spirit of Isa. 42.1 is now fulfilled.[14] Second, the Hebrew בחיר ('chosen one') which is in parallel with עבד in Isa. 42.1 can be translated as both ἐκλεκτός (as is the case in the LXX) and ἀγαπητός (as is the case in Mt. 12.18 which quotes Isa. 42.1). The latter, of course, is used in Mk 1.11.[15] Third, Jeremias argues that the oldest textual formulation of the voice from heaven at the baptism reads οὗτός ἐστιν ὁ ἐκλεκτός τοῦ θεοῦ (as it is found in the oldest MSS of Jn 1.34). This is a messianic title closest to Isa. 42.1 and suggests that the earliest reference to the voice at Jesus' baptism consisted of a verbatim quotation. In consistent fashion, pre-Christian Jewish references to Isa. 42.1 (and Isa. 43.10; 49.6; 52.13; 53.11) likewise associate the messiah with an 'Elect One' or 'Righteous One', but not with a 'Son'. Despite the small number of witnesses to ἐκλεκτός, Jeremias, leaning on the text-critical work of von Harnack, argues that the Greek, Syriac, and Latin textual history unanimously begins with this reading. According to Jeremias, the ἐκλεκτός reading was later replaced by ὁ υἱός in the fourth century when the Church responded to adoptionist Christology.[16] Fourth, it has been argued that since παῖς Christology is very common in the passion account, it should be read back into the baptism scene, especially if the baptism foreshadows the cross.[17]

This approach would remedy the theological problem often associated with Jesus' 'baptism of repentance for the forgiveness of sins' (Mk 1.4). In keeping

Deuterocanonical Books of the Old Testament [New York: Oxford University Press, 1991], p. 59) translate v. 13 as 'child' with a footnote reference to 'servant'.

12. G. Dalman, *The Words of Jesus Considered in the Light of Post-biblical Jewish Writings and the Aramaic Language* (Edinburgh: T&T Clark, 1902), pp. 276–80; C. Mauer, 'Knecht Gottes und Sohn Gottes im Passionsbericht des Markusevangeliums', *ZTK* 50 (1953), pp. 25–26.

13. J. Jeremias, 'παῖς θεοῦ', *TDNT* 5, p. 701. See also W. Bousset, *Kyrios Christos: A History of the Belief in Christ from the Beginnings of Christianity to Irenaeus* (trans. J.E. Steely; Nashville: Abingdon Press, 1970), pp. 97–98; O. Cullmann, *The Christology of the New Testament* (trans. S.C. Guthrie and C.A.M. Hall; Philadelphia: Westminster Press, 1963), p. 66; Dalman, *The Words of Jesus*, pp. 276–80;

14. Jeremias, 'παῖς θεοῦ', p. 701.

15. Jeremias, 'παῖς θεοῦ', pp. 701–702; Cullmann, *The Christology of the New Testament*, p. 66.

16. In addition to Acts 3.13, 26, 4.27, 30 and the quotations in Mt. 12.18, *Barn.* 6.1 and 9.2, παῖς θεοῦ as a designation for Jesus in Gentile Christian writings (up to 170 CE) is limited to eleven occurrences (five in the *Didache*, two in *1 Clement*, and four in the *Martyrdom of Polycarp*), each of which is in the context of worship and prayer (Eucharistic prayer, doxology and confession). Jeremias, 'παῖς θεοῦ', pp. 689, 702–703.

17. Mauer, 'Knecht Gottes und Sohn Gottes im Passionsbericht des Markusevangeliums', pp. 1–38.

with the Servant's role, the early audiences of Mark could have viewed Jesus' baptism as a vicarious event for the purpose of national restoration. Or the early audiences could have viewed Jesus' baptism as a catharsis, which resulted in a righteousness that allowed him to take on the mantle of God's servant. Whatever interpretation of the baptism one postulates, the underlying influence of Isa. 42.1 and its exegetical traditions coincides with not only the passion account, but the entire narrative.[18]

I mentioned at the beginning of this section that Isa. 42.1 as *the* echo is perhaps the most debated option. This is not to say, however, that the other two options are without their problems. The main reason why Isa. 42.1 has attracted more criticism is its lack of dictional coherence with Mk 1.11, as the following examples indicate. First, the suggestion that υἱός is a replacement of the original παῖς would be strengthened if other examples of this kind of practice were provided. The example of Jn 1.34 in which υἱός supposedly replaced ἐκλεκτός is not a parallel situation to Mk 1.11 since it has not been caused by a semantic problem.[19] Furthermore, as Metzger suggests, υἱός should be retained as the original on the basis of manuscript age and diversity. Its retention, of course, preserves the harmony of John's theological terminology.[20] Second, there is no evidence from the early church that the announcement of the voice in Mk 1.11 was understood apart from sonship.[21] Third, of the 807 times that עבד (Isa. 42.1) is translated into Greek, it is rendered as υἱός only once.[22] The example of Wisdom, where παῖδα κυρίου (2.13) and υἱός θεοῦ (2.18) are supposedly influenced by עבד from a Hebrew source, is on very shaky ground since we have no evidence that Wisdom was originally written in Hebrew. The writer could have just as well borrowed phraseology from the LXX.[23] For example, David Winston, favouring the Greek original, notices that Wis. 2.12 is a direct quotation from LXX Isa. 3.10 and considerably different from the Hebrew.[24] Finally, it can also be noticed that Matthew's quotation of Isa. 42.1 in 12.18 does not conform to Jesus' title at the description of the baptism, even though there does exist a thematic conformity.[25]

The evidence suggests that singling out Isa. 42.1 as the *only* echo is too reductionistic. Although the Isaianic servant motif is undoubtedly present in the baptismal scene, one cannot at the same time claim that it is the only motif. Moreover, if we consider the dictional connection between LXX Isa. 42.1 and Mk 1.11, the

---

18. E.g. Cullmann, *The Christology of the New Testament*, p. 67.

19. B. Lindars, *New Testament Apologetic: The Doctrinal Significance of the Old Testament Quotations* (London: SCM Press, 1973), p. 140.

20. B.M. Metzger, *A Textual Commentary of the Greek New Testament* (New York: United Bible Societies, 1975), p. 200.

21 I.H. Marshall, 'Son of God or Servant of Yahweh? – A Reconsideration of Mark 1.11', *NTS* 15 (1969), p. 328.

22. W. Zimmerli, 'παῖς θεοῦ Β', *TDNT* 5, p. 673.

23. Metzger and Murphy (eds), *The New Oxford Annotated Apocrypha*, p. 57.

24. D. Winston, *The Wisdom of Solomon* (AB, 43; New York: Doubleday, 1979), pp. 15–18.

25. Marshall, 'Son of God or Servant of Yahweh?', p. 332. See also Bretscher ('Exodus 4.22–23 and the Voice from Heaven', p. 304) who argues that Mt. 12.18 preserves a Greek version of Isa. 42.1 that had long been in use.

only similarity we encounter is ὁ...μου. Although it is easier to sustain the echo of Isa. 42.1 in Mk 1.10 based on the parallel of the descent of the Spirit, there really is no warrant to suggest the same for v. 11, whatever early version one proposes. The phrase 'I am well pleased' in Mark does not correspond to 'my soul is well pleased' (Hebrew), 'my soul accepts' (Greek), or 'my word is well pleased' (Aramaic).[26]

More recently, the case for the influence of the Isaianic servant in Mk 1.11 has been strengthen by Bruce Chilton, who claims that closer parallels are to be found in the Aramaic versions of Isa. 41.8–9 and 43.10 (see also 43.20 and 44.1–2) which in comparison to the Greek and Hebrew versions, read as follows:

Isa. 41.8–9

Aramaic – 'You, Israel my servant, Jacob that (or: in whom [ד]) I am well pleased with you... I said to you, you are my servant, I am well pleased with you...'
Hebrew – 'You, Israel my servant, Jacob that (or: in whom [אשר]) I chose you... I said to you, you are my servant, I chose you...'
Greek – 'And you Israel, my servant Jacob, whom I chose... I said to you, you are my servant, I chose you...'

Isa. 43.10

Aramaic – '...my servant the messiah that (or: in whom [ד]) I am well pleased with him...'
Hebrew – '...and my servant that (or: whom [אשר]) I chose...'
Greek – '...and my servant whom I chose...'

The clause 'in whom I am well pleased' in both Targumic renderings is closest in diction to Mark. In addition to this phrase, Chilton observes several other Targumic associations (not found in the other versions) which should also be considered as close parallels with Mark's baptismal account, such as the direct address (41.8, 9), the giving of the Spirit (42.1), and the identification of the servant as the messiah (43.10).[27] While there is more dictional coherence between Mk 1.11 and the Targumic version of Isa. 41.8–9 and 43.10 than the MT or LXX versions, Mark does not seem to be relying on an earlier form of the Targum. Instead, in a more general sense he seems to employ a tradition of the servant, which was later embedded in the Targum. For an audience member familiar with such a tradition (perhaps reiterated in the synagogue), the intimacy that Jesus shares with the Father by means of the heavenly voice (and throughout his ministry) may well have been compared to the intimate relationship between the servant and Yahweh in the Targum.[28]

---

26. B.D. Chilton, *A Galilean Rabbi and his Bible: Jesus' Use of the Interpreted Scripture of his Time* (Wilmington: Michael Glazier, 1984), p. 129.

27. Chilton, *A Galilean Rabbi and his Bible*, pp. 129–30.

28. Chilton, *A Galilean Rabbi and his Bible*, p. 131. Interestingly, the Targumic servant is nowhere identified with suffering as in the MT and LXX. He is rather the 'messianic servant' who will risk death in his ministry (p. 200). See also B.D. Chilton, *The Glory of Israel: The Theology and Provenience of the Isaiah Targum* (JSOTSup, 23; Sheffield: JSOT Press, 1983), pp. 93–96.

Whatever the exact text or version known to Mark and his audience, the implications of proposing the tradition of the Isaianic servant as the scriptural influence for Mk 1.11 are significant. If Mark's audience picked up on this echo, it would not have connected Jesus' baptism with an enthronement or a divine adoption.[29] Instead, Jesus' baptism (and hence his role) would have been associated with his new vocation as the one who recapitulates the Isaianic servant of God by giving his life for the sake of the nation. Early Jewish martyrdom ideology, which is evident in Mark's portrayal of Jesus (and the Baptist) as a pattern for his disciples to follow, could have conceivably provided the broader hermeneutical framework for understanding Jesus as a servant figure.[30]

The Binding of Isaac

Another option, which has been proposed for the underlying scriptural influence of the announcement of Mark's *bath qôl*, is the repeated announcement of God and the Angel of the Lord to Abraham in the story of the binding of Isaac in Gen. 22.[31] The diction in LXX Gen. 22.2, 12, 16 is very close to that of Mark:

Gen. 22.2:   ὃν υἱόν σου τὸν ἀγαπητόν
Gen. 22.12:   τοῦ υἱοῦ σου τοῦ ἀγαπητοῦ
Gen. 22.16:   τοῦ υἱοῦ σου τοῦ ἀγαπητοῦ
Mk 1.11:   ὁ υἱός μου ὁ ἀγαπητός

In addition to the diction, the thrice repeated announcement by a transcendent voice strengthens the possibility of Mark's audience picking up on this association if they were at all familiar with the story.

But if Mark and/or his audience associated the binding of Isaac with the baptism of Jesus it would probably not have been limited to the story as it is found in the MT or the LXX, for aside from the dictional parallel, there is very little theological or thematic resemblance. However, when the story is traced in Jewish exegesis contemporary with and subsequent to Mark, a whole new, rich and multi-dimensional portrait of Isaac emerges. By the first-century, Isaac serves as an exemplary figure, characterized by certain qualities that are similar to early Christian reflection about Jesus.

While it is too ambitious in this essay to examine all the references to the story of Isaac's sacrifice in post-biblical Jewish literature, a few examples should suffice in demonstrating the relevance of the story for both personal piety and national identity. I begin with texts that are generally contemporary with Mark.

One text which may have been influential for the construction of the Baptism scene is *T. Levi* 18.6–7, which contains a passing reference to the story of the binding of Isaac in a context that is possibly celebrating what was believed to be

---

29. Jeremias, 'παῖς θεοῦ', p. 702 n. 354.

30. R.E. Watts, *Isaiah's New Exodus and Mark* (WUNT, 2.88; Tübingen: Mohr–Siebeck, 1997), pp. 114–18.

31. Marshall, 'Son of God or Servant of Yahweh?', p. 334. See also E. Best, *The Temptation and the Passion: The Markan Soteriology* (SNTMS, 2; Cambridge: Cambridge University Press, 1965), pp. 169–72; C.H. Turner, 'ὁ υἱός μου ὁ ἀγαπητός', *JTS* 27 (1925–26), pp. 113–29.

the eschatological rise of Hasmonean priest-kings. Although this text does not develop the sacrifice theme as much as others, its similarities with Mark's baptism of Jesus are unmistakable.

> The heavens will be opened,
> and from the temple of glory sanctification will come upon him,
> with a fatherly voice, as from Abraham to Isaac.
> And the glory of the Most High shall burst forth upon him.
> and the spirit of understanding and sanctification
> shall rest upon him [in the water].[32]

Here the author compares the heavenly voice of assurance to that of Abraham when he says to Isaac in Gen. 22.8, 'God will provide for himself the lamb for the burnt offering my son'. It is not improbable to suggest that Mark and/or some members of his audience would have been influenced by this tradition of the coming priest-king whose divine appointment and empowerment was to result in an eternal priesthood.

Philo also provides a possible parallel to Mk 1.11 which, to my knowledge, is unique in the Judaism of his day. In his *On the Change of Names* 23.131, Philo magnifies Isaac's birth by calling him υἱός θεοῦ; and in *On the Cherubim* 45 he implies that Isaac's conception was a result of God's visitation to Sarah 'in her solitude'. Whatever Philo means by υἱός θεοῦ, clearly Isaac's role is perceived as being divinely ordained and having national significance.

In *Ant.* 1.222–36, Josephus provides an extended revision of the sacrifice story in which Isaac, who is portrayed in an intimate way as Abraham's only and beloved son, enthusiastically participates in the preparation of himself as a sacrifice. Despite the provision of the ram, Isaac's enthusiasm and piety are nevertheless efficacious not only with regard to his progeny, but on a national scale (*Ant.* 1.234–35). Aside from its sacrificial purpose, the exact implication for the nation, however, is difficult to explain. It is possible that Josephus views Isaac as a noble and courageous soldier who is willing to give his life as a martyr for the cause of the nation, which is not at the same time to be confused with an anti-Roman insurrectionist.[33] More likely, given Josephus' suppression of military imagery and the elevation of family honour in the farewell speech by Abraham to Isaac (*Ant.* 1.229–31), his rendition implies that the focus is on obedience and reward. Josephus' expanded and less barbaric, yet still historic, portrayal echoes a major theme of Israel's religious story: national restoration and prosperity can only be affected by obedience and submission to the will of God. If this is the case, then the Isaac story functions first to explain historically the subsequent prosperity of Israel, and second to give attention to Isaac as a relevant national icon or myth.

32. Translation is taken from H.C. Kee, 'Testaments of the Twelve Patriarchs', in J.A. Charlesworth (ed.), *The Old Testament Pseudepigrapha*. I. *Apocalyptic Literature and Testaments* (New York: Doubleday, 1983), p. 795. Aside from Christian interpolations like 'in the water', Kee dates the document to the early part of the second century BCE.

33. P.R. Davies and B.D. Chilton, 'The Aqedah: A Revisited Tradition History', *CBQ* 40 (1978), pp. 521–22.

The martyrdom motif is taken up more overtly in *4 Macc.* 13.8–17 and 16.15–23 where the story of Isaac's sacrifice functions as one biblical example, alongside others, which endorses the giving of one's life for the cause of righteousness. Although Isaac is not actually killed, his willingness to be killed serves as a pattern. By accepting their fate and not giving into the demands of their captors, and thereby demonstrating their readiness or willingness to be martyred, the Maccabean 'brothers' convey a personal piety, which has national implications. In *4 Maccabees*, not only does martyrdom (courage and endurance to the point of death) guarantee the immortality of the soul (e.g. 7.19; 16.25; 17.12; in contrast to the resurrection of the body in *2 Maccabees*), but it purifies the land and atones for the sins of the nation (e.g. 1.11; 17.21; 18.4). In 17.21 martyrdom is even referred to as a 'ransom' (ἀντίψυχος) for the sin of the nation, which is instrumental in defeating the tyrannical powers. Once again, it would not have been difficult for some members of Mark's audience to draw connections with the Markan Jesus who likewise dies for righteous convictions. Although Mark uses λύτρον (instead of ἀντίψυχος), the notion that his unwavering obedience which leads to death is significant for others (perhaps even for a redefined nation) is conveyed in 10.45. This is especially so if λύτρον is understood in its first-century popular usage as the purchase price for a slave's freedom.[34] In keeping with the motif of Jesus' supremacy over evil, if Jesus is the one who is stronger than the 'strong man' (i.e. Satan), then his obedience to the point of death can be viewed as effecting the liberation of those who are enslaved. Like the Maccabean martyrs, Jesus offers his life for the freedom of the oppressed.[35]

Apart from several passing echoes, other references to the story of Isaac's sacrifice in Jewish writings which are generally contemporary with (or prior to) Mark and may further represent popular traditions include the *Liber Antiquitatum Biblicarum* of Pseudo-Philo (18.5–6; 32.2–4; 40.2) where Isaac's willingness is deemed as the final atoning sacrifice, and 4Q225 (4QpsJubª) and *Jub.* 17.15–18.19, where in both accounts Prince Mastemah tests Abraham's convictions.

In rabbinic retellings, the story of the binding of Isaac usually contributes to the motif of religious piety and atonement instead of the political motif associated with martyrdom. As has been seen in earlier echoes, the focus on Isaac's piety, obedience and submission seems to atone for the sins of other Jews, but it is all the more a comment on post-70 CE Jewish identity and existence instead of national (i.e. political or military) liberation. Though rabbinic retellings are late, some which are consistent with much earlier retellings can be brought into the larger mix of popular interpretations accessible to Mark's audience.

One example is the tradition that was later embedded in the Targums. In Gen. 22.10, Isaac is portrayed as the paragon of obedience. Not only does he proceed willingly to the location of his own sacrifice once he learns that he may be the intended 'lamb of the burnt offering', but he even urges his father to tie him

---

34. A. Deissmann, *Light from the Ancient East: The New Testament Illustrated by Recently Discovered Texts of the Graeco-Roman World* (trans. L.R.M. Strachan; New York: George A. Doran, 1927), pp. 327–28. See also the entry in BAGD, 3rd edn.

35. C.A. Evans, *Mark 8.27–16.20* (WBC, 34B; Nashville: Thomas Nelson, 2001), p. 122.

securely and aids his father's task by extending his own neck. Moreover, as in Mark's baptism account, it is only the Targum, which includes direct speech from the *bath qôl. Tg. Neof.* Gen. 22.10 reads:[36]

> And Abraham stretched out his hand and took the knife to slaughter his son *Isaac. Isaac answered and said to his father Abraham: 'Father, tie me well lest I kick you and your offering be rendered unfit and we be thrust down into the pit of destruction in the world to come'. The eyes of Abraham were on the eyes of Isaac and the eyes of Isaac were scanning the angels on high. Abraham did not see them. In that hour a Bath Qol came forth from the heavens and said: 'Come, see two singular persons who are in the world; one slaughters and the other is being slaughtered. The one who slaughters does not hesitate and he who is being slaughtered stretches out his neck.* '[37]

Although the Targums were compiled quite some time after Mark, it is conceivable that public (i.e. synagogue) readings of Genesis 22, even during the time of Jesus, would have elaborated on Isaac as a model of obedience. While it is difficult to say if all the aspects of Neofiti's rendition date back to the first century, we can safely posit that at least Isaac's voluntary submission to be sacrificed is much older.[38] Furthermore, without positing too much and yet not omitting the numerous parallels between the Targums and the Gospels, it is conceivable on the basis of the dictional parallel between Mk 4.12 and *Tg. Isa.* 6.9–10 that Mark (and perhaps his audience) was familiar with traditions that were later embedded in the Targum.[39]

In the midrashim, Isaac's death takes on atoning significance on the basis of his exemplary submission to be bound. Once again, if this tradition was in circulation during the first century, then it would be easy to see why Mark would echo Gen. 22, especially since Jesus' baptism was connected with his atoning death (Mk 10.38). In *b. Rosh. Hash.* 16a, we read, 'The Holy One, blessed be He, said: "Sound before Me a ram's horn so that I may remember on your behalf the binding of Isaac the son of Abraham, and account it to you as if you had bound yourselves before Me"'.[40] In *Cant. R.* 14.1 a similar expression of a vicarious act is

---

36. *Tg. Ps.-J.* Gen. 22.10 is virtually identical, except for the explicit reference to the *bath qôl*.

37. Translation is taken from M. McNamara, *Targum Neofiti 1: Genesis* (Collegeville: Liturgical Press, 1987), pp. 117–18. Similar concepts of Isaac can be found in *TanB Wayyera*, Gen. 4, 'When he came to slaughter him, Isaac said to him: Bind me [sic] hand and foot because the instinct of life is strong. It is likely that before the knife comes, I would tremble and be disqualified as a sacrifice. Please <bind me>, my father, lest a blemish be inflicted upon me'. Taken from J.T. Townsend (trans.), *Midrash Tanhuma Vol 1* (Hoboken, NJ: KTAV, 1989), p. 130; *Pirqe R. El.* 31: 'O my father! Bind for me my two hands, and my two feet, so that I do not curse'. Taken from G. Friedlander (trans.), *Pirke de Rabbi Eliezer* (New York: Sepher-Hermon Press, 1981), p. 227; *Gen. R.* 56.8.

38. W.R. Stegner, 'The Baptism of Jesus: A Story Modeled on the Binding of Isaac', *BibRev* 1 (1985), p. 38. See also R. Hayward, 'The Present State of Research into the Targumic Account of the Sacrifice of Isaac', *JJS* 32 (1981), pp. 127–50.

39. Chilton, *A Galilean Rabbi and his Bible*, pp. 91–93. A pre-Christian dating has been vigorously argued on the basis of its similarity with the Qumran documents by M. McNamara, *The New Testament and the Palestinian Targum to the Pentateuch* (AnBib, 27; Rome: Biblical Institute Press, 1966), pp. 31–32.

40. Translation taken from I. Epstein (ed.), *The Babylonian Talmud* (London: Soncino Press, 1952).

observed: 'Cluster is unto me as a cluster of hennam. Cluster refers to Isaac, who was bound on the altar like a cluster of hennam (kofer): because he atones (*mekapper*) for the iniquities of Israel.'[41]

The substitutionary act of Isaac was also prominent in celebrations of the New Year and the Day of Atonement. In *Mek.* on Exod. 12.11–14 [*Pisha* 7], the blood of the paschal lamb is associated with the blood of Isaac;[42] and similarly in the Fragment Targum to Lev. 22.27, we read: 'The lamb was chosen (as the sacrificial animal) to recall the merit of the Lamb of Abraham, who bound himself upon the altar and stretched out his neck for the sake of thy name'.[43] Also, in *Lev. R.* 2.11 retellings of the offering of Isaac were part of the daily morning and evening sacrifices in the temple.[44] Although Isaac does not actually shed blood in these retellings, his unwavering willingness to do so together with the divine provision of the ram, function as the ideal sacrifice and fulfills the ancient stipulation of offering the first-born to Yahweh.

Given the extended and widespread interpretation of Isaac as the paragon of obedience (whether he is regarded as a martyr or not) who effects atonement, be it for the nation or just for the 'righteous', it is conceivable that the phraseology in Mk 1.11 which parallels LXX Gen. 22.2, 12, 16 in diction would have caused some members of Mark's audience to understand Jesus typologically as an Isaac figure. How far the typology would have been employed is, of course, difficult to know; but it is not inconceivable that for some it served as the hermeneutical key for understanding Jesus as the obedient one whose mission and death likewise effects atonement. Mark's characterization of Jesus as a pattern to follow lends itself nicely to this reading. The problem arises, as in the case of the Isaianic servant, when it is argued that this is *the* influence guiding the writing and/or hearing of the baptism account. While consistent with Mark's overall portrayal of Jesus, there is no conclusive evidence in the narrative that would constitute the binding of Isaac as the best option. Furthermore, proponents of this option need also to consider why such a prominent theme in early Judaism was not appropriated and

---

41. H. Freedman and M. Simon, *Midrash Rabbah Vol. 9* (London: Soncino Press, 1982).

42. J.Z. Lauterbach (trans.), *Mekilta de-Rabbi Ishmael Vol. 1* (Philadelphia: The Jewish Publication Society of America, 1976), p. 57. In *Gen. R.* on Gen. 22.12, Abraham is forbidden to shed even a drop of Isaac's blood. Lauterbach (p. 57 n. 7) suggests that it is possible that the *Mekilta* here follows R. Joshua who stated that one fourth of a log of Isaac's blood was shed on the altar.

43. Translation is taken from R.A. Rosenberg, 'Jesus, Isaac, and the "Suffering Servant"', *JBL* 84 (1965), p. 388.

44. J. Israllstam (trans.), *Midrash Rabbah: Leviticus* (London: Soncino Press, 1982), p. 31. Interestingly, in *Lev. R.* 2.10, it is stated that, 'Isaac fulfilled that which is written in the Torah, in that he cast himself before his father as a lamb that is to be sacrificed'. The fulfillment of the Law was implied due to Isaac's great love for God; and because of this it follows that Isaac would obey any divine wish. On Isaac being bound at the site of the temple, see also *Tg. Cant.* 3.6; *Frag. Tg.* Gen. 22.14; and the depiction of the *'Aqedah* at the entrance of the temple in the painting from the Dura Europos synagogue. See R.M. Jensen, 'Isaac as a Christological Symbol in Early Christian Art', *ARTS* 5.2 (1993), p. 11. Not surprisingly, Samaritan depictions located the binding of Isaac on Mount Gerizim, the site of the Samaritan temple. See V. Sussman, 'The Binding of Isaac as Depicted on a Samaritan Lamp', *IEJ* 48.3–4 (1998) pp. 183–89.

developed explicitly by Christian writers in the first-century.[45] The earliest explicit example of linking Isaac with Jesus is found in the second-century *Epistle of Barnabas* (7.3), and continues thereafter in subsequent Christian writings.[46]

The King as God's Son

The final option, which has both dictional and thematic coherence with Mk 1.11, is Ps. 2.7: 'He said to me,"You are my son, today I have begotten you"'. Psalm 2 is commonly placed within the thematic form group of royal psalms in which the king plays a significant role as the victor over rival kingdoms. The psalm begins by describing a rebellion by the kings of the earth against the Lord and his Anointed (vv. 1–3). The rebellion, however, is quickly silenced when Yahweh laughs and scoffs at the opposing monarchs, because he has installed his own king (vv. 4–6). This divinely appointed king not only receives Yahweh's full support in all that he requests, thus assuring victory over his opponents, but he also receives the privilege of sonship from the time of his coronation (vv. 7–9). The implicit metaphor of sonship, found in some sectors of the Ancient Near East, probably stems from the simile in 2 Sam. 7.14 where the title conveys Yahweh's loyalty.[47] The chosen king, and hence adopted son, becomes drawn to Yahweh's side and becomes the heir and representative of his divine rule. The king was not regarded as 'son of God' genetically, nor was he thought to become divine through the investiture; but rather, sonship was imputed to him through election. The common Israelite, at the enthronement festival where this psalm was probably sung, would have seen the enthronement of the new king as a sign of the continuation of the Davidic rule. It was a celebration of Yahweh's visitation and continuing presence in the so-called 'new birth' of a world king who will sit on Zion.[48]

Some have argued for Ps. 2.7 as the influence for the announcement by the *bath qôl* in Mark on the basis of the variant in Lk. 3.22 (par. to Mk 1.11), which is identical to LXX Ps. 2.7 (υἱός μου εἶ σύ ἐγὼ σήμερον γεγέννηκά σε).[49] If this is the case, then Luke understood Mark's account of the heavenly voice as a declaration of Jesus' enthronement. Though the variant is not commonly accepted as

45. N. Hillyer, 'The Servant of God', *EQ* 41 (1969), p. 158.

46. *Barn.* 7.3 reads, '... He [Christ] also Himself was to offer in sacrifice for our sins the vessel of the Spirit, in order that the type established in Isaac when he was offered upon the altar might be fully accomplished'. Translation taken from A. Roberts and J. Donaldson (eds), *The Ante-Nicene Fathers Vol. 1* (Grand Rapids: Eerdmans, 1987), p. 141.

47. H. Kraus, *Psalm 1–59: A Commentary* (trans. H.C. Oswald; Minneapolis: Augsburg Publishing House, 1988), p. 131; G. Cooke, 'The Israelite King as Son of God', *ZAW* 73 (1961), pp. 208–209.

48. Kraus, *Psalm 1–59*, p. 132. P.C. Craigie (*Psalms 1–50* [WBC; Waco, TX: Word Books, 1983] p. 67) suggests that the declaration of sonship should be viewed through the concept of covenant, which initiates and/or renews God's commitment to the Davidic dynasty.

49. J.A. Fitzmyer (*The Gospel According to Luke I-IX* [AB, 28; New York: Doubleday, 1970], p. 485) lists Grundmann, Harnack, Klostermann, Leaney, W. Manson, Moffatt, Streeter, and Zahn as supporters of the variant, which is found in Codex Bezae [D], some Old Latin texts, and some patristic writers. The variant reading is the result of *lectio difficilior*, meaning that later copyists tried to harmonize Luke's account with Mark's.

original, it should nevertheless be illustrative of early tendencies to see the heavenly voice as expressing messianic affirmation.

Opposition to this echo, however, has been quite strong. It is commonly argued that since Mark does not reproduce the LXX order (υἱός μου εἶ συ), his composition of the baptism scene was probably not influenced by this text.[50] Thus, the only part of the heavenly voice's announcement that coheres in diction with the psalm is υἱός μου. However, when the Targumic tradition is considered as a potential parallel, the argument based on the lack of diction is considerably weakened. An interesting phenomenon develops in some Targum literature with respect to the emphasis on the loving fatherhood of God. Although fatherhood is a common enough theme in the LXX and the MT,[51] it is not until one examines the later Aramaic paraphrases that one finds a striking emphasis on God's mercy, supplication, and especially love. For example, 'You are our Father' in Isa. 63.16 is rendered 'You are he whose love for us exceeds that of a father for his children' in the Targum. This development of tradition is plainly seen in Ps. 2.7 where 'The Lord said to me: "You are my son, this day I have begotten you"' is paraphrased in the Targum 'You are as dear to me as a son is to his father, as though I created you this day'.[52] The use of ὁ ἀγαπητός in Mk. 1.11, conveying the idea of uniqueness and intimacy, is not found in the MT or LXX; but the concept is present in the Targumic use of חבב ('to love', 'to make beloved').[53] Where the Targum differs from Mark is in its tendency to replace a straight declaration of sonship ('you are my son') with a comparative sense ('you are as a son to me'). This may not be a strong impediment, however, since Mark's affirmation of Jesus' sonship in his incipit removes the need for comparisons.

A number of years ago Joseph Fitzmyer argued that there is no evidence in pre-Christian Palestinian or Diaspora Judaism that 'son of God' in Psalm 2 was ever understood 'messianically'. The crux of the debate is Ps. 2.2 where the king is described as משיחו in the MT and τοῦ κυρίου αὐτοῦ in the LXX. Fitzmyer argued that 'son of God' may simply be a reference to an 'anointed' agent and not to a 'messiah'. If this is the case, then there would have been little precedent for Mark to rely on Ps. 2.7 as an expression of Jesus' messiahship.

Fitzmyer's general caution about drawing parallels between Jewish and Christian interpretations of scripture is wise in principle, but in this case his assessment may not be broad enough. The discovery of cave 4 has considerably changed the outlook on the 'son of God' as a messianic title in pre-Christian Judaism.[54] The availability of the entire text of 4Q246, which in its early stages was touted by

50. C.E.B. Cranfield, *The Gospel According to Saint Mark* (Cambridge: Cambridge University Press, 1983), p. 55; *idem.*, 'The Baptism of our Lord – A Study of St. Mark 1.9–11', *SJT* 8 (1955), pp. 59–60.

51. Exod. 4.22–23; Deut. 30.19; 32.5; Isa. 1.4; Hos. 2.1; 1 Chron. 29.10; etc.

52. E. Levine, *The Aramaic Version of the Bible* (New York: Walter de Gruyter, 1988), pp. 49–50.

53. R.A. Guelich, *Mark 1–8.26* (WBC, 34A; Dallas, TX: Word Books, 1989), p. 34.

54. J.A. Fitzmyer, *A Wandering Aramean: Collected Aramaic Sayings* (SBLMS, 25; Chico, CA: Scholars Press, 1979), p. 105.

some Christian scholars as evidence that 'son of God' was understood messianically by Second Temple Jews, has complicated the discussion considerably. The debate concerns whether or not 'son of God' refers to an antagonist figure such as 'antichrist' or a Seleucid king, or to a protagonist figure such as a divinely appointed agent, an heir to the throne of David, or the messiah. Surprisingly, Fitzmyer, who endorses a protagonist interpretation, comes very close to implying that the title refers to messiah.[55] But more than this, Fitzmyer's claim that pre-Christian Judaism did not associate 'son of God' with messiah does not appropriately consider other Qumran texts. In 4QFlor [4QMidrEschat[b]] (4Q174) we find an example of a midrash on 2 Sam. 7.10b-14 and the opening lines of Psalms 1–2 wherein Nathan's prophecy to David of a coming king is interpreted with a view to a figure who fits the role of messiah. Both the kingly figure and the Interpreter of the Law share in the future restoration of Israel. Moreover, as Donald Juel notices, 'the placement of a midrash on Psalms 1–2 immediately following the messianic interpretation of 2 Sam. 7.10–14 in 4QFlor [4QMidrEschat[b]] lends greater probability to the suggestion that 'the Son of God' was understood as royal – messianic – language.'[56] In the following quotation, the writer shows little hesitation in associating the divinely adopted son with the shoot (branch) of David, who is explicitly called the 'messiah of righteousness' in 4QpGen [4QpGen[a]] (4Q252).[57] 4QFlor [4QMidrEschat[b]] 1.10–11 reads:

> And the Lord declares to you that He will build you a house. And I will raise up your seed after you, and I will establish the throne of his kingdom for ever. I will be to him as a father, and he will be to me as son: He is the shoot of David who will stand with the Interpreter of the Law, who [will rule] in Zion in the latter days as it is written, 'And I will raise up the booth of David which is fallen': he is the booth (or branch) of David which was fallen, who will take office to save Israel.[58]

55. J.A. Fitzmyer, '4Q246: The "Son of God" Document from Qumran', *Bib* 74 (1993), pp. 153–74. On the debate, see J.J. Collins, *The Scepter and the Star: The Messiahs of the Dead Sea Scrolls and Other Ancient Literature* (New York: Doubleday, 1995), pp. 154–72.

56. D. Juel, *Messianic Exegesis: Christological Interpretation of the Old Testament in Early Christianity* (Philadelphia: Fortress Press, 1988), p. 68 n. 16.

57. Collins, *The Scepter and the Star*, p. 164. See also Juel, *Messianic Exegesis*, pp. 64–68; M. Hengel, *The Son of God: The Origin of Christology and the History of Jewish-Hellenistic Religion* (Philadelphia: Fortress Press, 1983), p. 44. Juel (p. 78) states that 'though the midrash on Psalms 1–2 that follows in 4QFlor [4QMidrEschat[b]] is unfortunately broken off, the reference to God's "begetting the Messiah" in 1QSa II [1QSa]...indicates that Ps. 2.7, in which God addresses the king as "my son," was likewise understood as furnishing stock messianic language'.

58. Translation taken from G.J. Brooke, *Exegesis at Qumran: 4QFlorilegium in its Jewish Context* (JSOTSup, 29; Sheffield: JSOT Press, 1985), p. 92. 4QFlor [4QMidrEschat[b]] 1.10–13 (an exposition of 2 Sam. 7) is concerned with the messianic prince expected from the line of David who will bring rule and restoration for Israel. A similar use of Psalm 2 and 2 Samuel 7 in apposition to one another is seen in Acts 13.33–37 and Heb. 1.5, both in reference to Jesus (p. 209). On 4QFlor [4QMidrEschat[b]] see also J. Allegro (ed.), *Discoveries in the Judean Desert of Jordan*. V. *Qumran Cave 4* (Oxford: Clarendon Press, 1968); J. Strugnell, 'Notes en marge du volume V des Discoveries in the Judean Desert of Jordan', *RQ* 29 (1970), pp. 163–279; Y. Yadin, 'A Midrash on 2 Sam. vii and Ps. i-ii (4QFlorilegium)', *IEJ* 9 (1959), pp. 95–98.

Another Qumran text, which associates 'son of God' with messiah, is 4QpsDan A[a] (4Q243) 1.6–2.4, which reads,

> [But your son] [7] shall be great upon the earth, [8] [O King! All (men) shall] make [peace], and all shall serve [9] [him. He shall be called the son of] the [G]reat [God], and by his name shall he be named (Col. II).[1]He shall be hailed (as) the Son of God, and they shall call him Son of the Most High. As comets (flash) [2] to the sight, so shall be their kingdom. (For some) year[s] they shall rule upon [3] the earth and shall trample everything (under foot); people shall trample upon people, city upon ci[t]y, [4] (*vocat*) until there arises the people of God, and everyone rests from the sword.[59]

Though there is no explicit mention of 'messiah' in this text, one can nevertheless draw the implication given the Palestinian apocalyptic context indicated by the titles for the royal successor.[60] They are probably a reference to the son of an enthroned king within the context of the Hasmonian rule; perhaps as Fitzmyer suggests, an heir to the throne of David, which would imply a messianic figure despite his own hesitation. [61]

A final example is 4Q369, which appears to connect 'you made him a firstborn son to you' with 'like him for a prince and ruler in all your earthly land'. Though this text is very fragmentary, Collins claims that this firstborn son who is a ruler must somehow be related to the Davidic line, be it past or present.[62]

Although late, rabbinic midrashim on Ps. 2.7 preserves a tradition which makes the link between sonship and messiah explicit. While there are some comparisons with Qumran exegesis (and Mark for that matter) that can tempt one to draw parallels, extreme caution needs to be exercised. Yet, at the same time, the similarities raise broader questions about the origins and influential trajectories of this exegesis. Should rabbinic exegesis be understood apart from nascent Christianity as it has traditionally been thought, or should Christianity and Judaism in late antiquity be viewed as much more integrated, as Daniel Boyarin has more recently argued?[63] I quote one part of a midrash (on Ps. 2.9) to show the extent of the similarity:

> In another comment, the verse is read *I will tell of the decree: The Lord said unto me: Thou art My son… Ask of Me and I will give the nations for thy inheritance, and the ends of the earth for thy possession* (Ps. 2.7, 8). R. Yudan said: 'All these godly promises are in the decree of the King, the King of kings, who will fulfill them for the lord Messiah. And why all this? Because the Messiah occupies himself with Torah'.
>
> Another comment on *Thou art my son*: God does not say, 'I have a son', but 'Thou art like a son to Me', as when a master wishing to give pleasure to his slave, says to him, 'Thou art as dear to me as a son…'

59. J.A. Fitzmyer, 'The Contribution of Qumran Aramaic to the Study of the New Testament', *NTS* 20 (1974), p. 393. Even though the interpretation of this text will be debated for some time to come given its fragmentary state, there is no doubt that the Aramaic titles, ברה די אל and בר עליון apply to some person in an apocalyptic context.

60. Hengel, *The Son of God*, p. 45.

61. Fitzmyer, 'The Contribution of Qumran Aramaic to the Study of the New Testament', p. 393.

62. Collins, *The Scepter and the Star*, p. 165.

63. D. Boyarin, *Dying for God: Martyrdom and the Making of Christianity and Judaism* (Stanford: Stanford University Press, 1999).

When the time comes, the Holy One, blessed be He, will say: 'I must create the Messiah – a new creation', As Scripture says, *'This day have I begotten thee'* – that is, on the very day of redemption, God will create the Messiah.[64]

Similarly in *b. Suk.* 52a, the royal son in Ps. 2.7 is the messiah, the son of David:

Our Rabbis taught, The Holy One, blessed be He, will say to the Messiah, the son of David (May he reveal himself speedily in our days!), 'Ask of me anything, and I will give it to thee', as it is said, I will tell of the decree etc. this day have I begotten thee, ask of me and I will give the nations for thy inheritance.[65]

That Mark relied on Ps. 2.7 or some exegetical tradition of it that connected 'son of God' with messiah is certainly conceivable in light of his lofty depiction of Jesus in the narrative. There are numerous instances throughout Mark's Gospel where one could argue that Jesus is subtly portrayed as a kingly figure, whether it is through irony such as the mocking of the crowd in the crucifixion scene and the inscription on the cross, through the secrecy motif which conveys to the reader/ hearer Jesus' messiahship, through his characterization as the divinely adopted agent who inaugurates the rule of God, through Bartimaeus' identification of Jesus as the son of David, through the future son of man sayings which depict Jesus sitting at the right hand of God, or possibly through the crowds' welcome when Jesus enters Jerusalem. Markan scholarship has repeatedly confirmed this portrayal, even if indirectly, through various critical methods. As a kingly figure, Jesus does not use the sword as other messianic figures, nor does he rule over or manipulate crowds. Those in Mark's audience who were familiar with Jewish traditions could have conceivably understood Jesus' baptism as a type of Davidic coronation.

A similar kind of association could have been made by Gentile members of Mark's audience as well. Although the evangelist was Jewish and primarily influ- enced by the Jewish scriptures and traditions, there are clear indications that he was also influenced by Roman culture (as were all Jews). One example where Jesus is probably portrayed as a king in accordance with Roman categories is Mark's incipit. At the beginning of his Gospel, the evangelist introduces Jesus as 'son of God' whose coming is 'the beginning of the good news' – as it was often said of Augustus (as is the case, for example, in the famous Priene calendar inscription). The incipit coupled with the Centurion's declaration that Jesus was the son of God at the end of the story would have undoubtedly been heard as a political challenge to Caesar, whether the story was performed in Rome or Syria. Since Roman coins, inscriptions, statues, and reliefs described both Augustus and Tiberius as gods or sons of God who are celebrated as bringing 'good news' to the empire, it is conceivable that Mark would have been heard as a subversive story wherein Jesus, not Caesar, brings ultimate peace.[66]

---

64. W.G. Braude, *The Midrash on Psalms* (New Haven, CT: Yale University Press, 1959), pp. 1.40–41.

65. Translation taken from Epstein, *The Babylonian Talmud.*

66. C.A. Evans, 'Mark's Incipit and the Priene Calendar Inscription: From Jewish Gospel to

Whatever the exact influence upon the author or specific association drawn by audience members, the point is that the designation 'son of God' as king conforms to the portrayal of Jesus in both the broader narrative and the socio-religious context.

3. *Concluding Remarks*

I have tried to show that at the level of Mark's performance, it is futile to engage in a search for *the* scriptural echo or influence at the root of the voice's announcement in Mk 1.11. Past attempts at uncovering *the* specific influence, be it a scripture text or a later interpretation of it, have been unyielding in their single-focused approach as if the evangelist's intention and the audience's interpretation are accessible to the modern reader. Investigations of embedded scripture texts and traditions by many modern scholars have assumed a literate ancient audience which would have been at home with the same kind of comparative preoccupation and skill which characterizes the modern reader who painstakingly dissects the text in isolation. But this neither reflects the oral culture in which Mark was performed, nor does it correctly portray the early audiences which could have drawn different association on different occasions of Mark's performance. Although I have dealt here with the so-called final form of Mark, in actuality Mark most likely would not have been performed exactly the same way each time. While the story line would have remained the same, specific terminology, body gestures and vocalization would have varied, for oral poets in the ancient world were not bound to texts. Moreover, the inclination toward originality at each performance did not require the introduction of new material, but it did require the performer(s) to incorporate traditional material in strategic ways in keeping with new situations and audiences.[67]

The narrative context in which the voice's announcement is embedded compounds the problem of 'certainty'. As a deconstructive tactic, I have first tried to make a case for the influence of each scriptural tradition, showing how Mark and/or his audience could have conceivably assumed the appropriate link with Jesus. In addition to dictional and thematic coherence, to use Chilton's terminology, I have then tried to briefly show that each option coheres with the portrayal of Jesus in the overall narrative. And herein lies the subversion of traditional historical-critical approaches. When two or more options are available and fit into the narrative, the historical-critical scholar attempts all the more to verify a single influence. The approach is not only myopic, but undermines the entire process. By trying to demonstrate the weaknesses of competing options, the historical-critic indirectly succeeds in showing the instability of his own position. When the whole narrative is brought into the mix, the historical-critic restricts himself to read

---

Greco-Roman Gospel', *JGRChJ* 1 (2000), pp. 67–81; J.D. Crossan and J.L. Reed, *In Search of Paul: How Jesus's Apostle Opposed Rome's Empire with God's Kingdom* (New York: HarperCollins, 2004), pp. 70–104, 235–49.

67. Ong, *Orality and Literacy*, pp. 57–67.

selectively in the same way that a redaction-critic might verify his results by pointing to one theological theme and conveniently omitting others. Beginning with a hypothesis and finding data to support it has long been shown to be problematic in the field of hermeneutics, and yet caution is still thrown to the wind.

In the end historical-criticism, which is indispensable for the study of embedded texts in the Gospels, can best benefit the interpretive enterprise by recognizing its myopia when confronted with a diversity of opinions on the meaning of an embedded scripture text. If the historical-critic grants appropriate consideration to literary approaches, such as narrative criticism, he will necessarily have to adopt the possibility of a plurality of meaning, however uncomfortable this may be.

Kingdom, Messianic Authority and the Re-constituting of God's People – Tracing The Function of Exodus Material in Mark's Narrative

Larry Perkins

Several major studies of Old Testament materials and themes that occur in the Markan narrative have appeared recently.[1] Each in its own way advances our understanding of the relationship between the Old and New Testaments, specifically in relation to Mark's Gospel. Concurrent with these studies has been the emergence of new forms of literary study of the Gospels. The term narrative criticism has come to denote one major application of these approaches. Many have applied narrative methodology to Mark's story,[2] resulting in helpful insights into this author's purpose and the rhetorical means he used to achieve this purpose.

The function and interpretation of embedded Exodus materials (direct quotes, allusions and parallel motifs)[3] with reference to the intention of the whole Markan narrative deserve further consideration, particularly as these materials help us understand more fully the author's development of several key themes – the kingdom of God, messianic authority and the re-constitution of God's people.[4] It is not sufficient to consider how a particular Exodus quote, allusion or motif functions

---

1. Some of the primary recent examples would include: Thomas R. Hatina, *In Search of Context: The Function of Scripture in Mark's Narrative* (JSNTSup, 232; SSEJC, 8; Sheffield : Sheffield Academic Press, 2002); Joel Marcus, *The Way of the Lord: Christological Exegesis of the Old Testament in the Gospel of Mark* (Louisville: Westminster/John Knox Press, 1992); Willard M. Swartley, *Israel's Scripture Traditions and the Synoptic Gospels: Story Shaping Story* (Peabody, MA: Hendrickson, 1994); Rikki E. Watts, *Isaiah's New Exodus in Mark* (WUNT, 2.88; Grand Rapids: Baker Academic, 1997).

2. Robert Fowler, *Let the Reader Understand. Reader-Response Criticism and the Gospel of Mark* (Harrisburg, PE: Trinity International Press, 1996); David Rhoads, Joanna Dewey and Donald Michie, *Mark as Story: An Introduction to the Narrative of a Gospel* (Minneapolis: Fortress Press, 2nd edn, 1999).

3. Most of the terminology employed in these materials in the Markan narrative probably comes directly from the Septuagint translation of Exodus (LXX Exodus) or perhaps Deuteronomy's rehearsal of Israel's Exodus experience (LXX Deuteronomy). In some contexts where Old Testament legal material is being referred to we cannot tell always whether LXX Exodus or LXX Deuteronomy is the immediate source. Furthermore, it is not always certain whether the narrator is quoting directly from the Septuagint translation or paraphrasing.

4. William R. Stegner, 'Jesus' Walking on the Water: Mark 6.45–52', in Craig A. Evans and W. Richard Stegner (eds), *The Gospels and the Scriptures of Israel* (JSNTSup, 104; Sheffield: Sheffield Academic Press, 1994), pp. 212–34.

in one limited context of Mark's narrative. Rather, the way the author has used this Exodus material to accomplish his overall narrative purpose must be defined if we are to appreciate fully the intertextual, narrative linkages[5] that serve to enrich the impact of this story upon early Christian readers or listeners.

Kee reminds us that Mark is quite intentional with respect to the incorporation of these Jewish scriptural materials into his narrative. Twice in his narrative the author tells us that Jesus' course follows divine necessity (9.11; 14.21) as expressed in the writings (καθὼς γέγραπται περὶ αὐτοῦ).[6]

Woven into Mark's narrative are both explicit and implicit references to Exodus material. Direct quotations from LXX Exodus include references to Moses' call narrative,[7] legal material,[8] and Israel's wilderness experience.[9] Allusions to specific personalities and events in the Exodus narrative include Moses,[10] Passover,[11] and the establishment of the covenant.[12] However, beyond this the Markan narrative incorporated motifs (i.e. wilderness, testing/temptation, feeding of multitudes, hardness of heart, miracles/signs, the journey, etc.) that also occur in the Exodus narrative. A significant question then is the degree to which the Markan author purposely used these quotes, allusions and motifs and incorporated them into his story because he wanted the reader to reflect upon key elements of Israel's experience expressed in the Exodus story as he or she was reading or hearing Mark's story.[13] A second question is the relationship between the explicit quotations from Exodus and the motifs in Exodus used in the Markan narrative. Are these two elements designed by the narrator to be complementary or do they serve different rhetorical and literary purposes? Finally, we should consider whether the Markan author desires his readers to understand the Exodus references through the grid of Isaiah 40–55 and its prophecies about a new exodus.

The occurrence of specific quotations from LXX Exodus in Mark shows clearly that the author certainly knew key portions of the Exodus narrative.

---

5. Swartley's phrase 'story shaping story' is a helpful way to conceive of these linkages.

6. Howard Clark Kee, 'The Function of Scriptural Quotations and Allusions in Mark 11–16', in E.E. Ellis and E. Gräßer (eds), *Jesus und Paulus* (Festschrift W.G. Kümmel; Göttingen: Vandenhoeck & Ruprecht, 1975), p. 167.

7. Mark 12.

8. Mark 2, 7, 10, and 12.

9. Mk 1.2.

10. Mk 9.2–7.

11. Mk 14.12ff.

12. Mk 14.22ff.

13. Some scholars (e.g. Stegner) presuppose that the Markan author used Jewish-Christian Greek materials in the formulation of his narrative. This raises the question of the degree to which the Markan author might be directly responsible for the embedding of Exodus materials in his narrative. However, moving such discussion from speculation to the point of probability is very difficult. In this article we have focused upon the occurrence of Exodus material in the Markan narrative without seeking to discern the tradition history that may have led either to the incorporation of Exodus material into the tradition or the incorporation of prior tradition in the Markan narrative.

LXX Exodus Text	Mark Text	Mark Context
3.6	12.26	Resurrection Conflict
3.15	12.26	Resurrection Conflict
20.12	7.10	Conflict over Tradition
20.12–16	10.19	Instruction to Rich Man
21.17	7.10	Conflict over Tradition
23.20	1.2	Introduction to the Gospel

Primary Markan references to LXX Exodus are to legal materials, fundamental to Judaism's understanding of its unique place, that Jesus used in situations of conflict with Jewish religious leaders (Mk 7.10; 12.26). Twice Jesus refers to the Ten Commandments. The conflict in Mark 7 concerns Jesus' laxness in not requiring his disciples to follow the Pharisaic practices of washing and maintaining ritual cleanness. Jesus in response accuses the Pharisees of hypocrisy in the way they apply the principle of *korban* and in that process 'annul' God's intent in the command to 'respect father and mother'.[14] Jesus also summarizes key parts of the Decalogue[15] in response to the Rich Man's question about eternal life (Mk 10.19). Here the conflict with the religious leaders is implicit in that this person's current religious beliefs probably reflect contemporary Jewish religious teaching.

The only specific quotation taken from LXX Exodus 1–15 occurs in Jesus' conflict with the Sadducees about the matter of resurrection. God's statement 'I am the God of Abraham and the God of Isaac and the God of Jacob' gives proof according to Jesus that these individuals still exist before God and therefore the book of Moses does support the idea of resurrection. He criticizes the Sadducees for their improper interpretation of the Scripture, as well as their deficient understanding of God's power. However, in the Markan narrative Jesus quotes no historical events recounted in Exodus 1–15. As well, no material from the building of the Tabernacle or Israel's idolatry in the Golden Calf episode is quoted.[16]

14. Whether the narrator is using material from LXX Exodus or the parallel passage in LXX Deuteronomy is open to debate. The fourth revised edition of *The Greek New Testament* in Mk 7.10 has σου. However, in Wevers' edition of the LXX Exodus, he omits σου. LXX Deut. 5.16, however, does have σου, meaning that the quotation in Mk 7.10 is exactly parallel with LXX Deuteronomy, but not with LXX Exodus. In 10.19 where the same command is quoted, the Markan narrative omits σου, paralleling the LXX Exodus form of the command, not LXX Deuteronomy. The presence or absence of the personal pronoun does not enable us to speak with conviction about LXX Exodus as the only source of this quotation in 7.10. However, the fact that Jesus in this context (7.10b) immediately quotes from LXX Exod. 21.17 would perhaps tip the scales in favour of an LXX Exodus source, rather than LXX Deuteronomy.

15. Again the question arises where the narrator is referring to LXX Exodus or LXX Deuteronomy. The Markan text uses μή plus the aorist subjunctive to express the prohibition whereas both LXX Exodus and LXX Deuteronomy use οὐ plus the future. The Second Gospel does not follow the order of the commands in either LXX Exodus or LXX Deuteronomy. Rather it follows the order of the Masoretic Hebrew text. Again, we find ourselves uncertain as to the source of this material. However, the Decalogue material does occur in LXX Exodus 20 and so we have warrant to examine how an LXX Exodus context might provide specific connotations for the larger Markan narrative.

16. The reference in LXX Exod. 32.34 to the divine messenger to assist Israel on its way to Canaan is similar in content to LXX Exod. 23.20, but quite different in wording: ἰδοὺ ὁ ἄγγελος μου

Most evaluations of Mk 1.2 consider that LXX Exod. 23.20 (conflated in some way with Mal. 3.1) is probably the source of the first part of this conflated quotation.[17]

a ἰδοὺ ἀποστέλλω τὸν ἄγγελόν μου πρὸ προσώπου σου, ὃς κατασκευάσει τὴν ὁδόν σου (Mk 1.2).
καὶ ἰδοὺ ἐγὼ ἀποστέλλω τὸν ἄγγελόν μου πρὸ προσώπου σου, ἵνα φυλάξῃ σε ἐν τῇ ὁδῷ, ὅπως εἰσαγάγῃ σε εἰς τὴν γῆν, ἣν ἡτοίμασά σοι (LXX Exod. 23.20).[18]

However, LXX Mal. 3.1a is also proposed as the source of this material:

ἰδοὺ ἐγὼ ἐξαποστέλλω τὸν ἄγγελόν μου, καὶ ἐπιβλέψεται ὁδὸν πρὸ προσώπου μου.

It is probably the case that the material in LXX Malachi is a later conscious patterning after LXX Exod. 23.20 and so it is appropriate to consider LXX Exod. 23.20 as the foundational source for terminology appropriated by the Malachi Greek translator for his own purposes. The word order of Mk 1.2, the form of the main verb ἀποστέλλω and the pronominal references would suggest that LXX Exod. 23.20 is the primary referent for Mark's author. However, the linkage of Mal. 3.1 with an Elijah persona in Mal. 4 and John the Baptist's identification by Jesus in Mark's narrative (9.8ff.) with the new Elijah makes the Malachi passage a secondary, but important referent.

The origin of ὃς κατασκευάσει τὴν ὁδόν σου in Mk 1.2c is puzzling. It diverges considerably from the LXX Exodus text (23.20) in which God promises to protect his people 'in the way' so that he leads them to the land he has prepared from them. The wording used by Mark's narrator in 1.2c affirms the messenger comes to assist another individual. The context makes clear that this individual is Jesus and the one who prepares the way is John. In this way the author redirects the reference in Exodus from the general people of God, whose way God's messenger prepares, to the specific person of Jesus. The phrase πρὸ προσώπου σου in LXX Exodus refers to Israel, but in Mark it refers to Jesus. The repetition of σου in Mk 1.2c continues to point the reader to God's actions on behalf of Jesus.

The LXX Malachi passage is also quite different from Mark's wording. In LXX Malachi God is speaking and he focuses attention on the messenger who will 'oversee a way before my [i.e. God's] face'. While the general impact of this messenger's activity will affect God's people, they are not the immediate agents or recipients of the action in this Malachi passage. God's messenger comes to

---

προπορεύσεται πρὸ προσώπου σου. The Markan narrator did not quote from LXX Exodus 32 in this instance. Swartley suggests that the Beelzeboul controversy and the exorcism in Mark 9, because of their position in the Markan structure, may reflect the Golden Calf episode in Israel's experience (*Israel's Scripture Traditions and the Synoptic Gospels*, pp. 52–53, 103–104). However, there is little if any specific indication in the Markan narrative to make these connections *pacem* Swartley.

17. Consider the comments by Marcus, *The Way of the Lord*, pp. 13ff.; Robert Guelich, *Mark 1–8.26* (WBC, 34A; Dallas, TX: Word Books, 1989), pp. 7ff.; and William Lane, *The Gospel According to Mark* (NICNT, Grand Rapids, Michigan: William B. Eerdmans Publishing Company, 1974), pp. 45ff., as exemplary of many others.

18. Quotations of Septuagint materials are taken from the Göttingen edition.

prepare God's way. In Mark's version God's messenger comes to prepare Jesus' way. In this sense, the Malachi rendering is closer to the Markan author's intent, but there is substantial divergence in terminology.[19]

Where then did the author derive this wording? Did he translate the Hebrew text of Exodus or Malachi afresh?[20] Did he have access to some other Greek translation? Is he reflecting some other interpretation of this text and presenting it in his own language? Perhaps Marcus and Watts are correct in suggesting that the author in 1.2c reflects the Hebrew text of Mal. 3.1 and prepared his own Greek translation.[21] It is interesting that both Matthew (11.10) and Luke (7.27) repeat the clause ὃς κατασκευάσει τὴν ὁδόν σου ἔμπροσθέν σου as part of a quotation in another context related to John the Baptist.[22] This might suggest that the Markan author did not create something new here, but rather was dependent upon a tradition that Matthew and Luke also accessed.[23]

Why does the author define his major character with reference to the Exodus narrative in this way? Apart from the fundamental emphasis upon God's sovereign involvement in Jesus' mission expressed in the ὁδός motif, what does the Exodus story contribute to our understanding of Jesus' mission? After all, presumably Mark could accomplish his narrative purpose relative to John the Baptist by using Isaiah's material only, just as Matthew and Luke do. But the Markan author is not content with this. It seems that he desires his readers to set the mission of Jesus within the larger story of Israel's formation as told in the Exodus narrative, but also to show that Jesus' mission is a separate, though connected, stage in God's plans for Israel. Jesus will affirm God's word as revealed to Moses. He will offer a revised interpretation and understanding of God's covenantal intent for Israel. The deliberate conflation of the Exodus text with the Isaiah quotation probably indicates that the author wanted his readers to see the new exodus of Isaiah as a revised exodus paradigm.[24]

---

19. Marcus (*The Way of the Lord*, p. 16) notes that both the Mal. 3.1 and Isa. 40.3 Hebrew texts have the phrase פנה דרך. LXX Isaiah renders this expression as ἑτοιμάσατε τὴν ὁδόν.

20. The Markan narrator seems to have facility in Aramaic and/or Hebrew given the various translations he provides of Aramaic expressions and Hebrew scripture quotations.

21. Marcus, *The Way of the Lord*, p. 16 and Watts, *Isaiah's New Exodus and Mark*, p. 62.

22. The source of the additional prepositional phrase ἔμπροσθέν σου is unclear, but it occurs in both Matthew and Luke. Perhaps it reflects πρὸ προσώπου μου in Mal. 3.1. Revisional activity in the Septuagint text was occurring in the pre-Christian era, with particular concern to bring the Greek text into more accurate alignment with the Hebrew text. Perhaps the Markan author's text of Malachi reflects this revisional activity.

23. The material in Matthew 11 and Luke 7 in which this quote is embedded is Q material. It is debated whether Mark also had access to some of this material. If Matthew and Luke are dependent upon Mark for this material, then we would expect it to occur in Matthew 3 and Luke 3, which parallel Mk 1.2–4.

24. Kee ('The Function of Scriptural Quotations and Allusions in Mark 11–16', pp. 176–77) notes that the Markan author frequently employs 'synthetic quotations'. He continues, 'The process in all of this is the interpretation of scripture by scripture, but with an eschatological aim that sees in Jesus the fulfillment of what can be discerned only when the synthesis of unrelated passages has been achieved and explained... Mark's sole concern is to demonstrate by appeal to scripture that in Jesus the divinely determined plan of redemption is in the process of accomplishment.'

The Markan author uses various conventions to designate these references to scripture materials as specific quotations: Καθὼς γέγραπται ἐν τῷ Ἡσαΐα τῷ προφήτη (Mk 1.2);[25] Μωϋσῆς γὰρ εἶπεν (Mk 7.10); τὰς ἐντολὰς οἶδας (Mk 10.19); and οὐκ ἀνέγνωτε ἐν τῇ βίβλῳ Μωϋσέως ἐπὶ τοῦ βάτου πῶς εἶπεν αὐτῷ ὁ θεὸς λέγων (Mk 12.26). In the case of Mk 1.2 the narrator directly makes reference to the scripture source so that the reader will know the context within which the actions of Jesus, 'Messiah, Son of God', should be understood. Perhaps in this way the narrator articulates the continuity of God's work with Israel, despite interventions such as the destruction of Jerusalem and the exile. In the other three instances (Mk 7.10; 10.19 and 12.26) Jesus is the speaker in the narrative. In two cases he refers to the 'book of Moses' or 'Moses' as the source of materials that he employs in debate with Jewish religious leaders (Pharisees and scribes, and Sadducees) regarding their improper use and interpretation of specific parts of the Jewish religious law (Mk 7.10; 12.26). In the other instance Jesus is responding to a question addressed to him by a wealthy Jewish man regarding the possession of 'eternal life'. In these settings the Markan narrative links Jesus with the Mosaic tradition, profiling Jesus as Moses' true interpreter.[26]

It is also possible that the Markan author has alluded to Exodus materials in three specific instances.[27]

25. The author assigns the entire quotation to Isaiah, even though part of it relates to Exodus. Whether this was a 'mistake' on the part of the author, or whether he chose to reference the source of the text that contributes most material to this conflated text, or whether he wanted his audience to understand the Exodus material in the light of Isaiah (as Watts suggests) is a matter of dispute. However, this is the only case in Mark's use of conflated material where he does ascribe a specific source to the material, as well as the only conflated text that does not occur on the lips of God (1.11) or Jesus (11.17; 12.1–12; 13.24–26; 14.62) or the Jerusalem crowd (11.1–11).

26. Jesus' use of the Exodus materials in 7.10 occurs also in the Matthaean parallel (15.4). His reference to the commands in Mk 10.19 is paralleled both in Mt. 19.15–16 and Lk. 18.20. The reference to Exodus in Mk 12.26 similarly occurs also both in Mt. 22.32 and Lk. 20.37. So the Markan author does not act uniquely in embedding these Exodus texts in his narrative. However, if we accept Markan priority as the solution to the synoptic relationship, then this writer may well have established the pattern followed by Matthew and Luke. The case of Mk 1.2 is more complex. Both Mt. (3.3) and Lk. (3.4–6) quote from Isaiah and explicitly mark the source as they seek to explain the appearance and function of John the Baptizer. Mark parallels this usage of Isaiah in Mk 1.2–3, using the same Isaiah materials with reference to John. However, he acts singularly when he adds the reference to Exod. 23.20 and/or Mal. 3.1 to the Isaiah material as further commentary upon John's appearance, as well as the significance of Jesus. Here he seems to have created a conflated text specifically for the purpose of introducing his narrative. Matthew (11.10) does incorporate this Exodus or Malachi material into a later section of his narrative as Jesus comments upon the significance of John after his arrest by Herod. Luke follows the same pattern in 7.26. Marcus (*The Way of the Lord*, p. 15) notes, 'the fusion of two or more scriptural passages into one conflated citation is a characteristic Markan method of biblical usage'.

27. Kee ('The Function of Scriptural Quotations and Allusions in Mark 11–16', pp. 169–71) notes Exod. 4.1 as possibly alluded to in Mk 13.11b and Exod. 26.31ff. as alluded to in the splitting of the temple curtain in Mk 15.38. In the case of Mk 15.38, the allusion to Exod. 26.31ff recounts the instructions to Moses for the weaving of the original tabernacle curtain, but there does not seem to be a specific allusion by the Markan author to this Exodus context. In Mk 13.11b Jesus seeks to assure his followers that when they are arrested the Holy Spirit will enable them to give a good account and so they should not be concerned about what they will say. In Exod. 4.1, Moses asks God for some answer to the anticipated scepticism by the Israelites' response to his claim that God has appeared to

Exodus	Mark	Context
20.8–10	2.27	Sabbath conflict
12.6, 14–20	14.12–13	Passover meal
24.8	14.24	Covenant in Jesus' blood

Within a series of conflict stories (Mark 2–3) the author includes an accusing question by the Pharisees concerning the action of Jesus' disciples who are plucking ears of corn on the Sabbath. The Jewish religious leaders construed this as work and a violation of Jewish Sabbath law. They explicitly criticized Jesus for his failure to discipline his followers. As Jesus concludes his response he asserts in Mk 2.27 that the Sabbath was made for people, not people for the Sabbath (τὸ σάββατον διὰ τὸν ἄνθρωπον ἐγένετο καὶ οὐχ ὁ ἄνθρωπος διὰ τὸ σάββατον). The definition of Sabbath as a holy day was included in the initial expression of the Ten Commandments (Exod. 20.8–10).[28]

Shortly after Jesus enters Jerusalem, he orders his followers to prepare the Passover celebration. In 14.1 we find a reference to τὸ πάσχα καὶ τὰ ἄζυμα. This reference is repeated in 14.12 (καὶ τῇ πρώτῃ ἡμέρᾳ τῶν ἀζύμων, ὅτε τὸ πάσχα ἔθυον). In the Markan narrative the final meal that Jesus has with his disciples before his death is the Passover meal. While this was a normal part of any Jewish person's annual religious practice, the origin of this ritual is recorded first in Exodus 12. The first Passover meal immediately precedes Israel's rescue from Egypt and occurs as God completes the work of the final plague, the killing of Egypt's firstborn. The roasted flesh of the lamb was eaten and its blood sprinkled on the doorposts. Unleavened bread also was a significant part of this meal. This ritual protected God's people from 'the destroyer'.

In Mark's narrative during the Passover meal celebration and just prior to his arrest, trial, death and resurrection, Jesus takes unleavened bread and wine and identifies them with his own body and blood 'of the covenant that is being poured out for many' (Mk 14.24). By infusing elements in the Passover meal with new meaning, Jesus defines his mission in reference to God's previous intervention for Israel's salvation. Jesus is about to die and he parallels his death with constitutive elements of the Passover ritual. As his followers partake of the bread and wine, in some sense his body and blood, they proleptically participate in the covenant that God establishes through Jesus' death.

The Markan author does not provide us with any specific editorial comment that leads us to see Jesus' imminent death typologically anticipated in the Passover. Rather, it is the action of Jesus himself defined in the narrative that leads readers to make these connections. If we presume that Jesus uses the phrase 'son of man'

---

him. However, in the Markan discourse there does not seem to be any indication that Jesus wants his followers to see in Moses an example of how God in the past has assisted his representatives.

28. These commandments are repeated by Moses to Israel in Deut. 5.12–14. It is not possible to discern definitively whether Jesus in his response is alluding specifically to the Exodus material or the Deuteronomy material.

in the narrative as a self-reference, then he previously has used sacrificial language to describe his death. In 10.45 he affirms that the son of man has come δοῦναι τὴν ψυχὴν αὐτοῦ λύτρον ἀντὶ πολλῶν. In 14.12 the Passover is specifically associated with sacrifice (ἔθυον). Jesus then links elements in the Passover meal with his body and blood 'that is poured out for many', again language that may reflect sacrifice. The conclusion is hard to avoid that Jesus in the Markan narrative wants his followers to interpret his coming death typologically with reference to the annual Passover sacrifice. If this is a correct conclusion, then Israel's Exodus story must be considered a template for understanding Jesus' mission. What is it that the author desires us to discern by this intertextual linkage in his narrative?

Jesus also in the narrative links the concept of covenant with his own death. As we have already seen, in Mk 14.24 Jesus regards his blood as the basis of a covenant (τοῦτό ἐστιν τὸ αἷμά μου τῆς διαθήκης τὸ ἐκχυννόμενον ὑπὲρ πολλῶν).[29] Of course, the concept of covenant was central to Israel's understanding of its relationship with God. Exodus recounts how God makes his covenant with Israel at Mount Sinai (Exodus 19–24). As Moses leads Israel to accept God's conditions for this relationship, he 'sacrificed young bulls as peace offerings to the Lord' (LXX Exodus 24.5). It is the blood of these sacrificed bulls that formed τὸ αἷμα τῆς διαθήκης, ἧς διέθετο κύριος πρὸς ὑμᾶς ('the blood of the covenant which the Lord has made with you') and Moses scattered the blood over the people. In a typologically similar way the Markan author suggests that the outpouring of Jesus' blood in his anticipated death created a covenant.

The Gospels of Matthew and Luke also use the participle (ἐκχυννόμενον) to describe what happens to the blood of Jesus in this covenant making. However, it is not the verb that the translator chooses in LXX Exod. 24.8 (τὸ αἷμα κατεσκέδασεν τοῦ λαοῦ—'scattered the blood over the people').[30] So why does Jesus in Mark's narrative choose this term? The verb does find use in one context of LXX Exodus where sacrificial blood is poured out and used in the consecration of the priests.[31] However, the Hebrew verb in this setting is different from that used

---

29. This is the only context in Mark's narrative where the term διαθήκη occurs. The expression 'the blood of covenant' also occurs in LXX Zech. 9.11 (καὶ σὺ ἐν αἵματι διαθήκης ἐξαπέστειλας δεσμίους σου).

30. The Hebrew narrative uses the expression זרק על המזבח ('dashed against the altar', NRSV) in Exod. 24.6 (LXX = προσέχεεν πρὸς τὸ θυσιαστήριον) and ויזרק על העם ('and dashed [it] on the people', NRSV) in Exod. 24.8 (LXX = κατεσκέδασεν τοῦ λαοῦ). The variation in translation equivalent by the Septuagint translator for the same Hebrew construction (presuming this translator had the same Hebrew text as we do), is not unusual for this translator, but does create, probably, an intended difference in meaning. Did the Markan author know the Hebrew text of Exodus and did he choose ἐκχύνω as a more suitable equivalent for the verb זרק in this statement by Jesus? If the Markan author has embedding traditional material in his narrative here, did Jesus himself generate this new interpretation of the Hebrew text or is this rendering generated through some other means?

31. In LXX Exod. 29.12 God gives Moses instructions for the consecration of Aaron and his sons to the priesthood. This includes sacrificing a bull: τὸ δὲ λοιπὸν πᾶν αἷμα ἐκχεεῖς παρὰ τὴν βάσιν τοῦ θυσιαστηρίου ('Then all the remaining blood you shall pour beside the base of the altar'). When Moses has the bronze laver made, he is to 'pour water into it' (30.18).

in Exod. 24.8.[32] We also find this Greek verb used to describe violent death, often of innocent victims.[33] In Matthew's Gospel Jesus warns the Jewish religious leaders: ὅπως ἔλθῃ ἐφ' ὑμᾶς πᾶν αἷμα δίκαιον ἐκχυννόμενον ἐπὶ τῆς γῆς ἀπὸ τοῦ αἵματος Ἄβελ τοῦ δικαίου ἕως τοῦ αἵματος Ζαχαρίου υἱοῦ Βαραχίου, ὃν ἐφονεύσατε... (23.35). Because they and their ancestors have killed innocent people, God will hold them accountable. Jesus' phrase in Mk 14.24 'my blood of the covenant' probably reflects Moses' action in Exod. 24.8 for reasons already specified. While this Gospel does not use the precise words from the Exodus narrative, the 'outpouring' of Jesus' own blood that is announced in the Markan narrative carries sacrificial overtones. However, it is also possible that simultaneously Jesus wants to reflect that his death will be violent and criminal, just like the death of other prophets in Israel's history. This nuance would not come from the Exodus material.[34] However, by this change in terminology perhaps the Markan author seeks to show how the establishment of this new covenant is different, though similar, to the first covenant. The involvement of the Messiah's violent death in this covenant making process underscores the seriousness of God's commitment to this new kingdom activity.

To this point we have observed the Markan author uses the Exodus material variously. The author begins the story by comparing God's action in providing a divine messenger to lead and protect Israel on its journey to Canaan, with God's action in sending John the Baptist as a messenger to prepare the way for Jesus Messiah and his new vision for God's people. This comparison invites the reader to set the entire story of Jesus that will unfold, in the referential context of the original Exodus narrative, but also in terms of its prophesied renewal in Isaiah. In addition we have found specific Exodus quotations employed by the key protagonist, Jesus, to critique the religious understanding and practices of two significant Jewish religious groups – Pharisees and Sadducees. In such conflicts Jesus critiques their interpretation and use of these sacred texts that define key elements of Second Temple Judaism and offers his own, authoritative, alternative meaning and application. In his response to the rich man, Jesus also uses a summary of the commands in Exodus 20 as a definition of Judaism and suggests that it is insufficient as a means to secure eternal life. Finally, through terminology chosen in Jesus' address to his followers at the Passover meal, the author again invites his reader to reflect upon the meaning of Jesus' death in the light of God's intentions in the original Exodus story when he constituted his people Israel.

Can we affirm then that this is in fact the author's intention – to encourage his readers to reflect upon Jesus' story in the light of the original Exodus story, that is the birth of Israel as God's specific people (and its recapitulation in the Isaianic prophetic material)? Both the author and his primary character draw our attention

---

32. The usual rendering of the verb זרק in LXX Exodus is προσχέειν (cf. 29.16 where Moses again pours the blood of a ram against the altar).

33. Ps. 105.38 (106.38) has ἐξέχεαν αἷμα ἀθῷον; and Jer. 7.6; 22.3 has αἷμα ἀθῷον μὴ ἐκχέητε.

34. Some would also discern in this language, particularly with the additional phrase ὑπέρ πολλῶν an allusion to Isa. 53.12 and a linkage with the suffering servant motif.

to Exodus parallels. Further, this occurs at the very beginning of the story (1.2) and just prior to the climactic event in the story – the death of Jesus (14.24). In between, Jesus challenges contemporary Jewish understanding of the founding principles that shaped Israel's identity – Sabbath keeping, cleanliness regulations, and God's covenant relationship with his people – based upon his interpretation of Exodus materials.

Is there further evidence that the Exodus narrative is used by the Markan author intentionally to inform our understanding of Jesus' mission? If so, what precisely does the author want the reader to discern through this comparison? What is the rhetorical agenda?

Perhaps further insight into these questions can be discerned by examining two additional categories of potential commonality between the Markan and Exodus narratives, namely similar motifs, and similar issues. By motifs I mean metaphors, geographical place, and characterization that are defined through similar terminology and used with literary intent in each narrative. For example, the episodic plague stories (Exodus 5–12) and divine interventions to assist Israel with food and water (Exodus 13–18) parallel in form and function many of the miracle and exorcism stories in Mark's narrative as demonstratations of God's kingly rule. The concept of God's σωτηρία (Exod. 14.13) expressed in the events of the Exodus generally coheres with Jesus' announcement of God's new kingdom activity and the salvific events integrated with his mission.[35] The revelations of God to Jesus at his baptism and transfiguration share similarities with God's self-revelations to Moses. In Exodus Moses' authority is a pivotal issue, just as the issue of Jesus' authority occupies a central place in Mark's Gospel.[36] God's primary work in Exodus is the formation of Israel as his special people. Similarly the Second Gospel enables the reader to discern how Jesus as Son of God forms the new family of God through his own life, death and resurrection. Did the author of Mark purposefully intend, indeed expect his early Christian audience to make these connections?

In terms of common motifs, Markan scholars such as Watts, Marcus, and Swartley previously have identified the following:

1. *Journey motif*: In Exodus, Israel journeys from Egypt into the wilderness and encamps at Sinai. In Mark Jesus journeys with his followers throughout Galilee and eventually goes to Jerusalem. A journey forms the backbone of the narrative structure in both cases. The use of ὁδός, especially in Mark 8–10, reflects the initial occurrences in the citations

---

35. Stegner ('Jesus' Walking on the Water: Mark 6.45–52', pp. 212–34) argues that the language found in Mk 6.45–52 deliberately incorporates key terminology used in Exodus 14 to describe the Exodus. I think his hypothesis in part depends upon how convincing one considers the proposed verbal connections. In the Markan narrative Jesus rescues the Twelve by walking to them on the sea. Certainly the element of rescue is common to both narratives and in this sense there are parallels. Whether the narrative shape of LXX Exodus 14 actually influenced the formulation of Mk 6.45–52 is more difficult to prove.

36. By issues I mean the common, key questions that each narrative seeks to address, such as the way God's people is constituted.

from Exodus and Isaiah in Mk 1.2–3. 'The way' in Exodus involves God's rescue of Israel out of Egypt, his personal guidance of them to Mt Sinai, as well as provision of his messenger to direct them to Canaan. In Isaiah 'the way' encompasses Israel's return from exile and her reconstitution in Palestine as God's people. 'The way' of Jesus, however, is radically different. He models the way his followers will go – through suffering to glory. Some consider this motif to be the primary paradigm that shapes the Markan understanding of Christology and discipleship.[37]

2. *Wilderness motif.*[38] In Exodus the locus of Israel's experience and journey is Egypt, the wilderness and Mt Sinai. The locus of Jesus' ministry vacillates between the villages and cities of Galilee and Jerusalem, and the uninhabited or wilderness areas of Galilee. John's ministry is located in 'the wilderness'. Although the wilderness is not the permanent locus of Jesus, the miracles in which he feeds large numbers of people 'in the wilderness' form significant parallels in this respect.

3. *Temptation or testing motif*: Several times in the Exodus narrative Israel tempts God and God tests Israel. In Mark, Jesus and his followers are tempted by Satan, sometimes through human agents. In specific contexts the author comments that characters in the story are motivated to 'test' Jesus (Pharisees in 8.11; Pharisees and Herodians in 12.13–17). Jesus is tested in Gethsemane, but the Markan author does not make explicit the source of this test. Conversely, sometimes it seems that elements of Jesus' teaching are intended to be 'tests' (e.g. the discussion of parables in Mk 4.10–12). Diverse groups or characters are tested or tempted in the Markan narrative.

4. *Plagues/miracles*: The power of God becomes evident in the Exodus narrative through the plagues brought against Pharaoh and the Egyptians, so that they will know the true God. He also performs various miracles for Israel to protect them (e.g. crossing the Red Sea), to nurture them (e.g. provision of food and water), and to guide them (e.g. validation of Moses as leader, pillar of fire and cloud). In the case of Mark's narrative Jesus directly heals, exorcizes, raises the dead, and feeds the multitudes. By these means he demonstrates that he is Israel's true shepherd possessing divine authority and urges Israel to follow him. Jesus' authority in these matters is in contrast with Moses who cannot initiate such miracles. The resurrection of Jesus at the conclusion of the Markan narrative presents a miracle of a different order and represents a major distinction

37. Cf. Swartley, *Israel's Scripture Traditions and the Synoptic Gospels*, pp. 98–115 and Marcus, *The Way of the Lord*, pp. 29–47.

38. Ulrich Mauser in *Christ in the Wilderness: The Wilderness Theme in the Second Gospel and its Basis in the Biblical Tradition* (Naperville, ID: Alec R. Allenson, 1963), p. 14, affirms that 'whenever the wilderness is mentioned, the thought of the New Testament writer is not directed to the geographical disposition of the country, but to the memory of the basic action of God which took place in the wilderness in the course of Israel's history'.

between Moses who died and was buried secretly by God and Jesus whom God resurrects.

5. *Self-revelation of God*: In Exodus, God appears to Moses in the burning bush, as well as at other times. He also reveals himself to the Israelite elders on Mount Sinai. In the Markan narrative God reveals himself directly to Jesus at his baptism, as well as to some of his followers on the Mount of Transfiguration.[39] In each narrative God vindicates the authority of his representatives, be it Moses or Jesus.[40] Perhaps, as Stegner suggests, God's revelation at the Exodus parallels, if not shapes, the account of Jesus' rescue of the Twelve in Mk 6.45ff.[41]

6. *Tabernacle/temple*: The latter part of the Exodus narrative focuses upon the construction of the tabernacle as the focus for Israel's covenant relationship with God – the tent of witness. In Mark 11–15, the temple in Jerusalem is a primary space in which the story takes place and a key focus in Jesus' teaching. However, in contrast with the Exodus construction of the tabernacle, Jesus prophesies the temple's destruction[42] and Jesus and the new people he is constituting will form a new temple not made with hands.

7. *Hardness of heart*: This motif could also be linked with the blindness motif in Mark's narrative. In Exodus, it is initially Pharaoh and the Egyptian leadership that demonstrate incredible stubbornness in their refusal to acknowledge God and accede to his demand to let Israel go. However, we find the concept transferred to Israel as they rebel against God in episodes such as the Golden Calf. In the Markan narrative hardheartedness exhibited by the Jewish religious leaders in their rejection of Jesus is emphasized. Jesus also warns his followers against spiritual stubbornness in relationship to their perception of the kind of Messiah he should be. The centrality of this motif in the Markan narrative and its terminology is unique within the Synoptic Gospels.[43]

---

39. Swartley, *Israel's Scripture Traditions and the Synoptic Gospels*, p. 103, provides a list of similarities that suggest some connection is intended to be made between Moses at Sinai and Jesus at the Mount of Transfiguration.

40. Some consider the exorcism following Jesus' Transfiguration to be an intentional parallel to the Golden Calf episode (Exodus 32–34). However, there seems to be little explicit material in Mark's narrative that would suggest this. Cf. Swartley, *Israel's Scripture Traditions and the Synoptic Gospels*, pp. 103–104.

41. Stegner, 'Jesus' Walking on the Water: Mark 6.45–52', pp. 212–34.

42. There is dispute as to whether Jesus taught that the temple was to be destroyed and replaced, rather than rebuilt or merely purified. In my opinion the intercalation of Jesus' action in the temple with the cursing of the fig tree, Jesus' quote from Jeremiah 7, the implications of the Tenant Farmers Parable (Mark 12) and the prophecies in Mk 13.1–5, indicate the temple's destruction and replacement with something quite different. Cf. Craig A. Evans, 'Jesus' Action in the Temple: Cleansing or Portent of Destruction?', *CBQ* 51 (1989), pp. 237–70.

43. Watts (*Isaiah's New Exodus and Mark*, chs. 7–8) shows how Isaiah's description of Israel's blindness and deafness is used by the Markan author (i.e. Mk 4.10–12; 8.14ff.) to explain the failure of Israel's leaders to respond to Jesus and the struggle the disciples have in understanding Jesus.

Sometimes in reference to these motifs the Markan author will use the same terminology that is found in LXX Exodus. At other times he will employ different terms, but the concept conveyed is the same. This list of motifs is not intended to be exhaustive, but rather suggestive of the extent to which the two narratives incorporate similar motifs. It seems that the extent of this is too great to suppose it is a literary coincidence or without rhetorical significance.

It is also the case that the primary character in each narrative shares a similar calling, role, and experiences. Moses' call to lead Israel has extraordinary features as he wrestles with God at the burning bush. Jesus' call is wrapped into the prophetic word of John the Baptist and his baptism in the Jordan River, as God announces his role and status as 'My beloved son in whom I am pleased'. We discern no reticence on Jesus' part, however, in assuming his vocation. Both Moses and Jesus function as prophets in their respective contexts. Jesus, how-ever, is never formally identified as a new Moses in Mark's narrative. Their pro-phetic office allows them to speak authoritatively for God and thus provide direc-tion for their followers. They bring God's word to the people with the expectation that Israel will honour and respond to this word. Mountains figure prominently in both instances (Sinai, Transfiguration) as places for significant revelation to these leaders. The conversation that Jesus has with Elijah and Moses (Mark 9) links their prophetic roles in some continuity.

Each divine representative experiences opposition to his leadership from his own people. For Moses the accusation is that he has led Israel into the desert to kill them through starvation, thirst, or some other means. In Jesus' case the rejec-tion is more substantial in that the religious leaders never admit that he is God's Messiah and therefore entirely reject him and his mission. Both are willing to give their lives for the survival of their people.

Finally, both characters exhibit divine power in accomplishing extraordinary acts. In the case of Moses sometimes these are acts of judgment (i.e. plagues) and sometimes acts of salvation (i.e. providing water from the rock, walking on dry land through the midst of the sea), but he is totally dependent upon God's initiative in each situation. Jesus does miracles that result in the healing and restoration of people and he has authority to initiate them. Only one is a curse, namely the with-ering of the fig tree, which the Markan author deliberately uses to symbolize the imminent, but future destruction of the Jerusalem temple.

But perhaps more significantly it is the role of Moses and Jesus as builders of God's people that brings them most closely together. In their respective narratives each functions to bring shape and definition to God's people through their personal leadership, courage, and piety. They bring God's authoritative word to bear on this huge task at great personal cost. In the Exodus narrative God's people are portrayed in widely contrasting terms. At times they are faithful, courageous, thankful followers of the God. At other times they are distrustful, fearful, and disobedient, willing to return to Egypt with all of its difficulties rather than

---

These linkages are no doubt present. However, it is also the case that the hardening of Pharaoh and Israel in the Exodus narrative provides another context as background for this motif in Mark's Gospel.

follow Moses, Yahweh's designated leader. They agree to the conditions God sets down for their covenantal relationship with him, but promptly seem to forget its essential character in the Golden Calf episode. At times God would rather destroy them and begin his program all over again with Moses as the starting point. Israel certainly struggles to grasp God's intention for them and equally struggles to fulfill what they do understand. Perhaps Moses' call to Israel in Exod. 32.16 'Who is on the Lord's side?' expresses the key challenge to Israel to express its faith in God.

As the Markan narrative unfolds, we find two segments within Israel – the religious leaders who regard themselves as the protectors and promoters of the Jewish heritage and the followers of Jesus who regard him as the true fulfillment of Judaism's fundamental dreams. Again the challenge issued is clear – who truly thinks the things of God (Mk 8.33)? If Jesus indeed reveals and embodies God's purposes (in ways that surpass Moses), then what are the implications for that part of Israel that seeks his death as a blasphemer? But for those who follow Jesus the way remains confused and uncertain, as well as their response to it. The motif of unbelief seems to gather intensity in the narrative as Jesus makes his mission more and more clear and it becomes less and less compatible with traditional Jewish messianic expectations, even to the point of the destruction of the very essence of Judaism, namely the temple and Jerusalem. Belief[44] and unbelief, hardness of heart and repentance, blindness and understanding, are all polarities that typify the responses to Jesus in Mark's narrative.

This leads us naturally to consider the theological issues raised by these two narratives. In the Markan narrative the primary issue, building on the blended citation in 1.2–3, gains definition in Jesus' inaugural message: 'The time stands fulfilled and the kingdom of God stands near. Repent and put trust in the good news' (1.15). When God addresses Moses at the burning bush, he says that,

> I have surely seen the affliction of My people who are in Egypt and have given heed to their cry because of their taskmaster, for I am aware of their sufferings. So I have come down to deliver them from the power of the Egyptians and to bring them up from that land to a good and spacious land, to a land flowing with milk and honey… Therefore, come now and I will send you to Pharaoh, so that you may bring my people, the sons of Israel, out of Egypt (Exod. 3.7–8, 10).

In both of these texts we discern God's decision to act on behalf of his people, a willingness to exercise his divine power to enable this, and a strong intent to form his people for future mission.[45] It is the formation of God's people as the

---

44. The verb πιστεύω occurs in LXX Exodus primarily in chapter 4 and once each in chapter 14 and 19. Apart from the usage in 4.31, the construction is πιστεύω + dative (personal pronoun). The concern primarily is for the people of Israel to have confidence in Moses, that in fact he is God's representative. Πίστις does not occur in LXX Exodus. In Mark's narrative the verb normally has no expressed object and so the reader has to supply the object of trust. The exceptions to this are 1.15 (ἐν τῷ εὐαγγελίῳ), 9.42 (εἰς ἐμέ – Jesus) and 11.31 (αὐτῷ – John the Baptist). In the longer ending, twice the simple dative completes the verb (16.13, 14).

45. Israel in Exodus is identified by God as 'my son, my firstborn' (Exod. 4.22). Jesus in Mark's narrative is identified by God as 'my beloved son in whom I am pleased' (Mk 1.11). So while there

expression of God's kingly rule that forms the heart and core of each narrative. Yet, in the case of the Markan narrative the role of Jesus in the re-constitution of God's people is quite different from that of Moses in the Exodus narrative. The death and resurrection of Jesus is a necessary part of the new covenant. A totally new part of the messianic construct is its two-stages – the incarnation and the parousia. As well, the nature of God's people changes fundamentally as they live in between these two stages of the messianic program. God purposefully includes Gentiles in this new configuration on equal terms with ethnic Jews. Although the Exodus material does envision that occasionally a Gentile will seek to align himself with Israel and be circumcised, this is not the primary intent for Israel's formation. Finally, the association of God's people with a specific place, that is, the Promised land or Mount Zion/Jerusalem, no longer is critical. Rather, as Jesus prophesies to his followers 'it is necessary for the gospel first to be proclaimed to all the nations' (13.10) and Jerusalem and the temple will be destroyed. Jesus' mission comprehends the entire world without specific localization. Those who follow Jesus find their inheritance defined as 'eternal life'.[46] 'New wine requires new wineskins.'

Some would suggest that the Markan narrative is in essence a midrash on the Exodus story. However, it is difficult to sustain this argument because the integration of the two narratives does not seem to be sufficiently detailed and deliberate to warrant such a conclusion. While there are many conceptual linkages, we cannot determine whether the Markan author deliberately structured his narrative literarily according to the Exodus narrative pattern. Nor does the pesher style of Old Testament citation and interpretation characterize this Gospel's narrative as the means of revealing the contemporary significance of the Exodus materials.[47] Nor is there any allegorizing tendency in the Markan materials with respect to the Exodus stories. Yet the Markan narrative in various ways indicates that Jesus' mission fulfills God's plan as outlined in the Old Testament. His mission is 'in accordance with' (κατά) God's prior revelation.[48]

are many similarities between the chief characters in these two narratives, there is also this fundamental difference. Jesus is God's son in a way that Moses never was. However, in the Golden Calf episode God does consider destroying Israel entirely and making from Moses 'a great nation' (Exod. 32.10), an option Moses pleads successfully with God to reject. In Jesus' case it is his sacrificial death and resurrection that will form the basis for a newly re-constituted people of God that incorporates Jew and Gentile.

46. Jesus tells Peter that his followers will receive 'in the age to come life eternal' (10.30). This comes at the conclusion of the story in which the rich man questions Jesus about 'inheriting eternal life' (10.17).

47. Kee ('The Function of Scriptural Quotations and Allusions in Mark 11–16', p. 179) conversely argues, 'the closest analogy is with the *pesher* exegesis from Qumran'. He does, however, note 'J.A. Fitzmyer is correct in distinguishing the *pesharim* which are commentaries on sequential portions of the biblical text from the use of isolated explicit quotations employed for interpretive purposes'. For Kee, 'it is not the form but the intention of the *pesher* method which concerns us, however'. While there are similarities of 'intention', we do not find in the Markan narrative with respect to Exodus materials the normal formulas associated with *pesher* exegesis in the Qumran materials nor commentary upon extended portions of the Exodus narrative.

48. Mk 1.2–3.

The narratological use of the Exodus materials in Mark's Gospel is intended both to compare and contrast the significance of these events in Israel's history with God's new work initiated in Jesus. Some things have not changed. Israel in Exodus and Israel in Mark demonstrate hard-heartedness in their response to God's revelations expressed through his chosen leaders. The challenge of faith emerges in both narratives. The ways of God in Exodus and Mark appear strange and confusing. In Exodus and in Mark God establishes new covenantal ways for his people to relate to him. Following God continues to be difficult and requires confidence in God's power, purpose, and goodness. John's prophecy that the 'one coming' would 'baptize in Holy Spirit' (Mk 1.8) indicates in another way the difference between the Exodus experience and the kingdom reality that Jesus promises and inaugurates.

I think it is probable that the Markan author understood the Exodus story in the light of its re-visioning in Isaiah 40.[49] However, I also think that the author considers Jesus and his good news as the true climax of Isaiah's re-visioning of the promises implicit in Israel's Exodus experience. Even in this, however, there is corrective because Israel in the first century, according to Jesus, did not comprehend the way God intended his revelation through Isaiah to be fulfilled. So the Markan story of Jesus provides for the author's readers the hermeneutical key for understanding God's ultimate purpose. This Gospel purpose has roots in the original Exodus; it has renewed emphasis in Isaiah's new exodus formulation; and it has final and clear articulation in the life and mission of Jesus. Each iteration, however, clarifies earlier components or adds new element.

The various layers of Exodus materials in Mark's narrative create complex tones. The author uses, perhaps exploits, these materials carefully, but his narrative structure is not bound by them. As with the parables Jesus tells, the author expects his audience to discern the spiritual dimensions that the Exodus quotations, allusions and motifs contribute to the Jesus story. By reflecting upon Israel's Exodus experience and Isaiah's prophecies of a new exodus in the light of Jesus' words and deeds, the Markan audience will understand more thoroughly and deeply the person and work of Jesus as Son of God, God's eschatological purposes, and within these purposes their potential role as Jesus' disciples (i.e. God's people). Jesus' message of God's kingly purpose, his authority and his intent to re-constitute God's people gains depth and perspective as the narrator sets Jesus' words and deeds in the larger frame of Israel's Exodus experience, its attendant narrative and Isaiah's reflections upon it.

---

49. Wright hypothesizes that Israel in the first century considered itself spiritually still to be in exile. He interprets Jesus' message and actions as expressed in Mark's narrative as reflecting the call to Israel to enter a new stage in God's program and resolve their spiritual exile by acclaiming Jesus as Messiah. The focus in this paper is on the Exodus materials, rather than Isaiah's prophetic application of the exodus motif to the exilic community. 'The exile is not yet really over. This perception of Israel's present condition was shared by writers across the board in second-temple Judaism' (N.T. Wright, *The New Testament and the People of God* [Minneapolis: Fortress Press, 1992], p. 269).

THE USE OF AUTHORITATIVE CITATIONS IN MARK'S GOSPEL AND ANCIENT BIOGRAPHY: A STUDY OF P.OXY. 1176

Stanley E. Porter

1. *Introduction*

Discussion continues around the topic of the genre of the Gospels, and Mark's Gospel in particular, since it is widely held that Mark's Gospel was written first and used by the other Synoptic evangelists. A good portion of this discussion contents itself simply with repeating the arguments of earlier generations or reaffirming positions already widely held, namely that Mark's Gospel (and by implication all of the Gospels)[1] is *sui generis*, the creation of a new kerygmatic literary form.[2] That this conclusion is still so glibly held is somewhat surprising, in the light of the issues raised by an apparently smaller, but still voluble, group that wishes to argue for the biographical character of the Gospels – if they are not biographies in and of themselves.[3] This is certainly not the place to engage in a full discussion of such topics – and the related secondary literature – as the issues surrounding ancient literary genres, the relation of history and biography, the question of whether any or all of the Gospels conform to such literary designations, and all of the distinguishing features that attend making such distinctions. What I wish to do here, however, is to examine the notion of the use of explicit citation and quotation within ancient biography and to compare this with the use of similar citations within Mark's Gospel. To do so requires that I first look at some basic generic distinctions from the ancients, and their suitability for application to the Gospels,

---

1.   Note that, logically, only the first Gospel can be unique, especially if there is a dependency relationship between the first and the subsequent Gospels. Therefore, if Mark's Gospel is written first, it would only be Mark's Gospel that is *sui generis*, and only for a short time. Matthew and Luke would be of the same type.

2.   As a recent proponent, see C.A. Evans, *Mark 8.26–16.20* (WBC, 34B; Nashville: Nelson, 2001), pp. lxiv–lxvii; but he does not respond to the proposal and argumentation of Burridge (see note below), even though he is mentioned in the bibliography.

3.   The distinction between 'biographical character' and 'biography' is a generic one, recognizing that biographical elements might be found in writings other than biographies. The most noteworthy of recent treatments, and one that recounts much of the pertinent literature – especially recent response to Burridge's book, in his added chapter to the revised edition – is R.A. Burridge, *What Are the Gospels? A Comparison with Graeco-Roman Biography* (Grand Rapids: Eerdmans; Dearborn, MI: Dove, 2nd edn, 2004 [1992]). He provides good bibliography regarding literary critical discussion of the concept of genre and the history of discussion of biography in the ancient world.

Mark's in particular. Then I will discuss one ancient source in particular, and compare it with examples from Mark.

2. *Ancient Literary Genres and Biography*

One of the bedeviling issues in generic discussion is the relation of modern categories of generic differentiation and ancient categories. As a result, moderns tend to differentiate history and biography as genres (while admitting that there may well be some overlap between them). The ancient Greeks, and the Romans who followed them, thought of historical writing in different terms.[4] The ancients thought of historical writing in terms of five major categories: genealogy, ethnography, history (accounts of men's [and it usually was men's] deeds or acts),[5] horography (local history), and chronography.[6] These literary genres of historical writing were all in place by the fifth century BCE. There are two observations relevant to this paper to note. The first is that there is no single category that was used to lump all of these five forms of historical writing together under one catch-all category. In that sense, there was no 'history' genre in the ancient world; although there were types of historical writing, called by various names. The second observation is that what we would call biography is not included within this set of five literary genres – even though at least one of the literary genres was concerned with the deeds or acts of men. This appears to have been a very specific type of historical writing, to be distinguished from the others, and not to be equated with biography, which was to develop independently, but with related though distinguishable emphases.[7]

---

4. My discussion here is dependent primarily upon the following: A. Momigliano, *The Development of Greek Biography* (Cambridge, MA: Harvard University Press, rev. edn, 1993), *passim*; C.W. Fornara, *The Nature of History in Ancient Greece and Rome* (Berkeley, CA: University of California Press, 1983), esp. pp. 1–46, 184–89; S. Hornblower, 'Introduction: Summary of the Papers; The Story of Greek Historiography; Intertextuality and the Greek Historians', in S. Hornblower (ed.), *Greek Historiography* (Oxford: Clarendon Press, 1994), pp. 1–72; D.S. Potter, *Literary Texts and the Roman Historian* (Approaching the Ancient World; London: Routledge, 1999), esp. pp. 9, 59–70, 144–45.

5. See Fornara, *Nature of History*, pp. 1–2, 3: Aristotle refers to history as concerned with men's acts, *praxeis* (*Rhetoric* 1.1360 A35), while Quintilian refers to 'the narration of deeds', *expositio rerum gestarum* (2.4.2), and Plutarch to 'great events and struggles' (*Alex*. 1.3). Plutarch (*Pompey* 8) also distinguishes between history depicting men's *praxeis* and biography illustrating a man's *ethos* (see P. Cox, *Biography in Late Antiquity: A Quest for the Holy Man* [Berkeley, CA: University of California Press, 1983], p. 12).

6. Here is not the place to engage in discussion over whether F. Jacoby ('Über die Entwicklung der griechischen Historiographie und der Plan einer neuen Sammlung der drieschischen Historiker-fragmente', *Klio* 9 [1909], pp. 1–44; *idem*, *Atthis: The Local Chronicles of Ancient Athens* [Oxford: Clarendon Press, 1949], where he re-iterates his defense of the priority of local history, especially regarding Athens) was correct in substituting contemporary history for history, and concluding that there was no 'history' *per se* as a genre of historical writing. Suffice it to say that recent scholarship seems to reject Jacoby on this point: Fornara, *Nature of History*, pp. 1–46, esp. pp. 2–3; Potter, *Literary Texts*, pp. 62–66.

7. It is worth noting, though only incidentally, that some of the debate about whether Luke is a

The development of biography in relation to, but independently of, history is worth recounting quickly, so as to emphasize the features that came to distinguish this literary genre in the ancient world. It was once thought that biography developed late as a literary genre, but recent scholarship places the emergence of biography in the fifth century BCE, that is, about the same time as historical writing, even though it did not really flourish until the Hellenistic period.[8] This same scholarship sees the origins of biography much earlier, quite possibly in the collecting of accounts and stories about people and in rhetoric, that is, speeches that were offered for or against a particular person.[9] Even though biography should be kept separate from biographical treatments in historical writings, it is clear that early writers such as Herodotus and Thucydides, as well as others, were interested in biographical matters. Momigliano defines a biography simply as 'An account of the life of a man from birth to death...'[10] However, he also notes that biography was not concerned with the description of an individual life simply for its own value as distinct from other individuals. Ancient biographers, he notes, were often concerned to write about men of the same 'type'.[11] The origins of biography are thus seen in what Fornara calls their 'ethical preoccupations'.[12] Fornara develops this notion further when he says that the deeds of a person were not considered of interest in themselves but as they enlightened understanding of that individual, especially that person's character. The result is that items not considered appropriate for historical writing, such that they might exemplify certain characteristics of the person, would be included in biography. The analysis of character thus explains the events in a biography. In Roman times, therefore, the discussion of the character of the ruler, the Caesar, was considered entirely appropriate, since it helped to explain the events of the most important person in the world of the time. Thus, biography was entirely appropriate to discussion of emperors and the like (as is found in Plutarch's *Lives of the Noble Greeks and Romans* or Suetonius' *Lives of the Twelve Caesars*). Noting the contradictory status of the biography within Roman literary life, Momigliano observes that during the imperial period the biography gained in prestige, so that it was 'the natural form of telling the story of a Caesar'. He also notes that biography also was a 'vehicle for unorthodox political and philosophic ideas'.[13]

As biography developed, several literary techniques became recognized as a part of the biographical approach. One of these was rhetorical elements, noted above as possibly one of the major sources of the development of biography. The

biography and Acts a history is disjunctive categorization (see Burridge, *What Are the Gospels?*, pp. 275–79), since there was no single word for historical writing among the ancient Greeks, and biography made use of so many of the features that were found in historical writing.

8.   Momigliano, *Development of Greek Biography*, p. 12. Momigliano notes that biography was not considered to be history writing by the ancients.

9.   Potter, *Literary Texts*, p. 67, who attributes this to Momigliano.

10.   Momigliano, *Development of Greek Biography*, p. 11.

11.   Momigliano, *Development of Greek Biography*, pp. 12–13.

12.   Fornara, *Nature of History*, p. 185.

13.   Momigliano, *Development of Greek Biography*, p. 99.

use of speeches was widespread in historical writing of the time (e.g. various types of speeches in a historian such as Thucydides),[14] but they were also used in biographies, in terms of the person offering speeches in one's own defense and against others.[15] A second is the genealogy. The genealogy is often thought to be one of the important precursors of biography, along with simply collecting together incidents and events related to a particular individual. The genealogy, as noted above, was one of the types of historical writing, in which emphasis was placed upon the 'family relationships of the heroes of mythical times', found for example in Homer's *Odyssey* (e.g. book 11), but brought to fruition in Hesiod's *Theogony*.[16] Genealogical elements are often found in biographies as well. A third element is the use of sources, and more particularly of direct citation or quotation. As Potter says, 'In terms of form, perhaps the most important point is that [biography] allowed for direct quotation of documents in a way that the generic rules for narrative history did not. It is not altogether clear why this should be so, but it may be that the tradition of the eyewitness memorialist influenced later practitioners in such a way that they too wished to include first-hand statements about their subject'.[17] To use the more recent language, biography, along with much historiography, availed itself of intertextuality between sources.[18] The use of these sources raises numerous questions (long well-known to biblical scholars) regarding orality and literacy, what it means to quote accurately, and how much of which sources would have been memorized and to what degree.[19]

In the light of the definition of biography in terms of the ethical implications of a study of an individual's character from birth to death, supported by rhetorical elements such as speeches, its use of genealogies, the typological nature of the character, and especially the use of direct quotation, it is not surprising that some ancient historians see the Gospels as forms of ancient biography.[20] Part of the potentially contradictory nature of the Gospels is reflected in the nature of narrative itself in the ancient world. There were the grand scale narratives, but there were also counter-narratives to the standard conception, something the biography was ideally suited to provide. As Potter says, 'Ultimately, the most powerful of these alternative narratives was that offered in the Christian gospels, and they in turn reshaped the world in which they were read'.[21] It is surprising, therefore, that there has not been a more widespread embracing of the Gospels as biography by New Testament scholars, even among those who recognize the counter-narrative nature of the Gospel accounts, going so far as to promote the

---

14. For discussion of speeches, see S.E. Porter, 'Thucydides 1.22.1 and Speeches in Acts: Is there a Thucydidean View?', *NovT* 32 (1990), pp. 121–42.

15. Potter, *Literary Texts*, p. 67.

16. Fornara, *Nature of History*, p. 4.

17. Potter, *Literary Texts*, p. 67.

18. See Hornblower, 'Introduction', p. 54–72. Cf. his comments on Acts in terms of eyewitnesses, p. 52

19. Hornblower, 'Introduction', pp. 63–64.

20. See Potter, *Literary Texts*, p. 145. However, some of his assumptions regarding the date of composition of the Gospels and the veracity of their historical content are certainly open to question.

21. Potter, *Literary Texts*, p. 9.

notion that at least Mark's Gospel was an 'apologetic that boldly challenges the emperor's claim to divinity and his demand for the absolute loyalty of his subjects'.[22] Biography was ideally suited for promoting the Caesar, so it should not be surprising that in the hands of early Christians it was ideally suited for promoting Jesus Christ instead of Caesar, as a form of counter narrative.

3. *Examples of Authoritative Citation in Mark and the Euripidean Biographer, Satyrus*

This paper, however, is in particular concerned with the use of authoritative citation within Mark's Gospel and ancient biographies. In discussing the Gospels and ancient literary practice, Potter observes the following:

> Chief among the techniques employed by the authors of the Gospels in their effort to convey an impression of authority is the use of direct quotation, which implies, as we have seen, direct access to a tradition and the use of documents. In this case, however, the documents are of a rather unusual sort: they are prophetic texts of the Jewish tradition. ...there can be little question that the word of a reliable prophet could be used to guarantee the truth value of a statement.[23]

There are several observations to make in the light of Potter's statement. The first is that some might be tempted to analyze the words of Jesus within Mark's Gospel as the kind of authoritative citation that the Gospel author has in mind. There is no doubt that the author does treat Jesus' statements as having a certain kind of authority. Instances where Jesus is cited in Mark as making a pronouncement that carries weight are numerous, and have rightly been discussed by scholars.[24] However, in terms of Mark as ancient biography and its use of authoritative citations, the kind of citations that seem most pertinent are not the statements that Jesus makes but the invoking of statements made by others held to be authoritative – here in particular Old Testament prophets – to substantiate the biographical account. The second observation concerns the role that these citations play. In ancient biographies, the authors cited others as a means of establishing the verisimilitude or veracity of an account.

There are a number of ancient biographies that could be brought into play for comparison with Mark's use of Old Testament citations.[25] Burridge discusses a number of examples, but, although he notes the use of sources in ancient biographies, he does not so far as I can tell deal in detail with the issue of authoritative

---

22. Evans, *Mark 8.27–16.20*, p. xi.

23. Potter, *Literary Texts*, p. 145.

24. The most recent major discussion of this is B. Chilton and C.A. Evans (eds), *Authenticating the Words of Jesus* (NTTS, 28.1; Leiden: Brill, 1999). I note, however, that there is no essay in that collection that addresses this issue in the terms presented above, apart from B.F. Meyer, 'How Jesus Charged Language with Meaning: A Study in Rhetoric', pp. 81–96.

25. The bibliography on Mark's use of the Old Testament is large. For a survey of recent accounts, see T.R. Hatina, *In Search of a Context: The Function of Scripture in Mark's Narrative* (JSNTSup, 232; SSEJC, 8; London: Sheffield Academic Press, 2002), pp. 8–48.

quotation.[26] There are of course the standard biographies often cited, such as those by Isocrates (*Evagoras*), Xenophon (*Agesilaus*), Cornelius Nepos (*Atticus*), Philo (*Moses*), Plutarch, Suetonius, Tacitus (*Life of Agricola*), Philostratus (*Life of Apollonius of Tyana*), Lucian (*Demonax*), and Diogenes Laertius (*Lives of the Eminent Philosophers*), among others.[27] Rarely introduced into the discussion of the Gospels are some of the fragmentary documents, such as P.Haun. 6 and P.Oxy. 1176 (an exception is Burridge).[28] P.Haun. 6 is interesting because – though highly fragmentary – it appears to be a combination of genealogies and interspersed short biographies. Though written in the second century CE, the account itself appears to date to around the third century BCE and the Ptolemaic times. Not surprisingly in the light of its condition, it is difficult to determine specifics, and there do not appear to be any determinable authoritative citations.

More useful for such discussion is P.Oxy. 1176 – although even Burridge, who treats this document, is hampered in his treatment by the fragmentary nature of the document.[29] This highly fragmentary and partial papyrus document is a life of Euripides by Satyrus, the biographer (this is identified from fr. 39 col. 23 line 1, which reads Σατύρου). In this work, of which we only have a part of the account of the life of Euripides, Satyrus wrote biographies of the three major tragedians, and this part concerning Euripides is at the end. The manuscript itself was copied in the second century CE, but reflects a text probably written in the third century BCE (or possibly the second).[30] Little is known of Satyrus, apart from his being either in the peripatetic school (Athenaeus 6.248d; 12.541c; 13.556a) or an Alexandrian,[31] and that he wrote a number of biographies that are cited by other ancient authors, such as Athenaeus and Diogenes Laertius, who refer to his works as οἱ βίοι (the editor notes that this papyrus refers, more correctly, to his βίων ἀναγραφή, 'register of lives', in fact, his sixth book, of Aeschylus, Sophocles and Euripides; fr. 39 col. 23 lines 2–5: βίων ἀναγ<ρ>αφή...Αἰσχύλου, Σοφοκλέους, Εὐριπίδου).[32] Satyrus was well known in the ancient world for having written,

---

26. Burridge, *What Are the Gospels?*, pp. 124–84, for the ten examples that he treats, and pp. 138–39, 221–22, on the use of sources.

27. Burridge, *What Are the Gospels?*, p. 285 n. 134, cites D. *Frickenschmidt, Evangelium als Biographie: Die vier Evangelien im Rahmen antiker Erzählkunst* (Tübingen: Francke Verlag, 1997), pp. 94–95 as listing 142 biographies that he uses in his study.

28. See T. Larsen (ed.), *Literarische Texte und Ptolemäische Urkunden* (Papyri Graecae Haunienses, 1; Copenhagen: Munksgaard, 1941; repr. Milan: Cisalpino-Goliardica, 1974), pp. 37–45; A.S. Hunt (ed.), *The Oxyrhynchus Papyri*, IX (London: Egypt Exploration Fund, 1912), pp. 124–82. See Momigliano, *Development of Greek Biography*, pp. 80–1, 85, 111, 115; Burridge, *What Are the Gospels?*, pp. 124–49 *passim* on P.Oxy. 1176.

29. As a result, Burridge is not able to include this document in a number of his analyses, such as content analysis, size (but cf. *What Are the Gospels?*, p. 135), structure, scale, and the like.

30. Hunt, *Oxyrhynchus Papyri*, p. 125. Cf. Momigliano, *Development of Greek Biography*, p. 111; Burridge, *What Are the Gospels?*, p. 126.

31. See Hunt, *Oxyrhynchus Papyri*, p. 125; Momigliano, *Development of Greek Biography*, pp. 80–81; S. West, 'Satyrus: Peripatetic or Alexandrian?', *GRBS* 15 (1974), pp. 279–87; Burridge, *What Are the Gospels?*, p. 126.

32. Hunt, *Oxyrhynchus Papyri*, p. 126. Hunt notes (pp. 124–25) that the scribe wrote the title of the work incorrectly.

among other things, biographies of monarchs, generals and other statesmen, orators, philosophers and poets.[33]

There are several features that distinguish this biography of Euripides and that merit its further attention for New Testament scholars. These include the fact that the biography of Euripides is written as a dialogue among three people (two of whom are named).[34] The account given is what the editor calls 'comprehensive', concerned with not only the major events in Euripides' life,[35] but with issues related to his writing of tragedy, his opinions on a range of topics, and, importantly to note, his character. The editor notes further that there does not appear to be any sign of original research by the author into Euripides' life, but that there is a large amount of use of anecdotes, not uncommon in writing of the time, as noted above, to help to reveal character.[36] As a result, some have accused Satyrus of manufacturing anecdotes on the basis of Euripides' own plays and the later response of Aristophanes, who singled out Euripides for ridicule in a number of his plays,[37] while also incorporating some of his dramatic techniques in the middle and new comedy.[38] Most importantly to note, perhaps, is the widespread use of quotations within the biography, both from Euripides and from other authors, some known and some now unknown.

In what remains of this papyrus – and as noted above, there was much more, possibly almost twice as much just for Euripides – there are a number of quotations from Euripides himself. These occur in the following places: fr. 37 col. 2 lines 19–28, a fragment from Euripides' *Pirithous* (Euripides, fr. 593); fr. 37 col. 3 lines 9–14, a fragment recorded by Clement of Alexandria (Euripides, fr. 912);[39] fr. 37 col. 3 lines 26–29, a citation of Euripides, *Troades* 886; fr. 38 col. 1 lines 16–24, a fragment recorded by Clement of Alexandria (*Stromata* 5.732; Euripides,

---

33. According to Burridge (*What Are the Gospels?*, p. 127 n. 13) these have been published in C.F. Kumaniecki (ed.), *De Satyro Peripatetico* (Polska Akademja Umiejetnosci Archiwum Filolgiczne, 8; Cracow: Getethner et Wolff, 1929).

34. The dialogue form was unusual this early, but as Momigliano shows (*Development of Greek Biography*, pp. 80, 115), does not compromise its being a biography – the dialogical form being taken up later by a number of authors (e.g. Sulpicius Severus, Palladius, Gregory the Great).

35. There are even some new events in Euripides's life included here, such as his being charged by Cleon with impiety (fr. 39 col. 10 lines 15–20).

36. Hunt, *Oxyrhynchus Papyri*, p. 127. Cf. Burridge, *What Are the Gospels?*, p. 138.

37. G. Murray (*Euripides and his Age* [London: Thornton Butterworth, 1913], pp. 23–27) notes that Satyrus shows 'a surprising indifference to historical fact' (p. 24). He notes that 'Euripides was, more than any other figure in ancient history, a constant butt for the attacks of comedy...most of the anecdotes about Euripides in Satyrus are simply the jokes of comedy treated as historical fact' (pp. 24–25; see also H.C. Baldry, *The Greek Tragic Theatre* [London: Chatto & Windus, rev. edn, 1981], *passim*). Murray cites as an example the story of the women attacking Euripides found in Aristophanes, *Thesmophorae* 374–75, 335–37, which is cited by Satyrus as apparently factual (fr. 39 col. 12 ll. 1–16; see below). Cf. also A. Lesky, *Greek Tragic Poetry* (trans. M. Dillon; New Haven, CT: Yale University Press, 1983 [1972]), p. 197, who notes that 'only two centuries separate Satyros from Euripides!' The reason that this carelessness is perhaps surprising to Murray is that it was not the norm in biographical research. See Cox, *Biography in Late Antiquity*, p. 6.

38. See D.W. Lucas, 'Euripides', in *OCD* (2nd edn), pp. 418–21, here p. 421.

39. Hunt (*Oxyrhynchus Papyri*, p. 172) does not give the specific reference in Clement.

fr. 913); fr. 38 col. 2 lines 14–29, a fragment recorded by Plutarch (*De aud. poet.* 14.36c; Euripides, fr. 960) in condensed form but here in expanded form; fr. 39 col. 4 lines 33–39, a previously unknown citation from Euripides; fr. 39 col. 6 lines 1–15, apparently a quotation from Euripides of an otherwise unknown passage; fr. 39 col. 11 lines 1–37, the entire column as extant, a fragment from Euripides' *Melannipe Desmotis*;[40] fr. 39 col. 17 lines 1–7, a fragment recorded by Stobaeus (*Florilegium* 38.8) from the *Ion* (Euripides, fr. 403.3–4); fr. 39 col. 17 lines 30–39, a fragment recorded by Clement of Alexandra (*Stromata* 4.642) from an unknown play; and fr. 39 col. 18 lines 7–8, a fragment also found in Clement.[41] What distinguishes each of these quotations is that they are apparently recognized by the author, Satyrus, as authoritative by virtue of their being from Euripides, and presented as such with no indication of doubt as to provenance or authenticity. In fact, in none of them is the author, Euripides, cited as the author, but they are simply cited (so far as this can be determined in a fragmentary text that sometimes does not have the introductory material), even though in some of the later authors Euripides is credited with the statement (e.g. fr. 38 col. 1 lines 16–24; fr. 38 col. 2 lines 14–29; and possibly others). Much more could be said about how this usage is similar to the way that Mark's Gospel presents the sayings of Jesus. Even though they are introduced as by Jesus, they are recorded as carrying an inherent authority by virtue of their being uttered by Jesus. However, this is not the areas that I wish to concentrate on in this paper.

More important for this paper is the fact there are also a number of citations by Satyrus from other authors. The major author cited is Euripides' nemesis but also promoter Aristophanes. However, there are others who are cited as well. They are worth examining in more detail, both to appreciate how these citations are utilized within Satyrus' biography itself and to note how these citations of authoritative sources are related to the use of sources in Mark's Gospel. I will take the quotations in the order of the narrative, although the fragmentary nature of the manuscript does not lend itself to the kind of broad contextual study that one would desire.[42] Along the way, I will draw attention to features that are paralleled in Mark's authoritative citation of Scriptures.[43] We unfortunately do not have at the outset of Satyrus' work anything like the authoritative initial citation of Mal. 3.1 and Isa. 40.3 (and possibly Exod. 23.20; see below) at the beginning of Mark's

---

40. The text of the play, as reconstructed and also found in a Berlin papyrus (P.Berol. 9772), is found in A.S. Hunt, *Fragmenta Tragica Papyracea* (Oxford: Clarendon Press, 1912), p. viii for introduction, and then the play; D.L. Page, *Select Papyri*. III. *Literary (Poetry)* (Cambridge, MA: Harvard University Press, 1941), 13, pp. 108–17. Cf. W. Schubart and U. Wilamowitz-Möllendorff, *Berliner Klassikertexte* II (Berlin: Weidmannsche, 1907), p. 125; A.W. Pickard-Cambridge, 'Tragedy', in J.U. Powell (ed.), *New Chapters in the History of Greek Literature*, Third Series (Oxford: Clarendon Press, 1933), pp. 68–155, here pp. 118–19.

41. Hunt (*Oxyrhynchus Papyri*, p. 180) does not give the specific reference.

42. I acknowledge use of the translation by Hunt, but have slightly modified it at some places.

43. I include the following in discussion, based upon the list provided in the *UBSGNT* 3rd edn: Mk 1.2–3; 4.12; 7.6–7, 10; 10.6–8, 19; 11.9–10, 17; 12.10–11, 19, 26, 29–30, 31, 36; 13.26; 14.27, 62; 15.34. There is dispute about a number of issues concerning the text cited, but these issues will only be raised incidentally as they are important for the topic of this paper.

Gospel, since we do not have the opening of the biography. Instead, I will examine instances where citation is made within the course of the developing biographical narrative.

Fr. 8 col. 2 lines 1–27: Euripides[44] '...in emulation of the beauties of Ion developed and perfected [tragedy] so as to leave no room for improvement to his successors. Such were the man's artistic qualities. Hence Aristophanes wishes to measure his tongue "By which such fine expressions were expunged".[45] And he was almost as great of soul also as in his poetry. For he contended, as we have said...'[46] This is the first fragment that is large enough to establish a significant portion of continuous text. The passage indicates that Satyrus is evaluating the artistic qualities of Euripides, and invokes an unknown statement by Aristophanes in support of this claim. In its style of attribution, this citation of Aristophanes is perhaps closest to only a few named citations in Mark's Gospel. Besides Mk 1.2–3, attributed to Isaiah the prophet (a fuller description of the speaker than is offered for Aristophanes), the only other citations that mention the specific personal source are: Mk 7.6–7, where the passage is attributed to Isaiah (Isa. 29.13); Mk 7.10, where the passage is attributed to Moses (Exod. 20.12; Deut. 5.16; Exod. 21.17); Mk 12.19, where it is attributed to Moses having written (Deut. 25.5; cf. Gen. 38.8); and Mk 12.36, where it is attributed to David (Ps. 110.1). This constitutes five of the eighteen direct citations in Mark's Gospel. In the same way that Satyrus can cite Aristophanes by name here, so can Mark single out the author of the statement. Similarly, just as we do not have attestation of this citation from Aristophanes, there is some textual novelty to be associated with several of these citations from Mark. For example, both the way in which the citation is made and the exact nature of the text cited in Mk 1.2–3 is still highly disputed, with numerous proposals being made (e.g. the use testimonia or ordering according to priority). None has commanded universal assent as a way of explaining how the quotation can be attributed to Isaiah but still begin with and consist of at least Mal. 3.1 and possibly Exod. 23.20.[47] For Satyrus, we presume that we have simply lost the original that he is citing, but there may be other explanations that reflect similar citation technique as found in Mark's Gospel. The author might be paraphrasing though claiming to quote, there may be a body of common material attributed to an author or authors that is drawn upon, or there may be other textual traditions now unknown to us. In any event, Satyrus's citation of Aristophanes is roughly paralleled in Markan citation technique.

Fr. 39 col. 2 lines 7–27: '...in the following way: "(A) When this is done in secret, whom dost thou fear? (B) The gods, who see more than men." Such a conception of the gods will be Socratic; for in truth what is invisible to mortals is to

---

44. The editor presumes that Euripides is the subject, since the fragment begins in the middle of the episode. This appears to be the case in the light of its continuation with Aristophanes being cited.

45. Hunt (*Oxyrhynchus Papyri*, p. 171) notes that the reconstruction of the citation is problematic, especially for the word translated 'fine' (λεπτά).

46. Hunt, *Oxyrhynchus Papyri*, p. 171.

47. See Hatina, *In Search of a Context*, pp. 139–53, esp. pp. 142–43. See also his treatment of Mk 7.6–7 on pp. 240–44.

the immortal gods easily seen. Moreover, the hatred of tyranny and the [condemnation of] democracies and oligarchies…' This citation is not otherwise known, according to the editor. The wording preceding the quotation does not give any indication that it is from Euripides, and while this is possible in the light of attributing such a conception to Socratic thought, it appears to function in the biography by defending Euripides rather than being his pronouncement. Noteworthy in this particular quotation is its use of the dialogue format between speakers A and B, consistent with the dialogue structure that is used throughout the biography. The ideas, but also the format, are Socratic in nature. In several places in Mark's Gospel, the use of authoritative citation is introduced in a dialogical format. The closest parallel to Satyrus's use is perhaps Mk 12.19 and 26, where Sadducees come to Jesus and they note that Moses wrote certain things (Deut. 25.5), and then they pose a question on the basis of this quotation. Jesus then answers them, including within his answer a citation from Exod. 3.6, 15–16. The citation in Satyrus is also not attributed except to say that it is Socratic in nature. This is similar to the 'informal'[48] style that Mark often uses, in which he does not specify a source. This type of citation is found in Mk 4.12, where Jesus cites Isa. 6.9–10; Mk 10.6–8, where Jesus, referring to God but not attributing the quotation to him, cites Gen. 1.27; 5.2; 2.24; Mk 13.26, where Jesus cites Dan. 7.13;[49] and Mk 14.62, where Jesus cites Ps. 110.1 and Dan. 7.13. The example of the crowd calling out to Jesus using Scripture (Mk 11.9–10, citing Ps. 118.25–26) could also be cited since the use is not labeled in the Gospel narrative as citation per se, but their conscious shouting draws attention to the passage in a way that is not done elsewhere. Satyrus' use of the quotation as an apparent means of reinforcing the Socratic viewpoint of Euripides[50] has the most similarities to how quotation is used in Mark by those in dialogue who are trying to create and defend arguments (e.g. Mk 12.19, 26). In this sense, Satyrus and Mark both exemplify the common appeal to authority by those involved in defending arguments.

Fr. 39 col. 4 lines 1–38: A comic poet is recorded as saying '"…not in this wise, but we are not also guilty of baseness when we put full trust in somebody whatever he says, speaking not what is base but having recourse to what is weak, and then each one accuses the assembly of which he was a member". (Diodorus) The comic poets, it seems, have said much both with severity and like statesmen. (A) Yes, of course. Euripides again admirably incites the youths to valour and courage, urging Spartan efforts upon them and emboldening the people thus: "Gain glory in the time to come by performing every day a labour…"' This example of the dialogical style of Satyrus incorporates both a quotation from Euripides (see above) and a citation from a comic poet. Neither the poet nor the passage from him are known elsewhere. However, there is an instructive interaction here between the use of the citation from the poet and the citation from Euripides. The citation from the poet is apparently designed to justify the behavior

---

48. The wording is Hatina's (*In Search of a Context*, p. 240), when he characterizes Mark's citing of Scripture.

49. It is noteworthy that, for example, the Holman Bible does not consider this a citation.

50. See Lucas, 'Euripides', p. 418.

of the people when they are misguided by demagogues. As Hunt paraphrases, 'we are weak, he says, but not base'. In response to the approval given to this statement by Diodorus, the other speaker agrees and cites a passage from Euripides that supports but actually moves beyond the original citation by not just excusing but commending behavior by the people. This usage is somewhat similar to the layered quotation pattern found in Mark in several places. For example, in Mark 7, Jesus first cites a passage from Isaiah (Mk 7.6–7; 29.13), points out the short-comings of the Pharisees to whom he is speaking, and then adds another citation from Moses (Mk 7.10; Exod. 20.12; Deut. 5.16; Exod. 21.17). The example of Mark 12 (discussed above) is also similar, when the Sadducees cite the passage from Moses (Mk 12.19; Gen. 38.8; Deut. 25.5) and Jesus answers, and in the course of doing so he cites a further passage from Moses (Mk 12.26; Exod. 3.6, 15–16). The citation after the fact by Diodorus of the comic poet is not found in Mark's Gospel, except possibly in Mk 15.34, where Jesus on the cross calls out (Ps. 22.1), and some of those standing nearby identify him, incorrectly it turns out, as calling out to Elijah.

    Fr. 39 col. 5 lines 12–27: 'The oboe-playing girls smile at you at the street corners. You ask who the *astynomi* are: you mean the men who clip the wings of liberty. If a man gains wealth, Pamphilius, you regard it not as property but as power.' A comic poet is again cited, although again it is unknown who the poet is and the lines are not found elsewhere. Hunt, based on a suggestion from Wilamowitz-Möllendorff, interprets the passage to mean that the *astynomi*, as tariff collectors, equalize status among rich and poor. The context is not clear, but apparently includes reference to Athenians who were standing around (lines 9–11), which is followed by brief words to introduce the quotation (καὶ δὴ καὶ τά). The way in which the quotation is introduced is more than by simply incorporating the quotation into the narrative, as is found, for example, in Mk 4.12 (Isa. 6.9–10) and especially 13.26 (Dan. 7.13). The introductory phrase may function similarly to the introductory words used in Mk 11.17 ('is it not written') or Mk 14.27 ('it is written'). Introductory words have a way of forcing the reader to prepare for the quotation to follow. The use of the particular quotation is also worth noting. The passage is used to illustrate a point in a particular way – it is an aphoristic example used for a specific crowd (if my reading of the context is correct). This is paralleled in Mk 14.27, where Jesus states that his followers will all fall away, but then he gives the aphoristic statement regarding striking the shepherd and the sheep being scattered (Zech. 13.7). In neither case is the quotation specific to the applied context, but it applies a generalized statement to a particular situation.

    Fr. 39 col. 7 lines 1–36: '[…the husband] against the wife, and the father against the son, and the servant against the master; or in the reversals of fortune, violations of virgins, substitutions of children, recognitions by means of rings and necklaces. For these are the things which comprise the New Comedy, and were brought to perfection by Euripides, Homer being the starting-point in this and in the colloquial arrangement of verses (?). And Philemon rightly gives him credit for this in the passage, "So says Euripides, who alone can speak…".' The first part of this passage is reminiscent of Mk 13.12, with the noteworthy difference that the passage in the Gospel is a serious warning to the readers while the treatment found in New Comedy derives comic value from the oppositions mentioned. Philemon, the New Comedy poet known for his moralizing,[51] is mentioned in the Γένος Εὐριπίδου 6,[52] although this particular quotation attributed to him is found nowhere else.[53] There is, of course, no exact parallel to Jesus being referred to by name in an Old Testament citation, but there are other Markan passages that have similar internal referential features. The quotation in Mk 1.2–3 (Mal. 3.1; Exod. 23.20; Isa. 40.3; see above for discussion) has an internal identification, in which the author introduces the book as concerning the good news of Jesus, and then cites a passage that quotes God as speaking of sending his messenger to prepare the way for the Lord (the references being taken to mean John the Baptist and Jesus); and Mk 12.36 asks how David can say 'the Lord declared to my Lord…', referring to himself (citing Ps. 110.1). A similar kind of internal identification is found in: Mk 11.9–10, when the people identify the one they are speaking of as 'he who comes in the name of the Lord' (citing Ps. 118.25–26); Mk 11.17, where Jesus cites a passage in which reference is made to 'my house' (Isa. 56.7); Mk 14.62, where Jesus' citation of Dan. 7.13 with reference to the son of man is in support of his positive answer to Pilate's question; and Mk 15.34, where Jesus cites Ps. 22.1 with 'my God why have you forsaken me?'. It appears that a common citational technique was to apply in a specific way a particular reference in a cited passage to the situation and the people involved in the narrative account.

Fr. 39 col. 8 lines 17–33: The fragmentary text probably speaks of a prosecution against Euripides, as he (Demosthenes?) does here in condemning the evil Aristogeiton, followed by citation of Demosthenes' *First Oration against Aristogeiton*: 'Now what is the defendant? "He is the watchdog of the democracy", some say. Of what sort? One whom does not bite at those he accuses of being wolves, but who himself devours sheep he claims to guard. For which of the orators has this one ever brought to trial? None…' (LCL modified). The context in Satyrus' biography is sufficiently unclear to determine the sense in which the quotation is being used, but it appears that it is invoked to condemn Euripides as one who is critical of others while being detrimental himself. There is no direct attribution of the quotation in the portion of the papyrus that is extant, but it appears that there was reference to Demosthenes earlier, and so this quotation would resemble those Markan citations that have direct attribution. The tenor of the use of the quotation is similar to that in Mk 12.19, when the Sadducees come to question Jesus and cite Moses to him in an attempt to trap him regarding Levirate marriage (Deut. 25.5).

---

51. See W.G. Arnott, 'Philemon (2)', in *OCD* (2nd edn), p. 813.

52. 'Thus Philemon loved him [Euripides] so as to dare to say this concerning him: "if, in truth, those who are dead have perception, men, as some say they do, I would lead the way in order to see Euripides".' On the 'Race', see Murray, *Euripides and his Age*, pp. 24–25.

53. This is not surprising since there are few quotations of him and very few papyri. For an example, see Page, *Select Papyri*, no. 50, pp. 238–39.

Fr. 39 col. 9 lines 4–32: '[Euripides] was the owner of a large cave there with the mouth towards the sea, and here he passed the day by himself engaged in constant thought or writing, despising everything that was not great and elevated. Aristophanes at least says, as though summoned as a witness for this very purpose: "As are his characters, so is the man". But once when witnessing a comedy he is said...' The quotation in lines 25–28, attributed to Aristophanes, is not known.[54] The sense of an attributed quotation 'witnessing' to the depiction is to be found in Mark's Gospel in a number of places: Mk 1.2–3, where 'it is written' in Isaiah (Exod. 23.20; Mal. 3.1; Isa. 40.3; see above); Mk 7.6–7, where again Isaiah prophesied, 'as it is written' (Isa. 29.13); Mk 11.17, where Jesus says that 'is it not written?' (Isa. 56.7); Mk 12.10–11, where Jesus asks whether his audience has 'read this Scripture' (Ps. 118.22–23); and Mk 14.27, where Jesus states that his disciples will flee, 'because it is written' (Zech. 13.7). The sense is that the citation was written in a way that has uncanny resemblance to the situation to which it is being applied.

Fr. 39 col. 12 lines 1–16: '[the council of the women enacted the following]: Timocleia presiding, Lusilla served as scribe, Sostrata moved: "if anyone councils any evil against this deme of women or with Euripides or the Medes calls for harm on any one"'. This is an abbreviated quotation of Aristophanes, *Thesmophorae* 374–75, 335–37. Hunt notes that this passage from Aristophanes was apparently cited in conjunction with the story of the attack on Euripides by the women.[55] The next episode – affirming Euripides' attitude toward women – recounts why Euripides was angry with them. It appears that his wife had been involved with another man in his house (lines 16–35). Regardless of whether this is the source of the story concerning Euripides, and it seems likely, the use of the quotation, since it begins in the middle of the account, is not attributed. Nevertheless, the use of an illustrative quotation of this sort is also found in Mark's Gospel. One example is Mk 10.19, where Jesus cites the commandments from Exod. 20.12–16 and Deut. 5.16–20, and then explains what the rich young man must do; another is Mk 12.29–31, where Jesus cites Deut. 6.4–5 and Lev. 19.18, but then the scribe responds by affirming and explaining what Jesus has said.

Fr. 39 col. 16 lines 1–17: The papyrus is fragmentary at this point, but it appears to have lines that read: 'Take some of Sophocles and Aeschylus, but put in a whole Euripides'. Hunt interprets this to mean that, whereas only a portion of the other two might be required in a recipe for a dish of poetry, it takes all of Euripides to reach their standard; in other words, Euripides is being deprecated.[56] The quotation is from an unknown comic poet, but the fragmentary state of the papyrus makes it impossible to know whether the quotation was introduced by name. The only place in Mark's Gospel where a quotation is used by Jesus' opponents against him is in Mk 12.19, where the Sadducees cite Gen. 38.8 and Deut. 25.5 regarding

---

54. According to Hunt (*Oxyrhynchus Papyri*, pp. 176–77), Wilamowitz-Möllendorff compares Aristophanes, *Thesmophorae* 149–50 to this passage as reflecting a similar sentiment.

55. Hunt, *Oxyrhynchus Papyri*, p. 178.

56. Hunt, *Oxyrhynchus Papyri*, p. 179.

Levirate marriage in an attempt to show Jesus up as not being adequate to explain the law.

Fr. 39 col. 17 lines 7–13: In this passage, a quotation from an unidentified Doric poet is interspersed between quotations of Euripides' own writings. Lines 1–7 quote Euripides, fr. 403.3–4 (Stobaeous, *Florilegium* 38.8) and lines 30–39 cite Euripides, fr. 911 (Clement of Alexandria, *Stromata* 4.642). Between these two, in lines 10–13, is found a quotation from the unidentified poet. The passage reads: '"…whatever part of the body it has taken for its habitation, in the hands, the inwards, or by the eyes", added mockingly to this, "where the dog as she sleeps puts her nose". These then, as I said, in their expression of views sought popular favour. He however, after putting in, so to speak, an obstructive plea, renounced Athens (Diodorus). What is the plea? (A) It was entered in the following choral ode: "wings of gold"…' The scatological lines by the Doric poet are added to Euripides' own material apparently to reinforce the depreciation of him, which resulted in his renouncing Athens and his leaving it. There is nothing exactly like this use of quotation in Mark's Gospel. However, in Mk 12.10–11, Jesus cites a passage from Ps. 118.22–23 that he applies to himself as a means of condemning those who were against him, and they realize that it is against them.

Fr. 40: Hunt believes that a lyric poet is cited,[57] who speaks of a person having a miserable life with disease in their dwelling. The text is too fragmentary to identify the author.

Fr. 41: Hunt believes that there may be a quotation here too, but only a couple of words are identifiable.[58]

The last example that I wish to cite is not a quotation in the formal sense, but the use of a proverbial statement in fr. 39 col. 21 lines 34–35: 'Hence they say the proverb is still in use among the Macedonians "Justice even for a dog"'. This is most obviously similar to Lk. 4.23: 'And he said to them, "Doubtless you will quote to me this proverb, 'Physician, heal yourself; what we have heard you did at Capernaum, do here also in your own country'"' (RSV). However, the usage of this proverb does vaguely resemble Mark's aphoristic statement spoken by Jesus in Mk 2.17: 'When Jesus heard this, he told them, "Those who are well don't need a doctor, but the sick do. I didn't come to call the righteous but sinners"' (Holman revised). The use of the proverbial statement is not widespread in either Satyrus's biography or the Gospels, but the limited use is similar.

4. *Conclusion*

This brief study has attempted to move beyond the standard discussion of the genre of Mark in terms of its relations to either biographical or non-biographical literature by examining a feature – the use of quotation – from the standpoint of its similarities to and differences from the use of citation and quotation in ancient

---

57. Hunt, *Oxyrhynchus Papyri*, p. 182.
58. Hunt, *Oxyrhynchus Papyri*, p. 182.

biography. Rather than treat one of the usual works that are entered into the discussion, I have brought a papyrus manuscript into the discussion that is often overlooked, and rarely examined in terms of its use of quotation. The fragmentary and incomplete nature of the document makes it problematic for comparison with Mark, with its well-established and well-documented textual history. Nevertheless, there are a number of features that show surprising overlap between the ways that quotations are used in the two sources. I did not examine in detail quotations from Euripides himself in Satyrus' biography of Euripides, but much more could be done with this usage in comparison with how the words of Jesus are cited in Mark's Gospel. One difference that will need to be taken into account is the fact that Satyrus' biography utilizes a dialogical approach, in which Euripides is not part of the narrative but is referred to in the third person and does not speak for himself except through direct citation. However, when one examines the use of other sources one notices that Mark in his use of a range of Old Testament citations mirrors the range of authors, some named and some unnamed, some known and others unknown, cited by Satyrus. Sometimes these quotations are introduced by name and sometimes they are not (and sometimes one cannot tell because of the fragmentary condition of the papyrus). These quotations are put to a variety of uses. Often they are used in support of the main character but sometimes they are used to deprecate him; sometimes they are used by opponents and sometimes they are used by supporters. Sometimes they are used to contrast arguments and sometimes they are used to build these arguments. The same uses that Satyrus evidences are to be found in the Gospel of Mark. This preliminary study has attempted to bring this papyrus document, apparently neglected in much recent Gospel discussion regarding genre, more into the mainstream of discussion. The purpose has been not just to inform study of ancient biography but to illustrate the diverse and complex yet apparently consistent use of authoritative citation in biographical literature of the ancient world.

'AFTER THREE DAYS HE WILL RISE': THE (DIS)APPROPRIATION OF HOSEA 6.2 IN THE MARKAN PASSION PREDICTIONS

Mark Proctor

1. *Introduction*

Jesus' third-day resurrection was for first-century believers an indispensable element of the Christian story that admitted of scriptural affirmation. That this was so can be seen from Paul's argument in 1 Cor. 15.1–28, where he uses the 'recognized fact' of Jesus' third-day resurrection to persuade the Corinthians about the truth of his eschatological claims.[1] Since Christ 'was raised on the third day in accordance with the Scriptures' (v. 4), Paul's Christian associates are justified in anticipating the future resurrection of deceased believers at the parousia.[2]

---

1. That Paul would use Jesus' resurrection as a premise for his argument suggests that those who denied the possibility of a general eschatological resurrection would at least affirm the content of the standard Easter kerygma. The rhetorical thrust of Paul's argument thus plays off his readers' acceptance of traditional teaching about Jesus' resurrection, something Paul realized his conversation partner(s) would be hard-pressed to deny without losing audience. Verse 3 speaks to the antiquity and significance of Jesus' third-day resurrection for Christian theology, and reveals that the information Paul shares in vv. 3b–7 does not reflect his independent thought but merely recapitulates a portion of what he inherited from primitive Christian tradition. Verse 1, moreover, suggests Paul made the Corinthian believers aware of these teachings from the earliest moments of their association. 1 Cor. 15.1–4 thus sets the *terminus ad quem* for the third-day resurrection motif prior to Paul's first visit to Corinth c.50 CE. W.L. Craig goes even farther by suggesting the formula in 1 Cor. 15.4b reaches back 'to within the first five years after Jesus' crucifixion' ('The Historicity of the Empty Tomb of Jesus', *NTS* 31 [1985], pp. 39–67 [39]). If so, Christian traditions do not (indeed cannot) get much older or more authoritative than the one Paul recites in 1 Cor. 15.4b. 'This is the kind of foundation-story with which a community is not at liberty to tamper… The heart of the formula is something Paul knows the Corinthians will have heard from everyone else as well as himself, and that he can appeal to it as unalterable Christian bedrock' (N.T. Wright, *The Resurrection of the Son of God* [*Christian Origins and the Question of God*, 3; Minneapolis: Fortress Press, 2003], pp. 318–19).

2. B.M. Metzger asks of 1 Cor. 15.4 'whether it is necessary to take κατὰ τὰς γραφάς as qualifying the entire preceding statement, ἐγήγερται τῇ ἡμέρᾳ τῇ τρίτῃ, or whether it is not possible to understand the two phrases (τῇ ἡμέρᾳ τῇ τρίτῃ and κατὰ τὰς γραφάς) as co-ordinate and separate qualifiers of the verb ἐγήγερται' ('A Suggestion Concerning the Meaning of I Cor XV.4b', *JTS* 8 [1957], pp. 118–23 [120]). If such were the case, the scriptural necessity to which Paul alludes would apply only to the resurrection and not its temporal qualifier. Metzger offers this argument as a means of simplifying the task of uncovering precisely what 'scriptures' satisfy Paul's claims in v. 4. The obvious problem with Metzger's hypothesis stems from the parallel expression κατὰ τὰς γραφάς in v. 3b, where the scriptural necessity of which Paul speaks clearly applies to the entirety of the thoughts preceding the phrase.

Christ's paradigmatic resurrection as 'the first fruits of those who have died' (v. 20) thus provides Paul and the letter's recipients with a confident assurance as they await the eschatological fulfillment of Isa. 25.8 and Hos. 13.14 (see vv. 54–56). Paul thus draws an analogy between Jesus' past victory over death and the future hope of deceased believers: Just as Jesus was raised on the third day, so deceased believers will be raised at his return. Both resurrections, moreover, find validation in the Old Testament.

Luke likewise affirms the scriptural necessity of Jesus' third-day resurrection in a pair of post-resurrection stories. When the Galilean women discover the empty tomb on the first day of the week, two men in dazzling clothes remind them of Jesus' previous instruction as a means of calming their fears: 'Remember how he told you, while he was still in Galilee, that the Son of Man must (δεῖ) be handed over to sinners, and be crucified, and on the third day rise again (τῇ τρίτῃ ἡμέρᾳ ἀναστῆναι)' (24.6–7).[3] Following Christ's conversation with Cleopas and another unnamed disciple on the road to Emmaus (in which he 'interpreted to them the things about himself in all the scriptures' [v. 27]), the risen Lord appears for the second time to the eleven in Jerusalem and defines the 'necessity' about which the angelic figures spoke in terms of scriptural fulfillment:

> Then he said to them, 'These are my words that I spoke to you while I was still with you – that everything written about me in the law of Moses, the prophets, and the psalms must (δεῖ) be fulfilled'. Then he opened their minds to understand the scriptures, and he said to them, 'Thus it is written, that the Messiah is to suffer and to rise from the dead on the third day (ἀναστῆναι ἐκ νεκρῶν τῇ τρίτῃ ἡμέρᾳ)' (24.44–46).

For Luke, Jesus' resurrection had to occur on the third day following his death, since that is what Scripture required.

Finally, Jn 2.19–22 links the concept of Jesus' third-day resurrection to scriptural fulfillment in the story of the temple's cleansing. In v. 19 Jesus tells the 'Jews' if they 'destroy this temple…in three days I will raise it up (ἐν τρισὶν ἡμέραις ἐγερῶ αὐτόν)'. The 'Jews', in characteristic fashion, fail to realize Jesus speaks not literally of the architectural edifice in which they stand, but metaphorically 'of the temple of his body' (v. 21). John links the dialogue's subject matter to Scripture in v. 22: 'After he was raised from the dead, his disciples remembered that he had said this; and they believed the scripture (τῇ γραφῇ) and the word that Jesus had spoken'. Since John uses γραφή in the singular ten more times when alluding to or quoting particular scriptural passages, concluding he had a specific biblical context in mind at 2.22 seems unavoidable.[4] According to John, not only did the disciples later recall Jesus' cryptic foretelling of the third-day resurrection, they also managed to link the Easter events to the fulfillment of a particular verse. Hence, representative passages from three major first-century Christian traditions (Pauline, Lukan, and Johannine) affirm the connection

---

3.   The 'necessity' δεῖ implies extends equally to all three phases of Jesus' passion: his betrayal, his crucifixion, and his third-day resurrection. The angelic figures' statement, moreover, recalls the wording of the Lukan passion predictions in 9.22 and 18.31–33. See also 9.44.

4.   See 2.22; 7.38, 42; 10.35; 13.18; 17.12; 19.24, 28, 36–37; 20.9.

between Jesus' third-day resurrection and the Old Testament. Early Christian authors writing before Mark (Paul), after Mark (Luke and John), and apart from Mark (Paul and John) agree not only that Jesus rose from the dead and did so on the third day, but that both things happened in accordance with the demands of Scripture.

Given the importance Paul, Luke, John, and others attribute to this bit of shared tradition, it comes as no surprise that the Gospel narratives agree on the timing of Jesus' emergence from the grave. Although John's protagonist dies in a different year than the Synoptic Christ, each evangelist narrates Jesus' death as occurring on Friday before sunset and they all have the women find the tomb empty just after daybreak on Sunday.[5] If one uses an inclusive means of counting days, the Gospel narratives concur with Paul, Luke, and John (and by extension the tradition[s] to which they were heir) in placing Jesus' resurrection 'on the third day' following his death: Friday being the first, Saturday the second, and Sunday the third.[6] Many first-century believers, it seems, considered the not-so-uncomplicated affirmation of Jesus' resurrection insufficient on its own, and so found it necessary to append a note about the timing of this miraculous event to the general declaration of its having occurred at all. According to Paul, Luke, and John, moreover, these same believers found confirmation of their third day temporal qualifier in Scripture. For the earliest Christians, it was important that believers understand Jesus 'rose on the third day in accordance with the Scriptures'.

That first-century Christians understood Jesus' story against a scriptural background is anything but a novel idea; for anyone with even a basic knowledge of the New Testament realizes that 'in general, the New Testament use of the Old is kerygmatic or Christocentric, and its kernel or core the Passion and Resurrection with their sequel'.[7] How ironic it is, therefore, that the New Testament authors neglected to divulge the precise scriptural basis for traditional affirmation of Jesus' third-day resurrection. Indeed, Mt. 12.40 alone cites a particular passage in connection with the third-day resurrection motif. While it is tempting to project Matthew's explicit citation of LXX Jon. 2.1 back onto preceding gospel tradition, S.V. McCasland cautions against doing so because 'this scripture began to be

5. The Gospels do not, however, depict the actual moment of Jesus' emergence from the grave (cf. Gos. Pet. 9.34–10.42). Since they merely describe the women's discovery of the empty tomb on the first day of the week, the evangelists appear content leaving the precise timing of Jesus' resurrection implicit in their narratives. This implicit timing, which finds confirmation in passages like Mt. 27.62–64 and Lk. 24.5–7, 45–46, coheres well with the temporal scheme of the pre-Pauline kerygmatic formula in 1 Cor. 15.4. Only one other New Testament passage outside the Gospels mentions Jesus' resurrection on the third-day, namely Acts 10.39b–40. Gospel passages linking the third-day motif with the topic of Jesus' resurrection include Mt. 12.40; 16.21; 17.22–23; 20.18–19; 26.60b–61?; 27.39–40?; Mk 8.31; 9.31; 10.32–34; 14.57–58?; 15.29–30?; Lk. 9.21–22; 13.32–33?; 18.31–33; 24.6, 21, 46; Jn 2.19–22.

6. The Greek expressions for 'today', 'tomorrow', and 'the day after tomorrow', were σήμερον, αὔριον, and τῇ τρίτῃ ἡμέρα (F. Field, *Notes on Select Passages of the Greek Testament: Chiefly with Reference to Recent English Versions* [Oxford: E. Pickard Hall, 1881], pp. 8–9).

7. M. Black, 'The Theological Appropriation of the Old Testament by the New Testament', *SJT* 39 (1986), pp. 1–17 (p. 5).

used comparatively late; Paul, Mark, Q and Luke all show no evidence of knowing of it; and it appears first in Matthew'.[8] So if LXX Jon. 2.1 did not provide the
initial scriptural validation for early Christian affirmation of Jesus' third-day resurrection, what text did?[9] The most likely candidate is Hos. 6.2, since this is the only
verse that combines the language of resurrection with a doubly precise third-day
temporal marker: 'After two days (μετὰ δύο ἡμέρας) he will heal us, on the third
day (ἐν τῇ ἡμέρᾳ τῇ τρίτῃ) we will rise up (ἀναστησόμεθα) and live (ζησόμεθα)
before him'.[10] Hence, H.E. Tödt states 'the scriptural text which is fundamental
for announcements of the resurrection is Hosea 6.2; the LXX furnishes a text which
includes both a span of time – after two days – and a point of time – on the third
day – and also the word ἀνίστημι, thus providing the elements which recur in
the phrases about the resurrection'.[11]

    Nevertheless, it remains at least marginally troubling that no New Testament
writer makes explicit use of this verse. What might explain the absence of any
quotation? H.K. McArthur hypothesizes that if Hos. 6.2 was absorbed into the
primitive kerygma at a sufficiently early date, this may have absolved the New
Testament writers of any responsibility to cite specific scriptural support.[12] Furthermore, since Hos. 6.2 employs plural verbs (ἀναστησόμεθα and ζησόμεθα), the
verse does not lend itself naturally to direct quotation and application to Jesus'
story. Those familiar with first-century exegetical practices realize Hos. 6.2's
corporate focus would hardly dissuade early Christians from using the verse for
Christological purposes, but it may at least have steered them away from any
straightforward citation. Yet even if the exact reason the New Testament lacks an
explicit use of Hos. 6.2 to interpret Jesus' story remains undiscovered, as long as
one takes Paul, Luke, and John at their word it must have been this passage that
corroborated early Christianity's teaching about his third-day resurrection; for no
other Scripture text could have done so.

    Comparing the passion predictions in Mk 8.31, 9.31, and 10.33–34 with the
importance Paul, Luke, John, and others attributed to the third-day resurrection
motif reveals a distinct peculiarity. Whereas the prevailing tradition claimed the

    8.   S.V. McCasland, 'The Scripture Basis of "On the Third Day"', *JBL* 48 (1929), pp. 124–37
(130). See also G. Strecker, 'The Passion- and Resurrection Predictions in Mark's Gospel (Mark 8.31;
9.31; 10.32–34)', *Int* 22 (1968), pp. 421–42 (p. 429 n. 20).
    9.   Wright attempts to avoid settling this issue directly by suggesting κατὰ τὰς γραφάς in 1
Cor. 15.4b 'looks back to the scriptural narrative as a whole, not simply to a handful of proof-texts'
(*Resurrection*, p. 321; see also Strecker, 'Passion- and Resurrection', p. 429 n. 20). While the plural
γραφάς might appear to support this conclusion, one should not forget 1 Cor. 15.4 speaks of two
distinct concepts: 'resurrection' and 'the third day'. Inasmuch as a plurality of individual 'scriptures'
might inform one idea or the other, the plural γραφάς seems required.
    10.   Although Matthew regards Jon. 2.1 as thematically *apropos*, it remains technically inaccurate.
Other possible but far less likely options include Lev. 23.11 and 4 Kgdms 20.5. For more on the
possible relevance of Lev. 23.4–21, see B.W. Bacon, '"Raised the Third Day"', *Expositor* 26 (1923),
pp. 426–41.
    11.   H.E. Tödt, *The Son of Man in the Synoptic Tradition* (trans. D.M. Barton; Philadelphia: West-
minster Press, 1965), p. 185.
    12.   H.K. McArthur, '"On the Third Day"', *NTS* 18 (1971–72), p. 85.

Lord arose 'on the third day', Mark has Jesus predict on three separate occasions that he would rise μετὰ τρεῖς ἡμέρας (i.e. 'after three days' or 'on the fourth day').[13] Mark's wording not only disagrees with the 'standard' way of speaking about the timing of Jesus' resurrection, it also stands in narrative tension with the temporal setting of his concluding pericope; for when the women go to anoint Jesus' corpse early on the first day of the week (i.e. 'on the third day' following his death), the tomb is already vacant. In a separate article I have argued Mark's use of μετὰ τρεῖς ἡμέρας in 8.31, 9.31, and 10.34 reflects his deliberate attempt to de-prioritize traditional Christian teaching about the resurrection by (a) eliminating from Jesus' passion predictions of any hint of temporal precision as a means of (b) subordinating the women's discovery of the empty tomb to the impending account of Jesus' tragic death.[14] Rather than parrot church tradition's specificity with regard to the moment of Christ's emergence from death, Mark has Jesus himself minimize the significance of the Easter events by saying only that his resurrection will occur 'an indeterminate amount of time after' (μετὰ τρεῖς ἡμέρας) his crucifixion. The circumstances that will culminate in Jesus' demise, by way of contrast, gain in detail with each consecutive prediction and fundamentally agree with the events of the Markan passion narrative. In this way, the second evangelist makes Jesus' traditional passion statements as passion-centered as possible. If so, what might Mark's Christological agenda entail for the standard early Christian exegetical treatment of Hos. 6.2?

Good reasons exist for suggesting not only Mark's general awareness of Hosea, but also his specific knowledge of LXX Hos. 6.2 and its Christological significance for the wider tradition. But where Mark's Christian contemporaries found in Hosea's text a temporal marker of sufficient accuracy to suit their particular theological needs, the second evangelist saw something that might draw his readers' attention away from his main literary goal. Mark's desire to downplay the significance of the empty tomb *vis-à-vis* the story of his protagonist's death thus

13. McArthur's suggestion that 'for Jewish thought "on the third day" and "after three days" could be treated as functional if not identical equivalents' ('"On the Third Day"', p. 85; see also C.S. Mann, *Mark: A New Translation with Introduction and Commentary* [AB, 27; New York: Doubleday, 1986] pp. 346–47, C.J. Cadoux, *The Historic Mission of Jesus: A Constructive Re-examination of the Eschatological Teaching in the Synoptic Gospels* [New York: Harper & Brothers, 1941], p. 286, D.J. Clark, 'After Three Days', *BT* 30 [1979], pp. 340–43 [341], and Field, *Notes on Select Passages*, p. 9) falters not only on the evidence of the Synoptic parallels (see Mt. 16.21; 17.23; 20.19; Lk. 9.22, 44; 18.33), but on the textual evidence for Mk 8.31, 9.31, and 10.34 as well (where large sections of the New Testament manuscript tradition express dissatisfaction with Mark's 'after three days' by emending his texts into conformity with what the scribes evidently considered the 'proper' way to word Jesus' predictions). Matthew quite possibly takes this 'harmonizing' approach toward understanding Mark's peculiar expression in the story of the guard at the tomb (Mt. 27.62–66), where he essentially equates μετὰ τρεῖς ἡμέρας with ἕως τῆς τρίτης ἡμέρας. The fact that Mt. 27.63 is the only New Testament passage apart from the Markan predictions to use the phrase 'after three days' in reference to Jesus' resurrection suggests Matthew here interprets the peculiar Markan temporal marker μετὰ τρεῖς ἡμέρας in such a way as to make it fundamentally indistinct from τῇ τρίτῃ ἡμέρᾳ.

14. M. Proctor, '"After Three Days" in Mark 8.31; 9.31; 10.34: Subordinating Jesus' Resurrection in the Second Gospel', *PRSt* 30 (2003), pp. 399–424.

precipitated an important change of wording in one of the gospel tradition's pivotal exegetical elements. While thinkers like Paul, Luke, and John relied heavily on the precision of Hos. 6.2's dual temporal expressions to lend scriptural support to their shared belief in Jesus' climactic resurrection on the third day, Mark (in an effort to focus his community's attention squarely on the cross and the spectacle of Jesus' ironic demise as the Son of God) used the general temporal phrase μετὰ τρεῖς ἡμέρας instead of the specific temporal marker ἐν τῇ ἡμέρᾳ τῇ τρίτῃ in the passion predictions and in so doing compromised Hos. 6.2's primary Christological appeal.[15] While Jesus' resurrection and Hos. 6.2's relevance for that traditional theme remained at least marginally relevant for Mark, the words μετὰ τρεῖς ἡμέρας in 8.31, 9.31, and 10.34 deprived the verse of its temporal precision. Mark's treatment of Hos. 6.2 thus becomes (at least with reference to the issue of Jesus' third-day resurrection) the prophet's undoing. In Jesus' own words, the Son of Man will not rise 'on the third day', but 'after three days'. Since within the context of Mark's gospel the only viable way to interpret μετὰ τρεῖς ἡμέρας is as an imprecise, non-literal expression meaning 'an indeterminate amount of time in the future', the evangelist's change of wording allows him the luxury of prioritizing his Christological themes (i.e. Jesus' death is more significant than his resurrection) at the level of the passion predictions yet keeps him from betraying the prevailing tradition altogether.[16] Whereas 1 Cor. 15.1–8 presents Jesus' death as on par with his burial, resurrection, and post-resurrection appearances, Mark wants the Son of Man's demise to serve as *the* focal point of the narrative. Mark does not 'mishandle' Hos. 6.2, but instead blends the language of the prophet's twin temporal expressions in such a way that his readers can no longer (mis)understand the resurrection as that which undoes the 'mistake' of Jesus' crucifixion. The events of Mk 16.1–8 are at best a denouement and at worst an anticlimax. By generalizing the meaning of the third-day temporal markers in Jesus' passion predictions, Mark lets go of that which made Hos. 6.2 most appealing to his contemporaries. Hosea's prediction of Jesus' resurrection remains, but its temporally precise meaning has been marginalized.

---

15. When compared with the actual wording of LXX Hos. 6.2, the relevant New Testament text forms appear fairly fluid. With the exception of the Markan passion predictions, however, the technical accuracy of Hosea's temporal marker remains uncompromised; i.e. outside of Mk 8.31, 9.31, and 10.34 Jesus always emerges from death 'on the (literal) third day' (see Mt. 16.21; 17.23; 20.19; 26.61?; 27.40?; Mk 14.58?; 15.29?; Lk. 9.22; 13.32; 18.33; 24.7, 21?, 46; Jn 2.19, 20; Acts 10.40; 1 Cor. 15.4). Verses with a question mark may not have felt the direct influence of the exegetical tradition surrounding Hos. 6.2. 1 Cor. 15.4 and Lk. 18.33 come closest to Hosea's text, since they lack only the preposition ἐν.

16. Mark is not an iconoclast. He has no interest in denying the resurrection, but thinks it less important than the work Jesus accomplishes on the cross as a 'ransom for the many' (10.45). He gives the nod to tradition by retaining the note about Jesus' resurrection in the predictions, but does not allow it to control the formation of his narrative in a rigorous manner.

2. Contextual Meaning and Christological Appeal: Early Christian Interest in Hosea 6.2

Apart from its combination of the temporal marker ἐν τῇ ἡμέρᾳ τῇ τρίτῃ with ἀναστησόμεθα, Hos. 6.2 had relatively little to offer early Christians as they endeavored to interpret Jesus' significance in light of Scripture. Historical-critical analysis of Hos. 5.15–6.6, for instance, recognizes that the oracular unit's predictive interests extend no farther than the decades immediately following the onset of the Syro-Ephraimite war (735–732 BCE). The prophet's concerns lay not in the realm of messianic eschatology but in Israel's immediate political future – a future Hosea thought would necessarily involve a prolonged period of divine chastisement at the hands of the Assyrian armies. H.W. Wolff offers a nice summary of Hos. 5.8–7.16's *Sitz im Leben*:

> The time was some point in 733, when Tiglath-pileser III came from the North and attacked the uppermost part of the Jordan Valley... Our text reflects in various aspects the time when Tiglath-pileser's attack brought about the end of the Syro-Ephraimite war... Immediately after the attack of Tiglath-pileser III, the revolution in Samaria, and the submission to Assyria, Hosea threatens further catastrophes. That is the essential content of his announcement of judgment.[17]

Concrete political circumstances in Palestine during the last few decades of the eighth century BCE thus provide the historical background against which Hos. 5.15–6.6 found its original meaning, and to this extent first-century CE Christological appropriations of Hos. 6.2 read like reverse anachronisms. Thinkers like Paul, Luke, and John read the verse forward through time and into the story of Jesus. They did not discover in Hos. 6.2 a ready-made, eschatological, and messianic text, but a piece of ancient political commentary with strong moral and religious overtones that happened to contain language useful for their theological purposes. Put simply, the 'historical' meaning of Hos. 6.2 could never have been made to serve Christian theology.

LXX Hos. 6.1–3 expresses hope for the northern kingdom's restoration after what is expected to be a rather brief period of punishment. As the seven first person plural verbs and three first person plural pronouns demonstrate, this text's primary interest lies with Israel's corporate welfare rather than the individual fate of some future messianic figure. The passage takes the form of a penitential liturgical psalm in which the speakers admit culpability (πορευθῶμεν and ἐπιστρέψωμεν) and acknowledge the onset of divine punishment (ἥρπακεν), but not without affirming their confident hope for renewal in the immediate future. They consider Israel's impending rediscovery (εὑρήσομεν) of God inevitable as the approaching dawn (ὡς ὄρθρον ἕτοιμον), and God's imminent appearance (ἥξει... ἡμῖν) certain as the annual cycle of the early and latter rains (v. 3). LXX Hos. 6.2

---

17. H.W. Wolff, *A Commentary on the Book of the Prophet Hosea* (trans. G. Stansell; Hermeneia; Philadelphia: Fortress Press, 1974), p. 111. See also D. Stuart, *Hosea-Jonah* (WBC, 31; Waco, TX: Word Books, 1987), pp. 101–102, and J.L. Mays, *Hosea: A Commentary* (OTL; Philadelphia: Westminster Press, 1969), p. 87.

establishes the anticipated time frame for the arrival of deliverance: 'After two days he will heal us, on the third day we will rise up and live before him!' (v. 2). As J.M. Perry points out, the temporal expressions μετὰ δύο ἡμέρας and ἐν τῇ ἡμέρᾳ τῇ τρίτῃ in v. 2 anticipate 'the conclusion of an uncertain but not too lengthy period of time (involving ambiguity and danger) as coming on the third of three figurative days'.[18] 'After two days' and 'on the third day' are thus prophetic shorthand for 'in the very near future'. Unlike the Gospel narratives, LXX Hos. 6.2 does not refer to a chronological interval equal to or slightly less than 72 hours. Instead, the denotatively exact figurative temporal expressions μετὰ δύο ἡμέρας and ἐν τῇ ἡμέρᾳ τῇ τρίτῃ connote nothing more precise than the idea 'not too long from now'.[19] The speakers' point is if the people repent, God will relent and will do so in short order.[20] 'Three days' is not too long for Israel to endure God's wrath, and the certain promise of complete restoration more than offsets the expected duration of their punishment. Hosea 6.1–3 thus presents the prayer of a penitent, yet naively optimistic people.

Contrary to the positive use early Christian writers made of this prayer, Hosea did not think the predictions of 6.1–3 would ever find fulfillment. If one views Hos. 5.15–6.6 as a diatribe, the content of 6.1–3 represents the false assumptions of a misinformed interlocutor.[21] While the verses may record sincere repentance,

18.   J.M. Perry, 'The Three Days in the Synoptic Passion Predictions', *CBQ* 48 (1986), pp. 637–54 (639); compare. Exod. 19.11. B. Lindars agrees that in Hos. 6.2 the Hebrew idiom 'after two days/on the third day' is 'always taken in the same sense as the better known שִׁלְשׁוֹם תְּמוֹל (lit. "yesterday, the third day") = "heretofore", "formerly", so that the words in their context mean national revival in the near future' (*New Testament Apologetic: The Doctrinal Significance of the Old Testament Quotations* [Philadelphia: Westminster Press, 1961], p. 61; see also P. Carrington, *According to Mark: A Running Commentary on the Oldest Gospel* [Cambridge: University Press, 1960], p. 180). J. Jeremias, moreover, suggests 'Semitic languages have no word for "several", "a few", "some", and use the expedient, *inter alia*, of saying "three" instead' (*New Testament Theology: The Proclamation of Jesus* [New York: Charles Scribner's Sons, 1971], p. 285; see also Mann, *Mark*, p. 344). While the first part of Jeremias' quote may admit of a technical inaccuracy (see H.F. Bayer, *Jesus' Predictions of Vindication and Resurrection: The Provenance, Meaning and Correlation of the Synoptic Predictions* [WUNT, 20; Tübingen: J.C.B. Mohr (Paul Siebeck), 1986], p. 206, and R.H. Gundry, *Mark: A Commentary on his Apology for the Cross* [Grand Rapids: Eerdmans, 1993], p. 447), the second part is absolutely true.

19.   For more on potential ambiguity in the numerical sequence 'x/x + 1' see W.M.W. Roth, 'The Numerical Sequence x/x + 1 in the Old Testament', *VT* 12 (1962), pp. 300–11, where he argues 'the meaning of the numerical sequence x/x + 1 distributed over the two halves of a verse exhibiting synonymous or synthetic parallelism must be determined by context' (p. 304).

20.   The statement thus seeks 'to link the acts of wounding and healing together as though they were an automatic sequence, an expected cycle of divine work on which the devotees of Yahweh could rely willy-nilly' (Mays, *Hosea*, p. 95; see also Wolff, *Hosea*, p. 118).

21.   The prophet makes similar use of mocking quotations elsewhere (see 2.5, 12b; 8.2; 9.7b; 10.3; 12.8; 13.14). The final example is particularly interesting because Hos. 13.14 constitutes the form-critical equivalent of Hos. 5.15–6.6 on a much smaller scale (5.15 = 13.14a; 6.1–3 = 13.14b; 6.4–6 = 13.14c), and since Paul quotes this verse approvingly in 1 Cor. 15.55. How ironic it is that early Christians read both Hos. 6.2 and 13.14b as positive statements confirming the truth of Christian theology. Reading Hos. 13.14 in this way is perhaps understandable in light of the LXX text (which changes the opening rhetorical questions into declarative statements and directs the final clause toward Death and Hades rather than Ephraim).

the hope they express in God's 'immediate' response to their cry for help remains delusional in light of the prophet's prevailing message of doom (see LXX Hos. 6.4–6). Hosea suggests it is now too late for Israel to do anything about God's impending judgment, the effects of which will endure until the nation has withered away to nothing.[22] LXX Hos. 5.15 characterizes the statement in 6.1–3 as one made out of a situation of absolute desperation, and to this extent differs by degree from the MT. Whereas YHWH vows in the Hebrew text to return to his place 'until they acknowledge their guilt and seek my face' (which of course leaves open the possibility for national renewal immediately following corporate repentance), the LXX states God's absence will persist 'until they disappear' (ἕως οὗ ἀφανισθῶσιν). LXX Hos. 5.15b, moreover, greatly accentuates the urgency of 6.1–3's plea for divine assistance: 'They will seek my face; in their affliction they will get up early in the morning (ὀρθριοῦσι), saying to me'. This use of ὀρθρίζω contrasts with the dawn imagery of 6.3 (ὡς ὄρθρον ἕτοιμον) and complements the light imagery of 6.5 (ὡς φῶς).[23] Divine judgment can neither be forestalled (indeed, the language of LXX 5.15b suggests it has already begun) nor foreshortened (the real matter at issue in 5.15–6.6), and the sooner Israel realizes the gravity of their situation the sooner they will be able to cope with grim reality. So not only are Hos. 6.2's twin figurative expressions for 'in the near future' incongruous with the chronology of the Gospel passion narratives, the prophet did not regard the oracular content of 6.1–3 as something anyone should take seriously; for these verses represent the sentimental, flippant, and wistful expressions of an overly optimistic people.

Finally, neither the 'reviving' (יְחַיֵּנוּ MT/ὑγιάσει LXX) nor the 'raising up' (יְקִמֵנוּ MT/ἀναστησόμεθα LXX) of Hos. 6.2 allude to the resuscitation of Israel and Judah's figurative corpse, but instead express hope for the people's quick recovery from a serious corporate illness. J. Wijngaards writes,

> The pi'el of *haiah* does not only denote the raising to life of dead persons (Is. xxvi 19; Am. v 2), but also sparing other people's lives or keeping them alive (Num. xxxi 15; Jos. ix 15; Is. vii 15). The qal form of *haiah* occasionally means no more than 'being cured from illness' (Jos. v 8; 2 Kgs viii 9; xx 7). Similarly, *qûm* and its hiphîl can be employed both in a true resurrection to life (Ps. Lxxxviii 11; 2 Kgs xiii 21; Is. xxvi 19; Am. v. 2) and in the rising from the bed of sickness (Ex. xxi 19; Ps. xli 9; Job xxiv 22; Dt. viii 27). In fact, the Hebrews made no absolute distinction between disease and death; Jahweh's healing power is often framed in terminology of 'reviving'. Moreover,–it is urged–the context does not speak of death, but of sickness, wounds and stripes, of healing and binding up (Hos. v 14; vi 1).[24]

22. That Israel will be made to endure a prolonged period of punishment is a recurrent them in Hosea (see 2.9–13; 3.1–5; 9.17; 10.11–12; 11.7; 12.6; 13.14). Even though the prophet anticipates a period of renewal for Israel (see 1.10–11; 2.14–23; 11.8–11; 14.4–7), it will take place only in the far distant eschatological future (see 3.5).

23. The MT of Hos.5.15b has only 'in their distress they will beg my favor'. LXX Hos. 5.15 thus presents the picture of a penitential Israel who gets up early in the morning just before sunrise in order to pray for divine restoration. Whereas the prayer in Hos. 6.1–3 mistakenly suggests God's provision of deliverance is as certain as the approaching dawn (ὄρθρον ἕτοιμον in v. 3), the prophet realizes instead that the light of day will bring only judgment (τὸ κρίμα μου ὡς φῶς ἐξελεύσεται in v. 5).

24. J. Wijngaards, 'Death and Resurrection in Covenantal Context (Hos. VI 2)', *VT* 17 (1967),

Hosea 6.2 thus concerns the welfare of a group of people who have been wounded but yet remain alive, and only this understanding of v. 2 is commensurate with the positive tone of the song's remaining portions. Since death is not within the purview of Hos. 6.1–3's enthusiastic singers, v. 2 cannot speak of resurrection from the dead; for doing so would entail their immediate demise, a notion they cannot entertain. 'Here, therefore, הׁיֹח pi'el does not mean "to make alive"; rather, it has its usual meaning of "preserve alive".'[25] This thesis finds confirmation in the LXX rendering ὑγιάσει ('he will heal'), which clearly has nothing to do with resurrection from the dead.[26] Although the Septuagint translators' selection of ἀναστησόμεθα to render יׁקמנו enabled early Christians to import the concept of resurrection from the dead into their Christological reading of Hos. 6.2, the verse never really had anything to say on the topic. Hosea does not portray the people as deceased, 'rather they are sorely wounded and Yahweh is expected to revive them by restoring their vitality and so saving them from death'.[27] Since the concept of resurrection from the dead is simply out of place in this eighth-century BCE text, those early Christians who used Hos. 6.2 to buttress their Christological claims about Jesus' emergence from death committed a second anachronism.

Hosea 6.2 thus became important for early Christians not because it predicted the future eschatological resurrection of a solitary messianic figure approximately 72 hours following his death, but simply because it linked what Christians could interpret as resurrection terminology with a pair of denotatively precise third-day temporal markers. This is as much grist as any first-century Christian could have hoped to grind out of Hos. 6.2, since all other aspects of the verse and its immediate context were ill-suited for Christological use. Even though Hosea never intended his readers to take the verse's predictive content seriously, early Christians nevertheless found value in its combination of ἀναστησόμεθα with ἐν τῇ ἡμέρᾳ τῇ τρίτῃ. The text's Christological relevance is therefore quite limited in scope, yet its importance for the traditional Christian project was necessarily immense. Whereas the notion of resurrection from the dead (corporate or otherwise) could be 'found' elsewhere in Scripture (Ezekiel 37, Daniel 12, etc.), the combination of what eventually came to be resurrection terminology with a third-day timeframe made Hos. 6.2 indispensable for Christians struggling to harmonize their story with the scriptural record. Early Christians thus appropriated Hos. 6.2 out of a concern to bolster the integrity of the gospel tradition, not for the sake of

pp. 226–39 (pp. 228–29). M.L. Barré argues that in Hos. 6.2 'the terms "within/after two days" and "on the third day" find their proper setting-in-life precisely in the context of medical prognosis... *Hence, on its "primary" level of meaning, Hos vi 2 clearly envisages the recovery of the sick; it has nothing to do with the resurrection of the dead*' ('New Light on the Interpretation of Hosea VI 2', *VT* 28 [1978], pp. 129–41 [140], emphasis his; see 2 Kgs 20.1, 5).

25. Wolff, *Hosea*, p. 117. See also W.R. Harper, *A Critical and Exegetical Commentary on Amos and Hosea* (Edinburgh: T&T Clark, 1979), p. 283, and Num. 31.15; Josh. 5.8; 9.15; 2 Kgs 8.9; 20.7; Isa. 7.31.

26. Ὑγιάζω occurs only here in Hosea, but all remaining LXX occurrences of the verb speak of physical healing rather than resurrection from the dead (see Lev. 13.18, 24, 37; Josh. 5.8; 4 Kgdms 20.7; Job 24.23; Ezek. 47.8–9, 11).

27. Mays, *Hosea*, p. 95. See also Wolff, *Hosea*, p. 117, and Ps. 41.4, 11.

the scriptural text itself. If it were the other way around (i.e. if consideration for the meaning of Scripture passages took precedence over maintaining the tradition), Christians would have seen Hos. 6.2 for what it is; namely, a remarkably poor fit with the story of Jesus.

3. *Temporal Ambiguity in the Passion Predictions:* *Mark's (Dis)Appropriation of Hosea 6.2*

Scholars wishing to comment on Mark's exegetical practices often find doing so a troublesome task. On the one hand, the Old Testament's importance for Markan theology is beyond doubt. As H.C. Kee suggests, 'the scriptures are indeed an indispensable presupposition of all that Mark wrote, and a necessary link with the biblical tradition that Mark sees redefined and comprehended through Jesus'.[28] Nevertheless, Mark's level of explicit interaction with Old Testament texts differs dramatically from that of the other evangelists, since he rarely uses quotations to interpret narrative events.[29] If Matthew's citation practices are analogous to the contemporary documentation habits of ambitious graduate students in 'dissertation mode', Mark's level of familiarity with and dependency on particular Old Testament texts frequently defies full explanation. For Mark, the Old Testament's influence often resides below the surface level of his narrative, so far in fact that at times one must wonder if Mark was aware of the precise connection between inherited Christian tradition and the sacred writings.[30] With this information in mind, D.M. Smith, Jr, makes the following observations about Mark's characteristic use of the Old Testament:

> Mark's view of the Old Testament is much less refined and programmatically formulated than that of his successors. Although Mark (through his introductory quotation and his appropriation of a traditional passion narrative replete with Old Testament references or allusions) reflects the primitive Christian idea that the event of Jesus' coming is the

28. H.C. Kee, 'The Function of Scriptural Quotations and Allusions in Mark 11–16', in E.E. Ellis and E. Gräßer (eds), *Jesus und Paulus* (Festschrift W.G. Kümmel; Göttingen: Vandenhoeck & Ruprecht, 1975), pp. 165–88 (p. 179).

29. H. Anderson notes that 'in direct contrast with Matthew's Gospel, there is a very low incidence of fulfillment קמל–מקל–πληροῦν phrases in Mark' ('The Old Testament in Mark's Gospel', in J.M. Efird [ed.], *The Use of the Old Testament in the New and Other Essays: Studies in Honor of William Franklin Stinespring* [Durham, NC: Duke University Press, 1972] pp. 280–306 [p. 281]; see 1.15; 14.49). With the important exception of 1.2–3, moreover, Mark places all his quotations on the lips of his characters. Hence, 'only at the very beginning...does *Mark himself* quote scripture and come near to the Matthaean type of formula quotation' (Anderson, 'Old Testament in Mark's Gospel', p. 281, emphasis his). Finally, the number of definite scripture quotations in Mark totals less than 40.

30. When commenting on the opening clause of Mk 14.21, for instance, E. Best suggests Mark left the reference to scripture vague 'because he himself did not know the precise reference' (*The Temptation and the Passion: The Markan Soteriology* [SNTSMS, 2; Cambridge: University Press, 1965] p. 151). S. Moyise, however, cautions the Second Gospel's readers against regarding Mark's relative paucity of direct editorial interaction with the Old Testament as indicating a lack of familiarity with Scripture, since 'there is in fact a rather extensive set of allusions and echoes that fill out Mark's narrative and engage the reader in a variety of ways' (*The Old Testament in the New: An Introduction* [New York: Continuum, 2001] p. 21).

fulfillment of Scripture and portrays Jesus as debating about the bearing of Scripture (especially the Law), he does not generally use the Old Testament to embellish and interpret the events of Jesus' Galilean ministry as extensively as does Matthew.[31]

For this reason the issue of Mark's theological appropriation of the Old Testament outside the passion narrative has never been a simple matter; for Mark made a habit of keeping his Old Testament sources outside the plain view of his readers (a fact that rings especially true on the level of the narrator's commentary). Given Mark's usual way of interacting with the Old Testament, is there any evidence to suggest he made a conscious decision to alter traditional Christian language related to the timing of Jesus' resurrection, and by extension also the standard treatment of Hos. 6.2? Was Mark aware the phrase μετὰ τρεῖς ἡμέρας in 8.31, 9.31, and 10.34 disagreed with normal first-century Christological expectations?

Answering this question partially involves assessing Hosea's importance for early Christian thought as a whole, since awareness of Hosea on the part of Mark's contemporaries increases the likelihood that the second evangelist also knew the prophet's work. Evidence from the rest of the New Testament confirms Hosea played an important role in the formation of early Christian theology since several New Testament writers from different traditions borrow directly from his oracular collection. In Rev. 6.15–16, for instance, when the Lamb opens the sixth seal the world's population hides 'in the caves and among the rocks of the mountains, *calling to the mountains and rocks, "Fall on us and hide us!"* ' Revelation 6.16a thus makes direct application of LXX Hos. 10.18, as does the Lukan Jesus in his dialogue with the daughters of Jerusalem: 'Daughters of Jerusalem, do not weep for me, but weep for yourselves and for your children. For the days are surely coming when they will say, "Blessed are the barren, and the wombs that never bore, and the breasts that never nursed". Then they will begin *to say to the mountains, "Fall on us"; and to the hills, "Cover us"* ' (Lk. 23.28–30).[32] 1 Peter 2.9–10 recalls Hosea's dealings with his daughter Lo-ruhamah ('not pitied') and son Lo-ammi ('not my people') in order to remind the audience of their special status *vis-à-vis* unbelievers. The words οὐκ ἠλεημένοι recall οὐκ ἠλεημένη of LXX Hos. 1.6; 2.25, and οὐ λαός finds direct parallel in οὐ λαός of LXX Hos. 1.9 and indirect parallel in οὐ–λαῷ–μου of LXX Hos. 2.25. The Petrine community thus viewed itself as the eschatological embodiment of the prophetic promises God makes to Hosea's children in LXX Hos. 2.25. Hence, elements of Hosea's thought managed to find their way into the eschatological teachings of the Lukan, Johannine, and Petrine communities.

Paul also quotes Hosea in a pair of letters. In Rom. 9.25–28 he uses Hosea 2 to explain God's extension of mercy to humanity:

---

31. D.M. Smith, 'The Use of the Old Testament in the New', in Efird (ed.), *Use of the Old Testament in the New*, pp. 3–65 (p. 42).

32. The texts of all three verses exhibit a high degree of verbatim agreement. The lack of any synoptic parallel for Lk. 23.27–31 indicates an independent (though hardly unique) interest in Hosea on Luke's part.

> As indeed he says in Hosea, 'Those who were not my people I will call "my people",
> and her who was not beloved I will call "beloved". 'And in the very place where it was
> said to them, "You are not my people", there they shall be called children of the living
> God.' And Isaiah cries out concerning Israel, 'Though the number of the children of
> Israel were like the sand of the sea, only a remnant of them will be saved; for the Lord
> will execute his sentence on the earth quickly and decisively'.

Verse 25 borrows from LXX Hos. 2.3, 25c, v. 26 quotes LXX Hos. 2.1b, and the words ὁ ἀριθμὸς τῶν υἱῶν Ἰσραὴλ ὡς ἡ ἄμμος τῆς θαλάσσης in v. 27 derive from Hos. 2.1a and combine with the content of LXX Isa. 10.22 to form a conflate quotation. The specificity of the citation formula at the beginning of v. 25, moreover, demonstrates Paul's knowledge of the quotation's exact source. Finally, in 1 Cor. 15.54–55 Paul quotes LXX Hos. 13.14 in anticipation of the believer's eschatological victory over death: 'When this perishable body puts on imperishability, and this mortal body puts on immortality, then the saying that is written will be fulfilled: "Death has been swallowed up in victory". "Where, O death, is your victory? Where, O death, is your sting?"'[33] Paul thus found Hosea's oracles helpful for both his soteriological and eschatological arguments.

Matthew uses Hos. 11.1 in his infancy narrative to explain why Joseph and Mary keep Jesus in Egypt until after Herod the Great's death. 'This was to fulfill what the Lord had spoken by the prophet (διὰ τοῦ προφήτου), "Out of Egypt have I called my son"' (2.15).[34] To the extent the first evangelist uses Hos. 11.1 to interpret the events of Jesus' 'life', Mt. 2.15 is similar to the standard early Christian treatment of Hos. 6.2. Although Matthew does not mention Hosea by name, his conjunction of the definite article τοῦ with the singular προφήτου suggests a certain level of familiarity with Hosea both on Matthew's part and the members of his community. Matthew quotes LXX Hos. 6.6 (the terminal verse of the oracular unit with which this paper is concerned) against the Pharisees in a pair of controversy dialogues. What Jesus' opponents in these stories fail to understand is that God desires mercy rather than sacrifice (see ἔλεος θέλω καὶ οὐ θυσίαν in 9.13 and 12.7). Since the Synoptic parallels to Mt. 9.9–13 (Mk 2.13–17; Lk. 5.27–32) and 12.1–8 (Mk 2.23–28; Lk. 6.1–5) bear no trace of a reference to Hos.6.6, concluding Matthew inserted these texts from Hosea on his own seems inescapable.[35] Hence, several New Testament documents (Matthew, Luke, Romans, 1 Corinthians, 1 Peter, and Revelation) representing a wide variety of traditions (Synoptic, Pauline, Petrine, and Johannine) found Hosea useful for a variety of purposes (eschatological, soteriological, and Christological).[36]

---

33. Since Hos. 13.14 is a sister text to Hos. 5.15–6.6, Paul's selection of Hos. 13.14 to speak about the eschatological resurrection in 1 Cor. 15.55 may confirm his awareness of Hos. 6.2's relevance for traditional teaching about Jesus' third-day resurrection (see 1 Cor. 15.4).

34. Matthew's quotation of Hos. 11.1 is closer to the MT than the LXX, which instead of reading 'and out of Egypt I called my son' has 'and out of Egypt I have called his children' (καὶ ἐξ Αἰγύπτου μετεκάλεσα τὰ τέκνα αὐτοῦ).

35. For more on Matthew's appropriation of Hos. 6.6, see D. Hill, 'On the Use and Meaning of Hosea VI. 6 in Matthew's Gospel', *NTS* 24 (1977–78), pp. 107–19.

36. There are, to be sure, other New Testament contexts that perhaps allude to passages from Hosea. Two of the more obvious examples include 2 Cor. 9.10/LXX Hos. 10.12 (both speak about reaping the

If Hosea's considerable influence on the wider New Testament tradition affords one the luxury of presupposing the second evangelist's general awareness of his work, is there any reason to think Mark found the prophet's oracles especially relevant for his own Christological project? Although the second evangelist does not make explicit use of Hosea to interpret Jesus' story (an unsurprising fact in light of the paucity of such citations in the Second Gospel), the contents of Mk 1.12–13 and 12.33 suggest the prophet's direct influence on the Markan narrative. In his comparatively brief account of the temptation, Mark states that following Jesus' baptism 'the Spirit immediately drove him out into the wilderness (αὐτον ἐκβάλλει εἰς τὴν ἔρημον). And he was in the wilderness (ἐν τῇ ἐρήμῳ) forty days, tempted (πειραζόμενος) by Satan; and he was with the wild beasts (μετὰ τῶν θηρίων); and the angels waited (διηκόνουν) on him' (1.12–13). Thematic and linguistic parallels between Hosea's story of God's firm but loving treatment of Gomer/Israel and the second evangelist's account of Jesus' temptation suggest LXX Hos. 2.16–20 helped shape Mk 1.12–13. LXX Hos. 2.16–20 differs considerably from the textual tradition preserved in the MT and reads as follows:

> Because of this, behold, I myself will lead her astray (πλανῶ) and put her in the wilderness (τάξω αὐτὴν εἰς ἔρημον). And I will speak to her heart and give her (δώσω αὐτῇ) the things belonging to her from that place and from the valley of Achor in order to open her understanding. And she will be humbled (ταπεινωθήσεται) there as in the days of her infancy and as in the days when she came up from the land of Egypt. And so it will be in that day, says the Lord, she will call me 'O, my husband', and will no longer call me 'Baalim'. And I will take up the names of the Baalim from out of her mouth, and their names will no longer be remembered. And I will make a covenant for them in that day with the beasts of the field (μετὰ τῶν θηρίων τοῦ ἀγροῦ) and with the birds of the air and with the reptiles of the earth.

As in Mk 1.12–13, LXX Hos. 2.16–20 describes God as aggressively maneuvering (πλανῶ = ἐκβάλλει) someone (Gomer/Israel - Jesus) into a wilderness setting (εἰς ἔρημον - εἰς τὴν ἔρημον) in order to humble or prove that person by testing (ταπεινωθήσεται – πειραζόμενος). A period of utter tranquility follows as God provides for (δώσω αὐτῇ – οἱ ἄγγελοι διηκόνουν) the object of his affection (Gomer/Israel [see LXX Hos. 2.21] – Jesus [see Mk 1.11]) and enables that person to live in peace with undomesticated wildlife (μετὰ τῶν θηρίων τοῦ ἀγροῦ – μετὰ τῶν θηρίων).[37] Whereas Hosea characterizes the eschatological

---

'fruit of righteousness' from God) and Heb. 13.15/LXX Hos. 14.3 (both describe 'the fruit of lips' as the appropriate 'sacrifice' to God).

37. With the exception of LXX Hos. 2.20, μετά occurs with θηρίον in the Septuagint only at Dan. 4.15, 17, and 33 in the predictions and descriptions of Nebuchadnezzar's period of insanity. The synonymous construct σύν + θηρίον is equally rare (see LXX Hos. 4.3; *3 Macc.* 5.47; 6.16). Mark's use of μετά to describe the nature of Jesus' association with the 'wild beasts' during his 40-day stay in the wilderness suggests he enjoyed a peaceful (rather than adversarial) relationship with the θηρίων; for 'elsewhere in Mark *einai meta tinos* generally has the sense of close, friendly association' (J. Marcus, *Mark 1–8: A New Translation with Introduction and Commentary* [AB, 27; New York: Doubleday, 2000], p. 168; see 1.20, 29, 36; 2.16, 19, 25; 3.6, 7, 14; 5.18, 24, 37, 40; 8.10, 38; 9.8; 11.11; 14.7, 14, 17–18, 20, 33, 43, 54, 67; 15.1, 7, 31). Mark uses κατά to describe an adversarial relationship (see 3.6; 9.40; 11.25; 14.55–57).

age as one in which Israel will peacefully coexist 'with the beasts of the field', Mark describes the dawn of this age as having already occurred in principle during the life of his protagonist.

Jesus' conversation with the scribe about the 'first commandment' in Mk 12.28–33 contains a second textual allusion to Hosea:

> One of the scribes...asked him, 'Which commandment is the first of all?' Jesus answered, 'The first is, "Hear, O Israel: the Lord our God, the Lord is one; you shall love the Lord your God with all your heart, and with all your soul, and with all your mind, and with all your strength". The second is this, "You shall love your neighbor as yourself". There is no other commandment greater than these.' Then the scribe said to him, 'You are right, Teacher; you have truly said that "he is one, and besides him there is no other"; and "to love him with all the heart, and with all the understanding, and with all the strength", and "to love one's neighbor as oneself", – *this is much more important than all whole burnt offerings and sacrifices*' (περισσότερόν ἐστιν πάντων τῶν ὁλοκαυτωμάτων καὶ θυσιῶν).

Jesus' response to the opening query and the scribe's complementary rejoinder comprise a scriptural collage that incorporates the repudiation of the sacrificial system in LXX Hos. 6.6: 'Because I desire mercy and not sacrifice (ἔλεος θέλω καὶ οὐ θυσίαν), and knowledge of God rather than whole burnt offerings (ἐπίγνωσιν θεοῦ ἢ ὁλοκαυτώματα)'.[38] Two things suggest Mk 12.33 constitutes an allusion to this verse: (1) Mark's use of τῶν ὁλοκαυτωμάτων καὶ θυσιῶν with the comparative expression περισσότερόν ἐστιν, and (2) his mention of loving God 'with all the mind' (ἐξ ὅλης τῆς διανοίας) in v. 30 and 'with all the understanding' (ἐξ ὅλης τῆς συνέσεως) in v. 33.

Although ὁλοκαύτωμα and θυσία occur together in numerous Septuagintal contexts,[39] only four passages present 'whole burnt offerings' and 'sacrifices' as of relatively little importance when compared with some more meaningful aspect of the religious life as in Mk 12.33. In 1 Kgdms 15.22 Samuel chides Saul for failing to follow his divinely sanctioned orders with regard to Amalek: 'Are whole burnt offerings and sacrifices as desirable to the Lord (εἰ θελητὸν τῷ κυρίῳ) as the one who hears the Lord's voice (ὡς τὸ ἀκοῦσαι φωνῆς κυρίου)? Behold, obedience is better than a good sacrifice (ἀκοὴ ὑπὲρ θυσίαν ἀγαθή), and listening is better than ram fat (ἡ ἐπακρόασις ὑπὲρ στέαρ κριῶν)'. Samuel's point is that those who carry out God's instructions will more readily receive divine approval than those forced to make ritual amends for sins committed; i.e. sacrifice is unnecessary so long as one obeys God's instructions. LXX Ps. 50.18–19, on the other hand, redefines sacrifice in non-ritualistic terms: 'For if you desired a sacrifice (ὅτι εἰ ἠθέλησας θυσίαν), I would have given it. You do not take pleasure in whole burnt offerings (ὁλοκαυτώματα οὐκ εὐδοκήσεις). A sacrifice to God is a broken spirit (θυσία τῷ θεῷ πνεῦμα συντετριμμένον); God will not reject a

---

38. Other Septuagintal texts informing the dialogue in Mk 12.30–33 include Lev. 19.18; Deut. 4.35; 6.4–5; Josh. 22.5; Isa. 45.21.

39. See Exod. 10.25; 18.12; Lev. 17.8; Num. 10.10; 15.3, 8; Judg. 13.23; 1 Kgdms 15.22; 4 Kgdms 5.17; 1 Chron. 29.21; 2 Chron. 7.1; Ps. 39.7; 49.8; 50.18–19; Isa. 1.11–17; 56.7; Jer. 6.20; 7.21–23; 14.12; Ezek. 44.11–13; Hos. 6.6; Amos 5.21–22; 1 Macc. 1.45.

broken and humbled heart'. The psalmist's use of ἐξουθενώσει in the last line of v. 19 suggests God abhors physical sacrifices. A dead animal does not a 'sacrifice' make, since it takes a 'penitent disposition' to get the deity's attention. So whereas God accepts contrite human supplicants, he 'rejects' whole burnt offerings and sacrifices with contempt. Isaiah 1.11–17 expresses God's frustration with Judah's countless sacrifices and asserts God's preference for moral behavior:

> What is the multitude of your sacrifices (πλῆθος τῶν θυσιῶν ὑμῶν) to me?... I am full of whole burnt offerings of rams (ὁλοκαυτωμάτων κριῶν) and sheep fat and bull's blood and no longer desire (οὐ βούλομαι) billy goats... Wash yourselves, become clean, put away evil from your souls and out of my sight, cease from your wrongdoings, learn to do good, seek justice, rescue the one who has been wronged, defend the orphan, and obtain justice for the widow.

In Isaiah's estimation, the benefits of Jerusalem's penitential cultus have reached their practical limit now that God is 'stuffed to the gills' (see πλήρης εἰμί in v. 11) with the blood and flesh of sacrificial animals. In order for Judah to avoid being 'devoured by the sword' (1.20), the people must stop sinning and start living ethical lives. Finally, LXX Hos. 6.6 affirms God's preference for 'mercy' (ἔλεος) instead of 'sacrifice' (θυσίαν) and for 'knowledge of God' (ἐπιγνωσιν θεοῦ) rather than 'whole burnt offerings' (ὁλοκαυτώματα).

Determining which if any of these four passages the evangelist had in mind while composing the scribe's rejoinder to Jesus' teaching on the 'first command-ment' would be difficult were it not for Mark's mention of loving God 'with the whole mind/understanding'; for the synonymous expressions ἐξ ὅλης τῆς δια-νοίας (v. 30) and ἐξ ὅλης τῆς συνέσεως (v. 33) provide a unique thematic link between the scribe's words and Hos. 6.6's positive regard for 'knowledge of God'. So although LXX Isa. 1.12–17 has the distinction of containing the quanti-tative term πλῆθος (parallel to πάντων in Mk 12.33), its preoccupation with ethical issues differs from Mark's concern for proper love of God and neighbor. LXX Ps. 50.18–19 drops from consideration for the same reason since it sets out to define what constitutes a proper penitential attitude rather than to proscribe vari-ous acceptable ways of loving the deity, and because the dialogue in Mk 12.28–34 has nothing to say about penitential guilt. Instead of love for God and neigh-bor, 1 Kgdms 15.22 speaks about the benefits of hearing (ἀκοῦσαι), obeying (ἀκόη), and listening to (ἡ ἐπακρόασις) the Lord's voice. Hence, if Mark had but one of these four passages in mind while writing 12.33b, LXX Hos. 6.6 repre-sents the best option since this Old Testament verse and no other (1) juxtaposes ὁλοκαύτωμα and θυσίον, (2) compares 'sacrifices' with a more valuable aspect of the religious life, and (3) provides a thematic link to the other side of the scribe's comparative clause via the words ἐπίγνωσιν θεοῦ.

If the preceding investigation of Mk 1.12–13 and 12.28–34 has confirmed Mark's positive appropriation of Hosea's oracular content for both narrative (12.33) and christological (1.12–13) purposes, can one also ascertain Mark's knowledge of LXX Hos. 6.2 and his awareness of that text's importance for the traditional note about the timing of Jesus' resurrection? Given the tradition-laden nature of Mk 8.31, 9.31, and 10.33–34, it would be surprising if Mark remained ignorant of the connection Paul and others made between Hos. 6.2 and Jesus' third-day resurrection.[40] Indeed, Mark's consistent use of ἀνίστημι and τρεῖς ἡμέρας probably reflects his direct knowledge of Hos. 6.2 as well as its importance for early Christian reflection on the third day resurrection motif. Whereas the New Testament writers typically prefer ἐγείρω when speaking about resurrection from the dead by a margin of 2.4.1, Mark's passion predictions make exclusive use of ἀνίστημι.[41] The ratio of ἐγείρω to ἀνίστημι in Mark, by way of contrast, stands at 1.5.1 in favor of ἀνίστημι. Dropping the Markan passion predictions from consideration has the effect of leveling off this ratio at an even

---

40. Eight aspects of Mk 8.31, 9.31, and 10.33–34 indicate the influence of early Christian traditions (exegetical or otherwise) on the Second Gospel's passion predictions:

1. Δεῖ in 8.31 suggests the idea of scriptural fulfillment, and in this way Mark subtly invokes early Christian exegetical musings about the passion.
2. The phrase ὁ υἱὸς τοῦ ἀνθρώπου, which Jesus uses to describe himself in all three predictions, echoes the story of the enigmatic figure of Daniel 7.
3. The words πολλὰ παθεῖν in 8.31 and the more specific list of 'sufferings' in 10.34 perhaps reflect the influence of Isaiah 53 and LXX Ps. 21.8 on Mark's thought.
4. Jesus' quotation of LXX Ps. 117.22 against the chief priests, scribes, and elders in Mk 12.10 helps confirm this verse as the scriptural tradition lying behind the Sanhedrin's anticipated 'rejection' (ἀποδοκιμασθῆναι) of Jesus in 8.31.
5. Mark's mention of the Sanhedrin's role in Jesus' passion at 8.31 and 10.33 reflects what by 70 CE had become a long-standing Christian polemical tradition charging the 'Jews' with responsibility for Jesus' death.
6. The evangelist's exclusive preference for ἀποκτείνω ('kill') over the more precise σταυρόω ('crucify') in all three predictions reflects the influence of a kerygmatic formula similar to the one Paul cites in 1 Thess. 2.15.
7. The words παραδίδοται εἰς χεῖρας ἀνθρώπων in 9.31 and the evangelist's use of παραδίδωμι in 10.33 play off early Christian kerygmatic formulations that spoke of Jesus' 'delivery' up to death (see LXX Isa. 53.6, 12; LXX Dan. 7.25; Rom. 4.25; 8.32; 1 Cor. 11.23).
8. Scholarship no longer regards Jesus' third prediction in Mk 10.33–34 as the *ex nihilo* creation of the evangelist; for if these verses reflect only Mark's compositional activity, one might expect to find a greater amount of narrative harmony between the third prediction and the passion narrative's plot development.

For a more complete discussion of each of these points, see Proctor, '"After Three Days"', pp. 401–409.

41. Passages using ἐγείρω to speak of resurrection from the dead include Mt. 10.8; 11.5; 12.42; 14.2; 16.21; 17.9, 23; 20.19; 26.32; 27.52, 63–64; 28.6–7; Mk 6.14, 16; 9.27?; 12.26; 14.28; 16.6; Lk. 7.14, 22; 8.54?; 9.7, 22; 11.31; 20.37; 24.6, 34; Jn 2.19–20, 22; 5.21; 12.1, 9, 17; 21.14; Acts 3.15; 4.10; 5.30; 10.40; 13.30, 37; 26.8; Rom. 4.24–25; 6.4, 9; 7.4; 8.11, 34; 10.9; 1 Cor. 6.14; 15.4, 12–17, 20, 29, 32, 35, 42–44, 52; 2 Cor. 1.9; 4.14; 5.15; Gal. 1.1; Eph. 1.20; 5.14; Col. 2.12; 1 Thess. 1.10; 2 Tim. 2.8; Heb. 11.19; Jas 5.15?; 1 Pet. 1.21. Ἀνίστημι, by way of comparison, means 'raised from the dead' less than half as many times (see Mk 8.31; 9.9–10, 27?, 31; 10.34; 12.23, 25; Lk. 9.8, 19; 11.32?; 16.31; 18.33; 24.7, 46; Jn 6.39–40, 44, 54; 20.9; Acts 2.24, 32; 9.40; 10.41; 13.33–34; 17.3, 31; Eph. 5.14; 1 Thess. 4.14, 16). These statistics yield a ratio of 2.4 uses of ἐγείρω to every 1 use of ἀνίστημι in New Testament passages speaking of resurrection from the dead. This ratio increases to 2.7.1 when one considers only references to Jesus' resurrection. Eliminating Mark's use of ἀνίστημι in 8.31, 9.31, 10.34 and parallels from the data pool, incidentally, yields an even greater ratio of 3.5.1. Hence, outside the context of Jesus' three passion predictions in Mark, the New Testament writers were at least 72 percent more likely to use ἐγείρω than ἀνίστημι when speaking of Jesus' resurrection from the dead.

1.1. Hence, while Mark makes statistically more frequent use of ἀνίστημι than ἐγείρω in resurrection contexts when compared with the other New Testament writers, it would be inaccurate to suggest he had a 'natural' editorial preference for ἀνίστημι when composing 8.31, 9.31, and 10.34. On the contrary, the data suggests the evangelist would have been just as likely to use one verb as the other. So what persuaded Mark to make exclusive use of ἀνίστημι in all three predictions?

Strecker contends Mark's use of ἀνίστημι in 8.31, 9.31, and 10.34 suggests the influence of source material, 'because the redactor prefers to use in a similar context the verb *egeirein*'.[42] LXX Hos. 6.2, with its use of ἀνίστημι rather than ἐγείρω, provides the source Strecker allows to remain unnamed.[43] Having considered Hosea's use of ἀνίστημι in 6.2 in light of the statistical preference for ἐγείρω in non-Markan New Testament contexts concerning Jesus' resurrection, Tödt concludes 'the earlier ἀνίστημι was superseded by the later ἐγείρω... The earliest, namely the Marcan form of the announcements of suffering denotes the resurrection of the Son of Man by the word ἀναστῆναι.'[44] Tödt therefore sees a direct link between Mark's use of ἀνίστημι in the passion predictions and the language of LXX Hos. 6.2.

Mark's consistent employment of ἀνίστημι in the passion predictions thus combines with his equally scripted use of the number 'three' (τρεῖς) and the noun 'day' (ἡμέρα) in such a way as to connect Jesus' statements in 8.31, 9.31, and 10.34 firmly to the traditional Christian exegetical treatment of Hos. 6.2, but not without making an immensely important adjustment. Whereas both Hos. 6.2 and the New Testament tradition speak of resurrection 'on the third day', the Second Gospel speaks instead of resurrection μετὰ τρεῖς ἡμέρας, or 'after three days'. This switch to μετὰ τρεῖς ἡμέρας, moreover, provides the only substantive example of a Markan divergence from the prevailing gospel tradition within Jesus' multi-layered passion statements. As R. McKinnis points out, 'this way of describing the resurrection...is unique and differs from the traditions which appear elsewhere in the early church'.[45] Hence, one finds in μετὰ τρεῖς ἡμέρας a Markan alteration of traditional language about Jesus' resurrection from the dead.

---

42. Strecker, 'Passion- and Resurrection Predictions', p. 430. If the 'similar context' to which Strecker refers is the passion narrative, he is correct; for in chapters 14–16 Mark makes exclusive use of ἐγείρω when speaking about Jesus' resurrection (see 14.28; 16.6). C.A. Evans (*Mark 8.27–16.20* [WBC, 34b; Nashville, TN: Thomas Nelson, 2001], p. 12) and Gundry (*Mark*, p. 430) concur. See also Rom. 4.24–25; 6.4; 1 Cor. 15.4, 15, 20; 1 Thess. 1.10. The only other context in which Mark broaches the topic of Jesus' resurrection is 9.9–10, where ἀνίστημι occurs twice. Yet given these verses' proximity to the first two passion predictions, the resurrection language of 8.31 and 9.31 probably influenced Mark's word choice in the closing verses of the transfiguration account. So while Strecker's comment may be slightly misleading with respect to the Second Gospel as a whole, one should not overlook the fact that in the rest of the New Testament ἐγείρω appears 49 times in reference to Jesus' resurrection to a mere 18 times for ἀνίστημι.

43. Gundry disagrees because Mark uses μετὰ τρεῖς ἡμέρας in the predictions rather than μετὰ δύο ἡμέρας, ἐν τῇ ἡμέρᾳ τῇ τρίτη as in LXX Hos. 6.2. Gundry's argument holds only so long as one cannot demonstrate Mark made an intentional break with traditional language about the timing of Jesus' resurrection at 8.31, 9.31, and 10.34.

44. Tödt, *Son of Man*, p. 185.

45. R. McKinnis, 'An Analysis of Mark X 32–34', *NovT* 18 (1976), pp. 81–100 (p. 96).

Mark's change of wording in the third-day temporal marker not only de-prioritizes Jesus' resurrection by suggesting it will happen only 'sometime in the indistinct future', it also robs this traditional aspect of Christian theology of its valuable prophetic underpinning. Although the Markan passion predictions preserve a portion of LXX Hos. 6.2's utility by having Jesus use ἀνίστημι when predicting his resurrection, the wording of the shared temporal marker nevertheless deprives the verse of its 'neat' or 'tidy' temporal precision and even uses LXX Hos. 6.2's own phraseology to do so. Whereas Hos. 6.2 spoke of resurrection 'after two' (μετὰ δύο) days, the Markan Jesus speaks instead of resurrection 'after three' (μετὰ τρεῖς). By altering the part of LXX Hos. 6.2 that would have enabled his readers to understand the passion predictions as climaxing with the all-too-familiar affirmation of Jesus' resurrection 'on the third day', Mark makes Hos. 6.2 serve his own christological purposes. There is no climactic note in the shared final clause of Mk 8.31, 9.31, and 10.34, no growing crescendo toward a miraculous act of divine reversal that renders the Son of Man's suffering acceptable. The Markan passion predictions, just like the Markan passion narrative, climax instead with the note about Jesus' death. For Mark, the Son of Man came to give his life as a ransom for the many, and so the story of Jesus' resurrection must not be allowed to detract attention from the story of the Son of God's crucifixion. Mark's effort to tone down the gospel tradition's emphasis on Jesus' resurrection therefore begins as early as Mk 8.31 with the evangelist's (dis)appropriation of LXX Hos. 6.2.

4. Conclusion: The Pragmatic Value of Inferring Intent

In the 1906–1907 Lowell lectures at Harvard University, W. James presented what in his estimation was destined to become a watershed work on how to go about resolving previously intractable metaphysical disputes. According to James, whenever confronted with incompatible philosophical claims, one need only ask which of the competing ideas admits of more practical import or utility. 'Try to interpret each notion by tracing its respective practical consequences. What difference would it practically make to any one if this notion rather than that notion were true? If no practical difference whatever can be traced, then the alternatives mean practically the same thing, and all dispute is idle.'[46] James therefore understood his pragmatic method as a verification process philosophers could use to discriminate between useful (i.e. 'true') and non-useful (i.e. 'false') ideas.

When dealing with ancient works like the Gospel of Mark, one frequently meets with questions that (like the metaphysical debates James wished to unravel) admit of no absolutely certain or verifiable answer; for the documents are old, their texts are uncertain, the communities and situations they originally addressed remain shrouded in obscurity, and their authors are no longer available for comment. Mark may have known nothing whatsoever of Hos. 6.2, but such a negative

---

46. W. James, *Pragmatism* (Great Books in Philosophy; Amherst, NY: Prometheus Books, 1991), p. 23.

proposition admits of considerably less practical merit than the alternative hypothesis. As long as there is as much evidence to suggest Mark's awareness of LXX Hos. 6.2 and its importance for first-century Christian theology as there is to deny it, scholars are better off thinking it so since this view alone can have the positive practical effect of promoting scholarly dialogue. It may be the case that Mark was such a poor writer that he unthinkingly substituted μετὰ τρεῖς ἡμέρας for the more traditional τῇ τρίτῃ (τῇ) ἡμέρᾳ, and did so for no particular reason. Yet is it not better to err on the side of giving him too much credit for creative thought than too little? Unnecessarily minimalistic or dismissive assessments of Mark's literary and theological skill serve only to truncate scholarly discussion on potentially viable issues, which is harmful not only for Biblical Studies but for every other academic discipline as well.

For this reason the current investigation of Mark's reaction to the traditional early Christian reading of LXX Hos. 6.2 sides with the general outlook of thinkers like Kee, who characterizes Mark's attitude toward available messianic models as indifferent except where such expectations served his particular narrative interests. 'Mark presents his christological portraits of Jesus, not by seeking to show how Jesus conformed to existing models of messianic or redemptive agents…but by redefining and reworking these to formulate his own.'[47] As J.D. Crossan suggests, Mark 'is not primarily interested in the apologetical and polemical value of Old Testament quotation to define and defend the Christian community over against Judaism…but as a weapon to define and defend the Christology he believes in'.[48] If the proposed reading of the temporal phrase μετὰ τρεῖς ἡμέρας in the passion predictions of 8.31, 9.31, and 10.34 is correct, Mark's treatment of the standard early Christian reading of LXX Hos. 6.2 provides an example of this phenomenon at work. Mark exegetically (dis)appropriated LXX Hos. 6.2 in these verses because doing so suited his theological interests, which (in contrast with other first-century Christologies) sought to subordinate all other aspects of Jesus' life and teachings to the cross.

---

47. Kee, 'Function of Scriptural Quotations', p. 186.
48. J.D. Crossan, 'Redaction and Citation in Mark 11.9–10 and 11.17', *BR* 17 (1972), pp. 33–50 (pp. 49–50). Crossan's article identifies two other pre-Markan exegetical traditions the second evangelist reworked for Christological reasons.

THE NARRATIVE ROLE OF JOHN AND JESUS IN MARK 1.1–15[1]

Tom Shepherd

1. *Introduction*

In the study of the Gospel of Mark, numerous questions have been raised concerning the introduction or prologue of the Gospel. In this short study we can only address a few of these questions. Does the prologue extend through v. 8, v. 11, v. 13, or v. 15, and what difference does answering the question make?[2] Is the first verse a title for the entire book or does it refer only to the prologue itself?[3] What role does the Scripture citation(s) play in 1.2–3?[4] And finally, what are the narrative characteristics of the passage?[5]

---

1. I wish to express thanks to Union College in Lincoln, Nebraska, for a generous grant of assistance towards writing this chapter.

2. See Leander Keck, 'The Introduction to Mark's Gospel', *NTS* 12 (1966), pp. 352–70; Frank Matera, 'The Prologue as the Interpretative Key to Mark's Gospel', *JSNT* 34 (1988), pp. 3–20; and Robert Tannehill, 'Beginning to Study "How Gospels Begin"', in Dennis Smith (ed.), *How Gospels Begin* (*Semeia* 52; Atlanta, GA: Scholars Press, 1991), pp. 185–92.

3. See James Edwards, *The Gospel According to Mark* (Grand Rapids: Eerdmans, 2002), pp. 23–6; Paul Danove, *Linguistics and Exegesis in the Gospel of Mark: Applications of a Case Frame Analysis* (JSNTSup, 218; Studies in New Testament Greek, 10; Sheffield: Sheffield Academic Press, 2001), pp. 79–83; N. Clayton Croy, 'Where the Gospel Text Begins: A Non-Theological Interpretation of Mark 1.1', *NovT* 53 (2, 2001), pp. 105–127; and M. Eugene Boring, 'Mark 1.1–15 and the Beginning of the Gospel', in Dennis Smith (ed.), *How Gospels Begin* (*Semeia* 52; Atlanta, GA: Scholars Press, 1991), pp. 43–81.

4. See Richard Schneck, *Isaiah in the Gospel of Mark I-VIII* (Vallejo, CA: BIBAL Press, 1994); Rikki Watts, *Isaiah's New Exodus in Mark* (Grand Rapids: Baker Academic, 2000); Ched Myers, *Binding the Strong Man: A Political Reading of Mark's Story of Jesus* (Maryknoll, NY: Orbis Books, 1988), pp. 121–27; P.J. Sankey, 'Promise and Fulfillment: Reader-Response to Mark 1.1–15', *JSNT* 58 (1995), pp. 3–18; and Steve Moyise, 'Is Mark's Opening Quotation the Key to his Use of Scripture?', *IBS* 20 (1998), pp. 146–58.

5. See Edwin Broadhead, *Mark* (Sheffield : Sheffield Academic Press, 2001), pp. 21–23; Donald Juel, 'The Gospel of Mark', in Charles Cousar (ed.), *Interpreting Biblical Texts*, (Nashville: Abingdon Press, 1999), pp. 53–64; Elizabeth Struthers Malbon, 'Ending at the Beginning: A Response', in Dennis Smith (ed.), *How Gospels Begin* (*Semeia* 52; Atlanta, GA: Scholars Press, 1991), pp. 175–84; Herman Waetjen, *A Reordering of Power: A Sociopolitical Reading of Mark's Gospel* (Minneapolis: Fortress Press, 1989), pp. 63–74; Elizabeth Struthers Malbon, ' "Reflected Christology": An Aspect of Narrative "Christology" in the Gospel of Mark', *Perspectives in Religious Studies* 26.2 (1999), pp. 127–45; Étienne Trocmé, *L'Évangile Selon Saint Marc* (Commentaire du Nouveau Testament II; Genève: Labor et Fides, 2000), pp. 21–31; Francis Moloney, *Beginning the Good News: A Narrative Approach* (Collegeville, MN: Liturgical Press, 1992), pp. 43–71; and John Donahue and Daniel Harrington, *The Gospel of Mark* (Sacra Pagina, 2; Collegeville, MN: Liturgical Press, 2002), p. 70. See

It is the goal of this study to present briefly the findings of a narrative analysis of Mk 1.1–15 in the standard categories of settings, characters, actions and plot, time relationships, and narrator/implied reader, and to suggest several ways this data may assist the scholarly debate over the passage. I fear that far too often narrative studies present interpretation of the narrative data without providing much of the raw analysis data itself that stands behind that interpretation. It seems preferable to me to present as much of the raw data as possible (and as is reasonable) so that others can both have the data in hand, and be able to critique the conclusions drawn from the data.

2. Settings[6]

Settings are usually the markers of a story's beginning and ending – its focalization and defocalization, though they can also serve as markers enhancing thematic concepts of a story. The settings serve both purposes in Mk 1.1–15, but the enhancement of thematic concepts seems to predominate. The settings and props are listed below in Tables 1 and 2. Those listed under 'sphere' are the cultural/religious settings or props.

Table 1. *Settings in Mark 1.1–15.*

Verse	Spatial	Temporal	Sphere
1		ἀρχή	Gospel
2	ἀποστέλλω πρὸ προσώπου Way	πρὸ προσώπου	In Isaiah
3	In the desert Way, paths		Straight
4	In the desert	ἐγένετο	Baptism, Repentance, Forgiveness
5	ἐξεπορεύετο πρός district of Judea in the Jordan		Being baptized, Confessing sins
7	ὀπίσω	ὀπίσω	
8		Baptized, He will baptize	
9	From Nazareth of Galilee In the Jordan	ἐγένετο In those days	Baptized
10	Coming up from the water		

also Robert Gundry's set of questions about this passage in his *Mark: A Commentary on his Apology for the Cross* (Grand Rapids: Eerdmans, 1993), pp. 29–30.

6.   At the end of this study I have placed an Appendix with definitions of narrative analysis terms as I use them in this study.

Verse	Spatial	Temporal	Sphere
	Heavens		
	Coming down		
11	From the heavens		Well pleased
12	Cast out into desert	εὐθύς	
13	In the desert	40 days	
14	Imprisoned	After	Gospel
	Into Galilee		
15		καιρός	βασιλεία τοῦ θεοῦ Repent, believe, in the Gospel

Table 2. *Props in Mark 1.1–15.*

Verse	Spatial	Sphere
6	Camel hairs, leather belt, locusts, wild honey	Camel hairs, leather belt, locusts, wild honey
7	Strap of sandal	Strap of sandal
8	With water	With water, with Holy Spirit
13	With wild beasts	With wild beasts

The settings enhance thematic concepts by placing special focus on two over-arching ideas – the eschatological time for change and the fulfillment of God's promises has arrived, and Jesus is the superior figure who will bring in the kingdom of God.

The focus on the eschatological times occurs in the references to the desert, in the cultural and religious settings noted under Sphere, and in the use of the term καιρός. The desert is the crucial location for action in the prologue. It was linked in Israelite history to God saving Israel from bondage in Egypt, and as a place of protection for and revelation to Elijah.[7] Alluding to this connection via the props that link John the Baptist to Elijah, the Evangelist presents the desert once again as an Exodus for God's people.[8]

The many cultural and religious settings noted under Sphere have an overwhelmingly consistent emphasis – a focus on a sacral world view with dominant ties to the Jewish heritage. The assumed context is a moral code in which human sinfulness is shameful and people are called to repentance. Baptism, repentance and forgiveness all fit into the eschatological perspective articulated by the settings.

The use of the temporal setting καιρός in 1.15 enhances the eschatological theme of repentance. Καιρός is used five times in Mark, usually with the sense

7. The props link John the Baptist to Elijah. See R.T. France, *The Gospel of Mark* (NIGTC; Grand Rapids: Eerdmans, 2002), pp. 56–58, who notes the link of the desert/wilderness with the concept of hope and a new exodus parallel to the outlook of the Qumran sect. Cf. Joel Marcus, *Mark 1–8* (AB, 27; New York: Doubleday, 2000), pp. 139–40 for various apocalyptic characteristics of the prologue.

8. Note how all of Judea and Jerusalem *go out* (ἐκπορεύομαι) to John the Baptist.

of the time for harvest, the determined or opportune time (11.13, 12.2, 13.33). It is a time for which one must be on guard and be awake to change (1.15, 13.33). In this sense καιρός comes as a conclusion or fulfillment of a period of time (such as a field of grain becomes ripe after a summer of maturation). The καιρός in this eschatological sense in 1.15 is what demands change – repentance and belief in the Gospel.

The concept of Jesus as superior is emphasized in two ways by settings – his position in relation to the sender and messenger in v. 2, and his location at the baptismal scene. The sender in v. 2 sends away (ἀποστέλλω) the messenger (ἄγγελος) 'before the face' of the 'you' character.[9] The picture created is that of a herald going before an important personage. Spatially this depiction places the 'you' character closer to the sender and thereby intimates Jesus' superiority.

At the baptismal scene Jesus comes *up* from the water while the Spirit comes *down* from the heavens. This pattern of telling suggests that Jesus has cosmic importance. Heaven and earth meet in him at his baptism.

But what of focalization and defocalization? One of the major difficulties in determining the length of the prologue is the way in which focalization and defocalization occur in the passage. Typical focalization brings together characters at a certain time and place. Action then takes place, and then the characters disperse (defocalization). However, in the prologue of Mark it does not occur that way. The book begins with the intriguing term ἀρχή which is then immediately followed by the introduction of Jesus Christ as the central character of the Gospel. But in v. 2 while Jesus is evidently still present, the focus shifts to the messenger figure, who will turn out to be John the Baptist. Jesus does not return to center stage in the story until v. 9. Thus, the story begins with an incomplete focalization on the main character, Jesus Christ.

The typical form of focalization appears in v. 4 with the appearance of John the Baptist in the desert preaching a baptism of repentance. Again, the typical form of focalization appears in v. 9 with the coming of Jesus to the Jordan for baptism. But then the problem arises of an incomplete defocalization of John the Baptist. Jesus is driven by the Spirit into the desert in v. 12 and then he enters Galilee in v. 14, all moving the story forward from the baptismal scene. However, v. 14 also notes that John has been thrown in prison. A gap is opened in the story as to just how this happened and what it portends – thus a sense of incomplete defocalization. We hear no more about John the Baptist until Mark 6 where his imprisonment and beheading are explained in graphic detail.

Why does the Evangelist begin his Gospel with incomplete focalization of Jesus and then leave us with incomplete defocalization of John the Baptist? There are likely theological reasons for both. The Evangelist wants us to know from the beginning that this book is about Jesus Christ. Thus, he must introduce Jesus first. However, it is obvious historically that John the Baptist preceded Jesus. The Evangelist goes out of his way to stress the relationship of John to Jesus, and the structure of the prologue emphasizes the central role of Jesus above John.

9. The 'you' figure in v. 2 is ambiguous at first, but later it becomes clear that he is Jesus. See below under 'Characters'.

The incomplete focalization of Jesus at the beginning serves notice from the start that Jesus is the central character.

But why the incomplete defocalization of John in 1.14? The Evangelist has talked about the 'Way of the Lord' in 1.3. We will eventually see that this 'Way' will lead Jesus to the cross. The Baptist precedes Jesus both as forerunner of the Gospel and as one who goes to death. By way of parallelism, the Evangelist will suggest that John's fate will become Jesus' fate. This is narrated when he returns to John's story in ch. 6.[10] The incomplete defocalization of John suggested by the gap in v. 14 serves as a pointer as to where the 'Way of the Lord' will lead.

3. *Characters*

The major characters of Mk 1.1–15 and their characterization are listed in Table 3 and the minor characters are listed in Table 4.[11]

Table 3. *Major Characters of Mark 1.1–15.*

Character	Characterization by Showing	Characterization by Telling
Jesus	Intimate of God (v. 2)	Christ (v. 1)
	Leader/King (vv. 2–3)	Lord (v. 3)
Humble/baptized (v. 9)	Stronger one (v. 7)	
Visionary (v. 10)	Follower of John (v. 7)	
Under Spirit (v. 12)	Baptizer with Spirit (v. 8)	
Tempted (v. 13)	Beloved son (v. 11)	
Weak/needy (v. 13)		
Authoritative (v. 15)		
Preacher (v. 15)		
God	Authoritative (v. 2)	Has beloved son (v. 11)
	Sender (v. 2)	
	Predictor (vv. 2–3)	
	Pleased with Jesus (v. 11)	
	King (v. 15)	
John the Baptist	Sent by God (v. 2)	Ἄγγελος (v. 2)
	Preparer of the way (v. 3)	Preparer of the way (v. 2)
	Preacher (v. 4)	Voice (v. 3)
	Authoritative/popular (v. 5)	John the Baptizer (v. 4)
	Ascetic (v. 6)	Unworthy to untie (v. 7)
	Elijah like (v. 6)	Baptizer with water (v. 8)
	Humble servant (v. 7)	
	Persecuted (v. 14)	
	Silenced (v. 14)	
Holy Spirit	Comes upon Jesus (v. 10)	Holy (v. 8)
	Authority over Jesus (v. 12)	Like Dove (v. 10)

10. See Tom Shepherd, *Markan Sandwich Stories: Narration, Definition, and Function* (Andrews University Seminary Doctoral Dissertation Series, 18; Berrien Springs, MI: Andrews University Press, 1993), pp. 172–209.

11. The characters of Mark 1.1–15 are not listed as major or minor solely on their role in this passage. Major characters also play an important role in the Gospel as a whole.

Table 4. *Minor Characters in Mark 1.1–15.*

Character	Characterization by Showing	Characterization by Telling
Isaiah	Prophet (vv. 2–3)	Prophet (v. 2)
Region of Judea and People of Jerusalem	Repentant (v. 5)	Confessors of sin (v. 5)
Satan	Tempter (v. 13)	

Jesus is the first character introduced in Mark and, not surprisingly, is the central figure of the prologue. It is striking the amount of characterization of Jesus which occurs in these few verses both by telling and showing. Many of the major Christological titles of Mark are presented here via telling – Christ, Lord, beloved son. This is quite impressive in light of the paucity of the titles in the majority of the book. The reader is informed from the start that Jesus is the Christ, a fact which takes characters in the story a great deal of time to figure out.

More than the Christological titles, however, it is striking how much characterization of Jesus occurs via showing. He is depicted as on intimate terms with God via the words of prophecy where God addresses him simply as 'you' in v. 2, and states that he will send his angel ahead of him.[12] Jesus is depicted in terms similar to an earthly potentate going out in his chariot, whose road has been prepared beforehand (vv. 2–3). He is a person who receives a vision from God in which he is addressed as beloved son (v. 11), and he brings an authoritative message about the kingdom of God (v. 15).

However, mixed in with these depictions of power are a number of pictures that suggest an opposing view of Jesus as weak, in need, or in submission.[13] These are especially displayed in the characterization by showing in contrast to the characterization by telling which tends to focus on Jesus' power. Jesus comes after John (ὀπίσω v. 7) and is baptized by John (v. 9). It must be noted that the Evangelist places the typical term for a disciple used of Jesus in v. 7 (ὀπίσω) within the context of John calling Jesus stronger than he. Furthermore, he tempers the sense of Jesus following John via the Scripture quotation in 1.2–3 which intimates that a greater personage follows those who prepare the way before him. Nevertheless, the terminology for a follower is still used. And it is compounded by the fact that Jesus is baptized by John. Further depictions of Jesus as weak or humble occur with him being ministered to by angels (suggesting a state of weakness or need). Add to this Jesus' submission to and direction by the Holy Spirit with the rather strong use of ἐκβάλλω, and then couple this with his subordination to God (God appears to be in charge of his 'way' in 1.1–3 and Jesus is called 'beloved son' in 1.11 suggesting that God is his Father) and the sense of Jesus being both a strong and weak or submissive character at the same time becomes

12. Cf. Marcus, *Mark 1–8*, p. 147.
13. Cf. Boring, 'Mark 1.1–15 and the Beginning of the Gospel', pp. 43–81, see especially, pp. 63–65.

evident. He is an extraordinary character, one with an intimate, primary relationship to God, and yet he is related to mankind and the world of people in such a way that humility, submission, and weakness are evident.

The depiction of John the Baptist carries some of the same paradoxical strong and weak characteristics. John is ἄγγελος, preparer of the way, the voice, sent by God, a great authoritative preacher, ascetic, and Elijah like. However, he is clearly depicted by both showing and telling to be inferior to Jesus, a humble servant, unworthy to even untie the thong of the sandal of the one to follow him, and finally imprisoned.

The Evangelist clearly sets out to draw a comparison and contrast between Jesus and John in the prologue. Throughout almost the entire passage (except for the description of John's ministry in 1.4–6, and Jesus' temptation in 1.12–13), there is always some parallel or contrast between them displayed. In the Scripture quotation God sends the ἄγγελος before his intimate relation to prepare the way. In John's preaching he depicts Jesus as superior. At the baptism John baptizes with water, but God sends down the Holy Spirit and addresses Jesus as 'beloved son'. In vv. 14–15 John is imprisoned, silenced it seems, and Jesus begins to preach boldly. The Evangelist wants the reader to know that Jesus is superior to John, even while he depicts Jesus as both a strong and weak character.

4. *Actions and Plot*

The details of actions in Mk 1.1–15 are found in Table 5.

Table 5. *Actions in Mark 1.1–15*

Ref.	Actor	Action	Duration	Frequency
1.1	Narrator	Beginning of Gospel	Pause	Single
1.2	Isaiah	It is written	Summary	Single
1.2	(God)	I am sending my angel	Tableau	Single
1.2	Angel	Who will prepare your way	Summary	Single
1.3	Voice	Crying in the wilderness	Tableau	Iterative
1.3	Voice	Prepare the way of the Lord	Tableau	Repeat
1.3	Voice	Make straight his paths	Tableau	Repeat
1.4	John	Baptizing and preaching	Summary	Iterative/repeat
1.5	Judea	Went out to him	Summary	Iterative
1.5	Judea	Were being baptized	Summary	Iterative/repeat
1.5	Judea	Confessing their sins	Summary	Iterative
1.6	Narrator	John's clothes and food	Pause	Iterative
1.7	John	Preached stronger one comes after me	Tableau	Single
1.7	John	I am not worthy to stoop and untie	Tableau	Single
1.8	John	I baptized with water	Tableau	Repeat
1.8	John	He will baptize with Holy Spirit	Summary	Single
1.9	Jesus	It occurred, he came	Summary	Single
1.9	Jesus	He was baptized by John	Summary	Single
1.10	Jesus	While coming up he saw heaven split	Tableau	Single
1.10	Spirit	Coming down like a dove	Tableau	Single
1.11	Voice	Came from heaven, son, well pleased	Tableau	Single

Ref.	Actor	Action	Duration	Frequency
1.12	Spirit	Casts him out into the desert	Summary	Single
1.13	Jesus	In the desert 40 days	Summary	Iterative
1.13	Jesus	Being tempted by Satan	Summary	Iterative
1.13	Angels	Were ministering to him	Summary	Iterative
1.14	John	Was handed over	Summary	Single
1.14	Jesus	Came into Galilee	Summary	Single
1.14	Jesus	Preaching the Gospel of God	Summary	Iterative
1.15	Jesus	Saying the time is fulfilled	Tableau	Repeat
1.15	Jesus	Kingdom of God is near	Tableau	Single
1.15	Jesus	Repent and believe the Gospel	Tableau	Single

Several points stand out in regards to the actions as depicted here. In the frequency data we note that in the first section of the prologue (vv. 1–8) there are a great number of repeats that take place. This is illustrative of the controlling role of the Scripture prophecy as quoted in 1.2–3.[14] These prophetic words become the direction within which the historical fulfillment in John's ministry finds its direction and meaning. This is all centered in the words καθώς γέγραπται. Interestingly, the καθώς reaches back into 1.1 to explain what the ἀρχὴ τοῦ εὐαγγελίου consists of or is based upon.[15] It is based upon the Scripture prophecy. Thus γέγραπται becomes the initial cause of the fulfillment (repeats of the prophecy's prediction) in the ministry of John.

However, when we see John's ministry unfold, we do not at first hear his voice. Ironically, his ministry is initially described in summary fashion – he preached, he baptized, but we do not hear his words. It is not until he describes the one to come after him that we actually hear words from his mouth. Thus, graphically, the Evangelist depicts the ministry of John focused on the fulfillment of the words of Scripture – preparing the way for the Lord.

In the duration data the typical pattern is summary statements followed by tableaus. It is interesting that the tableaus always involve someone speaking. We hear a number of voices. The first voice is the voice of God speaking through the prophet – 'I am sending my ἄγγελον who will prepare your way'. Then we hear the voice of the ἄγγελος in Scripture – 'Prepare the way of the Lord'. Then we

14. Cf. Donald Juel's comment, 'The citation from Isaiah and the scriptural echoes in the voice at Jesus' baptism are particularly significant as introducing the "script" by which the story will proceed. The story is driven by a kind of necessity: it has been written or, to put it another way, it has been promised' (*Mark*, p. 63).

15. Many take all of v. 1 to be a title for the book. However, it is more likely that ἀρχή points to the events of the prologue itself as the beginning of the Gospel. The key to the role of v. 1 is found in the use of καθώς in v. 2. Καθώς is used eight times in Mark (1.2, 4.33, 9.13, 11.6, 14.16, 14.21, 15.8, and 16.7). In every case, except possibly 4.33, it relates a current event (stated before καθώς) to a previous event (stated after καθώς). The previous event predicts in some way the current event. Three times καθώς introduces a quotation from Scripture (καθώς γέγραπται, 1.2, 9.13, and 14.21). In both 9.13 and 14.21 it is clear that the Scripture prophecy which follows καθώς is fulfilled by the event which precedes καθώς. Hence, it seems logical to expect the same in 1.2, in which case the beginning of the Gospel in 1.1 is the fulfillment of the Scripture prophecies quoted in 1.2–3. Thus 1.1 is intimately tied to 1.2–3 which is linked to 1.4–8 and the rest of the prologue. Cf. Gundy, *Mark*, pp. 30–31.

hear the voice of John himself – 'The mightier one is coming after me. I am not worthy to stoop and loose the thong of his sandal. I baptized you with water, but he will baptize you with the Holy Spirit.' Then we hear God's voice again – 'You are my beloved son, in whom I am well pleased'. And finally we hear Jesus' voice – 'The time is fulfilled, the kingdom of God is near, repent and believe the Gospel'. In each of these voices, save for the declaration about Jesus' sonship in 1.11, there is a sense of movement or motion. They speak of the Way of the Lord, a new direction which Jesus will follow and which he challenges other to follow. Combined with the testimony of these voices are statements of status – Jesus is the mightier one and the beloved son. Just where this Way will lead we are not explicitly told, but it is obvious that by 1.14–15 Jesus is on that Way.[16]

This leads us to a consideration of the plot of the prologue. Plot has to do with both direction and uncertainty of outcomes. These two concepts of direction and uncertainty are exactly what we meet in the concept of the Way of the Lord in the prologue. It is first described in the Scripture quotation with the metaphor of someone preparing the way for a royal figure. This is then tied into the ministry of John. Somehow his preaching of repentance, baptism, and the forgiveness of sin must prepare the way for what is to come. Then Jesus is linked into the scene through John's words about the mightier one. True to the plot theme of the Way of the Lord, John describes this mightier one as 'coming'. Jesus then proceeds to come to the Jordan for baptism, then is cast out into the desert, and then comes into Galilee preaching. The data already noted under characters above informs and helps to shape the plot. This Way of the Lord has an extraordinary figure walking it – Jesus, who is Christ, Lord, and beloved son, but who also experiences weakness and tempting in his life. The Way of the Lord does not appear to be an easy road. Indeed, the hints about John the Baptist and his comparison and contrast to Jesus imply that the Way of the Lord leads to difficulty and death.

We have suggested in discussing the plot that there are several unknowns in the prologue. These are best described as gaps – purposefully missing information which the narrator leaves out and which will be filled in later as the plot progresses. The gaps in the prologue include: What is the Way of the Lord, and where will it go? When will Jesus baptize with the Holy Spirit and what is that baptism?[17] Why is Jesus baptized? Why was God pleased with Jesus?[18] Why was John imprisoned? These gaps are either filled or expanded upon later in the narrative as Jesus proceeds on the Way of the Lord marked out for him. That they arise in the prologue suggests that the beginning of the Gospel lays out in cryptic form the major themes and directions of the book.

---

16. We noted above under 'settings' that the narrative points us toward the cross as the place where the Way will lead, but that becomes explicit only later in the Gospel.

17. It does not, as some suggest, occur within the pages of Mark. This baptism will take place later. See below under 'Time'.

18. Noted by Matera, 'The Prologue as the Interpretative Key to Mark's Gospel', p. 8.

5. *Time*

The analepses of Mk 1.1–15 are listed in Table 6. The prolepses are listed in Table 7.

Table 6. *Analepses in Mark 1.1–15.*

Ref.	Phrase	Type
1.2	'It is written…'	Mixed Analepsis
1.8	'I baptized you with water…'	Internal Repeating Homodiegetic Analepsis
1.15	'The time is fulfilled and the kingdom of God is near.'	Mixed Analepsis

Table 7. *Prolepses in Mark 1.1–15.*

Ref.	Phrase	Type
1.2	'I am sending my messenger before your face, who will prepare your way.'	Internal Homodiegetic Completing Prolepsis
	'A voice of one crying in the wilderness, "Prepare the way of the Lord".'	Internal Homodiegetic Completing Prolepsis
1.7	'The stronger one is coming after me…'	Internal Homodiegetic Completing Prolepsis
1.8	'…he will baptize you with the Holy Spirit.'	Mixed Prolepsis

Anachronies appear in stories for specific reasons.[19] Recognizing their presence and type is a first step in elucidating their purpose. Sometimes, as in our narrative, both analepses and prolepses work in concert to express the meaning the author wishes to convey. In 1.2–3 there is a conjunction of a mixed analepsis and two internal completing homodiegetic prolepses. 'It is written' is the mixed analepsis which points back to the Old Testament passages the Evangelist draws on. The writing of the Old Testament passages occurred long before Mark was penned. However, the Evangelist, using an intensive perfect, expresses his belief that the ancient writings continue to have authority in his time (thus, a mixed analepsis).

Although Mark refers to Isaiah, the quotation actually is a combination of three passages – Exod. 23.20, Mal. 3.1, and Isa. 40.3. The Exodus passage in its context

---

19. Notice that the controlling feature of narrative that determines if an anachrony occurs is story time – the historical time of the story world. An anachrony is a disorder in the telling of story time in the discourse. Thus, any telling of events out of order, be it ever so slight, fulfills the definition of an anachrony and its subcategories of analepsis and prolepsis. I have avoided here the use of the terms 'flashback' for an analepsis, and 'flashforward' for a prolepsis. The reason for this is that, as used here, the terms analepsis and prolepsis have a broader definition than either flashback or flashforward. The usual way of thinking of a flashback is that of an entire scene from the past that is told in the story's present, and a flashforward as a narrative shift to a future scene which is told in the story's present. However, the terms analepsis and prolepsis are more sensitive and cover more possibilities than only complete scenes which either take us backward or forward in time.

has God stating that he will send an angel before Israel to bring them into the Promised Land. In Mark we are not immediately told who the ἄγγελος will be, but later learn it is John the Baptist. In Malachi 2–3 there is an interesting mix of judgment and mercy. The prophecy of the coming messenger in 3.1 carries more of the message of judgment ('But who can endure the day of his coming?' 3.2). The Isaiah passage is in a context of comfort to God's people (Isa. 40.1–2), but also contains a message of the humbling of human pride (40.6–8).

This interesting combination of Old Testament passages, expressing both mercy and judgment, God's gentle watch care and guidance, and his punishment of evil, comes in to Mark as a prophecy being fulfilled. The combination of analepsis and prolepsis makes the striking point that what the Old Testament prophets foretold is now coming to pass. Whether the outcome will be mercy or judgment, or a combination of both, remains to be seen and reinforces the openness of the plot of both this passage and the Gospel of Mark as a whole.[20]

The next location for anachrony is in 1.7–8, and again there is a conjunction of an analepsis and two prolepses. The statement, 'I baptized you with water', is an internal repeating homodiegetic analepsis since it looks back to the Baptist's ministry of immersing people, but places it within the context of the ministry of the Coming One. This serves to reinterpret the significance of the Baptist's work and relates what he has done to what the Coming One will do.

'The stronger one is coming after me', is the first of two prolepses in 1.7–8. It is an internal completing homodiegetic prolepsis because it finally settles the relationship between Jesus and John and brings to closure the open question of just who the ἄγγελος and the 'Lord' of 1.2–3 are.[21] It is followed in 1.8 by a mixed analepsis, 'he will baptize you with the Holy Spirit'. It appears as though this predicted work of Jesus never occurs within the pages of the Gospel of Mark, thus it is a mixed analepsis. The truth of this claim is illustrated by Jesus' discussion with James and John in 10.35–40. There Jesus asks the two brothers if they are able to drink the cup he drinks or to be baptized with the baptism he is baptized with. They are ignorant of what his future holds, but he predicts, 'the cup which I drink you will drink and the baptism I am baptized with you will be baptized with'. Their experience of this baptism is clearly future, which is another mixed analepsis. It is narrated in the story's present, but its fulfillment is future.[22]

---

20. Cf. Watts, *Isaiah's New Exodus and Mark*, pp. 86–88.

21. Thus Mary Tolbert is correct in noting the ambiguity of 1.1–3, but I find unconvincing her chiastic structure for 1.1–13 and her application of ἄγγελος to Jesus instead of John in 1.1–3. John's statement in 1.7–8 that the stronger one will come after him links the Baptist to the preparatory role of the ἄγγελος of 1.1–3. This also makes much more sense of the position and role of John's ministry in 1.4–6. See Mary Tolbert, *Sowing the Gospel Mark's World in Literary-Historical Perspective* (Minneapolis: Fortress Press, 1989), pp. 108–13, 239–48. Note the reference to 'ambiguity at best' on p. 240.

22. It is interesting that, as Tolbert notes, there is irony between 1.7–8 and 1.9–10 in the way that John calls himself inferior to Jesus and yet baptizes him, and that Jesus is predicted to be the baptizer with the Holy Spirit, but is himself baptized by John. See Tolbert, *Sowing the Gospel*, p. 110. However, it is important to recognize that 1.9–10 is not the fulfillment of 1.7–8 but only its ironic contrast. John really is inferior to Jesus, and although Jesus is baptized with water and the Spirit descends on

This prediction of future baptism for the disciples is within the context of the second passion prediction. Clearly the baptism Jesus has in mind is tied to the cross. It seems reasonable to conclude that the baptism of the Spirit in 1.8 would also have some linkage to suffering for Jesus' sake.[23]

The final analepsis occurs in 1.15 when Jesus begins to preach the Gospel of God. He says that the time (καιρός) is fulfilled. As Marcus points out, καιρός can mean a 'decisive moment' or a 'span of time'.[24] The span of time seems more appropriate since 'fulfilled' suggests a time line coming to completion. This terminology of time fulfillment, combined with the call to repent and believe, fits well within an apocalyptic perspective. These words of Jesus have the same kind of ring to them as the opening verses of the prologue (1.1–3) which tells of prophecy fulfilling before your eyes and the concomitant call to prepare the way for the Lord. Furthermore, Jesus' words echo those of John the Baptist when he preaches a baptism of repentance.

The anachronies of the prologue tie the ἀρχή of the Gospel in to a panoramic view of time. The prologue looks back to the Old Testament prophecies and declares that they are coming to fulfillment now in the ministry of John the Baptist and Jesus. And the prologue looks forward to the powerful ministry of Jesus – a ministry more powerful than that of John, as baptism by the Spirit is more powerful than water baptism.

But there is also an interesting congruence that these anachronies produce. The prophecies of the past are brought into the present. The ministry of Jesus is linked to the ministry of John. And the future is tied to the present. The Gospel ties the past, the present, and the future together into one message of challenge, change, and hope based in belief.

6. *Narrator and Implied Reader*

The narrator of any story can be described by four characteristics – knowledge, intrusion, distance, and ideology. The narrator in Mark, in common with other biblical narrative, is omniscient. He knows where and when everything occurs, can see over long distances, and authoritatively tells the reader what everything means. He is privy to private statements between God and Jesus and informs the reader of these.

The prologue of Mark probably has the most intrusion of the narrator found anywhere in this Gospel. Verse 1 is entirely an intrusion by the narrator – informing the reader exactly who Jesus is. The narrator also uses the Scripture passage

---

him in 1.9–11, his deeper baptism occurs at the cross (note the reversal of the scene of 1.9–11 in 15.33–40 where Jesus cries for God – mistakenly understood by bystanders to be Jesus calling for Elijah [parallel John the Baptist in 1.9, cf. 9.11–13]; Jesus expires [ἐκπνέω – parallel to the cognate πνεῦμα in the descent of the Holy Spirit in 1.10]; the curtain is split [σχίζω, as the heavens are split in 1.10]; and the centurion calls Jesus Son of God [parallel to God's voice in 1.11]). The irony in 1.7–10 points to the aspect of weakness of the Messiah as noted above under characters.

23. Cf. 13.9–13 with its reference to witness, the Holy Spirit giving words, and suffering.
24. Marcus, *Mark 1–8*, p. 172.

of 1.2–3 to further inform the reader what to expect. Verse 6, describing the food and clothing of John the Baptist, could also be seen as narrator intrusion – a pause to better inform the reader just who John the Baptist is.

The narrator uses distance to draw the reader ever closer to characters. The spatial aspects of scenes always begin with a wide angle view from a distance. John is in the desert and all Judea goes out to him. However, the view draws in closer to John as we see baptisms taking place. And then we are able to see John's clothing and food, and finally we hear him speak. The distance moves from far away to close up.

The same happens with the scenes dealing with Jesus. First we are at a distance, he comes from Galilee. But shortly we are close up as John baptizes him and then we hear God's voice from heaven to Jesus. Then we back away with Jesus going out into the desert – this whole desert scene is presented at a greater distance. But then Jesus goes into Galilee and we hear his voice – another close up view.

Temporally, the distance of the implied author from the scene seems to be somewhat far. The story of the ἀρχή of the Gospel is in the implied author's past. Almost the entire narrative is told in the past tense. Mark 1.1–3 is a special sort of exception. There is no verb (stative or otherwise) in v. 1. This lends a certain timeless quality to 1.1–3. However, even here 1.1 is the ἀρχή of the Gospel. It is a starting point, and one clearly in the implied author's past.

It is interesting that 1.1–3 does not seem to be in the narrator's past. The timeless quality of these verses suggests that the narrator speaks of them as his present. This would suggest a triple layer to this story. The implied author is far, distant in some later present. The story itself is in the past, but the narrator is somewhere in between these two, in a reflective period at some distance from the beginning of the Gospel, and able to interpret for the reader what is going to happen and what it will mean, but not in the present of the implied author who seems to be in the same time period as the reader.

In terms of ideology, the narrator's viewpoint is quite clear. Jesus is the Christ, the hero of the story. The Old Testament is authoritative Scripture. There is right and there is wrong and there is a clear demarcation between who is on the right side and who is on the wrong side. There is a hierarchy of beings within a sacral world view. Heaven is God's place, earth is man's place. Jesus is somehow in between – affirmed as son from heaven, yet tempted on earth by Satan. A controversy rages over him as cosmic characters tempt him or support him.

The implied reader is expected to know Koine Greek, to have a sacral worldview, to know that Isaiah is authoritative Scripture, and to know and accept numerous biblical concepts such as baptism, sin, repentance, confession, belief, temptation, eschatology, and the kingdom of God.

The story telling in the prologue is both character elevating and reader elevating. It is character elevating in that the reader does not know for some time just who the ἄγγελος and the 'you' of 1.2 are. Nor does the reader know exactly where the Way of the Lord will lead, nor why John was arrested. However, the prologue is also reader elevating by way of the narrator aside in 1.1–3, and by hearing the voice of God to Jesus at the baptism, and by being able to observe, if at a distance, the temptation of Jesus in the wilderness.[25] While overall we may sense a quite overt reader elevating stance in the prologue, the more covert character elevating aspects of the prologue give clues to the reader that there may be surprises. The reader who forgets this even handed approach will likely be caught by surprise, not unlike the surprise of the cross to the disciples.[26]

7. *Summary and the Scholarly Debate*

What is the overall picture of the narrative which this analysis demonstrates? At the heart of the prologue is the role that Jesus will play in the Gospel. The narrator informs us from the beginning who he is. And two of the voices in the prologue emphasize his power – John the Baptist's words about Jesus as stronger one, and God's voice at the baptism about Jesus as beloved son.

But a 'role' includes more than status, it involves action as well. Jesus' status is settled from the beginning – he is Christ, Lord, stronger one, son – all signs of power. But Jesus' actions seem to point more in the direction of weakness – coming after John, being baptized, being cast out. He is powerful in action also, the voices in 1.1–3 and 1.14–15 point to this, but one cannot escape the sense of a strong and weak hero. This is underscored by the comparison the prologue makes between Jesus and John the Baptist. Both have characteristics of power and weakness.

This strong/weak character, Jesus, follows the Way of the Lord. The sense of journey, movement, change, occurs through the entire prologue, linked to concepts such as baptism, repentance, belief. The plot points in the same direction – we know that Jesus is amazingly strong, yet with connections to weakness, and that he is on a journey, the Way of the Lord that will lead him we know not where, but it seems a journey fraught with danger.

Besides the role of Jesus, the prologue emphasizes the perspective within which the Gospel will be displayed. Information from the settings and the time relationships points towards an eschatological perspective on the ministry of Jesus. Under settings the desert is the place of eschatological action. In time relationships the analepses and prolepses tie together the prophecies of the past with the present of Jesus and the future direction which his ministry will take giving a panoramic and eschatological perspective to the prologue.

25. See Matera, 'The Prologue as the Interpretative Key to Mark's Gospel', p. 5.

26. The even-handed approach to the story by the narrator is probably linked to the narrative strategy of both bonding the reader to the disciples and distancing the reader from them. It is a delicate balancing act which both affirms the disciples as the foundational witnesses of the Gospel and bonds us to them, and yet shows how Jesus called them and calls us to not only follow him, but follow him to the cross. Those who emphasize the reader elevating characteristics of Mark may be prone to see its message as a rejection of the disciples. But to take such a stance seems to me to parallel the pre-passion confidence of the disciples. It is to see the Gospel as an affirmation of wisdom rather than as a call to self denial.

Finally, the information about the narrator and implied reader point to both a reader elevating and character elevating story telling method. Congruent with the picture of the disciples in the rest of Mark, the reader both knows and does not know what will take place. Combining this with the apocalyptic viewpoint and Way of the Lord it is clear that Mark will both lead and challenge the reader to face the call to discipleship.

In summary we may say that the prologue focuses on the role of Jesus and places his Way within the perspective of Old Testament prophecy and the apocalyptic characteristics of the desert, the call to repentance, and fulfillment of the καιρός.

We turn briefly in conclusion to the questions raised at the beginning of this article. How long is the prologue? Does verse one serve as a title for the entire book? What role does the Scripture citation play? And what are the narrative characteristics of the passage?[27]

The length of the prologue is an important question because of the implications it carries for the development of characters and themes within the Gospel. An error in determining the length of the prologue could lead to a faulty understanding of the characters, misunderstanding of themes, or at least a failure to recognize logical linkages the narrative implies. The narrative analysis above points to 1.1–15 as the length of the prologue.[28] There are too many interconnections between John and Jesus in 1.1–13 to suggest that the prologue extends only through v. 8. Furthermore, the incomplete defocalization of John the Baptist in 1.14 and the way in which Jesus' words in 1.14–15 parallel 1.1–3, together suggest that vv. 14 and 15 should be included in the prologue.

Verse 1 serves as a heading to the prologue, not the entire book.[29] It has been demonstrated to be intimately tied to the Scripture citation in 1.2–3. Via parallel uses of καθώς elsewhere in Mark, we have noted that the event that precedes καθώς fulfills the event noted after καθώς. Verse 1 fulfills the Scripture citation, and the Scripture citation, along with the concept of the Way of the Lord, has been demonstrated to guide the direction of the development of the prologue.[30]

The intriguing article by Elizabeth Struthers Malbon on 'Reflected Christology' calls for special mention.[31] Malbon suggests that the implied author's voice appears in the words of Jesus and focuses on God while the narrator focuses on

---

27. Space does not allow for a full review and interaction with the scholarly literature. What follows are suggestions pertinent to the broader discussion of the passage.

28. Contra Gundry, *Mark*, p. 31, but in accord with Keck, 'The Introduction to Mark's Gospel', pp. 352–70. Though I think Keck is mistaken when he says the Gospel begins with Jesus' preaching (p. 359). It begins with the citation of prophecy from Isaiah (Exodus, and Malachi).

29. Contra Boring, 'Mark 1.1–15 and the Beginning of the Gospel', pp. 50–53, Matera, 'The Prologue as the Interpretative Key to Mark's Gospel', p. 6, and Edwards, *The Gospel According to Mark*, p. 23, but in concord with Danove, *Linguistics and Exegesis in the Gospel of Mark*, pp. 79–83.

30. Note Watts, *Isaiah's New Exodus and Mark*, pp. 86–88 and Moyise, 'Is Mark's Opening Quotation the Key to his Use of Scripture?', pp. 146–58 for additional concepts.

31. Malbon, '"Reflected Christology": An Aspect of Narrative "Christology" in the Gospel of Mark', pp. 127–45.

Jesus. Our research in this brief narrative study affirms Malbon's point and perhaps suggests a corollary.

In affirmation we note that Jesus' words in 1.14–15 do indeed focus on God. It is the 'gospel of God' that Jesus proclaims, not the 'gospel of Jesus Christ' as in 1.1. Indeed, almost the entire prologue in one way or another focuses on Jesus (the narrator's perspective).[32] However, as a corollary to Malbon's suggestion, we note the intriguing way that characterization by showing in the prologue tends to focus on Jesus' weakness while characterization by telling tends to focus on his strength. This would suggest that here in the prologue there is an intriguing dichotomy (not total, we must note) between who we are told Jesus is and what we see him do – not unlike Malbon's notation of the narrator's focus on Jesus and Jesus' own focus on God.

We also noted above the timeless quality of 1.1–3 and suggested that it presents the narrator's perspective in contrast to the time frame of the implied author. If this is the case, it seems that the focus on Jesus in 1.1–3 is the narrator's central perspective. This would also affirm Malbon's viewpoint that the narrator focuses on Jesus.

The narrative characteristics of the passage have been illustrated above in brief form. Delineating them and their interrelationships assists us in recognizing the thematic emphases of the prologue. At the heart of this introduction to Mark is Jesus displayed in parallel and contrast to John the Baptist. He is Christ, Lord, stronger one, son. He is baptized, cast out, tempted, served. The Way of the Lord in strength and weakness will lead to the cross. It is this irony of power in weakness that will be central to Mark's message and serve as its deepest call to discipleship.

8. *Appendix: Narrative Analysis Terminology*

Settings: The spatial, temporal, and cultural/religious locations where a story takes place.

Props: The moveable items within a setting where a story takes place.

Characters: The narrative representation of persons as perceived by the reader.

Actions: The events which take place in a story. In narrative criticism they are seen as the physical events, the speeches, and even the thoughts and feelings of characters which occur within the story. Actions can be described in terms of who does them (actor), the action itself, how long it takes to tell about the action in comparison with its actual time in the story world (*duration*),[33] and how often the action is noted in the narrative (*frequency*). Under duration we may speak of *pause* (discourse time continues, story time stops), *summary* (discourse time is less than story time),

---

32. Note the section dealing with John the Baptist. But as we have noted this relates to Jesus through the role of the forerunner.

33. Thus 'duration' describes the relationship between discourse time (the telling) and story time (the amount of time an event takes in the story world).

	tableau (we sense that discourse time = story time), *stretch* (discourse time is greater than story time), *ellipsis* (discourse time stops, story time continues). Under frequency we can speak of *singularity* (the action occurs once and is described once), *multiple singularity* (an action occurs numerous times and is recorded in the narrative the same number of times), *repeat* (the action occurs once and is described more than once in the narrative), *iterative* (the action occurs numerous times and is described once in the narrative).
Plot:	Where the story is going and the sensation of uncertainty about just how it will achieve its goal. The sense of direction in plot arises from the expression of some conflict which moves toward resolution.
Story Time:	The historical time within the story world.
Discourse Time:	The length of time taken to tell the story on the page.
Anachrony:	The telling of the events of a story in an order different than the story world's historical order. It is a disorder in the telling of story time in the discourse. Anachronies can be further classified as internal, external, or mixed and with subcategories in the internal classification of herterodiegetic or homodiegetic (which further divide into completing or repeating). In an *external anachrony*, the anachrony occurs completely outside the main story. In an *internal anachrony*, the anachrony occurs completely inside the main story. In a *mixed anachrony*, the anachrony crosses over from outside to inside or from inside to outside. In an *internal heterodiegetic anachrony*, the story line is different from that of the first story, while in an *internal homodiegetic anachrony*, the story deals with the same story as the first narrative. In an *internal homodiegetic completing anachrony*, gaps left out in the first telling of the main story are filled in. In an *internal homodiegetic repeating anachrony*, the meaning of the main story is modified by retelling of the event with a different perspective.
Analepsis:	An anachrony in which the telling of a story world event occurs later than its story time historical order. It is an event from the past, told in the story time's 'present'. The terminology for anachronies above applies to analepses.
Prolepsis:	An anachrony in which the telling of a story world event occurs earlier than its story time historical order. It is an event from the future, told in the story time's 'present'. The terminology for anachronies above applies to prolepses.
Author:	The actual person who wrote the work.
Implied Author:	The author as depicted or assumed in the written work.
Narrator:	The story teller of the work.

Narratee: The person assumed in the work to whom the narrator tells the story.

Implied
Reader: The reader as depicted or assumed in the written work.
Reader: The actual person who reads the work.

The Markan Interpretation of the Pentateuchal Food Laws[1]

Jesper Svartvik

'El hecho es que cada escritor *crea* a sus precursores. Su labor modifica nuestra concepción del pasado, como ha de modificar el futuro.'

('The fact is that each writer *creates* his precursors. Their work modifies our conception of the past, just as it is bound to modify the future.')

Jorge Luis Borges[2]

1. *Introduction*

At times biblical scholarship tends to arrive at a plateaux from where it is difficult to reach higher levels of insight.[3] Fortunately, this impasse is often overcome by the discovery of new documents or by the application of new methods. In this article it is argued that in order to further the discussion about the role of the Pentateuch in earliest Christianity, scholars will have to move beyond the study of separate quotations and references. Instead biblical scholarship is encouraged to adopt a more holistic perspective, which is presented in six programmatic points below, three of which in this particular case relate specifically to the Gospel of Mark and three to the Hebrew Bible in general. These recommendations constitute a tripartite method that includes textual, effectual and contextual perspectives. These suggestions are then put into practice in an interpretation of Mk 7.1–23, with particular emphasis on v. 15.[4]

2. *New Testament Scripture: Three Suggestions*

Text: Mark Is a Narrative Text and Must Be Read as Such
It is striking to what extent Mark has been read in the light of and therefore also in the shadow of the other canonical Gospels for almost two thousand years. The

1. Heartfelt thanks are due to Carole Gillis who corrected my English in this article.
2. J.L. Borges, 'Kafka y sus precursores', *Otras inquisiciones* (Madrid: Alianza Editorial, 1995), pp. 162–66 (p. 166). Translation: 'Kafka and his Precursors', in E. Weinberger (ed.), *The Total Library: Non-Fiction 1922–1986* (trans. E. Allen, S.J. Levine and E. Weinberger; London: Allen Lane, 2000), pp. 363–65 (p. 365).
3. T.R. Hatina, *In Search of a Context: The Function of Scripture in Mark's Narrative* (JSNTSup, 232; SSEJC, 8; London: Sheffield Academic Press, 2002), p. 45.
4. For an exhaustive tripartite examination of Mark 7.1–23, see J. Svartvik, *Mark and Mission: Mark 7.1–23 in its Narrative and Historical Contexts* (ConBNT, 32; Stockholm: Almqvist & Wiksell, 2000).

reason that Mark was neglected by early interpreters of the Bible was the result of the firm conviction that Mark was subordinate to the alleged eyewitness reports of Matthew and John. All this changed with the general acceptance of the two-source hypothesis, which would ultimately praise Mark to the skies as the premier Gospel. The portrayal of the *historical* Jesus could be rebuilt on this steady rock and nothing could prevail against it. Thus, none of the canonical Gospels has suffered more from the referential fallacy than has Mark, since it has been seen not as a text which should be understood on its own terms, but simply as a transparent film and a shortcut to history. But Mark is much more than a source for historical reconstruction of earliest Christianity; as all narrative texts, it is so much more than the sum of its parts.

When four score years of the twentieth century had passed, Markan scholars became interested in the text as a self-contained narrative. It is satisfactory to note that a growing number of scholars now argue that narrative criticism should be regarded as a necessary part not only of text-internal, but also of text-external investigations. If insufficient attention is paid to the Markan narrative, a large number of other topics hover in the air. Anyone interested in the history *behind* the text needs to first study carefully the story *in* the text: in a few words, textual analysis has operational priority over historical reconstruction.

Effect: The Markan Wirkungsgeschichte *Must Also Be Considered*

So far it has been argued that biblical scholarship makes great strides when Mark as an author is considered as a novelist and Mark as a work is approached with literary distinction. Indeed, in certain cases, Mark's *theological* agenda was soon forgotten (e.g. his apocalyptic emphasis), he has exercised a considerable *literary* influence, since he forged our understanding of the genre 'Gospel'. Reynolds Price has even called Mark '…the most enduringly powerful narrative in the history of Western civilisation, perhaps in the history of the world'.[5] This second point therefore concerns the role of the Markan readers. Texts never stand in splendid isolation – and biblical texts certainly do not constitute an exception to that rule. The earliest interpretation of Mark is found within the covers of the New Testament. It starts with the inner-canonical readings. Thus, *Redaktions–kritik* is the beginning of, but not the alternative to *Wirkungsgeschichte*.

Context: Early Christian Texts Must Not Be Isolated from Contemporary Judaism

Few would deny that second-temple Judaism has often fallen prey to New Testament scholarship. It is a sad irony that Jesus' own historical context is so often portrayed as his theological contrast. Two main factors have contributed to this understanding: first, Mark culminates with the death of Jesus. This emphasis

---

5.   R. Price, 'Foreword', in D. Rhoads and D. Michie, *Mark as Story: An Introduction to the Narrative of a Gospel* (Philadelphia: Fortress Press, 1982), pp. xi–xiii (p. xi).

on lethal causality facilitates the reading for those who are prone to see Jesus' contemporaries as his enemies, as if the entire Jewish people agitated for his execution. Secondly, the intense interest in the historicity behind the text has made some scholars forget that textual *dramatis personæ* are '...paper people, without flesh and blood'.[6] They are fabricated and '...do not "stand for" any real people in the world *outside the story*'.[7] The Markan antagonists belong to a textual world, in which they play a part necessary for the plot: they are the villains in the piece where Jesus is the hero. Their role is to create a contrast to the protagonist by leaving no room for doubt that only Jesus, not they, can rightly claim to have God's authority.

What is truly relieving in the contemporary reading of Mark is that both the text *per se* is freed from historicizing readings and that the Jews of Jesus' days are emancipated from the role of being the constant mirror image to the Markan protagonist and his followers.

3. *Hebrew Bible Scriptures: Three Suggestions*

Since the present volume seeks to further the understanding of how the Jewish Bible functions in, and contributes to, the narrative aspects of Markan narrative, it will prove fruitful to present three additional suggestions, which are all related to the study of the Scriptures.

Text: Not Only the Prophets and the Psalms, but Also the Pentateuch
First and foremost it is necessary to address the issue of the imbalance of scholarly interest in the different parts of the Hebrew Bible. Whereas the Prophets and the Psalms certainly play a dominant role in Christian theology and liturgy, the Pentateuch has been by far the most important in Jewish history. Hitherto the *Torah* has played a most modest role in Markan scholarship, sometimes discounted as something which simply hinders the boundlessness of Jesus' mission, at worst the target of an intra-Christian Law *vs.* Gospel projection. In order to further the contemporary study of Scripture within Scripture, more attention must be given to the totality of Scripture, as it was understood by the evolving rabbinic hermeneutics of *Torah*-centred Judaism.

Effect: Not Only the Text per se, but Also its Interpretation and Implementation.
Geoffrey H. Hartman has pointedly remarked that '...the proper task of midrashic or non-midrashic interpretation is to keep the Bible from becoming literature. Becoming literature might mean a material still capable of development turning

---

6. M. Bal, *Narratology: Introduction to the Theory of Narrative* (Toronto: University of Toronto Press, 2nd edn, 1997), p. 115. See also p. 122: '...a character is a construction, not a person'.

7. M.A. Powell, *What Is Narrative Criticism? A New Approach to the Bible* (London: SPCK, 1993), p. 66. For further comments, see P. Merenlahti, *Poetics for the Gospels? Rethinking Narrative Criticism* (London: T&T Clark, 2002), pp. 122ff.

into a closed corpus, a once-living but now fossilized deposit.'[8] By constantly commenting, elaborating, supplementing, questioning, defining, retracting, implementing the biblical texts, the rabbis kept them relevant despite the passage of time, shifting contexts and new circumstances. When the New Testament Gospels were written, the biblical texts already belonged to this thriving text-interpreting and *halakhah*-implementing community. There is, therefore, a problem imbedded in biblical scholarship which solely seeks to establish the role Scripture texts in the New Testament, as if these had not been interpreted in traditions, translations, *midrashim*, homilies, etc. It is actually quite remarkable how ineffectually the concept 'Old Testament' captures what the Scriptures meant to the contemporaries of Jesus. Thus, Markan scholarship needs to integrate the then evolving rabbinic scriptural hermeneutics.

It is well known how notoriously difficult it is to date sayings in the rabbinic texts, but it would be wrong, however, to draw the conclusion that the rabbinic texts cannot give us any evidence of the evolution until the *terminus ad quem*. No one would date all the *logia* in the Coptic *Gospel of Thomas* (NHC II.2) to 340 CE, that is, when the text was written down. What is needed, therefore, is to establish a plausible trajectory from *scriptura* to *rabbinica* which will help us establish the evolution of both *halakhah* and *aggadah* in New Testament times.

Context: Not Only Quotations, but Foundation.
Finally, it is also necessary to broaden the perspective. Scholars should not concentrate only on clear-cut quotations and references, but must consider that the Scriptures are intervowen into the New Testament. They are embedded in the Markan text to such an extent that they cannot be removed without destroying it. The role scripture plays in the New Testament is certainly neither a matter of antithesis nor of fulfilment, but rather of a shared symbolic universe. This, too, must be considered in future New Testament scholarship.

4. *Mark 7.1–23 as a Case Study for the Validity of the Tripartite Method*

The purpose of the remainder of this article is to exemplify how the preceding six textual, effectual and contextual recommendations could be implemented in New Testament scholarship by applying them to Mk 7.1–23 (with particular emphasis on v. 15), a pericope which has played an immensely important role in various quests for the historical Jesus, for the teaching of early Christianity and, indeed, even for *das Wesen des Christentums*. Before establishing the role of scriptural food laws in Mark, we need to address two issues:

First, the quest for the *ipsissima verba Jesu* seems to be a vain project, especially when one considers that the Gospels were written in Greek and that Jesus taught in Aramaic. What New Testament scholars should concentrate on is the *ipsissima structura*, by which is meant *the historical reconstruction, taking as its*

---

8.   G.H. Hartman, 'The Struggle for the Text', in G.H. Hartman and S. Budick (eds), *Midrash and Literature* (New Haven, CT: Yale University Press, 1986), pp. 3–18 (p. 9).

point of departure not the sifting of words, clauses and sentences, but a credible setting in which historically the reported deed could have been done or the reported saying could have been uttered. One should distinguish the *ipsissima structura Jesu*, which concerns the historical Jesus' context from the *ipsissima structura Marci*, which is the historical setting of the Markan narrative.

Secondly, it is necessary to describe briefly the mainstream interpretation of this pericope, which has dominated scholarship for centuries: its central ideas are (a) that the parabolic statement in Mk 7.15 is a crystal-clear and categorical abrogation of all Jewish food and purity laws and (b) that the historical Jesus must therefore have been exceedingly critical of the legal material in Jewish written texts and oral traditions. This article will seek to demonstrate that this interpretation does not hold up under critical scrutiny.

Text: The Markan 'Complot'

An author is never mightier than in the moment the features of the characters are being chiselled. As Robert Liddell points out, authors' only restraint when creating characters are their own nature, since they cannot make the characters more witty and intelligent than they are themselves.[9] It would be considerably difficult for the Evangelists to make alterations in the setting (the reader knowing that it took place in Galilee and Jerusalem) or the plot (the reader knowing that Jesus was put to death), but they certainly have more freedom of action when they describe the characters. And one must admit that Mark has been quite successful: the Markan antagonists are hostile from the first time they are presented. Consequently, the reader of the text becomes instantly hostile towards them.

An author is almost almighty in characterization, but not in plot; and Mark is no exception to this. Two reasons forced him to end his Gospel with the death of Jesus: first, he and his readers knew that *it had happened* and, secondly, he wanted his readers to believe that *it had to happen*.[10] To put it differently, both the actual death of Jesus and the cross *kerygma* preceded the narrative Gospels: as Frederick C. Grant once put it, '…the Gospel grew backwards'.[11] For these two reasons, one historical and one theological, there is a strong emphasis both on plot in his narrative and on – using the French word – *complot* in his plot.[12] There are numerous definitions of plot. Kieran Egan has presented one of the most practicable definitions: 'Plots, then, determine and provide rules for the sequencing

---

9. R. Liddell, *A Treatise on the Novel* (London: Alden, 1947), p. 105.

10. For a thought-provoking Borgesean interpretation of causality and the cross ('…whether Christ had allowed himself to be killed in order to save all mankind', p. 89), see J.L. Borges, 'The Gospel According to Mark', in *Brodie's Report. Including the Prose Fiction from In Praise of Darkness* (trans. A. Hurley; London: Penguin Books, 1998), pp. 84–90.

11. F.C. Grant, *The Earliest Gospel: Studies of the Evangelic Tradition at its Point of Crystallization in Writing* (New York and Nashville: Abingdon Press, 1943), p. 76.

12. The term 'plot' is often used – also in literature – as an expression parallel to the French word *complot*. Thus, we have a multitude of books on *The Plot to Assassinate John F. Kennedy, The Lincoln Murder Plot, The Plot to Kill Yitzhak Rabin/Malcolm X/Castro/Hitler*, etc. – and, of course, there was *The Gunpowder Plot* (5 November 1605). In other words, it is a time-honoured connotation of the word.

of narrative units – thereby creating a sense of causality'.[13] This article will concentrate on the narrative and theological dimensions of *causality* in the Markan
plot.

On the surface Mark is a conspiracy against the Nazarene, but on a deeper
level, the conspirators in the conspiracy are marionettes in a plot, where the script
was determined in advance. Hence, there are momentous machinations in Mark
and an essential interplay between causality and Christology. While Aristotle's
usage of μῦθος is wider than the machination connotation, his insistence on
coherence brings causality and conflict (problem and *dénouement*) closer to each
other than is generally done. The following discussion is influenced by the Aris-
totelian understanding of μῦθος.

In his oft-quoted two examples of the difference between a story and a plot,
E.M. Forster also stresses causality: '"[t]he king died and then the queen died" is
a story. "The king died and then the queen died of grief" is a plot.'[14] Now, how
could a Forsterean description of the Markan plot be formulated? 'A multitude of
Jewish parties and groups were determined to destroy Jesus and for that reason
he was executed' is a suggestion of a recapitulation of one significant trait of the
plot in Mark, a plot which simultaneously is a *complot*, a conspiracy. If we
remove the words 'for that reason' it is no longer a plot, only a story. Likewise, if
we remove the different Jewish groups from Mark, that is, chief priests, elders,
Herodians, Pharisees, Sadducees, and scribes, the text hovers in the air. Throughout the Gospel, hints are given to the reader, which serve to point out what will
eventually happen. By means of *predictions* (8.31, 9.31, 10.33–34), *provocations*
(11.12–26), *polemics* (2.1–3.6, 7.1–13, 8.11–13, 10.2–12, 11.27–33, 12.13–40),
public reactions (3.6, 11.18, 12.13) and *parables* (12.1–12), the reader gradually
realizes the lethal consequences of the conflict between the authorities and the
Authorized One, the protagonist who taught with the authority that the authorities
thought they had when teaching.

Thus, twice in the Gospel, representatives of Jewish groups line up and form a
queue in order to entrap Jesus in his talk and ministry. The reader of the Galilean
cycle (2.1–3.6) and Jerusalem cycle (11.12–12.12) is convinced that *all* the major
religious groups mentioned in Mark are part of the *complot* against Jesus:
Pharisees and Herodians in 3.6 and chief priests, scribes and elders in 11.18 and
12.27. The Sadducees alone (mentioned only once, i.e., in 12.18) are excluded.
Together these cycles serve the purpose of widening the gulf between Jesus and
the Jewish authorities, strengthening the idea of conspiracy against Jesus.

Most of the clashes relate to the interpretation of the *Torah* and to the authority with which Jesus interprets the sacred Scriptures. Nowhere in the entire Gospel
is the encounter more manifest than in the seventh chapter. When Jesus elsewhere discusses the Sabbath (2.23–3.6), divorce (10.1–12), resurrection (12.18–
27), the great commandment (12.28–34) and Christology (12.35–37), arguments
are based on the Scriptures. But in 7.14–23 we find nothing of that kind. *In fact,*

---

13. K. Egan, 'What is Plot?', *New Literary History* 9 (1978), pp. 455–73 (p. 470).

14. E.M. Forster, *Aspects of the Novel* (ed. Oliver Stalleybrass; London: Penguin Press, 1990),
p. 87.

a more anti-halakhic and antinomistic statement than 7.15 – as it is interpreted in the superstructure in v. 19b – cannot be found in the Gospels. The question therefore arises: if the purpose of the controversy cycles is to stress the antagonism between Jesus and different religious factions and if 7.15 is as alien to Jewish thought as has been suggested, *why is 7.1–23 not part of the controversy cycles?* In 3.6, 11.18, and 12.12, the reader is informed of the malicious intent of the religious leaders. They are in fact willing to kill Jesus, but hesitate because the people would be against it. However, when this dispute ends in 7.13, 'the Pharisees and some of the scribes' (7.1) leave the stage without uttering a single word. Indeed, vv. 14–23 are not even said to them, but to the crowds (vv. 14–15) and the disciples (vv. 17–23). All this indicates that the pericope, as it is situated in the Markan narrative, hardly stresses the gap between Jesus and the religious authorities. Put differently, nothing in 7.1–23 explains why the antagonists wanted to get rid of him. Instead, 7.1–23 is found between the two feeding narratives (6.34–44, 8.1–9) and is thus part of the so-called bread cycle (6.30–8.21).

Eighteen times – out of twenty-one in the whole Gospel – does ἄρτος occur in this cycle and the disciples are twice reproached for not understanding 'about the bread', once by the narrator (6.52) and once by Jesus (8.17 and 21). Both occasions take place during crossings of the Sea of Galilee by boat. The four most prominent interpretations of the two bread miracles are: (1) they are a reference or a pre-figuration of the Eucharist,[15] an illustration of the incomprehensible incomprehension of the disciples,[16] (3) they manifest the declining course of Jesus' miracles,[17] and (4) they serve as a justification for, or a retrospection of, Gentile mission.[18]

Each one of these four interpretations is plausible, but none is completely exhaustive. If, for example, the *only* underlying motif were the Eucharist, why does the text stress the importance of the bread (6.52) and the numbers of baskets and men being fed (8.18–21)? Or, if the purpose were solely to describe a declining activity of Jesus, how are we to explain the controversy with the Pharisees and some of the scribes (7.1–13)? The multiplicity of conceivable solutions serves as a warning to those who discredit all possibilities but one. The Eucharistic pattern should certainly be part of the frame of reference for a first-century Christian reader. Likewise, the disbelief of the disciples is such a distinguishable mark in

15. The main arguments concerning the Eucharist are collected by G.H. Boobyer, 'The Eucharistic Interpretation of the Miracles of the Loaves in St. Mark's Gospel', *JTS* 3 (1952), pp. 161–71 (pp. 162–68). Boobyer examines (a) the vocabulary and initial procedure, (b) the Johannine interpretation and (c) the Pauline reference to the manna as a type of Eucharist.

16. In spite of the fact that they had taken part in a miracle feeding of 5000 men, they are as dense before the second miracle (8.4) as before the first (6.37). See K.P. Donfried, 'The Feeding Narratives and the Marcan Community: Mark 6,30–45 and 8,1–10', in D. Lührmann and G. Strecker (eds), *Kirche: Festschrift für Günther Bornkamm zum 75. Geburtstag* (Tübingen: Mohr, 1980), pp. 95–103 (pp. 95, 101–103).

17. L.W. Countryman, 'How Many Baskets Full? Mark 8.14–21 and the Value of Miracles in Mark', *CBQ* 47 (1985), pp. 643–55 (pp. 647–50).

18. See, e.g., G. Rau, 'Das Markusevangelium: Komposition und Intention der ersten Darstellung christlicher Mission', *ANRW* 2.25.3 (1985), pp. 2036–257 (p. 2116).

the overall structure that a total absence in the bread cycle would be astonishing. The last-mentioned of these four motifs, however, stands out more clearly than the other three: The first is the choice of words: (a) χορτάζειν (6.42, 7.27; 8.4, 8) is a key-word which keeps the pericope together, (b) the expressions πάντες οἱ Ἰουδαῖοι (7.3) and Ἑλληνίς (7.26) are both *hapax legomena* in Mark, apart from the technical usage of Ἰουδαῖος in the fifteenth chapter. Seen apart from each other, they look arbitrary – kept together they form a pattern, sandwiched as they are between the two bread miracles ([i] a *Jewish* feeding, [ii] a discussion with representatives of 'all the *Jews*', [iii] a discussion with a *Gentile* woman, [iv] a *Gentile* feeding), (c) different words for the baskets: κόφινος when telling and retelling the first miracle (6.43 and 8.19) and σπυρίς when telling and retelling the second (8.8 and 8.20). Since Juvenal (*Sat.* 3.14) uses κόφινος to depict Jewish usage in Rome and σπυρίς is the ordinary Greek word for basket, the theory has been advanced that the two words also speak of a Jewish and a Gentile feeding. The second is the remarkable reluctance of Jesus to help the Syrophoenician woman's daughter, especially when compared with his attitude to the man, Legion, whom he voluntarily cures (5.1–20). The third is the narrator's interest in numbers (e.g. the very pigs of the herd are numbered in 5.13). In the bread cycle, the number of loaves (five in 6.38, seven in 8.5), dining guests (5,000 in 6.44, 4,000 in 8.9) and baskets of leftovers (twelve in 6.43, seven in 8.8) are accentuated. The most convincing explanation is to identify the twelve baskets of the first miracle with the twelve tribes of Israel and the seven of the second with the seventy nations of the world, that is, the Gentiles.[19] And the fourth motif has to do with how the narrator attributes substantial symbolism to the shores of the Sea of Galilee. It is emphasized that on the east side one finds swine herds and Greek cities, but on the west side, there are synagogues and so on. The Sea of Galilee serves as a boundary between the homeland and the foreign lands. The first miracle is thus meant for Jews on the west side of the sea and the second for Gentiles on the east side. *Hence, with key-words, effects of surprise, numbers and geography the narrator gives the reader a wider frame of interpretation than the text at first sight may seem to supply. These are all indications that a Jew-Gentile matrix can be found in the Markan bread cycle.*

The purpose of the Markan controversy cycles is to show the reader the lethal consequences of the conflict between protagonist and antagonists – *as early as in Galilee!* But there are no explicit or implicit references to the Passion in 7.1–23: no religious authorities gnash their teeth in the pericope (indeed, 7.14–23 is not even a controversy with the scribes and the Pharisees) and not a single trace of the saying can be found in the trial of Jesus. If not a syllable, not a sound of this anti-halakhic and antinomistic saying (as interpreted in v. 19b) is mentioned in the forensic Sanhedrin discussions, we must seek elsewhere for its narrative

---

19. Seven is the well-known number for completion and fullness. For biblical references, see, e.g., Gen. 10 (v. 2: the seven sons of Japheth. *Summa summarum* seventy nations are mentioned in the chapter – excluding Nimrod, who is an individual), Deut. 7.1 and Josh. 3.10 (the seven tribes in the Land).

context. The immediate context (chs. 6–8) proved to be the best narrative frame for the saying.

To narrative criticism belongs the question of genre, that is, readers' expectations and associations. Other scholars have suggested that Mark may be described as a Pauline Gospel.[20] In favour of this understanding are the facts (1) that both Paul and Mark emphasize the theological importance of Christ on the cross, rather than on the teachings of Jesus, (2) that both repudiate the actual followers of Jesus, and (3) that the *Gentiles* play an important role both in the letters written by the ἐθνῶν ἀπόστολος (Rom. 11.13) and in the Markan narrative. It seems highly arguable that a credible *ipsissima structura Marci* for our pericope is an outreach to Gentiles. What Paul states about the Gospel in Rom. 1.16, Mark depicts in his narrative about the Nazarene. *Mark is perhaps best described as a narrative presentation of, and a parallel to, the Pauline Gospel.*

Effect: Early Christian Parenesis

A survey of the *Wirkungsgeschichte* of Mk 7.15 (and its parallel in Mt. 15.11) during the first four centuries shows several interesting things:

(1) as Heikki Räisänen has pointed out, 'In fact, there is *no* evidence that *anybody*, conservative or radical, ever appealed to this saying in the course of the debates over Gentile mission and table fellowship during the first two decades or so in the early church.[21]

(2) A number of passages from the writings of the church fathers indicate that the saying was *enigmatic*. The best example of its vagueness is, no doubt, the correspondence between Athanasius and Ammoun in the middle of the fourth century.[22] This epistle shows that an unknown number of Egyptian ascetics interpreted the saying not as an exhortation to lenience concerning food laws (sc. what goes into a person), but to austerity concerning nocturnal emissions (sc. what goes out of a man).[23] Thus, they argued that the saying actually *reinforced* Levitical purity laws. Chrysostom stated that the saying is put forth as a riddle (ὡς ἐν αἰνίγματι).[24] Their understanding should be compared to the euphoria of modern biblical scholars at the alleged antinomistic unambiguousness of the saying.

(3) When Christian authors eventually began to quote or refer to this saying, they used it in two different ways in two different contexts. Whereas the first part of the saying was stressed in a few polemical texts against Judaism, a majority of

20. See, e.g., D.C. Sim, *The Gospel of Matthew and Christian Judaism: The History and Social Setting of the Matthean Community* (Edinburgh: T&T Clark, 1998), pp. 132ff. and especially p. 190 ('Mark's law-free attitude…clearly places him in the camp of the Pauline churches'.); J. Marcus, 'Mark – Interpreter of Paul', *NTS* 46 (2000), pp. 473–87. For further references, see Marcus, p. 474 n. 3.

21. H. Räisänen, *Jesus, Paul and Torah: Collected Essays* (trans. D.E. Orton; JSNTSup, 43; Sheffield: Sheffield Academic Press, 1992), p. 142.

22. *PG* 26.1169–176.

23. For once, 'man' actually has reference to only half of humankind.

24. In his *Expositions in the Psalms* 140 (LXX [=MT 141]; *PG* 55.432), Chrysostom first discusses Heb. 13.9, stating that the author of the epistle articulates his opinion as a riddle (ὡς ἐν αἰνίγματι) and then links this verse with the word μονονουχί to the saying in Mk 7.15/Mt. 15.11.

authors referred to the saying in intra-Christian parenesis whereby they empha-
sised the second part. Clement of Alexandria, Tertullian, John Chrysostom *et al.*
saw in the latter part of the saying a criticism of evil speakers.[25]

(4) Origen emphasized that while the historical Jesus did not oppose the Law,
post-Golgatha Christians, nevertheless, did not need to keep the Jewish Law,
since Jesus, through his sufferings on the cross (*and not through this saying!*),
liberated his disciples from the curse of the Law.[26] Thus, in a fascinating way he
outlines a Law-abiding Jesus within the boundaries of first-century Judaism, but
also a justification for Christians not observing Jewish *halakhah*. Thus, Origen
tried to have it both ways; it remains for his reader to decide whether one can
actually have it both ways.

To sum up, the survey of the application of the saying in early Christianity
indicates that *it was understood not in an absolute, but in a relative sense.* Thus,
both parts of the sayings are interesting and in need of a thorough investigation –
since it is then a question of a factual comparison between two valid categories:
not only 'what goes in' requires our attention, but also 'what goes out'.

Context: Establishing Contemporary Jewish Halakhah and Aggadah

New Testament scholars need to explore what contemporary Judaism taught
about 'what goes out' of a person.[27] The sages were certainly aware of the preva-
lence of evil speech (*b. Bab. Bat.* 165a):

אמר רב יהודה אמר רב רוב בגזל ומיעוט בעריות והכל בלשון הרע

> R. Judah said in the name of Rav: 'Most [people are guilty] of robbery, a minority of
> unchastity, and all of evil speech' (לשון הרע).

The aim is now to trace the development of this aggadic figure, the metaphor of
לשון הרע,[28] from the biblical epoch to the rabbinical period, in order to determine whether this and related aggadic teachings constitute not only a possible but
also a plausible *ipsissima structura Jesu* for the saying in Mk 7.15.

In the Hebrew Bible there are a large number of admonitions and prohibitions
of evil speech. The most common expression in biblical times was 'a lying tongue'
(לשון שקר).[29] Probably the most outright ban on evil speech is found in Lev.
19.16.[30] When we turn to the Septuagint, we see that in Sirach it becomes

---

25. For a compilation of all relevant passages, see Svartvik, *Mark and Mission*, pp. 168–73,
194–201.

26. Origen, *Commentary on Matthew* (*SC* 11.8).

27. For a thorough investigation into first-century *halakhah* and its discussion of what goes into a
person, see R.P. Booth, *Jesus and the Laws of Purity: Tradition History and Legal History in Mark 7*
(JSNTSup, 13; Sheffield: JSOT Press, 1986).

28. While the grammatically correct pronunciation of the *terminus technicus* ought to be *lᵉshon
hara'*, it is not unusual to see the transliteration *lashon hara'*. Ashkenazi parenetic literature trans-
literates *loshon hora*.

29. See Isa. 57.4; 59.3; Jer. 9.3, 5; Mic. 6.12; Ps. 109.2; 120.2; Prov. 6.17; 12.19; 17.4; 21.6; and
26.28. This expression occurs at least once in the Dead Sea Scrolls, see 4Q381, frag. 45.5:
...לשון שקר...

30. For a rabbinic application of the text, see *m. Sanh.* 3.7.

obvious that eventually religious writers found it necessary to extend the warn-ings of perilous speech. Sirach 19 deals with gossiping in general – it admonishes the readers not to repeat a conversation (19.7a) but rather to let it die within them-selves (19.10). Rabbinic Judaism used the concept לשון הרע to describe conver-sations which involve (a) what is not true and (b) true things which ought not to be said due to consideration for the one whom the speech concerns. In a word, לשון הרע is the usage of language in a damaging way.[31] That the religious lead-ership saw evil speech as highly amoral becomes obvious in *t. Peah* 1.2, perhaps the most amazing statement about evil speech in the whole tannaitic corpus:

על אלו דברים נפרעין מן האדם בעולם הזה והקרן
קיימת לו בעולם הבא על עבודה זרה ועל גלוי
עריות ועל שפיכות דמים ועל לשון הרע כנגד כולם

For these things they punish a person in this world, while the main [punishment] remains for the world to come: idolatry, incest, murder and evil speech, [which is] accounted equal to all of them together (כנגד כולם).

Whereas a number of verses in the Hebrew Bible and the LXX do discuss the topic of evil speech, most of them are to be found in the wisdom literature. As is well known, rabbinic Judaism takes as a starting point verses in the *Torah*, not the prophets or the writings. The rabbis therefore sorted out a few master stories in the Pentateuch in order to support their discourses against evil speech, the most important being Numbers 12. In that chapter it is recounted how Miriam, assisted by Aaron, spoke against Moses on account of the Cushite woman whom he had married. As a punishment for this behaviour Miriam was struck by a scale disease (צרעת) usually translated as 'leprosy'.[32] The rabbis had here a text which clearly stated that, Miriam was struck by the disease, Aaron lost his prophetic gift and Israel's arrival in the Land was delayed, all as a result of evil speech. The rabbis used this pericope when warning against detrimental speech.[33] It is interesting to note that even the *Torah* itself indicated that this pericope has a paradigmatic function. Although the original meaning of the hyper-textual comment in Deut. 24.9 – requesting the readers not to forget what God did to Miriam in the wilder-ness on the way out of Egypt – may not have been that one should avoid evil speech, it was nevertheless interpreted in this way eventually. Thus, the interplay

31. We owe this definition to Marc Bregman (private correspondence).

32. For an analysis of the etymology of the word, see J.F.A. Sawyer, 'A Note on the Etymology of Sara'at', *VT* 26 (1976), pp. 241–45. He argues that it was probably a neutral medical term originally (p. 245). For a comprehensive survey of the application of this word, see E.V. Hulse, 'The Nature of Biblical "Leprosy" and the Use of Alternative Medical Terms in Modern Translations of the Bible', *PEQ* 107 (1975), pp. 87–105. However, it is better either to keep the Hebrew word or to choose a descriptive expression: 'scale disease' (Milgrom), 'defiling afflictions' (Klawans) or 'repulsive scaly skin disease' (Hulse). See J. Milgrom, *Leviticus 1–16: A New Translation with Introduction and Com-mentary* (AB, 3; New York: Doubleday, 1991), pp. 775 and 817; J. Klawans, *Impurity and Sin in Ancient Judaism* (New York: Oxford University Press, 2000), p. 198 n. 43; and Hulse, 'Nature of Biblical "Leprosy"', p. 104.

33. For a survey of all the tannaitic and also of the most relevant amoraic texts, see Svartvik, *Mark and Mission*, pp. 375–402.

between Num. 12.1–16 and Deut. 24.9 led to Miriam being the warning example *par excellence* of what may happen due to evil speech.

Much can be said about the drawbacks of the metaphors being used – especially when one considers the tragic sense of guilt among the afflicted – but let it suffice now to sum up in three points what has been observed hitherto. First, there can be no doubt that the exhortations against evil speech in tannaitic times had called forth a specific and well-established *terminus technicus*, that is לשון הרע, which is wider in definition than the biblical expression לשון שקר since it comprises both true and untrue gossip. Secondly, it was seen that the rabbis were of the opinion that לשון הרע was one of the most serious sins. Indeed, they did not hesitate to compare it to the three cardinal sins (sc. idolatry, incest and bloodshed), and even to state that evil speech is as appalling as the three sins *together*. Thirdly, as early as in tannaitic literature, distinct proof was found of a special connection between malicious speech and an impure scale malady. In the aggadic realm, the rabbis said that the plagues which make a person ritually impure come only because of evil speech. *In brief, tannaitic aggadic texts teach that a person becomes impure by what goes out of the mouth.*[34]

5. General Conclusions

This article has drawn attention to a number of interesting observations, which make it difficult to adhere to the mainstream interpretation of the Pentateuchal food laws in Mk 7.1–23. The textual, effectual and contextual investigations have arrived at the followings results: (1) *Text*: Although Mark emphasizes causality to a remarkably high degree in his narrative, an abrogation of the Jewish food laws is not at stake in the trial. The setting, characters and plot suggest that the bread cycle in Mark 6–8 provides a narrative parallel to the Pauline mission to the Gentiles. (2) *Effect*: On the whole, this saying lacks *Wirkungsgeschichte* during the first decades. When the church fathers eventually did comment on the saying, they frequently put considerably more stress on the second part of the saying ('…but what goes out…') than on the first part ('…not what goes into…'). With such an emphasis, the kernel of the saying is that it serves as a warning against evil speech. (3) *Context*: A contextual analysis shows that the rabbinic aggadic metaphor of לשון הרע constitutes a close parallel to the enigmatic saying in Mk 7.15. Thus, the saying is best understood in a relative sense (*not so much… as*) rather than in an absolute sense (*nothing…*).

The emphasis in the present volume is on the narrative level, but it also encourages the contributors to go outside the text as well. By way of conclusion, it is suggested that the study of textual, effectual and contextual aspects provides us with the following trajectory of the saying in Mk 7.15: (1) If this statement goes all the way back to the teaching of the historical Jesus, it is best understood as a

34. It must be emphasized that this is not an halakhic saying – in the rabbinic corpus there are no purification ceremonies for evil speakers. Certainly there is the aggadic suggestion in *b. Arakh.* 16a (that the bells on the hem of the high priest's robe atone for the slanderer), but this is not halakhic purification jurisdiction, but aggadic atonement discourse.

statement which compares two valid aspects; it thereby emphasizes that avoiding evil speech is even more important than observing the food laws – not suggesting however that they be replaced.[35] The *ipsissima structura Jesu* is the ongoing discussion of contaminated foods and contaminating speech (לשון הרע). (2) The narrative analysis of the Markan narrative suggests that the contemporaneous aggadic metaphor לשון הרע is overshadowed by the inclusion of the Gentiles. Thus, the *ipsissima structura Marci* is the Pauline mission. (3) Interesting enough, the aggadic application of the saying reoccurs in early Christian literature, especially in parenetic homilies.

Sooner or later, students of the saying in Mk 7.15 stand at the crossroads: they have to decide whether the parabolic saying as part of the *ipsissima structura Jesu* is an awkward halakhic statement (*cleansing all foods*) or a credible aggadic instruction (*a warning of the perils of evil speech*). One purpose of this article has been to expose the numerous shortcomings of the first alternative and to demonstrate the force of the arguments in favour of the latter. Another purpose has been to illustrate the accuracy of Jorge Luis Borges's statement that writers create their precursors. When Matthew wrote his fifteenth chapter he also created Mark's seventh chapter (although this Gospel was written more than a decade earlier). The antinomistic features of the Markan Jesus were brought into relief by Matthew when, in his version of the very same pericope, he presented a Law-abiding protagonist. This is not to suggest that if Matthew had not written his Gospel, we would not perceive the specific nature of his Markan precursor; but it is to state that Matthew was instrumental in drawing attention to his Markan forerunner. How else should we explain the strange fact that for almost two millennia, people have read about Jesus of Nazareth in the Gospel of Matthew, but interpreted him according to Mark?

---

35. Cf. E.P. Sanders, *Jewish Law from Jesus to the Mishnah: Five Studies* (London: SCM Press; Philadelphia: Trinity Press International, 1990), p. 28: 'If, of course, we provide *a new context for the saying*, it can be saved as an authentic logion' (italics added).

BIBLIOGRAPHY

Allegro, J. (ed.), *Discoveries in the Judean Desert of Jordan V: Qumran Cave 4* (Oxford: Clarendon Press, 1968).

Anderson, H., 'The Old Testament in Mark's Gospel', in J.M. Efird [ed.], *The Use of the Old Testament in the New and Other Essays: Studies in Honor of William Franklin Stinespring* (Durham, NC: Duke University Press, 1972), pp. 280–306.

Anderson, J.C., 'Feminist Criticism: the Dancing Daughter', in J.C. Anderson and S.D. Moore (eds), *Mark & Method: New Approaches in Biblical Studies* (Minneapolis, MN: Fortress Press, 1992), pp. 103–34.

Arnott, W.G., 'Philemon (2)', in *OCD* (2nd edn, 1970), p. 813.

Aus, R., *Water into Wine and the Beheading of John the Baptist: Early Jewish-Christian Interpretation of Esther 1 in John 2.1–11 and Mark 6.17–29* (Brown Judaic Studies, 150; Atlanta, GA: Scholars Press, 1988).

Bacon, B.W., ' "Raised the Third Day" ', *Expositor* 26 (1923), pp. 426–41.

Bal, M., *Narratology: Introduction to the Theory of Narrative* (Toronto: University of Toronto Press, 1997, 2nd edn).

Baldry, H.C., *The Greek Tragic Theatre* (London: Chatto & Windus, rev. edn, 1981).

Barré, M.L., 'New Light on the Interpretation of Hosea VI 2', *VT* 28 (1978), pp. 129–41.

Barton, S.C., 'The Transfiguration of Christ according to Mark and Matthew: Christology and Anthropology', in F. Avemarie and H. Lichtenberger (eds), *Auferstehung–Resurrection: The Fourth Durham-Tübingen Research Symposium: Resurrection, Transfiguration and Exaltation in Old Testament, Ancient Judaism and Early Christianity* (Tübingen, September, 1999) (WUNT, 135; Tübingen: Mohr Siebeck, 2001), pp. 231–46.

Basser, H.W., 'The Jewish Roots of the Transfiguration', *Bible Review* 14/3 (1998), pp. 30–35.

Bauckham, R., 'Jesus and the Wild Animals (Mark 1.13): A Christological Image for an Ecological Age', in J. Green and M. Turner (eds), *Jesus of Nazareth: Lord and Christ. Essays on the Historical Jesus and New Testament Christology* (Grand Rapids, MI: Eerdmans; Carlisle: Paternoster Press, 1994), pp. 3–21.

Bayer, H.F., *Jesus' Predictions of Vindication and Resurrection: The Provenance, Meaning and Correlation of the Synoptic Predictions* (WUNT, 20; Tübingen: J.C.B. Mohr [Paul Siebeck], 1986).

Bellinger Jr, W. and W. Farmer (eds), *Jesus and the Suffering Servant: Isaiah 53 and Christian Origins* (Harrisburg, PA: Trinity Press International, 1998).

Berger, K., *Formgeschichte des Neuen Testaments* (Heidelberg: Quelle, 1984).

Best, E., *The Temptation and the Passion: The Markan Soteriology* (SNTMS, 2; Cambridge: Cambridge University Press, 1965).

Black, M., 'The Theological Appropriation of the Old Testament by the New Testament', *SJT* 39 (1986), pp. 1–17.

Bock, D. *Blasphemy and Exaltation in Judaism and the Final Examination of Jesus* (WUNT, II/106; Tübingen: Mohr/Siebeck, 1998).

Boobyer, G.H., 'The Eucharistic Interpretation of the Miracles of the Loaves in St. Mark's Gospel', *JTS* 3 (1952), pp. 161–71.

Booth, R.P., *Jesus and the Laws of Purity: Tradition History and Legal History in Mark 7* (JSNTSup, 13; Sheffield: JSOT Press, 1986).

Borges, J.L., 'Kafka y sus precursores', *Otras inquisiciones* (Madrid: Alianza Editorial, 1995), pp.162–66. Translation: 'Kafka and his Precursors', in E. Weinberger (ed.), *The Total Library: Non-Fiction 1922–1986* (trans. E. Allen, S.J. Levine and E. Weinberger; London: Allen Lane, 2000), pp. 363–65.

—'The Gospel According to Mark', in *Brodie's Report. Including the Prose Fiction from In Praise of Darkness* (trans. A. Hurley; London: Penguin Books, 1998), pp. 84–90.

Boring, M.E., 'The Paucity of Sayings in Mark: A Hypothesis', *SBL Seminar Papers* (Missoula, MT: Scholar's Press, 1977), pp. 371–77.

—*Sayings of the Risen Jesus: Christian Prophecy in the Synoptic Tradition* (SNTSMS, 46; Cambridge: Cambridge University Press, 1982).

—'Mark 1.1–15 and the Beginning of the Gospel', in Dennis Smith (ed.), *How Gospels Begin* (*Semeia* 52; Atlanta, GA: Scholars Press, 1991), pp. 43–81.

Bornkamm, G., *Jesus of Nazareth* (trans. I. and F. McLuskey with J. Robinson; New York: Harper & Row, 1960).

Bousset, W., Kyrios *Christos: A History of the Belief in Christ from the Beginnings of Christianity to Irenaeus* (trans. J.E. Steely; Nashville, TN: Abingdon Press, 1970).

Boyarin, D., *Dying for God: Martyrdom and the Making of Christianity and Judaism* (Stanford, CA: Stanford University Press, 1999).

Brandt, P.-Y., *L'identité de Jésus et l'identité de son disciple: Le récit de la transfiguration comme clef de lecture de l'Évangele de Marc* (NTOA, 50; Fribourg, Switzerland: Èditions Universitaires; Göttingen: Vandenhoeck & Ruprecht, 2002).

Braude, W.G., *The Midrash on Psalms* (New Haven, CT: Yale University Press, 1959).

Bretscher, P.G. 'Exodus 4.22–23 and the Voice from Heaven', *JBL* 87 (1968), pp. 309–11.

Broadhead, E.K., *Teaching with Authority: Miracles and Christology in the Gospel of Mark* (JSNTSup,74; Sheffield: Sheffield Academic Press, 1992).

—*Prophet, Son, Messiah: Narrative Form and Function in Mark 14–16* (JSNTSup, 97; Sheffield: Sheffield Academic Press, 1994).

—*Naming Jesus: Titular Christology in the Gospel of Mark* (JSNTSup, 175; Sheffield: Sheffield Academic Press, 1999).

—*Mark* (Chippenham, Wiltshire: Sheffield Academic Press, 2001).

Brooke, G.J., *Exegesis at Qumran: 4QFlorilegium in its Jewish Context* (JSOTSup 29; Sheffield: JSOT Press, 1985).

—'4Q254 Fragments 1 and 4, and 4Q254a: Some Preliminary Comments', in *Proceedings of the Eleventh World Congress of Jewish Studies* (Jerusalem: World Union of Jewish Studies, 1994), pp. 185–92.

Brown, R., *The Death of the Messiah* (New York: Doubleday, 1994).

Bruce, F.F., 'The Book of Zechariah and the Passion Narrative', *BJRL* 43 (1960–61), pp. 336–53.

—*New Testament Development of Old Testament Themes* (Grand Rapids, MI: Eerdmans, 1969).

Bultmann, R., *Theology of the New Testament* (trans. K. Grobel; New York: Scribner's, 1951).

Cadoux, C.J., *The Historic Mission of Jesus: A Constructive Re-Examination of the Eschatological Teaching in the Synoptic Gospels* (New York: Harper & Brothers, 1941)

Carlston, C.E., 'Transfiguration and Resurrection', *JBL* 80 (1961), pp. 233–40.

Carrington, P., *According to Mark: A Running Commentary on the Oldest Gospel* (Cambridge: University Press, 1960).

Casey, P.M., 'Culture and Historicity: The Cleansing of the Temple', *CBQ* 59 (1997), pp. 306–32).

Cathcart, K.J. and R.P. Gordon, *The Targum of the Minor Prophets* (ArBib, 14; Wilmington, NC: Glazier, 1989)

Chilton, B.D., 'The Transfiguration: Dominical Assurance and Apostolic Vision', *NTS* 27 (1981), pp. 114–24.

—*The Glory of Israel: The Theology and Provenience of the Isaiah Targum* (JSOTSup, 23; Sheffield: JSOT Press, 1983).

—*A Galilean Rabbi and His Bible: Jesus' Use of the Interpreted Scripture of His Time* (Wilmington, NC: Michael Glazier, 1984).

—*The Temple of Jesus: His Sacrificial Program within a Cultural History of Sacrifice* (University Park, PA: Penn State Press, 1992).

—*A Feast of Meanings: Eucharistic Theologies from Jesus through Johannine Circles* (NovTSup, 72; Leiden: Brill, 1994).

Clark, D.J., 'After Three Days', *BT* 30 (1979), pp. 340–43.

Clayton, N.C.', Where the Gospel Text Begins: A Non-Theological Interpretation of Mark 1.1', *NovT* 53 (2, 2001), pp. 105–27.

Collins, J.J., *The Scepter and the Star: The Messiahs of the Dead Sea Scrolls and Other Ancient Literature* (New York: Doubleday, 1995).

Colpe, C., 'ὁ υἱὸς τοῦ ἀνθρώπου', *TDNT* 8 (1972), pp. 400–77.

Cooke, G., 'The Israelite King as Son of God', *ZAW* 73 (1961), pp. 202–25.

Coune, M., 'Radieuse transfiguration. Mt 17,1–9; Mc 9,2–10; Lc 9,28–36', *AsSeign* 15 (1973), pp. 44–84.

Countryman, L.W., 'How Many Baskets Full? Mark 8.14–21 and the Value of Miracles in Mark', *CBQ* 47 (1985), pp. 643–55.

Cox, P., *Biography in Late Antiquity: A Quest for the Holy Man* (Berkeley, CA: University of California Press, 1983).

Craig, W.L., 'The Historicity of the Empty Tomb of Jesus', *NTS* 31 (1985), pp. 39–67.

Craigie, P.C., *Psalms 1–50* (WBC; Waco, TX: Word Books, 1983).

Cramer, J.A., (ed.), *Catenae graecorum patrum in novum testamentum* (Oxford: E. Typographeo Academico, 1844).

Cranfield, C.E.B., 'The Baptism of our Lord – A Study of St. Mark 1.9–11', *SJT* 8 (1955), pp. 53–63.

—*The Gospel According to Saint Mark* (Cambridge: Cambridge University Press, 1983).

Crossan, J.D., 'Redaction and Citation in Mark 11.9–10 and 11.17', *BR* 17 (1972), pp. 33–50.

Crossan, J.D. and J.L. Reed, *In Search of Paul: How Jesus's Apostle Opposed Rome's Empire with God's Kingdom* (New York: HarperCollins, 2004).

Cullmann, O., *The Christology of the New Testament* (trans. S. Guthrie and C. Hall; London: SCM Press, 1963).

Dalman, D., *The Words of Jesus Considered in the Light of Post-biblical Jewish Writings and the Aramaic Language* (Edinburgh: T&T Clark, 1902).

Danove, P., *Linguistics and Exegesis in the Gospel of Mark: Applications of a Case Frame Analysis* (JSNTSup, 218, Studies in New Testament Greek, 10; Sheffield: Sheffield Academic Press, 2001).

Davies, P.R. and B.D. Chilton, 'The Aqedah: A Revisited Tradition History', *CBQ* 40 (1978), pp. 521–22.

Deissmann, A., *Light From the Ancient East: The New Testament Illustrated by Recently Discovered Texts of the Graeco-Roman World* (trans. L.R.M. Strachan; New York: George A. Doran Co., 1927).

Denis, A.-M., *Fragmenta Pseudepigraphorum quae supersunt graeca* (PVTG, 3; Leiden: Brill, 1970)

Donahue, J.R., 'Recent Studies on the Origin of "Son of Man" in the Gospel', *CBQ* 48 (1986), pp. 484–98.

Donahue, J. and D. Harrington, *The Gospel of Mark* (Sacra Pagina, 2; Collegeville, MO: Liturgical Press, 2002).

Donfried, K.P., 'The Feeding Narratives and the Marcan Community: Mark 6,30–45 and 8,1–10', in D. Lührmann and G. Strecker (eds), *Kirche: Festschrift für Günther Bornkamm zum 75. Geburtstag* (Tübingen: Mohr, 1980), pp. 95–103.

Edwards, J.R., 'The Baptism of Jesus According to the Gospel of Mark', *JETS* 34 (1991), pp. 43–57.

—*The Gospel According to Mark* (PNTC; Grand Rapids, MI: Eerdmans, 2002).

Egan, K., 'What is Plot?', *New Literary History* 9 (1978), pp. 455–73.

Epstein I. (ed.), *The Babylonian Talmud* (London: Soncino Press, 1952).

Evans, C.A., 'Jesus' Action in the Temple: Cleansing or Portent of Destruction?', *CBQ* 51 (1989), pp. 237–70.

—'Jesus and the "Cave of Robbers": Toward a Jewish Context for the Temple Action', *BBR* 3 (1993), pp. 93–110.

—'"The Two Sons of Oil": Early Evidence of Messianic Interpretation of Zechariah 4.14 in 4Q254 4 2', in D.W. Parry and E. Ulrich (eds), *The Provo International Conference on the Dead Sea Scrolls: Technological Innovations, New Texts, and Reformulated Issues* (STDJ, 30; Leiden: Brill, 1998), pp. 566–75.

—'Jesus and Zechariah's Messianic Hope', in B.D. Chilton and C.A. Evans (eds), *Authenticating the Activities of Jesus* (NTTS, 28/2; Leiden: Brill, 1999), pp. 373–88.

—'Diarchic Messianism in the Dead Sea Scrolls and the Messianism of Jesus of Nazareth', in L.H. Schiffman, E. Tov, and J.C. VanderKam (eds), *The Dead Sea Scrolls: Fifty Years after Their Discovery. Proceedings of the Jerusalem Congress, July 20–25, 1997* (Jerusalem: Israel Exploration Society and the Israel Antiquities Authority, 2000), pp. 558–67.

—'Mark's Incipit and the Priene Calendar Inscription: From Jewish Gospel to Greco-Roman Gospel', *JGRChJ* 1 (2000), pp. 67–81;

—*Mark 8.27–16.20* (WBC, 34B; Nashville, TN: Thomas Nelson, 2001).

—'The Aramaic Psalter and the New Testament: Praising the Lord in History and Prophecy', in C.A. Evans (ed.), *From Prophecy to Testament: The Function of the Old Testament in the New* (Peabody, MA: Hendrickson, 2004), pp. 44–91.

Evans, C.F. '"I Will Go before You into Galilee"', *JTS* 5 (1954), pp. 3–18.

Field, F., *Notes on Select Passages of the Greek Testament: Chiefly with Reference to Recent English Versions* (Oxford: E. Pickard Hall, 1881).

Fitzmyer, J.A., *The Gospel According to Luke I–IX* (AB, 28; New York: Doubleday, 1970).

—'The Contribution of Qumran Aramaic to the Study of the New Testament', *NTS* 20 (1974), p. 393.

—*A Wandering Aramean: Collected Aramaic Sayings* (SBLMS, 25; Chico, CA: Scholars Press, 1979).

—'4Q246: The "Son of God" Document from Qumran', *Bib* 74 (1993), pp. 153–74.

—'Another View of the "Son of Man" Debate', *JSNT* 4 (1999), pp. 58–68.

Fletcher-Louis, C.H.T., 'The Revelation of the Sacral Son of Man: The Genre, History of Religious Context and the Meaning of the Transfiguration', in Avemarie and Lichtenberger (eds), *Auferstehung–Resurrection*, pp. 247–98;

Fornara, C.W., *The Nature of History in Ancient Greece and Rome* (Berkeley, CA: University of California Press, 1983)

Foster, E.M., *Aspects of the Novel* (ed. Oliver Stalleybrass; London: Penguin Press, 1990).

Fowler, R., *Let the Reader Understand. Reader-Response Criticism and the Gospel of Mark* (Harrisburg, PA: Trinity International Press, 1996).

France, R.T., *Jesus and the Old Testament* (London: Tyndale, 1971).

—*Divine Government. God's Kingship in the Gospel of Mark* (London: SPCK, 1990).

Freedman, H. and M. Simon, *Midrash Rabbah Vol. 9* (London: Soncino Press, 1982).

Frickenschmidt, D., *Evangelium als Biographie: Die vier Evangelien im Rahmen antiker Erzählkunst* (Tübingen: Francke Verlag, 1997).

Friedlander, G. (trans.), *Pirke de Rabbi Eliezer* (New York: Sepher-Hermon Press, 1981)

Gese, H., 'Psalm 22 und das Neue Testament: Der älteste Bericht vom Tode Jesu und die Entstehung des Herrenmahles', in *Vom Sinai zum Zion: Alttestamentliche Beiträge zur biblischen Theologie* (BEvT, 64; Munich: Kiaser, 1974), pp. 192–96.

Gnilka, J., 'Das Martyrium Johannes des Täufers (Mk 6,17–29)', in P. Hoffmann, N. Brox, and W. Pesch (eds), *Orientierung an Jesus: Zur Theologie der Synoptiker: Festschrift fur J. Schmid* (Freiburg: Herder, 1973).

Grant, F.C., *The Earliest Gospel: Studies of the Evangelic Tradition at its Point of Crystallization in Writing* (New York and Nashville: Abingdon Press, 1943)

Grant, M., Jesus. *An Historian's Review of the Gospels* (New York: Scribner's, 1977).

Grant, R.M., 'The Coming of the Kingdom', *JBL* 67 (1948), pp. 297–303

Guelich, R.A., *Mark 1–8.26* (WBC, 34A; Dallas: Word Books, 1989).

Gundry, R.H., *Mark: A Commentary on His Apology for the Cross* (Grand Rapids, MI: Eerdmans, 1993).

Haag, H., Der Gottesknecht bei Deuterojesaja (EdF, 233; Darmstadt: Wissenschaftliche Buchgesellschaft, 1985).

Hahn, F., *Christologische Hoheitstitel. Ihre Geschichte im frühen Christentum* (Göttingen: Vandenjoeck & Ruprecht, 1974).

Harper, W.R., *A Critical and Exegetical Commentary on Amos and Hosea* (ICC; Edinburgh : T&T Clark, 1905).

Hartman, G.H., 'The Struggle for the Text', in G.H. Hartman and S. Budick (eds), *Midrash and Literature* (New Haven, CT: Yale University Press, 1986) pp. 3–18.

Hartmann, M., *Der Tod Johannes' des Täufers: Eine exegetische und rezeptionsgeschichtliche Studie auf dem Hintergrund narrativer, intertextueller und kulturanthropologischer Zugänge* (Stuttgarter Biblische Beiträge, 45; Stuttgart: Katholisches Bibelwerk, 2001).

Hatina, T.R. 'Intertextuality and Historical Criticism in New Testament Studies: Is There a Relationship?', *BibInt* 7 (1999), 28–43.

—*In Search of a Context: The Function of Scripture in Mark's Narrative* (JSNTSup, 232; SSEJC, 8; London: Sheffield Academic Press, 2002).

Hayward, R., 'The Present State of Research into the Targumic Account of the Sacrifice of Isaac', *JJS* 32 (1981), pp. 127–50.

Heil, J.P., *The Transfiguration of Jesus: Narrative Meaning and Function of Mark 9.2–8, Matt 17.1–8 and Luke 9.28–36* (AnBib, 144; Rome: Biblical Institute Press, 2000).

Hengel, M., *Crucifixion* (trans. J. Bowden; Philadelphia, PA: Fortress, 1977).

—*The Son of God: The Origin of Christology and the History of Jewish-Hellenistic Religion* (Philadelphia, PA: Fortress Press, 1983).

Heschel, A., *The Prophets* (New York: Harper & Row, 1962).

Hill, D., 'On the Use and Meaning of Hosea VI. 6 in Matthew's Gospel', *NTS* 24 (1977–78), pp. 107–19.

Hillyer. N., 'The Servant of God', *EQ* 41 (1969) pp. 143–160.

Hoehner, H., *Herod Antipas* (SNTSMS, 17; Cambridge: Cambridge University Press, 1972).

Hooker, M.D., *Jesus and the Servant* (London: SPCK, 1959).

—'Mark', in D.A. Carson and H.G.M. Williamson (eds), *It is Written: Scripture Citing Scripture. Essays in Honour of Barnabas Lindars* (Cambridge: Cambridge University Press, 1988), pp. 220–30.

—*The Gospel According to Saint Mark* (BNTC; London: A. & C. Black, 1991).

Horbury, W., *Jewish Messianism and the Cult of Christ* (London: SCM Press, 1998).

Hornblower, S., 'Introduction: Summary of the Papers; The Story of Greek Historiography; Intertextuality and the Greek Historians', in S. Hornblower (ed.), *Greek Historiography* (Oxford: Clarendon Press, 1994), pp. 1–72;

Hulse, E.V., 'The Nature of Biblical "Leprosy" and the Use of Alternative Medical Terms in Modern Translations of the Bible', *PEQ* 107 (1975), pp. 87–105.

Hunt, A.S., (ed.), *The Oxyrhynchus Papyri*, IX (London: Egypt Exploration Fund, 1912).

Hunt, A.S., *Fragmenta Tragica Papyracea* (Oxford: Clarendon Press, 1912)

Hurtado, L.W., *Mark* (NIBC; Peabody, MA: Hendrickson, 1989).

—*Lord Jesus Christ. Devotion to Jesus in Earliest Christianity* (Grand Rapids, MI: Eerdmans, 2003).

Israllstam J. (trans.), *Midrash Rabbah: Leviticus* (London: Soncino Press, 1982).

Jacoby, F., 'Über die Entwicklung der griechischen Historiographie und der Plan einer neuen Sammlung der drieschischen Historikerfragmente', *Klio* 9 (1909), pp. 1–44.

—*Atthis: The Local Chronicles of Ancient Athens* (Oxford: Clarendon Press, 1949).

James, W., *Pragmatism* (Great Books in Philosophy; Amherst, NY: Prometheus Books, 1991).

Jensen, R.M., 'Isaac as a Christological Symbol in Early Christian Art', *ARTS* 5.2 (1993), pp. 6–12.

Jeremias, J., *New Testament Theology: The Proclamation of Jesus* (New York: Charles Scribner's Sons, 1971).

—'παῖς θεοῦ', *TDNT* 5 (1967), pp. 677–717.

de Jonge, H.J., 'The Cleansing of the Temple in Mark 11.15 and Zechariah 14.21', in Christopher Tuckett (ed.), *The Book of Zechariah and its Influence: Papers of the Oxford-Leiden Conference* (Aldershot: Ashgate, 2003), pp. 87–100.

de Jonge, M., 'Mark 14.25 among Jesus' Words about the Kingdom of God', in W.L. Petersen *et al.* (eds), *Sayings of Jesus: Canonical and Non-Canonical. Essays in Honour of Tjitze Baarda* (NovTSup, 89; Leiden: Brill, 1997), pp. 123–35.

Juel, D., *Messianic Exegesis: Christological Interpretation of the Old Testament in Early Christianity* (Philadelphia, PA: Fortress Press, 1988).

—'The Gospel of Mark', in Charles Cousar (ed.), *Interpreting Biblical Texts*, (Nashville, TN: Abingdon Press, 1999), pp. 53–64.

Kaspar, W., *Jesus the Christ* (trans. V. Green; New York: Paulist Press, 1977)

Kee, H.C., 'The Function of Scriptural Quotations and Allusions in Mark 11–16', in E. E. Ellis and E. Gräßer (eds), *Jesus und Paulus* (Festschrift W.G. Kümmel; Göttingen: Vandenhoeck & Ruprecht, 1975), pp. 165–88.

—'Testaments of the Twelve Patriarchs', in J.A. Charlesworth (ed.), *The Old Testament Pseudepigrapha. I. Apocalyptic Literature and Testaments* (New York: Doubleday, 1983), p. 775–828.

Kelber, W., *The Oral and Written Gospel* (Philadelphia, PA: Fortress Press, 1983).

Kermode, F., *The Genesis of Secrecy: On the Interpretation of Narrative* (Cambridge, MA: Harvard University Press, 1979).

Kim, S., 'Jesus—The Son of God, the Stone, the Son of Man, and the Servant: The Role of Zechariah in the Self-Identification of Jesus', in G.F. Hawthorne and O. Betz (eds), *Tradition and Interpretation in the New Testament: Essays in Honor of E. Earle Ellis for His 60th Birthday* (Tübingen: Mohr; Grand Rapids, MI: Eerdmans, 1987), pp. 134–48.

Klawans, J., *Impurity and Sin in Ancient Judaism* (New York: Oxford University Press, 2000).

Kraus, H., *Psalm 1–59: A Commentary* (trans. H.C. Oswald; Minneapolis, MN: Augsburg Publishing House, 1988)

Kumaniecki, C.F., (ed.), *De Satyro Peripatetico* (Polska Akademja Umiejetnosci Archiwum Filolgiczne, 8; Cracow: Getethner et Wolff, 1929).

Lane, W.L., *The Gospel according to Mark* (NICNT; Grand Rapids, MI: Eerdmans, 1974).

Larsen, T., (ed.), *Literarische Texte und Ptolemäische Urkunden* (Papyri Graecae Haunienses, 1; Copenhagen: Munksgaard, 1941; repr. Milan: Cisalpino-Goliardica, 1974).

Lauterbach, J.Z. (trans.), *Mekilta de-Rabbi Ishmael Vol. 1* (Philadelphia, PA: The Jewish Publication Society of America, 1976).

LaVerdiere, E., *The Beginning of the Gospel: Introducing the Gospel According to Mark.* I. *Mark 1–8.21* (Collegeville, MN: Liturgical Press, 1999)

Leander, K., 'The Introduction to Mark's Gospel', *NTS* 12 (1966), pp. 352–70.

Lesky, A., *Greek Tragic Poetry* (trans. M. Dillon; New Haven, CT: Yale University Press, 1983 [1972]).

Levine, E., *The Aramaic Version of the Bible* (New York: Walter de Gruyter, 1988).

Liddell, R., *A Treatise on the Novel* (London: Alden, 1947).

Lindars, B., *New Testament Apologetic: The Doctrinal Significance of the Old Testament Quotations* (Philadelphia, PA: Westminster Press, 1961).

—*New Testament Apologetic: The Doctrinal Significance of the Old Testament Quotations* (London: SCM Press, 1973).

—*Jesus Son of Man: A Fresh Examination of the Son of Man Sayings in the Gospels* (London: SPCK, 1983).

Lucas, D.W., 'Euripides', in *OCD* (2nd edn, 1970), pp. 418–21.

Luz, U., 'Das Geheimnismotiv und die markinische Christologie', *ZNW* 56 (1965), pp. 361–64.

Malbon, E.S., 'Ending at the Beginning: A Response', in Dennis Smith (ed.), *How Gospels Begin* (*Semeia* 52; Atlanta, GA: Scholars Press, 1991), pp. 175–84.

—'Echoes and Foreshadowings in Mark 4–8: Reading and Rereading', *JBL* 112 (1993), pp. 211–30.

—' "Reflected Christology": An Aspect of Narrative "Christology" in the Gospel of Mark', *Perspectives in Religious Studies* 26.2 (1999), pp. 127–45.

Mann, C.S. *Mark: A New Translation with Introduction and Commentary* (AB, 27; New York: Doubleday, 1986).

Marcus, J., 'Mark 14.61: "Are you the Messiah-Son-of-God?" ', *NovT* 31 (1988), pp. 125–41.

—*The Way of the Lord: Christological Exegesis of the Old Testament in the Gospel of Mark* (Louisville, KY: Westminster/John Knox Press, 1992).

—*Mark 1–8: A New Translation with Introduction and Commentary* (AB, 27; New York: Doubleday, 2000).

—'Mark—Interpreter of Paul', *NTS* 46 (2000), pp. 473–87.

Marshall, I.H., 'Son of God or Servant of Yahweh? – A Reconsideration of Mark 1.11', *NTS* 15 (1969), pp. 326–36.

Marxsen, W., *Mark the Evangelist* (trans. Roy A. Harrisville; New York: Abingdon, 1969).

Matera, F., *The Kingship of Jesus: Composition and Theology in Mark 15* (SBLDS, 66; Chico, CA: Scholars Press, 1982).

—'The Prologue as the Interpretative Key to Mark's Gospel', *JSNT* 34 (1988), pp. 3–20.

Mauer, C., 'Knecht Gottes und Sohn Gottes im Passionsbericht des Markusevangeliums', *ZTK* 50 (1953), pp. 1–38.

Mauser, U., *Christ in the Wilderness The Wilderness Theme in the Second Gospel and its Basis in the Biblical Tradition* (Naperville, ID: Alec R. Allenson, 1963).

Mays, J.L., *Hosea: A Commentary* (OTL; Philadelphia, PA: Westminster, 1969).

McArthur, H.K., '"On the Third Day"', *NTS* 18 (1971–1972), pp. 81–86.

McCasland, S.V., 'The Scripture Basis of "On the Third Day"', *JBL* 48 (1929), pp. 124–37.

McCurley Jr, F.R., '"And after Six Days" (Mark 9.2): A Semitic Literary Device', *JBL* 93 (1974), pp. 67–81.

McKinnis, R., 'An Analysis of Mark X 32–34', *NovT* 18 (1976), pp. 81–100.

McNamara, M., *The New Testament and the Palestinian Targum to the Pentateuch* (AnBib, 27; Rome: Biblical Institute Press, 1966).

—*Targum and Testament. Aramaic Paraphrases of the Hebrew Bible: A Light on the New Testament* (Shannon: Irish University Press, 1972).

—*Targum Neofiti 1: Genesis* (The Aramaic Bible 1A; Collegeville: Liturgical Press, 1992).

Meier, J.P., *A Marginal Jew. II. Mentor, Message, and Miracles* (ABRL; New York: Doubleday, 1994).

Merenlahti, P., *Poetics for the Gospels? Rethinking Narrative Criticism* (London: T&T Clark, 2002).

Metzger, B.M., 'A Suggestion Concerning the Meaning of I Cor XV.4b', *JTS* 8 (1957), pp. 118–23.

—*A Textual Commentary of the Greek New Testament* (New York: United Bible Societies, 1975).

Metzger, B.M. and R.E. Murphy, *The New Oxford Annotated Apocrypha: The Apocryphal/ Deuterocanonical Books of the Old Testament* (New York: Oxford University Press, 1991)

Meyers, C., *Binding the Strong Man: A Political Reading of Mark's Story of Jesus* (Maryknoll, NY: Orbis Books, 1988)

Meyers, C.L. and E.M. Meyers, *Haggai, Zechariah 1–8* (AB, 25B; New York: Doubleday, 1987).

Milgrom, J., *Leviticus 1–16. A New Translation with Introduction and Commentary* (AB, 3; New York: Doubleday, 1991).

Moloney, F., *Beginning the Good News: A Narrative Approach* (Collegeville, MO: Liturgical Press, 1992).

Momigliano, A., *The Development of Greek Biography* (Cambridge, MA: Harvard University Press, rev. edn, 1993)

Moo, D., *The Old Testament in the Gospel Passion Narratives* (Sheffield: Almond Press, 1983).

Moss, C.R., 'The Transfiguration: An Exercise in Markan Accommodation', *BibInt* 12 (2004), pp. 69–89.

Moyise, Steve, 'Is Mark's Opening Quotation the Key to his Use of Scripture?', *IBS* 20 (1998), pp. 146–58.

—*The Old Testament in the New: An Introduction* (New York: Continuum, 2001).

Murray, G., (*Euripides and his Age* (London: Thornton Butterworth, 1913).

Nickelsburg, G., 'Son of Man', *ABD* 4, pp. 137–50.

Ong, W.J., *Orality and Literacy: The Technologizing of the Word* (New York: Routledge, 2002).

Page, D.L., *Select Papyri*. III. *Literary (Poetry)* (Cambridge, MA: Harvard University Press, 1941).

Perrin, N., 'Mark 14.62: The End Product of a Christian Pesher Tradition?', in *A Modern Pilgrimage in New Testament Christology* (Philadelphia, PA: Fortress Press, 1974).

—'The High Priest's Question and Jesus' Answer', in W. Kelber (ed.), *The Passion in Mark: Studies on Mark 14–16* (Philadelphia, PA: Fortress Press, 1976), pp. 80–91.

Perry, J.M., 'The Three Days in the Synoptic Passion Predictions', *CBQ* 48 (1986), pp. 637–54.

Pesch, R., *Das Markusevangelium* (HTKNT; Freiburg: Herder, 1980).

—*Das Markusevangelium, 2. Teil* (HKNT, II/2; Freiburg: Herder, 1984).

Petersen, D.L., *Zechariah 9–14 and Malachi* (OTL; Louisville, KY: Westminster John Knox Press, 1995).

Pickard-Cambridge, A.W., 'Tragedy', in J.U. Powell (ed.), *New Chapters in the History of Greek Literature*, Third Series (Oxford: Clarendon Press, 1933), pp. 68–155.

Poirier, J.C., 'Two Transfigurations (Mark 8.31–9.8 and Zechariah 3–4)' (unpublished paper, read at the Colloquium Biblicum Lovaniense XLV, 1996).

—'The Endtime Return of Elijah and Moses at Qumran', *DSD* 10 (2003), pp. 221–42.

—'Jewish and Christian Tradition in the Transfiguration', *RB* 111 (2004), pp. 516–30.

Potter, D.S., *Literary Texts and the Roman Historian* (Approaching the Ancient World; London: Routledge, 1999).

Powell, M.A., *What is Narrative Criticism? A New Approach to the Bible* (London: SPCK, 1993).

Price, R., 'Foreword', in D. Rhoads and D. Michie, *Mark as Story: An Introduction to the Narrative of a Gospel* (Philadelphia, PA: Fortress Press, 1982), pp. xi–xiii.

Proctor, M., ' "After Three Days" in Mark 8.31; 9.31; 10.34: Subordinating Jesus' Resurrection in the Second Gospel', *PRSt* 30 (2003), pp. 399–424.

Propkes, W., *Christus Traditus.* (ATANT, 49; Zurich: Zwingli, 1949).

Räisänen, H., *Jesus, Paul and Torah: Collected Essays* (trans. D.E. Orton; JSNTSup, 43; Sheffield: Sheffield Academic Press, 1992).

Rau, G., 'Das Markusevangelium: Komposition und Intention der ersten Darstellung christlicher Mission', *ANRW* 2.25.3 (1985), pp. 2036–257.

Reumann, J.H., 'Psalm 22 at the Cross: Lament and Thanksgiving for Jesus Christ', *Int* 28 (1974), pp. 39–58.

Rhoads, D., J. Dewey and D. Michie, *Mark as Story. An Introduction to the Narrative of a Gospel* (Minneapolis, MN: Fortress Press, 2nd edn, 1999).

Roberts, A. and J. Donaldson (eds), *The Ante-Nicene Fathers Vol. 1* (Grand Rapids, MI: Eerdmans, 1987).

Robinson, J.M., 'Jesus: From Easter to Valentinus (or the Apostles' Creed)', *JBL* 101 (1982), pp. 5–37.

Robinson, J., P. Hoffman and J. Kloppenborg (eds), *The Critical Edition of Q* (Leuven: Peeters, 2000).

Rosenberg, R.A., 'Jesus, Isaac, and the "Suffering Servant" ', *JBL* 84 (1965), pp. 381–88.

Roth, C. "The Cleansing of the Temple and Zechariah xiv 21," *NovT* 4 (1960), pp. 172–79.

Sanders, E.P., *Jesus and Judaism* (London: SCM Press; Philadelphia, PA: Fortress Press, 1985).

—*Jewish Law from Jesus to the Mishnah: Five Studies* (London: SCM Press; Philadelphia, PA: Trinity Press International, 1990).

Sankey, P.J., 'Promise and Fulfillment: Reader-Response to Mark 1.1–15', *JSNT* 58 (1995), pp. 3–18.

Sawyer, J.F.A., 'A Note on the Etymology of Sara'at', *VT* 26 (1976), pp. 241–45.

Schildgen, B.D., 'A Blind Promise: Mark's Retrieval of Esther', *Poetics Today* 15 (1994), pp. 115–31.

Schlatter, A., *Der Evangelist Matthaeus: Seine Sprache, sein Ziel, seine Selbstaendigkeit* (Stuttgart: Calwer, 1948).

Schmithals, W., 'Der Markusschluß, die Verklärungsgeschichte und die Aussendung der Zwölf', *ZTK* (1972), pp. 379–411.

Schneck, R., *Isaiah in the Gospel of Mark I–VIII* (Vallejo, CA: BIBAL Press, 1994)

Schubart, W. and U. Wilamowitz-Möllendorff, *Berliner Klassikertexte* (vol. 2; Berlin: Weidmannsche, 1907).

Schulz, S. S., 'Markus und das Alte Testament', *ZTK* 58 (1961), 184–97.

Seeley, D., 'Jesus' Temple Act', *CBQ* 55 (1993), pp. 263–83.

Senior, D.P., *The Passion of Jesus in the Gospel of Mark* (Wilmington, NC: Michael Glazier, 1984).

Shepherd, Tom, *Markan Sandwich Stories: Narration, Definition, and Function* (Andrews University Seminary Doctoral Dissertation Series, 18; Berrien Springs, MI: Andrews University Press, 1993).

Sim, D.C., *The Gospel of Matthew and Christian Judaism: The History and Social Setting of the Matthean Community* (Edinburgh: T&T Clark, 1998).

Smith, D.M., 'The Use of the Old Testament in the New', in J.M. Efird (ed.), *The Use of the Old Testament in the New and Other Essays: Studies in Honor of William Franklin Stinespring* (Durham, NC: Duke University Press, 1972), pp. 3–65.

de Souza Nogueira, P.A., 'Visionary Elements in the Transfiguration Narrative', in C. Rowland and J. Barton (eds), *Apocalyptic in History and Tradition* (JSPSup, 43; Sheffield: Sheffield Academic Press, 2002), pp. 142–50.

Stegner, W.R., 'The Baptism of Jesus: A Story Modeled on the Binding of Isaac', *BibRev* 1 (1985), pp. 331–47.

—'Jesus' Walking on the Water: Mark 6.45–52', in Craig A. Evans and W. Richard Stegner (eds), *The Gospels and the Scriptures of Israel* (JSNTSup, 104, Sheffield: Sheffield Academic Press, 1994), pp. 212–34.

Stein, R.H., 'Is the Transfiguration (Mark 9.2–8) a Misplaced Resurrection-Account?', *JBL* 95 (1976), pp. 79–96.

Strecker, G., 'The Passion and Resurrection Predictions in Mark's Gospel (Mark 8.31; 9.31; 10.32–34)', *Int* 22 (1968), pp. 421–42.

Strugnell, J., 'Notes en marge du volume V des Discoveries in the Judean Desert of Jordan', *RQ* 29 (1970), pp. 163–279.

Stuart, D., *Hosea-Jonah* (WBC, 31; Waco, TX: Word Books, 1987).

Suhl, A., *Die Funktion der alttestamentlichen Zitate und Anspielungen im Markusevangelium* (Gütersloh: Mohn, 1965).

Sussman, V., 'The Binding of Isaac as Depicted on a Samaritan Lamp', *IEJ* 48.3–4 (1998), pp. 183–89.

Svartvik, J., *Mark and Mission: Mark 7.1–23 in its Narrative and Historical Contexts* (ConBNT, 32; Stockholm: Almqvist & Wiksell International, 2000).

Swartley, W.M., *Israel's Scripture Traditions and the Synoptic Gospels: Story Shaping Story* (Peabody, MA: Hendrickson, 1994)

Tannehill, R., 'Beginning to Study "How Gospels Begin"', in Dennis Smith (ed.), *How Gospels Begin* (Semeia 52; Atlanta: Scholars Press, 1991), pp. 185–92.

Taylor, J.E., *The Immerser: John the Baptist within Second Temple Judaism* (Studying the Historical Jesus; Grand Rapids, MI: Eerdmans, 1997).

Taylor, Vincent, *The Gospel According to St. Mark* (London: MacMillan, 2nd edn, 1966).

Theissen, G., *The Gospels in Context: Social and Political History in the Synoptic Tradition* (Minneapolis, MN: Fortress Press, 1991).

—*Social Reality and the Early Christians* (Minneapolis, MN: Fortress Press, 1992).

Tödt, H.E., *The Son of Man in the Synoptic Tradition* (trans. D.M. Barton; Philadelphia, PA: Westminster Press, 1965).

Tolbert, M., *Sowing the Gospel Mark's World in Literary-Historical Perspective* (Minneapolis, MN: Fortress Press, 1989)

Townsend, J.T. (trans.), *Midrash Tanhuma Vol 1* (Hoboken, NJ: KTAV, 1989).

Trocmé, É., *L'Évangile Selon Saint Marc* (Commentaire du Nouveau Testament II; Genève: Labor et Fides, 2000).

Turner, C.H., 'ὁ υἱός μου ὁ ἀγαπητός', *JTS* 27 (1925–26), pp. 113–29.

Vermes, G., *Jesus the Jew: A Historian's Readings of the Gospels* (London: Collins, 1973).

—'The "Son of Man" Debate', *JSNT* 1 (1978), pp. 19–32.

Waetjen, H., *A Reordering of Power: A Sociopolitical Reading of Mark's Gospel* (Minneapolis, MN: Fortress Press, 1989).

Walker, W., 'The Son of Man: Some Recent Developments', *CBQ* 45 (1983), pp. 584–607.

Walton, J., 'The Imagery of the Substitute King Ritual in Isaiah's Fourth Servant Song', *JBL* 122 (2003), pp. 734–43.

Watson, F., 'The Social Function of Mark's Secrecy Theme', *JSNT* 24 (1985), pp. 49–69.

Watts, J.D.W., *Isaiah 34–66* (WBC, 25; Waco, TX: Word Books, 1987).

Watts, R.E., *Isaiah's New Exodus and Mark* (WUNT, 2.88; Tübingen: Mohr, 1997).

Webb, R.L., *John the Baptizer and Prophet: A Socio-Historical Study* (JSNTSup, 26: Sheffield: JSOT Press, 1991).

Weeden, T.J., *Mark—Traditions in Conflict* (Philadelphia, PA: Fortress Press, 1971).

West, S., 'Satyrus: Peripatetic or Alexandrian?', *GRBS* 15 (1974), pp. 279–87.

Wijngaards, J., 'Death and Resurrection in Covenantal Context (Hos. VI 2)', *VT* 17 (1967), pp. 226–39.

Winks R.W. and S.P. Mattern-Parkes, *The Ancient Mediterranean World: From the Stone Age to A.D. 600* (Oxford: Oxford University Press, 2004).

Winston D., *The Wisdom of Solomon* (AB, 43; New York: Doubleday, 1979).

Wolff, H.W., *A Commentary on the Book of the Prophet Hosea* (trans. G. Stansell; Hermeneia; Philadelphia, PA: Fortress Press, 1974)

Wrede, William, *The Messianic Secret* (trans. J.C.G. Greig; Cambridge, James Clark, 1971 [1901]).

Wright, N.T., *The New Testament and the People of God* (Minneapolis, MN: Fortress Press, 1992).

—*The Resurrection of the Son of God* (Christian Origins and the Question of God, 3; Minneapolis, MN: Fortress Press, 2003).

Yadin, Y., 'A Midrash on 2 Sam. vii and Ps. i–ii (4QFlorilegium)', *IEJ* 9 (1959), pp. 95–98.

Zimmerli, W., 'παῖς θεοῦ Β', *TDNT* 5 (1967), p. 673–77.

INDEXES

INDEX OF REFERENCES

BIBLE

OTHER ANCIENT SOURCES

INDEX OF AUTHORS